Yale Historical Publications, Miscellany, 113

Plantation Slavery on the East Coast of Africa

FREDERICK COOPER

New Haven and London   Yale University Press

1977

Published under the direction of the Department of History of Yale University with assistance from the income of the Frederick John Kingsbury Memorial Fund

Designed by John O. C. McCrillis
and set in Baskerville type.
Printed in the United States of America by
The Vail-Ballou Press, Inc., Binghamton, New York.

Published in Great Britain, Europe, Africa, and Asia (except Japan) by Yale University Press, Ltd., London. Distributed in Latin America by Kaiman & Polon, Inc., New York City; in Australia and New Zealand by Book & Film Services, N.S.W., Australia; and in Japan by Harper & Row, Publishers, Tokyo Office.

Library of Congress Cataloging in Publication Data

Cooper, Frederick, 1947–
    Plantation slavery on the east coast of Africa.

    (Yale historical publications: Miscellany; 113)
    Bibliography: p.
    Includes index.
    1. Slavery in Africa, East—History   2. Slavery and Islam—Africa, East.   3. Plantation life—Africa, East—History.   I. Title.   II. Series.
HT1326.C66   301.44'93'0967   76-41398
ISBN 0-300-02041-4

TO

RUTH AND JACK

Contents

Tables

Maps

Preface

This is a study of how Africans and Arabs living on Africa's east coast used slave labor to build a plantation economy, and of the society that developed from the meeting and confrontation of masters and slaves. My desire to pursue this subject arose from a simultaneous fascination with the cosmopolitan culture of the East African coast and with the diverse forms of the institution of slavery in different historical situations. The study of African societies can, I think, be enhanced by awareness of what they share with and where they differ from other parts of the world; while the provocative work of students of plantation slavery in the Americas can be enhanced by a look beyond the relatively narrow range of social, economic, and political structures found among Europe's offshoots.

I am focusing on a broad region of Africa that embraces a variety of local situations. It was, however, united by a common language and a modicum of cultural unity with important local variations. In the nineteenth century, it was part of a single trading network and a single political entity, the Sultanate of Zanzibar, whose power over local communities was more than nominal and less than effective. Studying slavery in a number of localities within a region makes it possible to understand the factors which shaped particular practices. I have studied four areas within this region: the islands of Zanzibar and Pemba, where Omani Arabs built up the clove industry on the labor of slaves imported from Central Africa, and two towns in what is now Kenya, Mombasa and Malindi, which local people and immigrants—African and Arab—turned into centers of grain and coconut production. No one area is typical of the coast, but these four, I think, embrace the range of responses to agricultural development. More local studies, especially of complex regions like the Pangani Valley, would add to the picture.

The study of coastal slavery begins in the late eighteenth and early nineteenth centuries with an analysis of slavery in Oman, where the founders of Zanzibar's plantations originated. It then examines the process of agricultural development, between approximately 1820 and 1850 on the islands and 1840 and 1885 on the mainland, and looks at the agricultural economy in a period of internal difficulties and external pressure up to the takeover of East Africa by European powers around 1890. It is equally important—but more difficult—to place the information on the organization of slave labor, the material conditions of slaves, and the social life of slaves, in a chronological framework. In addition to the "before" data on Oman, there is much more "after" data on slavery in the developed plantation economy from the 1870s onward, but there is less data on the actual process of change in the nature of slavery. It is hard to fix a closing date. Slavery gradually declined as an economic institution in the 1890s and was abolished in 1897 in Zanzibar and 1907 in Kenya, but its death as a social institution was even more prolonged. The process of decline will be the subject of a later study.

I have had the good fortune to learn much about agriculture, slavery, and coastal society from the elders of Mombasa and Malindi (Zanzibar has been off bounds for researchers). The experience of working with them in pursuit of a shared goal of preserving knowledge of the past has helped make this endeavor personally valuable to me. I deeply appreciate the time and effort which these men, the sons of slaves as well as slaveholders, gave me. I have included a list of the names of informants in the Note on Sources and wish to express my gratitude to all of them. Here, I would like to say a special word about three of them, as individuals and as surrogates for the others.

Al-Amin Said Al-Mandhry was more of a teacher than an informant. I came to him many times for insight into Islamic law, coastal culture, agriculture, slavery, and the history of Mombasa. Mohamed Maawia introduced me to his home town, Malindi. Not only was his understanding of the economy and society of the town impressive, but he also helped me meet the elders of his community, the Washella, and people from other communal groups as well. Finally, Awade Maktub, born of slave ancestry in the declining years of slavery, provided me with a view of Malindi from the point of view of the people who worked in the fields.

I am also grateful to the many archivists and librarians, whose institutions are mentioned in the Bibliography, for helping me locate obscure material. I am especially glad to have had the opportunity to work in the archives and government offices in Kenya. Mohamed Maawia deserves another word of thanks in his capacity as an official of the Mombasa Land Office, where he helped me work with an extraordinary source of information on the coastal economy. I would like to thank Dr. Farouk Topan for showing me the illuminating biography of his grandfather, Tharia Topan, written by Dr. Topan's father.

I have also benefited from being a research associate of the Department of History of the University of Nairobi, in particular from the advice and criticism of Kenyan scholars, and the opportunity to have a scholarly base in Kenya. Fortunately, my stay on the coast of Kenya overlapped the field work of several other students of coastal history, and the atmosphere of common effort that existed among us was intellectually healthy and personally rewarding. I would like to thank Peter Koffsky, William McKay, Karim Janmohamed, and Margaret Strobel for sharing notes, leads on informants, and ideas with me. Margaret Strobel's generosity with her notes on interviews with Swahili women, as well as her own insights, helped me learn about problems that would have been virtually impossible for a male researcher to study in coastal society.

In addition, I want to thank my mother, Ruth Cooper, for translating some lengthy and important works in German, and William Freund for giving me a summary of a thesis in Dutch.

Finally, my teachers, colleagues, and friends have given me much thoughtful criticism of various versions of this book. Different drafts of the manuscript in its voluminous entirety were read by Norman Bennett, David Brion Davis, Steven Feierman, William Freund, Carla Glassman, Margaret Jean Hay, Peter Koffsky, William McKay, David Robinson, Margaret Strobel, Leonard Thompson, Carol Wasserloos, Marcia Wright, Marguerite Ylvisaker, and John Zarwan. The comparative dimension of this study was also helped along by Benjamin Braude, Emilia Viotti da Costa, Gavin Hambly, and C. Duncan Rice. Leonard Thompson deserves a special word of thanks, not only for his advice, criticism, and encouragement during and after my days as a graduate student, but for generously fulfilling the obligations of a patron without expecting me to behave in the role of a client.

F.C.

Cambridge, Massachusetts
1976

Swahili Terms

I have usually used Swahili words in forms that would be acceptable to coastal people. Plurals are generally formed by altering or adding a prefix to a root. Plurals are shown below in parentheses.

hamali (mahamali): port worker, carrier
heshima: respect, honor, dignity, rank
huru (mahuru): manumitted slave
kibarua (vibarua): day-laborer (lower status than hamali)
mkulia (wakulia): slave who was brought up locally (i.e. who was
    bought as a child)
mtama (mitama): millet
mtumwa (watumwa): slave
mwungwana (waungwana): free person without slave descent
mzalia (wazalia): locally born slave, person of slave descent
nokoa (manokoa): supervisor on a plantation
shamba (mashamba): farm or plantation
toro (watoro): runaway slave

Arabic Terms

imam: prayer leader in a mosque, also used to refer to the re-
    ligious leader of Oman before the Al-Busaidi dynasty
kadi: judge under Islamic law
seyyid: lord or master, honorary title used by Omanis, especially
    for the Sultan of Muscat and Zanzibar

Money and Weights

Currency is expressed in Maria Theresa Dollars (M.T. Dollars or $). They were officially exchanged at par with United States dollars during the nineteenth century, although the actual rate varied. $1 was worth 2⅛ rupees, while its value against the pound sterling was relatively steady at $4.75 until the early 1870s, when it began to fall to $6–$6.50 in the early 1890s. Currency and price levels have not been studied systematically on the coast, and all statistics and trends should be taken to be rough.

Small amounts of currency are expressed in pice, at the rate of 128 pice to one dollar.

The only local weight used here is the frasila, equal to 35 pounds.

Abbreviations Used in the Notes

a/c   Adjudication Cause: records of hearings on applications for land titles on the coast of Kenya, 1912–24, Land Office, Mombasa

ADM   Admiralty files, Public Record Office, London

AN   Archives Nationales, Paris

CMS   Church Missionary Society Archives, London

CO   Colonial Office files, Public Record Office, London

CP   Coast Province Collection, Kenya National Archives, Nairobi

FO   Foreign Office files, Public Record Office, London

FOCP   Foreign Office Confidential Prints, Slave Trade and Africa Series, Public Record Office, London

Ind. Off.   India Office Records and Library, London

INA   Indian National Archives, Foreign Department, excerpts from material on Zanzibar, prepared by Dr. Abdul Sheriff, microfilm in the library of the University of Dar es Salaam

KNA   Kenya National Archives, Nairobi (except for Coast Province Collection)

MAE   Archives du Ministère des Affaires Etrangèrcs, Paris (Correspondance Commerciale, Zanzibar, unless otherwise noted)

MAL   Notes of interviews at Malindi, Kenya, 1972–73. Numbers refer to the list of informants in the Note on Sources, pp. 275–78.

MSA   Notes of interviews in Mombasa, Kenya, 1972–73. Numbers refer to the list of informants in the Note on Sources, pp. 279–81.

NEMA   *New England Merchants in Africa: A History through Documents 1802 to 1865*, ed. Norman R. Bennett and George E. Brooks, Jr. (Boston: Boston University Press, 1965)

O.I.   Océan Indien file, Archives de l'Ancien Ministère d'Outre-Mer, Paris

PP   Parliamentary Papers

Reg., Mal   Registers of Deeds pertaining to Malindi, 1903–, kept in Mombasa Land Office. In citations, the letter *A* after a number refers to the volumes on land transactions, while *B* refers to the volumes of miscellaneous deeds.

Reg., Msa   Registers of Deeds pertaining to Mombasa 1891–, kept in Mombasa Land Office. Letters *A* and *B* in citations are used as above

Réunion   Réunion file, Archives de l'Ancien Ministère d'Outre-Mer, Paris

RGS   Royal Geographical Society, London

St. Esprit Archives de la Congregation du St. Esprit, Paris

TBGS   *Transactions of the Bombay Geographical Society*

UMCA   Universities' Mission to Central Africa, London

US Consul   Dispatches from United States Consuls in Zanzibar, National Archives, Washington

Introduction:
Plantation Slavery in Comparative Perspective

People of diverse races and cultures, in all parts of the world and in all periods of history, have devised a variety of ways to force others to work for them. Even in societies where all inhabitants toiled together in the fields, political leaders sometimes mobilized kinsmen, clients, subjects, or slaves to build their homes or perform other special tasks. In many places, powerful groups captured weaker outsiders and set them to work on the most tedious or unpleasant duties that needed to be done. In other situations, landowners reduced their own subjects to serfdom and enjoyed the fruits of their toils.

As these forms of unfree labor were abolished in the name of humanity or progress, the concentration of land and other means of production in a limited number of hands left more and more people with no choice but wage labor. In modern industrial society, people find themselves part of a system that demands work not only for survival but in response to deeply ingrained and carefully nurtured social values emphasizing work and success for their own sake. Labor for the benefit of others has always had an element of compulsion, whether the pain of the whip, the fear of starvation, or the pressures of social conventions and ideology.

Slavery is one form of labor. It is not the only one responsible for vast human suffering and its abolition has not always relieved the misery of its victims. Yet it, more than any other form of exploitation, has captured the imagination of those who were sensitive to the subservience of man to man. A slaveowner not only controlled the labor of his slave; he possessed him as a commodity that could be bought and sold. The enslaved person was not only alienated from his labor but from his home and society—forcefully transported to a strange region and made to start his life anew under his owner's personal control and within his owner's social and cultural milieu. The slave auction, the gang of men and women toiling under the overseer's watchful eye, and the whipping post, were the most vivid symbols imaginable of the subordination of humanity to the greed of the wealthy and the powerful.[1]

1. The most universal characteristic of slavery is that, in M. I. Finley's words, "The slave is an outsider: that alone permits not only his uprooting but also his reduction from a person to a thing which can be owned." A slave's person, not just his labor, was

1

In another sense, slavery, more than other forms of labor, recognized the humanity of the worker. He was not simply a factor of production with whom the employer maintained a limited relationship for a portion of each day, but a part of the master's household, plantation, or factory. If slaves had less control over their own lives than other members of society, their owners also had greater responsibility for their welfare, and even for their actions toward others. The master derived not only labor from his slaves but the satisfactions, problems, and status of having dependents.[2]

Dependence and labor are two dimensions of slavery found in varying degrees in different slave systems. Slaves were closest to being pure economic objects in the sugar islands of the Caribbean, where high profits, readily available replenishments for the labor force, and the planters' belief that the best home for a plantation owner was London or Paris, combined to maximize the economic dimension of slave-ownership and to minimize the social.[3] On the other hand, in Cuba before the days of sugar, or in Virginia and northeastern Brazil after the plantation economy was at its peak, slavery was more of an organic social institution.[4] Slaves were valued not just for the commodities they

---

exchangeable property in both Roman and Islamic law, but nowhere have slaves been treated—legally or socially—*purely* as property. Equally important was the slave's kinlessness. Generally obtained by purchase or capture from outside the boundaries of the society (although a social pariah could become a slave as well), the slave lacked the protection of membership in a social group. M. I. Finley, "Slavery," in *International Encyclopedia of the Social Sciences* (New York, 1968), 14: 307–08; David Brion Davis, *The Problem of Slavery in Western Culture* (Ithaca, N.Y., 1966).

2. A dependent, to borrow Marc Bloch's phrase, is "the 'man' of another man." Dependence expresses subordination regardless of the nature of the bond: "the count was the 'man' of the king, as the serf was the 'man' of his manorial lord." The importance of the concept is its ambiguity: it expresses a diffuse, variable tie, rather than a functionally specific relationship. Marc Bloch, *Feudal Society: The Growth of Ties of Dependence*, trans. L. A. Manyon (Chicago, 1961), p. 145. In feudal society, such ties were pervasive; in modern society specific relationships predominate.

3. For an introduction to these comparative problems, see Eugene D. Genovese, *The World the Slaveholders Made* (New York, 1969), and Laura Foner and Eugene Genovese, eds., *Slavery in the New World: A Reader in Comparative History* (Englewood Cliffs, N.J., 1969). Among the best studies of the sugar islands are Richard S. Dunn, *Sugar and Slaves: The Rise of the Planter Class in the English West Indies, 1624–1713* (Chapel Hill, N.C., 1972); Orlando Patterson, *The Sociology of Slavery: An Analysis of the Origins, Development and Structure of Negro Slave Society in Jamaica* (Rutherford, N.J., 1967); and Franklin W. Knight, *Slave Society in Cuba During the Nineteenth Century* (Madison, Wis., 1970). Yet even in these islands, a social order developed, shaped by the cultures of the European planters, African slaves, and local conditions. Edward Brathwaite, *The Development of Creole Society in Jamaica 1770–1820* (Oxford, 1971).

4. David Brion Davis, "The Comparative Approach to American History: Slavery," in Foner and Genovese, p. 67; Herbert Klein, *Slavery in the Americas: A Comparative Study of*

produced but for the satisfaction of having people at one's command. Profit and prestige were by no means incompatible—plantation life and cotton were equally important to defining the civilization of the Southern United States.[5]

Virtually all of the lively and penetrating debate on comparative slavery that has taken place during the past fifteen years centers on white, Christian slaveowning classes, whose plantations grew out of the dynamic economic system of early-modern Europe. Comparisons have therefore covered a relatively narrow range of political, social, and economic structures. This book focuses on similar problems in a different setting: slaveowners who were black or brown, who were Muslim, and whose economy was part of the Indian Ocean commercial system.

In the nineteenth century, slaves on the East African coast became enmeshed in a developing plantation economy that in many ways resembled the plantation economies of the Western Hemisphere. Plantations were large-scale, specialized units that developed in order to serve the needs of a vast and widespread market for particular commodities. Plantations were concentrated where conditions were best suited to the crops they grew and where transportation networks could link them with the markets they served. Because vast quantities of cheap labor had to be brought to those areas, slavery was the key to plantation development in both the New World and the coast of East Africa. Slaves could be brought from places where they were plentiful to places where they were needed without paying them enough to make them want to go. And as outsiders, they were in a poor position to resist the regimentation and discipline that were the hallmarks of plantation organization. And the plantation became a social unit: the entire lives of slaves were linked to it and to these relations of subordination.[6]

In East Africa, plantations developed in places where soil and climate were ideal for particular crops—cloves on the islands of Zanzibar and Pemba, grain and coconuts on the adjacent mainland—and at a time when expanding trade routes had linked these areas with markets and

Virginia and Cuba (Chicago, 1967); Gilberto Freyre, *The Masters and the Slaves: A Study in the Development of Brazilian Civilization*, trans. Samuel Putnam, abridged from 2d ed. (New York, 1964).

5. For different views of the slave South, see Robert W. Fogel and Stanley L. Engerman, *Time on the Cross: The Economics of American Negro Slavery* (Boston, 1974), and Eugene Genovese, *Roll, Jordan, Roll: The World the Slaves Made* (New York, 1974).

6. Where plantations did not use slave labor, they relied on coolies—semifree outsiders—or else they either took advantage of an impoverished peasantry or created one. Jay R. Mandle, "The Plantation Economy: An Essay in Definition," in Eugene D. Genovese, ed., *The Slave Economies* (New York, 1973), 1: 214–28. See also W. O. Jones, "Plantations," in *International Encyclopedia of the Social Sciences* (New York, 1968), 12: 154, and P. P. Courtenay, *Plantation Agriculture* (London, 1965), p. 7.

sources of labor. Planters, like those of the Western Hemisphere, often came from distant lands, attracted by the possibility of profits. Long-time residents of coastal towns also found new sources of wealth in the nearby fields. As in the Americas, slaveowners soon learned that local or neighboring peoples were too independent or too scattered to make an adequate labor force and they turned to distant lands to find workers—the far interior of East and Central Africa. The slave trade gave planters great flexibility in labor recruitment and, even more important, workers with no local roots except those they established through their owners.

Because coastal slaves in the nineteenth century lived and worked on plantations, their living conditions were in some respects closer to those of slaves in antebellum Alabama than to conditions facing nonagricultural slaves in African societies twenty miles from the coast. Nevertheless, coastal society brought as much to plantation life as the plantations brought to it. A planter and his dependents were part of a particular social and political context, one very different from nineteenth-century Alabama.

Many of the slaveholders of East Africa came from Arabia, especially from its southeastern corner, Oman. Others were Swahili, a mixed people who were the products of centuries of intermarriage and cultural interaction between Africans, Arabs, Persians, and others in the trading centers of the coast. Ethnically, linguistically, and culturally, the Swahili were closer to their African than to their Asian forebears. Coastal towns remained cosmopolitan centers throughout their history, and even when the Sultan of Oman conquered most of the ports in the late eighteenth and early nineteenth centuries, the towns kept their individual character and defacto independence. Within towns, Swahili and Arabs were both divided into distinct subgroups with close ties within themselves and with looser affiliations to related groups in other coastal towns or in Arabia.[7]

What most clearly distinguished this society—and others in Africa and the Middle East—from the societies of early-modern Europe was the internal development and functional importance of kinship and communal groups. Extended families were more important than nu-

7. Historical and anthropological studies of Swahili culture are sadly lacking. For an introduction, see A. H. J. Prins, *The Swahili-Speaking Peoples of Zanzibar and the East African Coast* (London, 1961); and N. Chittick, "The Coast before the Arrival of the Portuguese," and F. J. Berg, "The Coast from the Portuguese Invasion," in B. A. Ogot, ed., *Zamani: A Survey of East African History*, new ed. (Nairobi, 1974), pp. 98–134; J. deV. Allen, "Swahili Culture Reconsidered: Some Historical Implications of the Material Culture of the Northern Kenya Coast in the Eighteenth and Nineteenth Centuries," *Azania* 9(1974): 105–37; and Ann Patricia Caplan, *Choice and Constraint in a Swahili Community: Property, Hierarchy, and Cognatic Descent on the East African Coast* (London, 1975).

clear ones, and even wider groupings acknowledging descent from a common ancestor had a strong sense of social solidarity and political loyalty. The structure of kinship groups in Africa and Arabia varied greatly, as did the ways in which they fit into larger political entities. Wider social groups—often kinship groups that had incorporated strangers or federations of different groups—frequently became, over time, closely knit bodies that shared a sense of common origins and identity and stuck together against outsiders: these were "communal groups." [8]

Both the institutions of state and the concept of a loyal citizenry were in general much weaker in Africa and Arabia than in sixteenth- and seventeenth-century Europe, so that the collective strength of kinship and communal groups was the principal form of protection a person had. If an individual or group tried to dominate a region, it had to reckon with the fact that its subjects were also members of their own groups and would have divided loyalties. Conflict was endemic—both among groups, and between the forces for centralization and independence.

In some societies, the balance of power among kinship groups and the ties that cut across kinship lines produced an equilibrium. But in other cases, conflict could lead to a fundamental change in the distribution of power and the development of institutions by which one group dominated others.[9] The stakes of conflict were often high. Kinship might be a nucleus of support, but the capacity of kinship groups to expand was biologically limited. The recruitment of followers was for kings and kinsmen a vital part of politics.

Followers could be recruited in a variety of ways, and one of them was the slave market. Slaves were outsiders, with no ties except to their master and through him to his kinship and communal groups. In many African and Arabian polities, the dimension of dependency that is always part of slavery was thus strongly accentuated. The traumata of capture, transportation, and sale severed slaves from the social fabric of their original communities. For protection against new misfortunes, for access to land, for family and social life, and for peace with the local spirits and gods, they had to look to their masters. Slaves served conflicting roles. Incorporated into kinship groups, they enhanced their

8. Where such groups were distinguished by culture, language, race, and/or religion from one another, they can be termed "ethnic groups." Both must be distinguished from "kinship groups," which are simply descendants of common ancestors. On the East African coast, kinship groups were relatively unimportant politically, and communal groups were the primary foci of loyalty, group identity, and political action.

9. P. C. Lloyd, "Conflict Theory and Yoruba Kingdoms," in I. M. Lewis, ed., *History and Social Anthropology* (London, 1968), pp. 25–62.

size, productivity, reproductive capacity, and fighting potential. Attached to an ambitious individual, they gave him wealth and power that
could be used to establish his independence of his own kinship group
and to subordinate others.

In short, the personal bond between a master and his slaves could be
as important as any specific tasks that slaves performed. Before the
nineteenth century, slaves in Oman and on the east coast of Africa performed a great variety of functions. Many were domestic servants, concubines, artisans, and common laborers. Others were soldiers for local
rulers or ship captains for merchants. All conveyed prestige and political power by their presence. No labor-intensive industries had yet
emerged. The concept of slavery—although it emphasized the low
status and personal dependence of the slave upon his master—did not
identify slavery with menial labor. But slavery, in East Africa and Arabia as much as in the Americas, signified subordination. Slaves could be
placed in positions of trust precisely because their subordination to
their masters was, in the society's own terms, so extreme.

If slaves' dependence could be exploited for social and political ends,
it could also be mobilized to serve economic objectives when circumstances changed. This book examines that process. It assesses the impact of a changing market for agricultural produce, and a consequent
shift in emphasis among the functions slaves performed in an established form of slavery that had long stressed the role of slaves as
dependents.

Expanding trade along the East African coast in the late eighteenth
and early nineteenth centuries set the stage for the transformation of
small-scale coastal agriculture into a plantation system. On the islands
of Zanzibar and Pemba, two decades of experimentation by Omanis
with clove cultivation led to a major breakthrough in the 1840s. On the
adjacent mainland, Swahili and Arabs brought more and more land
under grain cultivation—while planting more coconut trees—between,
roughly, 1840 and the 1880s. The basis of this transformation was slave
labor.

The first half of this book focuses on the changes—and the limits of
change—in coastal agriculture, as well as on the impact those changes
had on social structure. The second half examines the lives of the
slaves: the conditions under which they lived and worked within the
new plantation regime, and their place in coastal society.

This study is at the intersection of two sets of scholarly investigations,
which unfortunately remain ignorant—in some cases by deliberate
choice—of one another. Plantation slavery has been examined at length
by historians of the Americas, who if they looked at African slavery at

all, used it as a benign foil against which the economic exploitation and inhumanity of American slavery stood out.[10] Africanists have begun to study the diverse roles and statuses of slaves in African societies. With some exceptions, they have also stressed the contrast between slavery as a social institution in Africa and as an economic one in the Americas. Most Africanists have treated slavery more as an aspect of culture than as a response to economic and political incentives arising out of changing historical circumstances.[11]

Had Africanists paid more attention to their Americanist colleagues they might have avoided some of the misinterpretations which the lengthy debate on slavery in the Americas has uncovered. They would have learned that the dichotomy between the social and economic aspects of slavery is false—that slavery almost invariably has elements of both. They might have avoided seeing forms of slavery as static and culturally determined. Americanists, on their part, might have seen that the wide contrasts within the Western Hemisphere are part of an even wider spectrum and that the racial dimension of American slavery—with which they have almost obsessively been concerned—is part of a broader context of exploitation and subordination.

This is not the place to survey past analyses of slavery, but only to search for useful questions and approaches that will assist in the study of particular slave societies and to begin to situate slavery on the East African coast in respect to the range of variations that exists. The debate on comparative slavery in the Americas provides revealing examples of how slavery can be studied and how it shouldn't be.

Frank Tannenbaum and Stanley Elkins, in their pioneering efforts to compare slavery in different parts of the Americas, stress the importance of the institutions of the Catholic Church and the Crown in Spanish and Portuguese South America and their absence in North America. The Church had its own institutional interests and recognized all people as potential additions to its membership, while Catholic ideology encouraged Latin Americans to see social distinctions as part of an organic social hierarchy. Protestant churches, even though internally more democratic, lacked the Catholic Church's worldwide perspective, were more easily influenced by slaveholding parishioners, and also were more discriminating about who should be allowed to join.

10. See, for example, Eugene Genovese, *The Political Economy of Slavery* (New York, 1965), p. 80, and Gary B. Nash, *Red, White, and Black* (Englewood Cliffs, N.J., 1975), p. 159.

11. Many contributors to a recent and sophisticated book on African slavery write in the "anthropological present," as if slavery could be divorced from time, and the half-century since slavery was abolished could be ignored. Claude Meillassoux, ed., *L'esclavage en Afrique précoloniale* (Paris, 1975). For more on the economic-social dichotomy, see below.

Similarly, the Portuguese and Spanish monarchs had an interest in reserving the right to control all their subjects, slave or free, while the strength of local government in the British colonies and ex-colonies put slaves under the effective legal and administrative domination of planter classes.

As a result, the economic interests of slaveholders in North America were not subject to the institutional restraints of their counterparts to the south. These institutions may not have prevented slaves from being overworked or punished, but they did insist that slaves be regarded as human. Ideologically, therefore, slaves were regarded not as chattels but as dependent members of society; legally, they had the protection of slave codes that were not entirely the product of the planter class; and socially, they had a better chance to be accepted as citizens once they were freed.[12]

Critics have argued, first of all, that the strength of Church and Crown in Portugal, Spain, and colonial capitals did not mean their presence was felt in remote plantation areas. Whatever slave codes said, they may have had little effect on what slaves actually experienced. The evidence suggests that, under certain conditions, slaves in Iberian areas suffered brutal treatment.[13] Second, even if the institutions had some influence on slaveholders, Tannenbaum and Elkins ignore the economic forces pushing them in other directions. When the sugar market was booming, God and Country could be set aside. On the other hand, Protestantism could become part of a paternalistic ethos—if other factors encouraged it. In its own way, the society built by Anglo-Saxons in the Southern United States was as paternalistic as Brazil ever was, while both Englishmen and Spaniards created some of the world's most dehumanizing plantation societies on the sugar islands of the Caribbean.[14] Still, most critics of Tannenbaum and Elkins have attacked only their exclusive emphasis on institutional factors and have not denied the importance—within a broader context—of religion, law, and government toward shaping attitudes, ideologies, and patterns of behavior in slave societies.[15]

Elkins and Tannenbaum, as well as their critics, have much to tell the

12. Frank Tannenbaum, *Slave and Citizen: The Negro in the Americas* (New York, 1946); Stanley M. Elkins, *Slavery: A Problem in American Institutional and Intellectual Life* (Chicago, 1959).

13. Davis, *Problem*, pp. 223–61; Knight, *Slave Society in Cuba*; Stanley J. Stein, *Vassouras: A Brazilian Coffee County, 1850–1900* (Cambridge, Mass., 1957); Charles R. Boxer, *The Golden Age of Brazil, 1695–1750* (Berkeley, Calif., 1962).

14. Sidney W. Mintz, "Slavery and Emergent Capitalisms," in Foner and Genovese, pp. 27–37; Genovese, *World*, p. 96; and Genovese, *Roll*, passim.

15. See especially Genovese, "Materialism and Idealism in the History of Negro Slavery in the Americas," in Foner and Genovese, p. 241, and Genovese, *Roll*, p. 179.

student of slavery on the East African coast. They point up the importance of asking whether Islamic law and theology provided norms of treating slaves and attitudes toward slaves' place in society that blunted the impact of the plantation economy. In fact, the coast was even less secular than Catholic countries of early-modern Europe, and Islamic law provided what amounts to a slave code that enshrined the conception of slavery of a period before the rise of plantation slavery. Islam insisted that slaves be treated kindly and that they be incorporated into the Muslim community, even if it explicitly defined slaves' social inferiority. In the Tannenbaum-Elkins approach, Muslims were more Catholic than the Catholics.

Yet the role of Islam among the peoples of the Indian Ocean must be approached as cautiously as that of Christianity in Atlantic societies. Profit could undermine piety, and laws could be ignored. It is important to ask not only what Islamic texts had to say about slavery, but whether these precepts were vital and accepted parts of nineteenth-century East African society or mere anachronisms. By itself, Islam might mean little, but if reinforced by other elements it might have helped to shape the ways slaveowners regarded their own role in society and that of their slaves.

Other scholars have gone beyond institutions to examine attitudes that were deeply ingrained in certain cultures. Since the 1950s, historians of the United States have debated whether English racial preconceptions were responsible for the creation of the repressive apparatus of black slavery, or whether such prejudices grew out of experiences with a system of labor that was chosen for economic motives.[16] Winthrop Jordan admits that prejudice and slavery, over time, reinforced each other; but his own emphasis is on his discovery that Englishmen, in their initial encounters with Africans, found them loathsome and inferior. In this early attitude he finds "the indispensable key to the degradation of Africans in English America." [17]

But the fundamental question about prejudice is what one makes of it. Prejudice—a hostile attitude toward other people's distinc-

16. Oscar and Mary Handlin, "Origins of the Southern Labor System," *William and Mary Quarterly*, 3d ser., 7 (1950): 199–22; Carl N. Degler, "Slavery and the Genesis of American Race Prejudice," *Comparative Studies in Society and History* 2 (1959): 49–67.

17. Had he termed attitudes "*an* indispensable key" Jordan would have been on firmer ground. Instead, he dismisses the importance of the economic roles of slaves by saying, "It may be take as given. . . ." Yet even if slaves were exploited everywhere, different economic situations had differing impacts on racial attitudes. Winthrop D. Jordan, *The White Man's Burden: Historical Origins of Racism in the United States* (New York, 1974), p. 50. A fuller version of Jordan's work was published as *White Over Black: American Attitudes Towards the Negro, 1550–1812* (Chapel Hill, N.C., 1968).

tiveness—is not the same as racism—a systematic ideology justifying domination of one group by another on the grounds of the subordinate group's inherent inferiority. An explanation of what turned prejudice into racism must focus on the conditions that made an ideology of domination both desirable and possible; and in large part those conditions derived from the way labor was exploited and controlled.[18]

In both North and South America, early settlers experimented with virtually every possible source of labor: they may have had qualms about treating indentured servants ruthlessly because they were white, or Indian slaves because they were noble savages, but they did it anyway. However, as the economic importance of slavery grew from a source of labor for the diverse tasks facing new settlers to the basis of a plantation economy, the advantages of African slaves became paramount: they were the most available and the easiest to control.[19] In turn, the overwhelming association of blacks with a menial role in the economy reinforced the idea of black inferiority. Moreover, large numbers of brutally exploited slaves posed a very real menace to the safety and way of life of the dominant class. Landowners came to need poor whites less as workers and more as allies. On their part, poor whites, especially in a competitive society like the United States, saw blacks—freedmen as well as slaves—as potential threats to their livelihood and status.[20] Prejudice, exploitation, and repression were all mutually reinforcing: racism emerged out of a dialectical process.

Such an analysis could be applied to any plantation society, but the variety of forms that race relations took during and after slavery belies

18. For a penetrating critique of Jordan, see George M. Fredrickson, "Why Blacks Were Left Out," *New York Review of Books*, February 7, 1974, pp. 23–24. On the concept of ideology—as distinct from attitudes—see Clifford Geertz, "Ideology as a Cultural System," in David A. Apter, ed., *Ideology and Discontent* (New York, 1964), pp. 47–76. A further problem with Jordan's emphasis on attitudes is his failure to specify who held them. He tries to explain a society's prejudices by reference to an elite's writings.

19. These lessons were learned by experience, for Indians and Englishmen generally proved to be intractable servants. Unlike Indians, Africans had no place to flee, and unlike English servants, they could not blend in with the free population, lacked familiarity with the slaveowners' culture, and, having been violently wrenched from their home, had no expectations that they had rights (including freedom at the end of the indenture) which their masters could unfairly deny. Slaves did resist oppression, but rarely effectively.

20. A comparative treatment of the early years of New World slavery may be found in C. Duncan Rice, *The Rise and Fall of Black Slavery* (New York, 1975), pp. 24–62. For North American studies, see Peter Wood, *Black Majority: Negroes in Colonial South Carolina from 1670 through the Stono Rebellion* (New York, 1974); T. H. Breen, "A Changing Labor Force and Race Relations in Virginia, 1660–1710," *Journal of Social History* 7 (1973): 3–25; and Edmund S. Morgan, *American Slavery-American Freedom: The Ordeal of Colonial Virginia* (New York, 1975).

its simplicity.[21] Racial inequality, discrimination, and antagonism existed throughout the Western Hemisphere, but racial groups were not always defined in the same way and the ideologies of ruling classes stressed race to differing degrees. In the United States, a sharp division between black and white has long prevailed, while in the British Caribbean and Iberian South America, people were classified into three groups—black, mulatto, and white—which were often fuzzy along the edges.

Such differences cannot readily be explained in terms of differences in economic organization.[22] Nor can ideological differences be reduced to mere reflections of differing economic orders. The planters of the Southern United States tended increasingly in the nineteenth century to rationalize its hegemony on the grounds of racial superiority. As American political ideas increasingly stressed equality, proslavery ideologues made it more and more clear that such ideas applied to whites alone. In Brazil, the racial component was less prominent and the class component more so—slaves were part of a wider hierarchy effectively controlled by a small elite.[23] Attitudes did not determine the nature of slavery, nor did the particular ways in which slaves were exploited uniquely determine attitudes and ideologies.

In studying the East African coast, the historian faces similar problems in deciphering the relationship between particular forms of slavery and conceptions people had of slaves, blacks, and the master-slave relationship. Racial prejudice was not unique to the European mind. Bernard Lewis has shown how widespread the belief in the inferiority

21. Jordan's approach is hard to apply comparatively. The early impressions Portuguese had of Africans did not differ drastically from those of the English, yet race relations evolved in different ways (Emilia Viotti da Costa, personal communication). II. Hoetink's argument that Northern and Southern Europeans had different somatic norms is also hard to correlate with forms of slavery or race relations. *Caribbean Race Relations: A Study of Two Variants,* trans. Eva M. Hooykaas (London, 1967).

22. For this reason, some economic determinists have tried to minimize such differences, although not persuasively. Marvin Harris, *Patterns of Race in the Americas* (New York, 1964). For discussions of two- versus three-tiered systems, see Carl N. Degler, *Neither Black nor White: Slavery and Race Relations in Brazil and the United States* (New York, 1971), and Winthrop D. Jordan, "American Chiaroscuro: The Status and Definition of Mulattoes in the British Colonies," in Foner and Genovese, pp. 189–201.

23. The importance of democratic beliefs and politics, status competition among whites, and pressure from abolitionists in shaping racist ideology in the Southern United States is emphasized by George M. Fredrickson, *The Black Image in the White Mind: The Debate on Afro-American Character and Destiny 1817–1914* (New York, 1917), esp. chapter 2. The ideological differences in Brazil did not mean that prejudice was absent or that poverty and a black skin did not tend to go together. See Degler, *Neither Black nor White.* I am also indebted to Emilia Viotti da Costa for sharing with me some of the ideas that will appear in her forthcoming book on Brazilian slavery.

of blacks was in the Islamic world.[24] However, like Jordan, he fails to show what prejudice meant to the structure of particular Islamic societies. The problem is to analyze the connection of slavery and race with the boundaries of social groups. In terms of how people thought and acted, how was society divided—into black and brown,, slave or free, or into communal groups that incorporated both slaveowners and slaves? What was the influence of experiences Arabs and Swahili had with slavery before the expansion of agriculture?

Particularly in Arabia, slaves included whites and Asians as well as light- and dark-skinned Africans. There were tendencies to associate blacks with menial roles and low status, but the legal category of slave was not identified with any particular race or any particular occupation. However, plantation development implied the importation of vast numbers of black Africans to serve in the fields of their Arab and racially mixed masters. The economic process appears similar to that of the Americas, but its outcome was different from both the two-tiered racial hierarchy of North America and the three-tiered version of the Caribbean and South America.

Neither institutions nor attitudes can by themselves explain why slavery took particular forms in certain societies. Economic determinists such as Eric Williams and Marvin Harris have similarly failed to explain the variations in plantation societies in terms of variations in markets.[25] The attempt of Robert Fogel and Stanley Engerman to see plantation organization and slave life as direct consequences of capitalist rationality has likewise given a distorted view of slavery, particularly the place of profit-maximization and efficiency in the value-structure of the plantation class, the meaning of subordination, the complexities of the master-slave relationship, and the ways in which slaves tried to make the best of their situation.[26]

Even if profit was not the sole determinant of plantation agriculture, the expansion of European capitalism was a powerful force pushing Western slaveowners to develop a regimented, closely supervised, intensely employed labor force. Did the expanding market of nineteenth-century East Africa—although different from the capitalist economy

24. Bernard Lewis, *Race and Color in Islam* (New York, 1971).

25. Harris, *Patterns of Race;* Eric Williams, *Capitalism and Slavery* (New York, 1944). See the penetrating critique of economic determinism from a Marxist perspective in Genovese's, "Materialism," in Foner and Genovese, pp. 238–55.

26. Fogel and Engerman. See the criticisms of their approach in Herbert G. Gutman, *Slavery and the Numbers Game: A Critique of Time on the Cross* (Urbana, Ill., 1975), as well as the much fuller account of plantation society in Genovese, *Roll.* Fogel and Engerman are quite right in seeing slaveowners as men concerned with profit and efficiency, but they fail to see slaveowners as part of a society.

and bourgeois culture of Europe—have a similar effect? Some societies encouraged profit-maximizing more than others, in non-Western as well as Western cultures.[27] One must ask, what opportunities for consumption and investment existed for the person who acquired wealth? To what extent could the need to run an efficient enterprise be ignored without falling victim to competitors and creditors? Did the expansion of agriculture create a planter class or just planters—in other words, did ownership of land and slaves define the dominant group in society, or were such factors as family, religious learning, and having personal followers, important bases of stratification? It is essential not only to examine the changing agricultural economy but its changing meaning to coastal society.

The studies of comparative slavery in the Americas suggest that those scholars who have emphasized the determining role of institutions, attitudes, and markets have—in common with many modern social scientists—emphasized correlation at the expense of process. They have tried to show that a particular variable—say, the Catholic church—is associated with a particular form of slavery. The problem with this approach is not merely that it ignores other variables, but that it fails to show how they interact and influence one another.

For example, the development of rice cultivation in colonial South Carolina affected more than the way slaves worked. From the founding of the colony, slaves had served a variety of needs in a frontier situation—from cutting trees to fighting Indians. They faced hard work and severe, if irregular, punishment, but not a rigid mechanism of social control. They often lived in remote areas, free from constant supervision, grew their own food on plots that effectively belonged to them, and exercised considerable initiative in doing their work. But as rice began to overshadow the other facets of South Carolina's economy, slaves were increasingly relegated to a specific role in the economy—that of field workers. The apparatus of control tightened: slaves lost their own plots and came under close supervision. As their independence in daily life was narrowed, whites tended to think of slaves less as

27. A number of economic anthropologists, notably Karl Polanyi, have argued that societies with nonexistent or limited markets allocate goods and services on the basis of social considerations, whereas modern societies follow economic rationality. Such concepts are of little use to the historian interested in change, for some "primitive" economies are quite responsive to changes in supply or demand while "modern" economies are filled with irrationalities. For a critique of this view and an impressive application of economic principles to African economic history, see A. G. Hopkins, *An Economic History of West Africa* (London 1973), p. 6 and chapter 2. Particular modes of production and particular social contexts must be analyzed, not such catch-alls as "traditional" or "modern," "Western" or "non-Western" societies.

useful and loyal servants on the frontier, but as degraded—and resentful—laborers. Their fear, which was quite justified, led to further repression and more fear. By 1740, in the aftermath of a slave rebellion and its repression, economic roles, the slaves' patterns of living, the master-slave relationship, and interracial attitudes had all changed.[28]

In Brazil, the various factors combined differently. Coming from a more patriarchal, traditional society than the English settlers of the United States and living scattered in a large country with a feeble central government, the Portuguese colonists made their plantations into personal domains. The planter's own family, clients, loyal freed slaves, and slaves were all part of a hierarchy. Isolated and often feuding with one another, plantations were political organizations as well as economic and social ones. The planter's following, slaves and ex-slaves included, occasionally participated in the fights between slaveowners, although their military role was much weaker than in many African and Middle Eastern societies.

But if masters were patriarchs, they were generally stern patriarchs, and often greedy ones as well. Economic decline in northeast Brazil reinforced the social dimension of the estate and helped create the myth of relaxed, sensuous slaveowners, but the rise of the coffee industry in the south in the nineteenth century turned slaves into regimented, overworked, brutalized economic objects. The older heritage still survived in such practices as miscegenation and manumission, but coffee had undermined a seigneurial culture, just as rural isolation and stagnation had reinforced it.[29]

The complex interrelation of specific economic conditions and broader social structures has led John Lombardi to urge scholars to avoid writing about "slave systems" altogether, and to discuss instead particular occupational categories and environments—plantation workers, artisans, and urban workers, both slave and free.[30] Indeed, such concepts as "the Latin American slave system"—or "Islamic slavery" or "African slavery"—correspond to no real society or culture, and so mean little. And to look at slavery as one form of labor is as valid as to look at labor as one dimension of slavery. But Lombardi narrows the

28. Wood. On the impact of economic change on social relations and racial attitudes in colonial Virginia and nineteenth-century Cuba, see Morgan and Knight.

29. The views of Boxer and Stein might be compared with those of Freyre. See also Genovese, *World*, pp. 71–95; da Costa's forthcoming book; and—on Latin America generally—Robert Brent Toplin, ed., *Slavery and Race Relations in Latin America* (Westport, Conn., 1974).

30. John V. Lombardi, "Comparative Slave Systems in the Americas: A Critical Review," in Richard Graham and Peter H. Smith, eds., *New Approaches to Latin American History* (Austin, Tex., 1974), pp. 156–74, esp. p. 170. This approach is particularly valuable in the many cases in South America, both urban and rural, where slaves were only one part of a complexly structured work force.

scope of inquiry too far. Slaveowners and slaves participated in cultures that transcended their particular situations and the particular tasks that slaves performed. It is important to ask if a set of behavior patterns, expectations, and attitudes toward slaves became part of the culture of a particular slaveowning class. Especially where slavery dominated all other forms of labor, as on the plantations of the Americas and the East African coast, it is indeed necessary to understand the slave system.

To analyze a slave system is to unravel general patterns of economic activities, social relationships, and ideology. It entails understanding the place of slavery in the economy and in society. It involves studying the conflict among opposing conceptions of slavery held by different groups within a society—especially the daily struggle between masters and slaves to alter the demands being made upon slaves and whatever rights or privileges they might have. It involves analyzing the ways in which the various influences on slavery—economic, institutional, social, political, and ideological—reinforced, contradicted, or transformed one another. And, as Eugene Genovese has emphasized, it requires understanding the dynamics of the master-slave relationship itself: how slaveowners, whatever their background and whatever their motives for employing slaves, tried to create some kind of social order and how slaves tried to bend that order when it could not be broken.[31]

If plantation slavery turns out on close examination to be a social as well as an economic institution, slavery in a large number of African societies turns out to be an economic as well as a social phenomenon. Slavery in Africa took on a great variety of forms, but beneath the variations lies a common thread: the multiple and changing ways in which the slave's extreme subordination, in each society's own terms, could be exploited in changing historical situations.

As in the Americas, the slave was most often an outsider, that is, someone from outside the society's kinship structure. He could be a local person who had been totally removed from his kinship group in compensation for a crime which he or a kinsman had committed or for some other reason, but wherever slaves were numerous, the majority were either captured or purchased.[32] Slavery began with violence, and that trauma was the first step in incorporating slaves into the master's

31. Genovese, *World,* p. 96.

32. With relatively fragile apparatuses of government, few African rulers could have afforded to pervert the system of justice to supply large numbers of slaves from within their own society. So strong was the association of capture with enslavement that French colonial officials—and some modern scholars—preferred the word *captive* to *slave.* Meillassoux, pp. 12–13; Michael Mason, "Captive and Client Labour and the Economy of the Bida Emirate: 1857–1901," *Journal of African History* 14 (1973): 453–71.

society on the master's terms. The question is: on what basis were they incorporated into their new society, and to serve what ends?

Paul Bohannan and Philip Curtin write, "The object in buying a slave was to increase the size of one's own group, more often for prestige or military power than for the sake of wealth. Women were therefore more desirable than men, but men and women alike were assimilated into the master's social group."[33] This picture does fit peoples like the Ila of Central Africa, where the social fabric was made up of kinship groups cross-cut by marriage and other ties, and where the economy was not highly differentiated. Most slaves were bought from neighboring peoples, and youth was the most desirable attribute. New slaves were immediately adopted into the owner's kinship group and fully included in the group's rituals.

Little separated the lives of children brought into the kinship group from those born into it. Adult slaves relieved their owners of certain arduous tasks, but all Ila worked in the fields. Slaves could marry free Ila, but this was not the preferred pattern. In general, slaves' relationships developed within the most closely related kin group; they did not participate in the activities of broader kinship groupings to the same extent as the free. By the second generation, such distinctions were virtually nonexistent for the children of slave-free marriages and had become blurred even for the child of two slaves.[34]

Slavery among the Ila was primarily a way of adding members to kinship groups, but Arthur Tuden and Leonard Plotnicov could hardly have been more wrong in claiming that the Ila represented "the general condition of slavery in Africa."[35] They and similar societies were all the way at one end of the spectrum. Only if one assumes that all African societies were made up of kinship groups in perfect equilibrium, with no concentrations of power and no economic differentiation, will the conditions underlying Ila slavery apply generally. Africanists have in recent years emphasized the ability of African leaders to build powerful states and of African entrepreneurs to find new ways of amassing wealth, but most have preferred to ignore the fact that in Africa, as in most of the world, wealth and power also meant exploitation and subordination. The use of slaves was not the only route to power, and slaves were not the only exploited people, but the complexities of African societies were reflected in the diverse forms of slavery.

33. Paul Bohannon and Philip D. Curtin, *Africa and Africans* (Garden City, N.Y., 1971), p. 265.

34. Arthur Tuden, "Slavery and Social Stratification among the Ila of Central Africa," in Arthur Tuden and Leonard Plotnicov, eds., *Social Stratification in Africa* (New York, 1970), pp. 47–58.

35. Tuden and Plotnicov, "Introduction," ibid., p. 13.

The social egalitarianism of the Ila was not true of all African societies, and not all incorporated slaves as near-equals. Even if the life-style of slaves was similar to that of free people, they were often excluded from certain rituals, barred from marrying free people, and considered to belong to sublineages of lower status within their owner's kinship group. In some cases, slaves were gradually accepted as members of their new society; in others, second-generation slaves advanced to a more equal status; but in some, slave ancestry remained a stigma. It did not always define a distinct social category, as slave ancestry did in the United States, but it was a mark of low status, often expressed in the reluctance of free people to marry the descendants of slaves.[36] In hierarchical societies, slave status was a very important part of a wider system of stratification.[37]

Sexual subordination was often an important dimension of slavery, particularly because it gave the master-father fuller control of his offspring than he had over the children of his free wives. In matrilineal societies like the Yao of East Central Africa, children normally were considered members of their mother's kinship group, and the father, no matter how wealthy he became, had trouble converting wealth into strengthening his own kinship group. But slave-mothers, with no kinship group of their own, produced children for the master's own kinship group.[38] Sexual exploitation of slaves in such societies thus had very different social implications from American slaveowners' unions with their slaves, but in either case, control of reproduction was adapted to the social conditions of the master's society.

Politically, most African societies were differentiated. In small-scale societies, the emergence of a powerful man depended on his ability to recruit personal followers. In flexible situations, a variety of people, through ambition, desire for material rewards, or detachment from their own kinship groups, sought to join the entourage of powerful chiefs; but the strength of ties to kinship groups and local chiefs created structural obstacles to the acquisition of followers loyal to one man. Because slaves could be obtained by an individual on the market

36. The variety of forms of slave status in African societies may be seen in the essays in Meillassoux and Suzanne Miers and Igor Kopytoff, eds., *Slavery in Africa: Historical and Anthropological Perspectives* (Madison, Wis., 1977). I have examined the literature, as well as conceptual problems and approaches, in "Studying Slavery in Africa: Some Criticisms and Comparisons," paper presented to the Program of African Studies, Northwestern University, 9 February 1976.

37. M. G. Smith, "The Hausa System of Social Status," *Africa* 29 (1959): 239–51.

38. The importance of the master's control over reproduction is stressed by Meillassoux, esp. pp. 24–25. On slavery among the matrilineal Yao, see E. A. Alpers, "Trade, State, and Society among the Yao in the Nineteenth Century," *Journal of African History* 10 (1969): 410–13.

and because they were not part of local groups, they made good henchmen. While in the stable politics of kinship among the Ila, slaves
strengthened lineages, in the unstable situation of the Nyamwezi in the
nineteenth century, slaves strengthened aspiring chiefs in their struggles against the traditional order and each other. Some slaves were set
to work farming—freeing the chief and his entourage from normal agricultural activities and contributing to his wealth. Others became part
of the entourage itself—hunting, fighting, and intimidating.[39]

In more structured kingdoms, slave-henchman could be made into
officers of state and soldiers.[40] In the intricate administrative system of
the Hausa-Fulani, certain offices of state were reserved for free people,
some for slaves, and some—including several of the most important—
for eunuchs. These categories could balance each other, preventing a
slave-bureaucracy or slave-army from worming its way into power, as
did the Mamluks.[41]

The slave as a man of power seems totally out of keeping with Western ideas of the slave as a degraded and troublesome chattel. What the
paradox shows, however, is how well those rulers who used slave-subor-
dinates understood the meaning of slavery. Unlike members of other
kinship groups, slaves had no divided affiliations, and unlike the king's
own relatives, they stood no chance of succeeding him. Because the
status of slavery was inherently marginal and because the overwhelming majority of slaves faced a hard life, the incentives to serve one's
king and master loyally were strong.

Economically, most African societies were more complex than the
Ila. Where markets existed for local produce, African farmers
frequently responded by intensifying the scale of production. Kinship
ties and clientage could be mobilized to provide labor, but regular military campaigns and slave-trading networks made slaves the most flexible source of labor.[42] In the Sudanic areas of West Africa, urban concentrations and intricate trading networks within the Sudan, and
between it and the forest region to the south and the desert to the

39. Andrew Roberts, "Nyamwezi Trade," in Richard Gray and David Birmingham,
eds., *Pre-Colonial African Trade* (London, 1970), pp. 59–61.

40. Large domestic retinues, concubines, and eunuchs were also important symbols of
a king's prestige. See the descriptions of a number of West African courts in Allan G. B.
Fisher and Humphrey J. Fisher, *Slavery and Muslim Society in Africa* (Garden City, N.Y.,
1971), pp. 119–22, 169.

41. M. G. Smith, *Government in Zazzau* (Oxford, 1960). On slave-officials in the Sudanic
empires, see Nehemia Levtzion, *Ancient Ghana and Mali* (London, 1973), pp. 112–13, and
on slave-soldiers in other African kingdoms, see E. A. Oroge, "The Institution of Slavery
in Yorubaland with Particular Reference to the Nineteenth Century" (Ph.D. diss., University of Birmingham, 1971), pp. 2–112.

42. On the economic choices involved in creating a labor force, see Hopkins,
pp. 23–27.

north, made the cultivation of grain and other products an important source of income for the elite.[43] Not only did a substantial portion of the population in parts of the Sudan consist of slaves—50 percent in the region of Zaria, among the Hausa in northern Nigeria—but their ownership was concentrated in a few hands. Some owned hundreds.

The arrangements under which slaves worked varied. Sometimes, they were settled in villages, where they had a large measure of day-to-day independence but had to work their masters' fields as well as their own, or else set aside substantial amounts of produce for their owners. In Zaria, the bulk of the ruler's property consisted of slave settlements, and on the estates of prominent families slaves often worked under their owners' watchful eyes. These slaves thus farmed under different conditions than ordinary people. While locally born slaves were clearly demarcated from newly imported ones, both were part of a social category distinct from the free. Even manumission did not end the slave's dependent relationship with his master, and after the abolition of slavery by the British, most slaves had limited access to land and no place in Hausa society except through their ex-masters.[44] Different as Hausa slavery was from that of any society in the Americas, slaveowning was as vital a part of the economic, political, and social dominance of a ruling class as it was in the Southern United States.

In a great variety of historical circumstances in both Africa and the Americas, slaves served different functions and occupied different social positions. What they shared was the most fundamental element of slavery. As Moses Finley writes:

> What sets the slave apart from all other forms of involuntary labor is that, in the strictest sense, he is an outsider. He is brought into a new society violently and traumatically; he is cut off from all traditional human ties of kin and nation and even his own religion; he is prevented, insofar as that is possible, from creating new ties, except to his masters, and in consequence his descendants are as much outsiders, as unrooted as he was.[45]

43. The importance of slave labor to the economy of the medieval Sudan is emphasized by Levtzion, pp. 117–18, and for a later period, William A. Brown, "The Caliphate of Hamdullahi ca. 1818–1864: A Study in African History and Oral Tradition" (Ph.D. diss., University of Wisconsin, 1969), pp. 114–16, 124, 136. See also Meillassoux, pp. 16–17, and several of the papers in his collection.

44. For a fascinating description of life in a slave-owning household, see Mary Smith, *Baba of Karo: A Woman of the Moslem Hausa* (New York, 1964), pp. 35, 41–42, 44. See also M. G. Smith, "Slavery and Emancipation in Two Societies," *Social and Economic Studies* 3 (1954): 253, 264, 273–75, and *Zazzau*, pp. 353–57. Other instances of relatively intense use of slave labor are described in Meillassoux, pp. 159–60, 234.

45. Moses I. Finley, "The Idea of Slavery: Critique of David Brion Davis' *The Problem of Slavery in Western Culture*," in Foner and Genovese, p. 260.

Finley's last phrase takes him too far: slaves were everywhere incorporated into their new society. But his emphasis on their rootlessness does explain why their masters—whether motivated by greed, political ambition, or lineage solidarity—were able to exploit slaves more fully than they could people with firm roots in the society and culture, and why the masters could largely control the process of incorporation. It is not so much a question of a neat distinction between the slaves and the "free," as of a gradation of powerlessness. In some situations, the lower orders of a society were able to differentiate themselves from a still lower stratum of foreign slaves and their descendants; in others, the weakness of the "free" allowed them and slaves to be submerged in a wider subordinate stratum; and in others, slaves eventually were absorbed with only marginal liabilities into the society's basic social groups. As items of trade, sowers of their owners' grain, retainers of their king, or mothers of their masters' children, slaves experienced the extremes of subordination.

Part 1

Agricultural Development on the
East African Coast

1 The Arabs of Oman and the Growth of Trade in East Africa

The slaveowners and the slaves of East Africa were Muslims. They all shared the beliefs, laws, and traditions of a universalistic religious community. The first plantations were built by Omanis, who also brought with them their own experiences and values. Economic change was to bring its own imperatives, but the religious values and the particular experiences of the Omanis were a crucial point of departure for a changing society.

SLAVERY AND ISLAM

Addressing the question of whether the economy of the medieval Islamic world was a "just economy," Maxime Rodinson concludes:

> Like every body of moral and religious doctrines, it [Islam] can do no more than, at best, limit, among a certain number of the rich and powerful, the tendency to abuse the power and wealth they possess. . . . Familiarity with Islamic history suggests only that Islam's capacity is of the same order of magnitude as that of its rival ideologies, in other words, a very weak one.[1]

Like slaves, serfs, peasants, and workers throughout the world, the slaves on the plantations of the coast of East Africa could not expect to be treated kindly because of their masters' religious convictions. However, if, instead of trying to isolate the effects of religion on the character of slavery, one examines it within its economic and social context, religion's relevance again becomes apparent.

There is no such concept as "Islamic slavery," any more than there is a "Christian slavery" or a "pagan slavery"; yet the fact that coastal slaveowners and slaves were Muslims, not Christians or pagans, is an important one. However responsive to economic incentives they are, people still perceive their environments and their actions through normative frameworks. However greedy or vain, people in all but the most extreme circumstances seek the approval of their peers and attempt to

1. Maxime Rodinson, *Islam and Capitalism*, trans. Brian Pearce (New York, 1973), p. 72.

devise ideologies to convince themselves and those beneath them of the righteousness of their hegemony. Islam was crucial to the conceptions slaveholders had of themselves, their slaves, the master-slave relationship, and the social order. Behavior that appears to a modern historian as a response to complex economic, political, and social imperatives appeared to an insider as obedience to the will of God.

Islam differed from the religions of many African peoples in that it had a written tradition. Oral traditions have a tenacity of their own, but written ones have an even greater fixity. In studying a changing African slave system, it is important to note that a detailed set of doctrines governing the place of slaves in society was developed centuries before the first clove tree was planted. Such moral and legal codes could be reinterpreted or ignored—as they often were—but each generation of slaveowners had to evaluate its actions against the original texts.

Islam differed from Christianity—especially from the form to which it had evolved by the plantation era—in that it drew no distinction between church and state. The laws which the *kadis* (judges) of nineteenth-century East Africa enforced were derived by jurists, mainly in the first few centuries after Mohammed, from Koranic precepts. To the temporal sanctions facing the violator of the law could be added the threat of further punishment in the next world. This was certainly no guarantee that the laws would be obeyed, but the sacred origin of the law contrasts sharply with the cases where slave codes were written by planter-dominated local assemblies.

The view of slavery that came down to generations of Muslims—as expressed in the Koran and in the sayings of the Prophet—reflected the changing nature of Arabian society in the seventh century A.D. Arabia had long been divided into ethnic and kinship groups that frequently fought among themselves. The expansion of trade, particularly in the region of Mecca, helped to create a need for more inclusive types of relationships and less disruptive means of settling disputes. Koranic views of slavery reflect both the needs of individuals and groups for laborers and dependents, and the need to establish a Muslim community based on common values and a common institutional framework.[2]

Slavery had existed in pre-Islamic Arabia and was regarded by Muslims as a legitimate and moral institution. It became enshrined in the Koran, and legal commentators later worked out detailed regulations

2. Eric R. Wolf, "The Social Organization of Mecca and the Origins of Islam," *Southwestern Journal of Anthropology* 7 (1951): 331–50; W. Robertson Smith, *Kinship and Marriage in Early Arabia* (Cambridge, 1885); W. Montgomery Watt, *Muhammad at Mecca* (Oxford, 1953); Maxime Rodinson, *Mahomet* (Paris, 1961); Joseph Schacht, *The Origins of Muhammadan Jurisprudence* (Oxford, 1967).

governing social interaction between the free and the slaves and defining the slaves' place in society. They had little to say about the conditions of labor, for at the time most slaves were domestics or artisans: the question of industrial discipline did not arise.[3]

As befits a community seeking to maintain internal order, the enslavement of Muslims was forbidden. Only foreigners at war with the Muslims could be taken as slaves. As a member of a growing community, the captor or purchaser of a slave was required to convert him to Islam. The slave became a member of the Islamic community, aspiring to the same heavenly reward: he was a spiritual equal. At the same time, the slaveowners' requirements for loyal followers were reflected in the Koran's emphasis that slaves were socially subordinate and had to obey their masters. Certain rights of slaves were circumscribed, such as the right to own property, but what rights they had—including food, shelter, and marriage—were guaranteed. The master was responsible for the slave's economic transactions and crimes against others. This concern with the slaves' dependence on their masters within community norms did not negate the blunt fact of slavery—slaves could be bought and sold. Nor did conversion or local birth end slavery; only the master could do that. The slave was simultaneously exchangeable property, a dependent, a person with specified rights, and a member of the Muslim community.[4]

One aspect of the master-slave relationship treated in great detail was concubinage. Briefly, men were only allowed to have four wives, but they could take an unlimited number of concubines from among their own slaves. The law gave a special status to concubines who had borne their masters children, forbidding the owners to sell them and providing for their manumission upon the masters' deaths. Unlike the laws and customs of Christian nations, Islamic law defined the children of a master by his concubines—provided he acknowledged his paternity—to be legitimate and legally the equals of the offspring of his free wives.[5] The typical European image of concubinage—a lecherous old Arab taking lascivious delight in his vast harem—misses the social significance of slavery. For the master, the social advantages of having children were as important as the pleasure of begetting them; for the master's kinsmen, concubinage provided a way of enlarging the group as a

3. My understanding of Islamic theories of slavery and the variety of ways they were practiced owes much to an unpublished paper of Gavin R. G. Hambly, "Islamic Slavery: An Overview," presented to a faculty seminar at Yale University in 1972. See also R. Brunschvig, " 'Abd," *Encyclopedia of Islam* (Leiden, 1960), 1: 25–31.

4. Hambly; Brunschvig, pp. 24–40; Reuben Levy, *The Social Structure of Islam* (Cambridge, 1957), pp. 75–77.

5. Hambly; Levy, pp. 64, 77, 117–18; Brunschvig, pp. 28–29.

whole; and for the slave, subordination included the master's control of her womb.[6]

The fact that Islam regulated slavery may have been just as significant as the content of the regulations. Because slavery was clearly sanctioned within its prescribed limits, Muslims did not have to search for rationales for enslaving outsiders. The slaves' inferiority was part of the social order. Where slavery's ethical foundations were less secure and where the sense of hierarchy was crumbling, it could become difficult, ideologically, to defend slavery without arguing that slaves were not fully human. Such arguments did not take place in a vacuum, but it is worth noting that Islam was at one pole in sanctifying slavery as part of a social order, while Protestantism was at the other extreme, and Catholicism in the middle. Islam, in East Africa and elsewhere, never provided the ideological basis for an abolitionist movement, but neither did it foster systematic doctrines justifying slavery on the basis of the slaves' racial inferiority.[7]

Islamic history provides enough examples to demonstrate that the Koranic emphasis on the social position of slaves and its insistence on their spiritual equality was no guarantee against economic exploitation or ethnic antagonism.[8] However, the economies of the Middle East—unlike those of early-modern Europe—rarely created the conditions for the reduction of slaves to economic objects. Slavery, as in Mecca, was more often a concomitant of urban, commercial prosperity than a source or rural, agricultural income. Slaves were most often artisans, domestics, and concubines. Many helped in trading operations, while others served their masters as soldiers or henchmen. Dependent on their masters for all the benefits of life, slaves proved to be loyal followers, capable of serving their masters in a great variety of ways.[9]

6. This descent rule was not unique to Islam, but is found in many societies where kinship groups were structurally important. The significance of the master's control over the slave's reproductive capacity is emphasized, in the case of African societies, by Meillassoux in his introduction to *L'esclavage en Afrique précoloniale*, pp. 24–25.

7. On the connection between the Enlightenment, religious thought, abolitionist movements, and race, see Davis, *The Problem of Slavery in Western Culture*. The ways in which different intellectual traditions viewed the place of the slave in the social order cannot be isolated from economic and social change. See David B. Davis, *The Problem of Slavery in the Age of Revolution, 1770–1823* (Ithaca, N.Y., 1975).

8. In the salt-flats of Iraq in the ninth century A.D. the intense exploitation of African slaves provoked a severe revolt. See Bernard Lewis, *The Arabs in History* (New York, 1958), pp. 103–06.

9. Claude Cahen, "Economy, Society, Institutions," in P. M. Holt, A. K. S. Lambton, and B. Lewis, eds., *The Cambridge History of Islam* (Cambridge, 1970), 2: 516; Hambly; and Brunschvig, pp. 31–39. Among the case studies of slavery in various Islamic societies are: S. D. Goitein, "Slaves and Slave Girls in the Cairo Geniza Records," *Arabica* 9 (1962): 120; C. E. Bosworth, "Ghaznevid Military Organization," *Der Islam* 36 (1960): 37–77; David

The emphasis Islam placed on integrating slaves into the Muslim community did not prevent invidious distinctions from being made against these newcomers. However, the pattern of expansion of Islamic societies did not create the overwhelming association of being a slave with being black that the development of American plantations fostered. "White barbarians," Turks, and Slavs were enslaved as well as brown-skinned Ethiopians and black Africans. Elaborate stereotypes developed regarding the talents and weaknesses of slaves from different ethnic groups. Blacks, as Bernard Lewis has explained, generally were looked down upon.[10] Yet by law a slave was a slave, and in practice the absence of a distinct economic role for slaves reduced the impetus to associate a particular race with a particular occupation. The prevalence of concubinage meant that even members of the slaveowning group were likely to become darker.[11] The association of blackness with low-status slaves was a tendency, but color itself did not define social groups.[12]

The heritage of Mohammed's Arabia and the classical period of Islam—expressed in the Koran, the sayings of the Prophet, the works of legal scholars, and oral traditions—is to this day a strong and vital one. But Islam was not transmitted as an inviolable entity across time, space, and cultural differences. Just as Islam had developed in a particular social environment, so its impact on the East African coast depended on the local situation in the nineteenth century. It also depended on the experiences, habits, and conventions of the people who helped shape the changing situation on the coast.

Ayalon, *L'esclavage du Mamelouk* (Jerusalem, 1951); and Allen Meyers, "The ʿAbīd 'L-Buhārī: Slave Soldiers and Statecraft in Morocco, 1672–1790" (Ph.D. diss., Cornell University, 1974).

10. The stereotypes regarding slaves developed as part of a wider pattern of discrimination and prejudice against non-Arabs as the Islamic community expanded. Blacks stood out among non-Arabs because a distinctive appearance went along with the fact of subordination. Arabs also had less respect for the power and civilization of Africa than for other regions, while the abundance and relatively low price of black slaves made them preferable for low-status jobs. In short, the particularities of the processes of conquest and enslavement account for the tendency to look down on black slaves. Lewis, *Race and Color in Islam*, esp. pp. 25–29, 38, 64–65.

11. In some cases the child of a black concubine was looked down upon, but in others the children of slave mothers, including Africans, attained high positions. Lewis, *Race*, pp. 94–95; Levy, p. 64; Ignaz Goldziher, *Muslim Studies*, trans. C. R. Barber and S. M. Stern (Chicago, 1967), pp. 120–21.

12. Lewis, unfortunately, fails to go beyond his exposé of Arab prejudice into an analysis of its significance for social structure (*Race*, passim). For a discussion of how people in one part of the Islamic world defined the major structural divisions in society, see Albert Hourani, "Race and Related Ideas in the Near East," in Melvin M. Tumin, ed., *Comparative Perspectives on Race Relations* (Boston, 1969), pp. 162–63.

The Society and Economy of Oman

Omanis played a catalytic role in the economic development of the East African coast, and founded the first clove plantations on Zanzibar. Moreover, much more is known about slavery in Oman than slavery among the Swahili before the nineteenth century.

The Arabs of Oman belonged to one of several groups that had split off from the orthodox Caliphate in the generations after the Prophet's death. The Ibadis—found in parts of Algeria and Libya as well as Oman—denied the right of hereditary succession to the Caliphate and argued that only the community of the faithful could elect a leader. He could command obedience only when he himself remained faithful to the law. Puritanical and ascetic, they believed in rigid adherence to the laws as laid down by Mohammed and saw the creation of a truly Islamic social order, the imamate (after *iman*, "religious leader of the community"), as the only earthly task for man.[13] Ibadis "abominate Luxury and Pride," remarked an eighteenth-century European visitor to Oman.[14] Ibadi legal writing retained the egalitarian emphasis of Mohammed to a greater degree than other schools of law. In Ibadi theory, even a slave could aspire to be imam, the leader of the faithful.[15]

The Omanis were divided into a number of communal groups, such as Al-Ya'rubi, Al-Busaidi, Al-Mandhry, Al-Mazrui, and Al-Harthi. Although all of them had undoubtedly absorbed members of various origins, each claimed common descent and a common historical tradition. They were the primary focus of political loyalty. The group was obliged to fight for the individual and the individual for the group. Partly because the Ibadi imamate had never developed into a strong temporal authority commanding loyalty to the state, the communal groups remained strong. The imam tended to come from one particular group, but his power was weak, feuds chronic, and dynasties unstable.[16]

13. Elie Adib Salem, *Political Theory and Institutions of the Khawārij* (Baltimore, 1956), pp. 14–29; Tedeusz Lewicki, "Al-Ibadiyya," *Encyclopedia of Islam* (Leiden, 1971), 3: 652; Robert G. Landen, *Oman Since 1856: Disruptive Modernization in a Traditional Arab Society* (Princeton, N.J., 1967), p. 45; Wendell Phillips, *Oman: A History* (London, 1967), pp. 8–9.

14. Alexander Hamilton, *A New Account of the East Indies 1688–1723* (Edinburgh, 1727), 1: 62.

15. Salem, pp. 56–57, 62; Landen, pp. 42–44; Lewicki, p. 658; T. Lewicki, "The Ibadites of Arabia and Africa," *Cahiers d'Histoire Mondiale* 13 (1971): 556; Interview with Abdalla Saleh Al-Farsy, MSA 21. The Hadramaut, the southern portion of the Arabian peninsula, was more hierarchical. R. B. Serjeant, "Société et gouvernement en Arabie du Sud," *Arabica* 14 (1967): 285–91.

16. For analyses of Omani society and politics, see Landen; R. D. Bathurst, "The Ya'rubi Dynasty of Oman" (D. Phil. diss., Oxford University, 1967), and J. B. Kelly, *Sultanate and Imamate in Oman* (London, 1959). The centrality of communal conflict to Omani history is clear in the chronicle of Salil-ibn-Razik, *History of the Imams and Seyyids of 'Oman from A.D. 661–1856*, ed. and trans. G. P. Badger (London, 1871).

Map 1 : The Indian Ocean

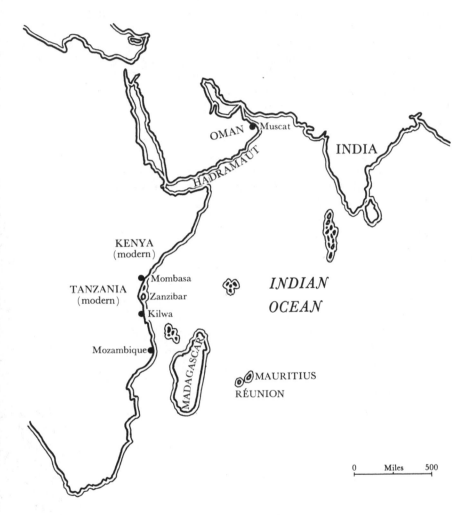

The ascetic Ibadis of Oman were favored with better material circumstances than many other Arabs. Parts of their country had enough water for the cultivation of subsistence crops and date palms. Most important, Oman occupied a position commanding the junction of the Persian Gulf with the Indian Ocean. Sailing vessels traveling between East Africa and India crept along the coast, passing Oman, while much trade from Turkey, Persia, and other areas near the gulf had to pass Oman's main port and capital, Muscat.[17]

As early as the first century A.D., Omanis were sailing and even settling along the East African coast, seeking the luxury goods from the hinterland. The trade sometimes prospered and sometimes stagnated, particularly during the period of Portuguese hegemony in the Indian Ocean in the sixteenth and seventeenth centuries.[18] The subsequent decline of Portuguese power enabled the Omanis to reassert themselves. They expelled the last Portuguese forces from Muscat by 1650 and set about strengthening their military position in the Persian Gulf area and in East Africa. Omani seamen developed improved sailing vessels and used them in raids and trade. The imam himself became a wealthy merchant and owner of ships, date plantations, and slaves.[19]

However, Oman remained torn by internecine warfare. Omanis in the interior did not feel as much as their urban brethren the moderating influences of commercial success and were truer to Ibadi conceptions of the imamate. The imam's preoccupation with his own business affairs, religious disagreement, and urban-rural conflict, superimposed on communal feuds, were too much for the reigning Al-Ya'rubi dynasty to handle and led to Persian intervention and domination in the 1730s and 1740s.[20] When Oman emerged from the debacle, it was under the rule of a forceful, dynamic, and ruthless ruler from a rival group, Ahmed bin Said Al-Busaidi.

Al-Busaidi rule did not mean the end of communal wars or religious differences, but the new dynasty was at least sufficiently strong to retain political power in Oman, to regain military hegemony in the Persian Gulf, and to provide the stability necessary for trade to expand.[21] Ahmed bin Said himself did not take the title of *imam* but styled himself

17. Landen, passim.

18. Ibid., pp. 52–53; Justus Strandes, *The Portuguese Period in East Africa*, trans. J. F. Wallwork (Nairobi, 1961); Charles R. Boxer and Carlos de Azevedo, *Fort Jesus and the Portuguese in Mombasa 1593–1729* (London, 1960).

19. Landen, pp. 54–55; Bathurst, pp. 173–76.

20. Salil-ibn-Razik; pp. 92–93; Bathurst, p. 205; Landen, pp. 56–58; Phillips, pp. 53–56.

21. Carsten Niebuhr, *Travels through Arabia* (Edinburgh, 1792), 2:120–22; Landen, pp. 58–61.

Seyyid, meaning "lord" or "master." [22] He became, besides a strong military leader, a prosperous trader. His successors followed in his footsteps.[23]

By 1800 the Arabs of Oman were considered the "best mariners in all Arabia" and were sailing throughout the Indian Ocean. British authorities in Bombay anxiously observed the "amazing increase in the shipping and navigation of the Subjects of the Imam of Muscat." More and more of the local sailing vessels, dhows, plied the ocean routes, and Omanis even began to use square-rigged vessels built for them in India.[24]

The port of Muscat was essentially an entrepôt. Arab traders brought cowrie shells, rice, wood, wax, hides, and—of greatest importance— ivory and slaves from East Africa. European products, metals, cloth, rice, sugar, and other goods came from India. Pearls and drugs came from Persia and coffee from the Hadramaut. All imports were redistributed widely. Trade had become "a never failing source of wealth." [25] Customs revenues have been variously estimated at $47,000 (1765), $141,000 (1802), and $180,000 (ca. 1815). Officials in Bengal in 1807 noted that an "enormous and annually increasing capital" was invested in Arab trade with the Indian subcontinent alone.[26]

22. This term should be carefully distinguished from the way *seyyid* is used in the Hadramaut, where it refers to a descendant of the Prophet. In Oman, it is a more general term of respect that was adopted by the Al-Busaidi dynasty. Later, the term *Sultan* came into use, and is still used by East Africans to refer to the ruler of Oman and Zanzibar. See J. B. Kelly, *Britain and the Persian Gulf 1795–1880* (Oxford, 1968), p. 12.

23. On Al-Busaidi business activity, see Niebuhr, 2: 122; Edmund Roberts to Louis McLane, 14 May 1834, *NEMA,* p. 156; A. de Gobineau, *Trois ans en Asie, de 1855 à 1858* (Paris, 1823), 1: 109; S. B. Miles, *The Countries and Tribes of the Persian Gulf* (London, 1919; repr. 1966), pp. 266–67; Phillips, pp. 62–68.

24. Niebuhr, 2: 123; Samuel Manesty and Harford Jones, "Report on British Trade with Persia and Arabia," 15 December 1790, Ind. Off., G/29/21, pp. 210–11, 223. "Report on the External Commerce under the Presidency of Bombay, 1803/04," Ind. Off., P/419/41, par. 49, 52, 53; Seton to Bombay, 9 July 1802, Bombay Political Consultations, Proceedings for 27 August 1802, Ind. Off., P/381/33, p. 3613; W. F. W. Owen, *Narrative of Voyages to Explore the Shores of Africa, Arabia and Madagascar* (London, 1833), 1: 334.

25. Seton to Bombay, p. 3615; "External Commerce, Bombay," par. 56; Niebuhr, 2: 116; Owen, 1: 340; J. S. Buckingham, "Voyage from Bushire to Muscat," *Oriental Herald* 22 (1829): 89; Manesty and Jones, pp. 210–11; M. Hugo, "Notes Extraites de la 5ᵉ lettre d'un officier de cavalerie sur ses voyages en Afrique et en Asie," 1772, Colonies F2C/12, AN. See also Landen, pp. 61–63; Kelly, *Britain,* pp. 14–16; and Abdul Mohamed Hussein Sheriff, "The Rise of a Commercial Empire: An Aspect of the Economic History of Zanzibar, 1770–1873" (Ph.D. diss., University of London, 1971), pp. 42–43.

26. Niebuhr, 2: 116; Seton to Bombay, p. 3609; Vincenzo Maurizi, *History of Seyd Said, Sultan of Muscat* (London, 1819), p. 29; "Report on the External Commerce of Bengal, 1806–7," Ind. Off., P/174/18, par. 59, 65.

The large commercial expansion in the Indian Ocean during the eighteenth century resulted from several factors: a revival of older patterns of trade in the wake of Portuguese decline, increasing demand for ivory and other African produce in India and Europe, a demand for slaves by Europeans and Asians, the availability of Indian capital to finance trade, and the initiative of Africans in bringing goods from the interior to coastal ports. Oman's catalytic role followed from its renewed political vigor, which enabled her merchants and sailors to take advantage of her geographical position and allowed the Sultan to extend his political control to key East African ports, including Zanzibar and Kilwa in the late eighteenth century. A progressive Sultan, himself a trader, kept duties and exactions low, gave his own and foreign merchants free rein, and provided them with security in Muscat and the major ports of East Africa. However, the Omani governors of these ports did not penetrate inland and left local communal groups a large measure of independence. The Omani empire was a network of ports, held together more by shared commercial interests than by a state structure.[27]

Despite the increased scale of commerce and the wealth flowing into it, the extent of structural change within Oman was limited. Not all the benefits of Muscat's role as emporium fell into Arab hands. Indian merchants—numbering about 1,200 in the late eighteenth century and 4,000 in the early nineteenth—dominated certain branches of trade, such as pearls and coffee, and were among the major shipowners.[28] The job of collecting customs revenue was entrusted to an Indian. Most important, Indians were the "Bankers of Arabia," who provided much of the capital used in commerce. Even the Sultan, the richest merchant of all, turned to Indians to finance his trading ventures.[29]

The commercial activities of Omanis were directed toward the exchange centers of Oman and East Africa, the carrying trade itself, and later toward up-country caravans. Much of their success was within the familiar role of merchant-adventurer. The trading voyage was neither a specialized nor a regularized business. Dhows—constrained by the monsoon winds to making only one round trip between Arabia and Africa each year—stopped along the way, buying and selling as the opportunity arose. Dhows were not tied to trade in any one type of merchandise but generally carried a variety of goods.[30] Captain and crew

27. Sheriff; Landen; Edward A. Alpers, *Ivory and Slaves in East Central Africa* (Berkeley, Calif. 1975); C. S. Nicholls, *The Swahili Coast: Politics, Diplomacy and Trade on the East African Littoral, 1798–1856* (London, 1971).

28. Niebuhr, 2: 116; Maurizi, p. 23; "External Commerce, Bombay," par. 54; J. R. Wellsted, *Travels in Arabia* (London, 1838), 1: 19, 23–24.

29. Maurizi, p. 29; Owen, 1: 340.

30. Wellsted, 1: 23–24. Wellsted's description is similar to that of Alan Villiers a cen-

were often personal dependents of the owner—bound to him either because they were his slaves or because of long-term indebtedness.[31]

External commerce did not transform the internal economy of Oman. Date production may have increased in the early nineteenth century, probably owing to improved access to markets, more capital to invest, and better supplies of slaves, but it remained a small fraction of Muscat's commerce.[32] Oman had no other economically important agricultural products or industry and internal trade was modest.[33]

That money was being brought into Oman did not mean that the antimaterialist values of the Ibadis were completely negated. To be sure, Muscat contained a number of wealthy men whose fortunes were linked to trade, while a substantial proportion of the population enjoyed "independence and comfort." [34] However, most observers were struck by the simplicity of life and the modesty of dress, houses, and mosques, even in the port of Muscat. Some attributed this indifference to display to the Ibadi creed, for the Omanis remained pious.[35] In fact, Ibadi political and social ideals remained strong enough to reassert themselves in mid-nineteenth century in the form of a powerful, and partly successful, movement to restore the old imamate. In the interior, the social structure was still dominated by the various communal groups, living off pastoralism and small-scale agriculture, often fighting with one another and with the Sultan. Even the inhabitants of the coast—urban life and business notwithstanding—kept close personal and political ties with their homelands. New social groups did not emerge.[36]

Although Al-Busaidi Sultans dropped the title of *imam,* they stuck to other qualities of the old-fashioned ruler. They recruited personal ar-

tury later. "Some Aspects of the Arab Dhow Trade," *The Middle East Journal* 2 (1948): 400–04.

31. Horace B. Putnam, Journal, 1847, Essex Institute, *NEMA,* p. 404. On slaves as sailors, see the next section. Relations of dependence, underscored by perpetual indebtedness, characterize the twentieth-century dhow trade as well. Villiers, pp. 403–04, 410–11; A. H. J. Prins, *Sailing from Lamu: A Study of Maritime Culture in Islamic East Africa* (Assen, 1965), pp. 213–14.

32. Captain Loarer, "Ile de Zanguébar," O.I., 5/23, notebook 5; "Report on the External Commerce under the Presidency of Bombay," 1807–08, 1808–09, table 3; Buckingham, p. 89; Wellsted, 1: 279, Sheriff, p. 41.

33. Wellsted, 1: 317; A. Germain, "Quelques mots sur l'Oman et le Sultan de Maskate," *Bulletin de la Société de Géographie* (Paris), 5th ser. 16 (1868): 344.

34. Wellsted, 1: 347–48. See also Sheriff, pp. 33–35, 41–43, and Landen, pp. 60–63.

35. Niebuhr, 2: 188; Maurizi, pp. 104, 111–12; Germain, p. 352. Hugo, 1772, Colonies F2C/12, AN. Perhaps asceticism indirectly contributed to economic development by encouraging—as in Protestant Europe—investment instead of consumption. Ibadis from North Africa were also notably successful in commerce. Lewicki, "Ibadites," pp. 51–130.

36. Wellsted, 1: 232–33, 366. On urban-rural and commercial-purist conflict, see Landen, passim, and J. B. Kelly, *Sultanate,* pp. 5–6.

mies, relying in part on slaves, while they also sought to appease the communal groups and leading families, relying on personal connections and the distribution of wealth to cement bonds with their supporters. Heads of leading groups and families behaved in a like manner toward their followers.[37] The politics of patrimonialism still flourished.

Like Europeans in the fifteenth to eighteenth centuries, Omanis at the dawn of the nineteenth century were extending their horizons to distant lands in search of items to trade. However, in Europe, long-distance trade went hand-in-hand with the restructuring of agriculture, labor, internal markets, state organization, and social values. Omani entrepreneurship brought in wealth, but no innovations and only modest expansion in agriculture, no breakthroughs in a limited domestic market, greater dependence on foreigners for financial transactions, and only moderate changes in social values and institutions. Fundamental changes in the organization of production—forcing the restructuring of social relationships—came about only in the nineteenth century, and principally among those Omanis who emigrated to East Africa.

SLAVES IN OMANI SOCIETY

Slavery was an old institution in Southern Arabia—older than the Islamic religion—and by the late eighteenth century it was a pervasive one as well. Slaves were "very numerous," and a "great mart for slaves" flourished in Muscat. One imam reputedly owned 700 male slaves.[38]

A large number of these slaves were house servants. Arabs had two or more servants; the rich often had dozens; and the Sultan himself, over a hundred.[39] Certain servants held responsible positions in large households. However, the amount of work demanded of servants was not great, for the "wants of any individual are few." [40] A large personal retinue was a better sign of importance than material objects, and servants were intended as much for display as for relief from the drudgery of daily life.[41]

37. Wellsted, 1: 349, 380–81; Germain, pp. 352–53. See also Kelly, *Sultanate,* p. 5.

38. Irfan Shahid, "Pre-Islamic Arabia," in Holt et al., *Cambridge History,* 1: 7; Hamilton, 1: 63; Salil-ibn-Razik, pp. 92–93, 165; Maurizi, pp. 131–32; James B. Fraser, *Narrative of a Journey into Khorosan in the Years 1821 and 1822* (London, 1825), p. 6; Edmund Roberts, *Embassy to the Eastern Courts of Cochin-China, Siam and Muscat, 1832–4* (New York, 1837), p. 334. Wellsted, in 1838, estimated that 4,000 slaves were sold in Muscat each year (1: 388).

39. Wellsted, 1: 195, 390–91; Memorandum by J. S. Buckingham, 20 June 1842, in FO 54/4; R. Mignan, *A Winter Journey through Russia, the Caucasian Alps and Georgia, thence . . . into Koordistan* (London, 1839), 2: 239–40.

40. Maurizi, p. 104. Buckingham, "Voyage," p. 92; Wellsted, 1: 390–91.

41. A similar conclusion was reached by an ethnographic survey. "Eastern Arabia," in Human Relations Area Files, Subcontractor's Monograph 51 (1956), pp. 178–79.

Other slaves were trained to be sailors. If they proved their loyalty, they could be put in command of ships and entrusted with valuable merchandise.[42] Sultans made some of their slaves into soldiers. One reportedly had a guard of 100 slaves armed with guns, and Ahmed bin Said Al-Busaidi, when he became Sultan, bought 1,000 East African slaves and 100 Nubians to guard his fortress. Even in the nineteenth century, Seyyid Said bin Sultan employed slaves as soldiers. Slave-soldiers who distinguished themselves could be made into officers or even governors of cities.[43] In a society as divided as Oman, a Sultan could trust a slave more than a free subject.

Concubinage was common. Omanis who could afford it preferred brown-skinned, Caucasian-featured Ethiopian women and were willing to pay more for them than for Central African slaves.[44] The price differential is clear evidence that Arabs were color-conscious, but their children by mothers of all races were accepted as legitimate. The Islamic laws of concubinage meant that color was not a good indicator of status. The "pure Arab element" in the Omani population was "remarkably small."[45]

The most important productive role for slaves was on the date plantations. In the interior, farming communities, although they possessed slaves, did not require much labor to handle the scale of cultivation in which they were engaged.[46] On the coastal belt, date palms were grown on individually owned plantations. The trees were a favorite investment and the produce a cash crop.[47] Some estates had 3,000 to 5,000 trees, while one imam allegedly planted 30,000 date palms and owned

42. Memorandum by E. C. Ross, incl. Ross to Argyll, 25 January 1873, Letters from the Persian Gulf, Ind. Off., L/P&S/9/22; Wellsted, 1: 391; Mignan, 2: 240.

43. Hamilton, 1: 66; Salil-ibn-Razik, p. 165; Wellsted, 1: 381; Maurizi, pp. 29–30; Buckingham Memorandum. Seyyid Said's governor of Zanzibar was an Ethiopian slave. See chapter 5.

44. Wellsted, in 1838, wrote that Galla slaves from Ethiopia sold for $100 to $150, whereas black slaves from the Zanzibar coast were worth $40–60 (1: 389; see also Buckingham, "Voyage," p. 92). Ethiopian males also commanded a high price and were often used in responsible jobs in the household or business. Buckingham, "Voyage," p. 93; Kemball to Robertson, 8 July 1842, PP 1843, LIX, 337, p. 26.

45. A. S. G. Jayakar, "Medical Topography of Muscat," Muscat Annual Report, 1876/77, p. 102, Ind. Off.; Hugo, 1772, Colonies F2C/12, AN. Wellsted also notes that the Arabs of the hinterland were fairer than those of the coast, suggesting that miscegenation with Africans was more frequent among the Omanis who were most active in trade and hence the wealthiest. His reference to the purity of Arabian descent among the "highest orders" of Omanis apparently refers to leaders of interior communal groups (1: 17, 33).

46. Wellsted, 1: 52–53. Wellsted's references to slaves in the interior do not indicate any role for them in agriculture. Ibid., pp. 63–64, 70, 187. For more recent information on agriculture in the interior of Oman, see Human Area Relations Files 51, pp. 164–65.

47. Wellsted, 1: 189, 347–48; Fraser, p. 18; Muscat, Annual Report, 1876/77, p. 79, Ind. Off.

1,700 slaves.[48] Few Omanis, however, cultivated dates on this scale, and some landowners leased their estates to tenants rather than farming it with the aid of their own slaves.[49]

The date tree is not a difficult tree to cultivate. With some exaggeration, a visitor wrote that it "yields its nutritious and abundant produce almost spontaneously," so that the agriculturalist was "free from the life of severe and unremitted toil, to which so large a portion of the population of Europe is always condemned." [50] Contemporary observers occasionally saw slaves in date groves and on other farms, but reported no evidence that slaves were closely supervised or overworked.[51] This situation was not necessarily the result of their masters' benevolence but of the limited demands of Omani agriculture.

The evidence from European visitors to Oman on the treatment of slaves is subjective and general. However, in so far as it is valid, there is virtual unanimity that slaves, whether house servants or field hands, were treated with "kindness," "consideration," or even "indulgence." "Public opinion," wrote a British official, condemned cruelty to slaves. Some observers claimed that slaves were treated as members of the families they served.[52] According to the explorer J. R. Wellsted, a slave who was mistreated could go to the kadi and demand a public sale. Although the master could sell, exchange, or punish slaves, he could not inflict the death penalty on his slaves without public trial. Young slaves were given an Islamic education and the children of slaves, unless they were freed, were treated with more familiarity than new slaves and given work in the house.[53] The data, while not conclusive, suggest that

48. Fraser, pp. 16–18; Bathurst, p. 205; Seton to Bombay, 9 July 1808, Bombay Political Consultations, Proceedings for 27 August 1802, Ind. Off., P/381/33, p. 2609. Some of the wealthiest Omani families now in Mombasa used to have date plantations in Oman. MSA 14 and MSA 27.

49. Wellsted, 1: 347–48; Fraser, p. 18.

50. Maurizi, p. 110. A detailed commercial report by the French consul in 1900 indicated that in good date country a single worker could care for 1,000 palms. Where well-water was required, he could still tend 200 trees. Ottavi, "Report commercial sur l'Oman et Mascate," 1900, MAE, Correspondence Commerciale, Mascate, II. For more on the requirements of date cultivation, see Human Area Relations Files 51, p. 179, and F. S. Vidal, "Date Culture in the Oasis of Al-Hasa," in Abdulla M. Lutifiyya and Charles W. Churchill, eds., Readings in Arab and Middle Eastern Societies and Cultures (The Hague, 1970), pp. 209–10.

51. Fraser, p. 18; Ross Memorandum; diary of Lieutenant-Colonel Disbrowe, entry for 16 April 1865, PP 1867–68, LXIV, 657, p. 126.

52. Fraser, p. 18; Ross Memorandum; Wellsted, 1: 390–91; Mignan, 2: 239–40; W. G. Palgrave, A Narrative of a Year's Journey through Central and Eastern Arabia (1862–63) (London, 1865), 2: 272; Germain, p. 351.

53. Wellsted, 1: 390–91; Ross Memorandum.

slaves, although regarded as inferiors, at least had the mixed benefits of paternalism.[54]

Manumission was apparently common. William G. Palgrave, who visited Oman in 1862–63, claimed that most slaves who did not die young were eventually freed, so that about one-fourth of the population of Oman consisted of freed African slaves and their descendants. The death of the master was the principal occasion for freeing slaves.[55] Some freed slaves settled in the countryside, sometimes intermingled with the free population, sometimes living in separate villages. In Muscat, most ex-slaves worked as servants, water carriers, gardeners, sailors, and the like.[56] A few, mainly Ethiopian ex-servants, were able to become substantial merchants.[57] Freed slaves, in practice, were less than the equals of their former masters. A slave, whatever Ibadi theory maintained, could never have become imam, and few had the opportunity to acquire wealth or the esteem of their fellow Muslims.

The Arabs of Oman were familiar with slavery as an institution and with African slaves as people. They used slaves to perform a variety of tasks, but the position of slaves was conditioned by the absence of labor-intensive industries. It was perfectly normal for slaves to serve as ship captains and soldiers, not just as menial laborers. Religious texts and social norms treated slaves as social inferiors, not as degraded and inherently inferior beings, while the economic situation did not foster the belief that slaves were capable only of mindless labor under close supervision. Slaves were as much an item of consumption—as domestics or living displays of wealth—as of production. In a society divided into feuding communal groups, slaves were valued as reliable soldiers and trusted retainers. Never considered the social equals of their masters, the slaves of Oman were above all else an integral part of a hierarchical social order.[58]

54. The only contrary evidence comes from British ships later in the nineteenth century, which picked up slaves who had fled their masters, sometimes complaining of mistreatment. Commander Needham to Sir F. Richards, 10 May 1887, FOCP 5616, p. 85; "Précis on the Slave Trade, 1906," Ind. Off., p. 52. An earlier source, however, claimed that desertion was rare. Germain, p. 351.

55. Palgrave, Narrative, 2: 272; Germain, p. 351; Wellsted, 1: 390.

56. W. G. Palgrave, "Observations Made in Central, Eastern and Southern Arabia during a journey through that Country in 1862 and 1863," Journal of the RGS 34 (1864): 151–52; de Gobineau, 1: 113; Palgrave, Narrative, 2: 272, 366; Germain, p. 351; Maurizi, pp. 100–01; J. B. F. Osgood, Notes of Travel or Recollections of Majunga, Zanzibar, Muscat, Aden, Mocha and Other Eastern Ports (Salem, Mass., 1854), pp. 92–93.

57. Buckingham, "Voyage," pp. 92–93.

58. In the adjacent portion of Southern Arabia, the Hadramaut, where many immigrants to East Africa also originated, slavery did not involve labor-intensive industry. Foreign observers thought it basically similar to slavery in Oman. Wellsted, 2: 434;

TRADE ON THE EAST COAST OF AFRICA, 1800–1860

Omani initiative in the seaborne trade would have meant little had it not been for the growth of trading centers on the East African coast and of trade routes to the interior. The coastal towns, inhabited by ethnically mixed populations speaking the Swahili language, jealously guarded their political independence during the centuries of foreign commercial activity. They farmed, fished, and actively traded, obtaining products like ivory, rhinoceros horn, and slaves from the peoples of the interior. For their part, hinterland peoples like the Yao were expanding their regional trading networks to more profitable markets. It was on commercial cooperation across land and sea that the long history of trade in African produce was based.[59]

The expansion of a commercial network centered on Zanzibar in the late eighteenth and early nineteenth centuries laid the foundations for the development of plantation agriculture. The growth of the dhow and caravan trade linked the East African coast with sources of slaves in the interior of Africa and potential markets throughout the Indian Ocean trading system. Commerce provided capital for investment in agriculture. Yet despite its profitability, trade was a risky business, subject to the dangers of travel across stormy seas and war-torn lands, buffeted by competition from Indians and intermittent bursts of activity against the slave trade by the British. In part, the decision of Omanis to invest in clove plantations may have reflected a choice of life-style: once a viable source of income was found, traders may have preferred to settle down to a more relaxed life on their estates.[60] Plantation development can also be explained as an economic decision to diversify sources

---

J. Theodore Bent, "Expedition to the Hadramut," *The Geographical Journal* 4 (1894): 322. See also Serjeant, p. 287, and "Southern Arabia," Human Area Relations Files Sub-contractor's Monograph 52 (1956), p. 130.

59. Alpers emphasizes the initiatives of the interior peoples in commercial development, even though their entrepreneurship ended by tying their economies to the needs of distant areas over which they had no control. On economic and political relationships between coastal towns and their hinterlands, see the following Ph.D. dissertations: William Francis McKay, "A Precolonial History of the Southern Kenya Coast," Boston University, 1975; F. J. Berg, "Mombasa under the Busaidi Sultanate: The City and Its Hinterland in the Nineteenth Century," University of Wisconsin, 1971; Marguerite Ylvisaker, "The Political and Economic Relationship of the Lamu Archipelago to the Adjacent Kenya Coast in the Nineteenth Century," Boston University, 1975; Thomas Spear, "The Kaya Complex: A History of the Mijikenda Peoples of the Kenya Coast to 1900," University of Wisconsin, 1974.

60. There is no direct evidence on the motivation of clove planters, such as diaries or record books. The economic reasons behind the development of clove production are inferred from timing and from the economic situation in general.

of income in an uncertain world. Yet the growth of clove planting did not represent a retreat from commerce. Omanis took to clove growing slowly and cautiously while continuing to trade.[61]

Of the many East African commodities that contributed to Indian Ocean commerce, ivory and slaves were the most important. Yao and other African traders had, since the seventeenth century, found eager customers for ivory among Portuguese and Indian traders in towns along the southern coast, while ports like Mombasa on the northern coast had valuable trading relationships with their hinterlands. Omani domination of the northern ports from mid-eighteenth century onward provided Arab and Indian traders with the security they needed, and Oman's takeover of Kilwa offered Yao traders better conditions than the Portuguese to the south. Moreover, the rising demand for ivory in India, Europe, and the United States, combined with the declining price of cotton goods—the leading import—meant that terms of trade for coastal merchants were generally good in the first half of the nineteenth century.[62] Much of this trade came to be directed through the principal Omani entrepôt, Zanzibar, and the expansion of commerce can be seen in the figures on customs revenues, as shown in Table 1:1.

Oman, Persian Gulf countries, and India had long imported slaves. This trade continued, and probably increased, in the early nineteenth century.[63] The development of European sugar plantations on the islands of Bourbon and Ile de France further stimulated the slave trade. The slave population of the islands grew from nothing to over 100,000 in the course of the eighteenth century. Slaves were also exported to Brazil and the Caribbean, mainly in the nineteenth century, although not on the scale of the West African slave trade.[64] Mozambique was exporting an average of 5,400 slaves per year between 1786 and 1794,

61. My interpretation differs from that of Abdul Sheriff, who argues that the inability of Omanis to compete with Indians in the ivory trade, and the decline of the European slave trade, both of which occurred around the 1820s, induced Omanis to seek a new source of income: Omanis became planters because they failed as traders. Sheriff fails to note, as described in the next chapter, that the peak of clove planting occurred between 1835 and 1845, nearly two decades after the events which supposedly brought it about. He also overestimates the importance to Zanzibar of the European slave trade, while he underestimates the trade to Arabia. Finally, his persuasive evidence of increasing Indian participation in commerce, and above all in finance, does not imply a corresponding decline in profits made by Omanis. For a more complete analysis, see Frederick Cooper, "Plantation Slavery on the East Coast of Africa in the Nineteenth Century" (Ph.D. diss., Yale University, 1974), pp. 74–101.

62. Sheriff, pp. 101, 124–26, 207–14, 267; Alpers, pp. 166, 234–35.

63. The French were attracted to Kilwa because of the well-developed Arab slave trade there. Alpers, p. 150.

64. Auguste Toussaint, *Histoire des îles mascareignes* (Paris, 1972), pp. 335–36; Alpers, pp. 127, 185–89, 210–18.

TABLE 1:1

THE SULTAN'S INCOME FROM CUSTOMS AT ZANZIBAR

M.T. Dollars

1807–08	30–40,000
1811	60,000
1819	80,000
1834	150,000
1842	150,000*
1844	125,000
1862	200,000

SOURCES: Henry Salt, *A Voyage to Abyssinia and Travels into the Interior of that Country* (London, 1814; repr. 1967), p. 91; Captain Smee, "Observations during a voyage of research on the East Coast of Africa from Cape Gardafui south to the island of Zanzibar" (1811), reprinted in Richard Burton, *Zanzibar, City, Island, Coast* (London, 1872), 2:491; Fortené Albrand, "Extraits d'une memoire sur Zanzibar et sur Quiloa," *Bulletin de la Société de Géographie* (Paris), 2d ser. 10 (1838): p. 78; Captain H. Hart, "Extracts from Brief Notes of a Visit to Zanzibar . . . 1834," in Papers of Sir John Gray, Royal Commonwealth Society, London, Box B1; Atkins Hamerton to Aberdeen, 21 May 1842, FO 54/4; Michael W. Shepard, "Log Book of Bark *Star, 1844,*" copy in Gray Papers, Box B2; Speer to Seward, 26 November 1862, US Consul, 4.

* The total revenue of the Sultan, of which duties were the largest, but not the only, portion.

while Kilwa and Zanzibar were selling to Europeans at most 2,500 per year, and probably less.[65]

Numerically, the European slave trade was more important to the southern—Portuguese-dominated—section of the coast than to the northern region, where Omanis held sway. But, as with ivory, African traders were acutely sensitive to changing trading conditions in different ports and could redirect the traffic as circumstances warranted. The main significance of the European demand for slaves—added to the Asian markets—was the stimulus it gave to the creation of a slave-trading infrastructure linking hinterland sources with coastal markets.[66] The growing African commitment to international trade

65. These estimates come from Alpers, pp. 185–87, 191–92. The best evidence for Kilwa is a figure of 1,500 from the 1770s. Some Portuguese trade may later have been attracted to Kilwa, but there is also reason to believe that the French slave trade was not very important to the Zanzibari economy around 1800. A French slaver reported in 1804 that his attempts to buy slaves were discouraged, while the slave trade with Muslims was being promoted. Report of Captain P. Dallons, reprinted in G. S. P. Freeman-Grenville, *The East African Coast: Select Documents* (Oxford, 1962), pp. 198–201. A similar conclusion is reached by J.-M. Filliot, *La traite des esclaves vers les mascareignes au XVIIIe siècle* (Paris, 1974), p. 174.

66. Coming at the time when Omani power in East Africa was being consolidated, the French slave trade may have helped to motivate Oman to maintain close control of Kilwa,

brought people like the Makua in the nearby hinterland, and later those living near Lake Nyasa, to coastal ports, where they were sent wherever people were willing to pay for them.[67]

Slaves—and ivory—were brought to Kilwa and other ports by people like the Yao. For them, trade not only presented opportunities to obtain desirable goods, but also gave leaders the chance to enhance their power by redistributing some of their new-found wealth and by buying guns. The high stakes of defeat left others with little choice but to raid and trade. Only well into the nineteenth century did Swahili and Arabs mount expeditions and found inland bases to trade for ivory and slaves and, less often and generally with local allies, to raid for slaves. Through a complex series of transactions, slaves—captured in wars and raids or obtained by other means—ended up on the coast and eventually in Zanzibar. Rapid rise and fall of political fortunes—and general insecurity—affected a widening portion of East Central Africa in the nineteenth century. Both this state of conflict and flux and the developing networks for bringing human and other produce to the coast contributed to the Zanzibari economy.[68]

As the trade routes expanded into the interior of East Africa, the system of distribution of ivory and slaves became increasingly centered on Zanzibar. The development of Zanzibar as an entrepôt was in part the result of Omani policies to concentrate trade in the area of tightest Omani control and the importance of protection to Indian, Omani, and other traders. More fundamentally, the rise of Zanzibar was a consequence of geography. With a fine harbor, Zanzibar was more accessible and safer than other ports. Above all, the necessity that sailors follow the patterns of the monsoon winds made the entrepôt economically viable.

Along the East African coast, winds blow from the north from roughly November to March and from the south from April to September. It is difficult to sail against these winds, but during periods of variable winds small coasting vessels can shuttle between Zanzibar and the adjacent mainland. This permitted goods to be stockpiled in Zanzibar so that the large dhows could pick up all their loads there and use the short periods of monsoon winds to maximum efficiency. Coastal

---

while it induced Indian and Omani traders to install themselves in what later became Zanzibar's main supplier of slaves.

67. Alpers, passim.

68. The best synthesis of the connection between the European and Omani trading systems and events in the interior is Alpers. See also Andrew Roberts, ed., *Tanzania Before 1900* (Nairobi, 1968); Richard Gray and David Birmingham, eds., *Pre-Colonial African Trade* (London, 1970); papers of a Boston University conference reprinted in *African Historical Studies* 4 (1971): 477–657; and Steven Feierman, *The Shambaa Kingdom: A History* (Madison, Wis., 1974).

ports did not lose their importance—and some thrived on the shipment of goods from the mainland to the island—but Zanzibar came to be the commercial center of East Africa. More and more Omanis settled there, and Sultan Seyyid Said bin Sultan, the most active Omani trader of all, moved his capital to the island.[69]

As in Oman itself, Indians took on some of the more lucrative roles in the economy. Growing from "a few adventurers" in 1811 to a prosperous and permanent community of nearly 2,000 in 1850, Indians—both Muslim and Hindu—specialized in the tasks of the merchant-broker and, most important, the financier. They advanced goods, for example, to Arab or Swahili caravan leaders who were headed up country. The loan plus interest was repaid when the caravan returned, frequently with the proviso that produce had to be sold through the creditor.

Omanis by no means ignored merchandising and money-lending—the Sultan himself was one of the largest and most innovative businessmen in Zanzibar—but the tendency for Indians to predominate in the more capitalistic roles was evident in the first half of the nineteenth century. Omanis showed daring and initiative above all within the dhow and caravan trades.[70] Still, these areas of Omani predominance were profitable and expanding. A skillful up-country trader, such as Tippu Tip, even if he borrowed from an Indian, could be very successful.[71] Omanis continued to profit from commerce throughout the century.

The vagaries of the trade in slaves had the greatest impact on the growth of plantation agriculture, and here too the continuities stand out. To be sure, the trade to the Mascerene islands declined because of the Napoleonic wars and subsequent British measures against the trade, but it had never been very large at Zanzibar and Kilwa. Nor was its decline complete, for the French devised a "free labor" system by

69. Sheriff, pp. 24, 28–29; Nicholls, pp. 74–77; Walter T. Brown, "The Politics of Business: Relations between Zanzibar and Bagamoyo in the Late Nineteenth Century," *African Historical Studies* 4 (1971):631–44. For an introduction to Zanzibar, see Sir John Gray, *A History of Zanzibar from the Middle Ages to 1856* (London, 1962).

70. The best treatment of the role of Indians in the coastal economy is Sheriff. A full explanation of the reasons for their success in the nineteenth century has yet to be made, but forthcoming studies by Edward Alpers on an earlier period and by John Zarwan on the twentieth century should shed new light on this question.

71. For the career of a successful Omani trader, see *Maisha ya Hamed bin Muhammed el Murjebi yaani Tippu Tip kwaa maneno yake mwenyewe*, ed. and trans. W. H. Whiteley (Nairobi, 1966). Other Zanzibari Arabs became wealthy and powerful trader-chiefs in up-country towns. Some are mentioned by Richard Burton, *The Lake Regions of Central Africa* (London, 1860), 1: 323, 327, 329; 2: 228. Omani merchants on the coast are mentioned by Loarer, O.I., 5/23, notebook 1. See also Sheriff, pp. 39–41, and Alpers, p. 131.

which slaves of Zanzibari Arabs "volunteered" to go to the French-held islands before their masters were paid.[72] More important to Zanzibar was the slave trade to Arabia and the Persian Gulf.

A precise analysis of the northern slave trade, as the English called it, is impossible in the absence of the kind of statistical data used by Philip Curtin in his study of the Atlantic slave trade.[73] The available figures are nothing more than rough estimates by visitors and naval officers who at no point actually counted slaves or saw import-export data. Most such estimates claim that between 7,000 and 20,000 slaves passed through Zanzibar each year between 1811 and 1860, but the higher estimates, at least, are inflated.[74] However, if the quantitative information of visitors to Zanzibar is not accurate, their impressions are clear: the slave trade from Zanzibar to Oman and the Persian Gulf was a big business throughout the first half of the nineteenth century. For the 1860s, customs figures indicate that up to 20,000 slaves entered Zanzibar each year.[75] These figures reflect the demands of plantation agriculture near mid-century, but these high levels of importations grew out of an older, and substantial, trade in slaves to the north.

Even though the business of selling slaves remained important, the slave dhow did not always experience smooth sailing. Slave supplies always depended on unpredictable events in the interior, and cargoes of humans could perish. Slave traders also had to face the external factor. The British banned the export of slaves to Mauritius in 1821 and a year later pressured the Sultan of Oman to sign a treaty officially ending the export of slaves to all Christian nations, India and the Mascerenes included (see Appendix 2). These measures did not eliminate,

72. French and Spanish slavers were also involved in a blatantly illegal form of slave trading. For references to the continuation of the European slave trade up to 1860, see Cooper, "Plantation Slavery," p. 83, nn. 136–38.

73. Philip D. Curtin, *The Atlantic Slave Trade: A Census* (Madison, Wis., 1969).

74. These estimates are tabulated in Cooper, table 2, p. 85. These figures are for imports, but the local demand for slaves was low until the clove harvests became important in the mid-1840s. Sheriff, who is rightly skeptical of exaggerated estimates of the slave trade, probably goes too far in the other direction. In his attempt to calculate the number of slaves who arrived in Arabia, he relies on observers in Arabian cities or on the routes; yet slaves were widely dispersed in the Persian Gulf region, while the inability of European vessels to track slave dhows was made clear by experiences in the 1870s. The figures he uses to try to calculate the labor requirements of date fields are almost completely arbitrary, and he underestimates the importance of domestic and other nonproductive slaves to Omani society. The prosperity of traders may well have been translated into increasing imports of slaves—one of the best forms of both investment and consumption. However, much work is needed on the economies of the Gulf states before their slave-buying practices can be properly analyzed.

75. The available observer accounts of the Zanzibar slave trade before 1860 are listed in Cooper, "Plantation Slavery," p. 86. For the 1860s, see below, chapter 2.

but they did curtail, the European slave trade. As a result, prices fell to $20 per slave in Zanzibar in 1822, as opposed to $25 a few years earlier.[76] The decline in prices may well have encouraged slave buyers in the Persian Gulf and Oman, and it may have influenced the Sultan and a few Arabs in Zanzibar to carry out the first experiments with clove cultivation in the 1820s.

The drop in slave prices was temporary, although prices constantly fluctuated. In time, the slave traders realized that the British were doing little to enforce the 1822 treaty, while exports to the Islamic north remained legal. Zanzibar was still an entrepôt for the slave trade. A British naval officer, Commander Fremantle, who visited Zanzibar just after the 1842 trading season, noted that "only a small portion" of the slaves brought to Zanzibar stayed there. The rest—numbering 20,000 in his exaggerated estimate—were sent to Oman and neighboring ports.[77] A few years later, when demands for agricultural labor may well have increased, two Frenchmen independently estimated that one-third or more of the 12,000 to 16,000 slaves imported to Zanzibar stayed there—the majority still fed the export trade.[78]

A significant local demand for slaves, then, coexisted with a large external trade. Before the mid-1840s the relationship between the two could be close. Atkins Hamerton, British Consul to Zanzibar, wrote in 1842 that on arrival male slaves were sold to various plantations or kept by their owners as domestics, field hands, or artisans. They were then sold off as the opportunity arose or when the owner needed cash. Female slaves might be used as concubines and then, if they had not borne children, resold.[79] Later on, observers reported that it was considered a disgrace for a slaveowner to sell a domestic slave.[80] This dif-

76. I am ordinarily skeptical of comparing prices given by different observers. But when the source specifically mentions that prices were declining, as is the case here, I am willing to give his evidence more credence. Massieu to Ministre de la Marine et des Colonies, 9 October 1822, O.I., 17/89.

77. Extracts of a report by Admiral Fremantle to Admiral King, incl. Admiralty to FO, 11 January 1843, FO 54/5.

78. Extract of a report by Cap. Romain Desfossés, commander of the naval station of Bourbon and Madagascar to Ministre de la Marine et des Colonies, 11 February 1846, O.I., 15/65. Loarer, 1847, O.I., 5/23, notebook 5. For the views of two American consuls, see Waters Papers, Notes, 18 October 1842, and Ward to State Department, 21 February 1846, US Consul, 2, *NEMA*, pp. 253, 357.

79. Hamerton to Bombay, 2 January 1842, PP 1884, xlviii, 1, p. 419. In the interior of both West and East Africa, slave-trading peoples frequently used slaves for a few months or even years before selling them. See the summary of narratives of ex-slaves in Alpers, p. 240, and Philip D. Curtin, ed., *Africa Remembered: Narratives by West Africans from the Era of the Slave Trade* (Madison, Wis., 1968).

80. Loarer, O. I., 5/23, notebook 5; Burton, *Zanzibar*, 1: 352; James Christie, "Slavery in Zanzibar As It Is," in Bishop E. Steere, ed., *The East African Slave Trade* (London,

ference suggests an alteration in the values of Omanis living in Zanzibar as their orientation shifted—in a slow and incomplete fashion—from trading in slaves to owning them. After the 1840s, as the possession of slaves became more important, Zanzibaris tended to regard slaves more as a permanent part of the social order and less as a commodity temporarily in their custody.

This slow process of change was accentuated in 1847 by the second flurry of British antislave-trade activity. The Sultan of Zanzibar, Seyyid Said, was induced to sign a treaty banning the export of slaves beyond his dominions within East Africa. The slave trade to the Persian Gulf and Arabia was now illegal.[81] The French explorer Loarer, whose visit coincided with the imposition of the treaty, reported a drop of 25 percent in the price of slaves from 1845–46 levels.[82] Hamerton felt that the elimination of the northern slave trade had knocked the bottom out of the slave market. Imports to Zanzibar were "not one-tenth" of what they had been before the treaty went into effect.[83]

Loarer, however, claimed that the number of slaves exported from Kilwa did not decline significantly, because proprietors in Zanzibar and Pemba took advantage of the drop in prices to buy "unaccustomed quantities of slaves." Their response to increased supplies and lowered prices of slaves was responsible, in Loarer's view, for the agricultural development of Zanzibar.[84] Clove planting, as the next chapter will show, was by then well under way, but the enlarged supplies of slaves came at the moment when many more slaves were needed to gather the expanding harvests. Loarer's view of a logical and rapid reaction to a changing economic situation was nearer the mark than Hamerton's picture of collapse.

However, the shift away from the northern slave trade in 1847 was again temporary. Slave traders soon realized that the British were making no serious efforts to prevent slave dhows from reaching Arabia and the Gulf. In the first season after the treaty, Arabs took few slaves to Arabia, but by the next year they were carrying slaves again.[85]

Loarer felt that the growth of the clove industry would produce too many cloves for even the increased number of slaves—100,000 in his

---

1871), p. 45. This ideal was still violated at times. See the testimony of Consul Churchill before the Select Committee on the slave trade, PP 1871, XII, 1, p. 29, and G. L. Sulivan, *Dhow Chasing in Zanzibar Waters* (London, 1873), p. 202.

81. On the treaty, negotiated in 1845, and effective two years later, see Gray, pp. 245–48.

82. Loarer, "Ports au Sud de Zanguebar," O.I., 2/10, notebook B.

83. Hamerton to Palmerston, 10 February 1848, FO 84/737; same to same, 20 August 1850, FO 84/815; Ludwig Krapf, Journal, 18 February 1850, CMS CA 5/016/175.

84. Loarer, O.I., 2/10, notebook B; O.I., 5/23, notebook 5.

85. Ibid.

estimate—to pick.[86] But another Frenchman, writing in 1854, found that Zanzibar was amply stocked with slaves; planters from Réunion, he thought, might be able to obtain the surplus as "free laborers." At that time, according to still another French naval officer, Zanzibar was importing roughly 15,000 slaves each year and retaining half of them.[87] At the end of the decade, the British consul also thought that half the imports, which totaled some 20,000 per year, supplied Zanzibar's own needs. The value of the slaves cited in import statistics for 1861–62 came to $120,000.[88] Slave trading, for both local use and export, was a big business. It remained that way until effective antislave trade measures were finally taken in the 1870s.

The problem with Omani commerce—in slaves and other products— was its uncertainty. Despite the opportunities offered by expanding trade, the Omani trader still had to worry about competition from foreigners and the whims of a distant power. Other sources of income were desirable, and the investment of profits in agriculture was familiar and socially acceptable to people originating in a date-growing country. Omani Arabs, especially in the periods of antislave trade measures in the 1820s and 1840s, looked toward agriculture. They took to clove growing over several decades, a pace which suggests an effort to find a safe investment for trading profits. As a consequence, the transition of the Zanzibari economy from trading to farming was halting and incomplete.

The ups and downs of the slave trade provided the means of agricultural development as well as an incentive for it. An infrastructure capable of bringing slaves from distant regions was organized. When slave prices fell temporarily, slaves could be profitably diverted to agriculture.

An infrastructure also existed for the disposal of agricultural produce. Dhows were not built to carry specific commodities and could be loaded with whatever was most profitable. Expanding trading networks put the fertile areas of East Africa in communication with parts of Arabia and Asia where spices and grain were wanted. Omanis continued to trade throughout the century, but many invested their profits in agriculture. The development of plantations owed more to positive incentives than negative ones, to the commercial value of cloves, coconuts, grain, and sesame.

86. Ibid., notebook 4.

87. Cap. Fournier to Ministre de la Marine et des Colonies, extract, 12 July 1854, Réunion, 135/1035. Cap. Laguerre to Ministre de la Marine et des Colonies, 4 January 1854, ibid.

88. Rigby to Anderson, 14 May 1861, FO 84/1146; R. L. Playfair, "Extracts from the Administration Report of the Political Agent for the two past Years Ending with the 31st of May 1864," *TBGS* 17 (1864): 280.

2 Traders and Planters: The Development of Clove Cultivation in Zanzibar, 1810–1872

By 1850, Omani immigrants to Zanzibar almost completely dominated the world market in a crop they had never planted a half-century before. They responded to the extraordinary prices which spices commanded and to the opportunities that the development of the Indian Ocean trading network offered. With virtually perfect soil and climate for the delicate clove tree and with ready access to labor, Zanzibaris were able to produce cloves under plantation conditions: on a large scale with a disciplined labor-force. In so doing, Omanis were not only changing the way they earned money but the way they lived. Urban society, the dhow voyage, and the caravan did not lose their importance, but the plantation eventually became a way of life.

Yet the profits that cloves brought did not begin a continuous or radical restructuring of the economy, social groups, or values. The very success of the plantation economy sent prices plummeting by mid-century and reduced the incentives to expand or intensify production. After 1872, as chapter 4 will show, external pressures and internal economic weaknesses constrained further development. The slave plantation remained viable as much because of its ability to support itself with a rich variety of crops as because of its specialized productive role. Its work-force became part of the dependent following that wealthy and prestigious Omanis had long sought, even though slaveowners now had to be concerned with their slaves as workers. By 1872, Zanzibar's cloves dominated the spice markets of the world, but the clove plantation's impact on the economy and society of Zanzibar, while substantial, was not so complete.

THE BEGINNINGS OF AGRICULTURAL DEVELOPMENT, 1810–1850

Zanzibar is the Garden of Eden of East Africa. Today, as in the past, the density and variety of fruit-bearing trees and field crops is extraordinary. Before the days of cloves, the Arab and Swahili populations of Zanzibar grew crops such as fruits, cassava, millet, and rice. Coconut products were all that Zanzibar contributed to the export trade.[1] Early

1. M. Morice, Questions and Observations, 1777, in G. S. P. Freeman-Grenville, *The French at Kilwa Island* (Oxford, 1965), p. 181; Captain Smee, "Observations during a

visitors were not impressed by the extent or intensity of cultivation, despite the island's natural endowments. Two British naval officers, Smee and Hardy, who visited Zanzibar in 1811, found that it was "at present not half cultivated" and that little effort was put into what farming there was. In 1819, a Frenchman named Fortené Albrand also found that large portions of the island were covered with forest, while cultivation was "very negligent and the means which are used are primitive and defective." Land was not considered valuable except in the immediate vicinity of the port. Elsewhere, anyone could obtain land for growing rice by giving the local Swahili chief some rice each year. Only a small number of Omani Arabs, living near the port, had "large landed property." Slaves were used in agriculture, but Smee and Albrand both stress that the state of the farming economy was such that "the operations of agriculture are not numerous." Cassava and fruit, the principal crops, were easy to grow, so that the work was "not very tiring," and discipline "indulgent." [2]

Pemba was even more fertile and more important as a grain producer than its sister island. In Portuguese times, Pemba supplied Mombasa with rice; she still did so in the 1820s.[3] A small number of Arabs, as well as Wapemba, the Swahili of Pemba island, lived interspersed among one another, cultivating rice and other produce.[4]

Before 1820, the crop that was to transform the Zanzibari economy was being grown in a few places in the Indian Ocean region. Cloves were indigenous to some of the Moluccas islands in southeast Asia. They were first used by the Chinese, at least as early as the first century B.C. Arab traders introduced them to Europe, and small quantities were regularly imported after the eighth century A.D., at a very high cost. After the Dutch occupied the Moluccas, they attempted to restrict cultivation to one island and gain a monopoly of this spice. However,

---

voyage of research on the East Coast of Africa from Cape Gardafui south to the island of Zanzibar," reprinted in Richard Burton, Zanzibar, City, Island, Coast (London, 1872), 2: 494, 500; Fortené Albrand, "Extraits d'un memoire sur Zanzibar et sur Quiloa," Bulletin de la Société de Géographie (Paris), 2d ser. 10 (1838): 69.

2. Albrand, pp. 66, 70–71, 73; Smee's logbook, 20 March 1811, Ind. Off., L/MAR/c/586, p. 87; Report of Lieut. Hardy, ibid., p. 167; Smee, in Burton, Zanzibar, 2: 494–95, 500.

3. Gray, A History of Zanzibar, pp. 63, 68, 78; Captain W. Fisher of H. M. S. Racehorse, Report, incl. Bertie to Pole, 11 January 1810, ADM 1/62; "Note by Cap. Owen on Replies of Prince Membarrook," incl. Cole to Bathurst, 19 June 1824, CO 167/72. On grain shipments to Mombasa, see chapter 3.

4. John Middleton, Land Tenure in Zanzibar (London, 1961), pp. 52–53; Zanzibar Protectorate, "Report on the Inquiry into claims to certain land at or near Ngezi, Vitongoji, in the Mudiria of Chake Chake in the District of Pemba," by John Gray (Zanzibar, 1956), pp. 30–31; Oscar Baumann, Die Insel Pemba (Leipzig, 1899), pp. 9–10.

Map 2 : Zanzibar and Pemba

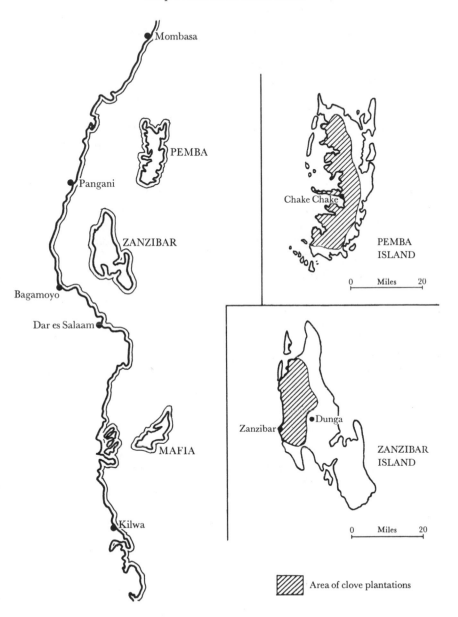

Mombasa

PEMBA

Pangani

ZANZIBAR

Bagamoyo

Dar es Salaam

MAFIA

Kilwa

Chake Chake

PEMBA
ISLAND

0   Miles   20

Zanzibar●   ●Dunga

ZANZIBAR
ISLAND

0   Miles   20

Area of clove plantations

cloves spread to Penang and later to Ile de France and Bourbon. By 1800, Bourbon was producing cloves on a commercial basis, and in 1813 Ile de France was exporting 20,000 pounds of cloves annually.[5]

In 1819, Albrand saw "several clove trees" in Zanzibar, noting that they had been brought from Réunion by two Frenchmen seven years earlier.[6] However, Zanzibari traditions credit the introduction of cloves to an Omani named Saleh bin Haramil Al-Abry, who got the shoots from French contacts in Réunion.[7] Either Saleh grew Zanzibar's first clove trees or else he gave them to the Sultan; but in any case Saleh's plantations were confiscated by Seyyid Said, ostensibly as punishment for slave dealing in violation of the 1822 accords with England.[8]

It takes the clove tree at least six years to reach the bearing state, and longer to attain maximum productivity. Cloves are a form of investment that pays off only in the long run. The people of Zanzibar, who had other sources of income, took to cloves only slowly. The Sultan— an imaginative businessman who experimented with sugar and indigo as well—was responsible for the clove industry's initial development. As late as 1840, two-thirds of the 8,000 frasilas (a frasila is about 35 pounds) being produced in Zanzibar came from the Sultan's plantations.[9] He reportedly acquired forty-five plantations, and visitors were struck both by the immense scale of his enterprise and the "admirable

5. H. N. Ridley, *Spices* (London, 1912), pp. 158–61; Madeleine Ly-Tio-Fane, *Mauritius and the Spice Trade: The Odyssey of Pierre Poivre* (Port Louis, Mauritius, 1958), pp. 1–18. See also Louis Malleret, *Pierre Poivre* (Paris, 1974).

6. Albrand, pp. 69–70; Albrand to Milius, 1 June 1819, Réunion, 72/472; another Frenchman also saw only a few clove trees—Fremelin to Milius, 22 May 1819, incl. Milius to Ministre de la Marine et des Colonies, June, 1819, Réunion, 72/472.

7. Abdulla Saleh Farsy, *Seyyid Said bin Sultan* (Zanzibar, 1942), p. 29. Farsy dates these events after the arrival of *Seyyid* Said in Zanzibar in 1828, but since cloves were seen in Zanzibar as early as 1819, his dating is in error. See also F. B. Pearce, *Zanzibar: The Island Metropolis of Eastern Africa* (London, 1920), p. 297.

8. Saleh had turned the shoots over to the Sultan because he was seeking a pardon for earlier misdeeds, but he apparently got caught violating the Sultan's wishes again. Charles Guillain, *Documents sur l'histoire, la géographie et le commerce de l'Afrique orientale* (Paris, 1856–58), vol. 2/1, p. 50. See also Gray, pp. 129, 153, and Sheriff, "Rise of a Commercial Empire," pp. 176–80.

9. Loarer, O.I., 5/23, notebook 4. A French visitor in 1822, before the Sultan had settled permanently, noted that Seyyid Said's governor was "almost the only person on the island" growing cloves. Massieu to Ministre de la Marine, 9 October 1822, O.I., 17/89. Later visitors observed the Sultan's thriving clove trees, but did not consider cloves to be important to the population at large. Edmund Roberts to Levi Woodbury, 19 December 1828, copy in papers of Sir John Gray, Royal Commonwealth Society, London; Captain H. Hart, "Extracts from Brief Notes of a Visit to Zanzibar," 1834, copy in Gray Papers; Lieut. Wolf, "Narrative of a Voyage to explore the shores of Africa, Arabia and Madagascar, performed by His Majesty's Ships *Leven* and *Barracouta*, under the direction of Captain W. F. W. Owen, R.N.," *Journal of the RGS* 3 (1833): 211.

neatness and beauty" of his clove plantations.[10] One visitor asserted —somewhat credulously perhaps—that Seyyid Said had 6,000 to 7,000 slaves on one plantation alone, while the Sultan's daughter later wrote that most plantations had 50 to 60 slaves, with 500 on the major ones. Each was supervised by an Arab overseer.[11]

Only in the mid-1830s did Zanzibar's clove trees begin to produce large harvests. The Sultan's main plantation, as of 1835, had 4,000 trees, each producing six pounds of cloves annually.[12] Statistics from Bombay, a leading consumer of cloves, show the first major impact of developments in Zanzibar in 1837–38, when $29,000 worth were imported. Five years later, imports from Zanzibar totaled $97,000, dwarfing all other sources.[13] The estimates by various visitors of Zanzibar's clove exports, shown in Table 2:1, indicate a tremendous expansion in the 1840s, leveling off after 1850. The peak of planting must therefore have occurred between 1835 and 1845.[14] This coincides with a period when the entrepôt trade—stimulated by the arrival of American merchantmen—was doing well. Trade and agriculture went hand in hand.

It was during this same period that clove cultivation spread from the Sultan's plantations to the *mashamba* (farms or plantations) of a large proportion of the Omani community. Although Seyyid Said's estates were producing more cloves than ever, his share of the market fell from two-thirds in 1840 to one-third in 1845. After his property was divided among his many children upon his death in 1856, his succes-

10. W. S. W. Ruschenberger, *A Voyage Round the World including an Embassy to Muscat and Siam in 1835, 1836 and 1837* (Philadelphia, 1838), p. 50; Richard Waters, Journal, 2 August 1837, quoted in Philip Northway, "Salem and the Zanzibar-East African Trade," *Essex Institute Historical Collections* 90 (1954): 384; Guillain, vol. 2/1, pp. 50–51. See also Farsy, p. 61, and Emily Ruete, *Memoirs of an Arabian Princess: An Autobiography* (New York, 1888), p. 87. When Seyyid Said died, his plantations and houses were worth $173,933 out of a total estate of $425,363, the only other comparable item being the navy, which he owned personally. Rigby to Bombay, 18 September 1860, reprinted in William Coghlan, "Proceedings connected with the Commission appointed by the Government to investigate and report on the Disputes between the Rulers of Muscat and Zanzibar" (Bombay, 1861), Ind. Off., L/P&S/5/145, p. 113.

11. Guillain, vol. 2/1, p. 48; Ruete, p. 87. Emily Ruete, or Bi Salima, was a daughter of Seyyid Said by a concubine. She eloped with a German merchant, causing what must have been the biggest sex scandal in Zanzibari history.

12. Ruschenberger, pp. 50, 51.

13. Bombay's imports from Zanzibar exceeded those of Ile de France and Bourbon for the first time in 1837–38. By 1843–44, imports from those islands and elsewhere had trailed off to virtually nothing. Bombay Commerce, Ind. Off., P/419/56–87.

14. Loarer in fact dates the introduction of cloves from 1831 to 1832, but this reflects the real breakthrough in planting rather than the actual introduction. "Ile," O.I., 5/23 notebook 4. See also Com. Fremantle, "Extract from Report to Admiral King," 20 May 1842, incl. Admiralty to FO, 11 January 1843, FO 54/5.

sor's estates—large as they were—accounted for about 6 percent of the $232,087 worth of exports.[15]

TABLE 2:1

CLOVE EXPORTS OF ZANZIBAR, 1839–1856

Year	Volume (Frasilas)	Price ($ per frasila)
1839–40	9,000	5–5½
1843–44	30,000	4
1846–47	97,000	
1849	120–150,000	
1852–53	128,000	
1853–54	140,000	
1856	142,857	2–3

SOURCES: Loarer, "Ile de Zanguébar," O.I., 5/23, notebook 4; Guillain "Rapport Commercial," O.I. 2/10, 1:15; Burton, Zanzibar, 1:364–65; Sheriff, p. 186, n. 55.

Whether the Sultan took specific action such as distributing seedlings to encourage clove planting is not known, but his general interest in expanding the commerce and productivity of his dominions is well documented. He did avoid taxing cloves produced in Zanzibar, although there was a tax on cloves from Pemba, and above all he demonstrated that selling cloves was a profitable enterprise.[16]

The lesson was well learned. In 1835, the American W. S. W. Ruschenberger observed that cloves "are found to thrive so well that almost everybody on the island is now clearing away the cocoanut to make way for them." Loarer, in the late 1840s, wrote:

> The easy profits which plantations of clove trees provided after the first years caused all the inhabitants of Zanzibar to turn their eyes towards this crop. On all sides, people were cutting down coconut trees, fruit trees of all varieties, even orange trees. They were neglecting the cultivation of cassava, potatoes, and grains in order to plant clove trees. . . . One only saw this tree in all of the deforested part of the island.

15. Loarer, O.I., 5/23 notebook 4, Playfair, "Extract from the Administration Report . . . 1864," pp. 280, 284. Loarer's figures are roughly consistent with those given by Charles Guillain, "Rapport Commercial," O.I., 2/10, vol. 1, and C. Ward to Abbot, 13 March 1851, US Consul, 3, NEMA, p. 479.

16. Loarer, O.I., 5/23, notebooks 2, 4. Burton wrote that, as of 1857, plantation owners were required to plant three clove trees for every coconut tree. Zanzibar, 1: 218–19.

Loarer's colleague Guillain asserted that everyone with a little extra land planted clove trees.[17] Other visitors and consuls noted that rice and other grains were being neglected in favor of cloves—so much so that these staples now had to be imported.[18]

Not only did farmers switch to cloves, but traders invested in them as well. Arabs would participate in three or four caravans to the interior of Africa, invest the profits in land, and become clove cultivators. Some people with relatively small land holdings began to prefer this activity to the strain of the caravan.[19] Even some Indians invested in clove mashamba.[20]

By the 1840s, the leading Arab families of Zanzibar had become deeply involved in plantation ownership. According to an American whaler who spent several months in Zanzibar in 1842, wealthy Arabs possessing 200 to 300 slaves owned most of the plantations. Arabs were "generally the lords of the soil," wrote the American consul.[21] Among the leading planters were members of the Sultan's family and entourage. One close associate reputedly owned 12,000 clove trees, and the Sultan's prime minister, Seyyid Suleiman bin Hemed, was producing 5,000 to 6,000 frasilas of cloves per year toward the end of the decade.[22]

The oldest Omani communal group in Zanzibar and the leading rivals of the Al-Busaidi, the Al-Harthi, became the proprietors of "large landed estates and numerous slaves." Their leader allegedly owned 1,500 slaves.[23] The other leading Omani groups of Zanzibar

17. Ruschenberger, p. 51; Loarer, O.I., 5/23, notebook 4; Guillain, *Documents,* vol. 2/1, p. 145.

18. Guillain, "Rapport Commercial," O.I., 2/10, vol. 1; Hamerton to Aberdeen, 2 January 1844, FO 54/6; Osgood, *Notes of Travel,* p. 23; Lewis Pelly, "Remarks on the Tribes, Trade, and Resources around the Shore Line of the Persian Gulf," *TBGS* 18 (1863): 66. Sheriff doubts that clove growing reduced rice production, on the basis that cloves are grown on hills or ridges while rice is grown in valleys. However, the fact that simultaneous production was theoretically possible does not mean that people were oblivious to the comparative advantage of the more profitable clove crop. Sheriff, p. 187.

19. Loarer, O.I., 5/23, notebook 1.

20. Ibid.; Mohamed Hussein Tharia Topan, "Biography of Sir Tharia Topan Knight," MS (1960–63), p. 86; Charles Ward to Buchanan, 7 March 1847, US Consul, 2, *NEMA,* p. 376.

21. The whaler visited a number of plantations himself. J. Ross Browne, *Etchings of a Whaling Cruise with Notes of a Sojourn on the Island of Zanzibar, etc.* (Cambridge, Mass., 1846; repr. 1968), pp. 434–35, 438–40. Ward to State Department, 7 March 1847, US Consul, 2.

22. Loarer, O.I., 5/23, notebook 4; Richard Waters, Journal, 15 October 1839, *NEMA,* p. 212; Adrien Germain, "Note sur Zanzibar et la Côte Orientale d'Afrique," *Bulletin de la Société de Géographie* (Paris), 5th ser. 16 (1868): 534.

23. Rigby to Bombay, 4 April 1859, encl. to Secret Letter 57 of 23 May 1859, Ind. Off., L/P&S/5/140; Rigby to Anderson, 26 July 1859, Political Consultation of 30 September 1859, INA, Reel 1.

and Pemba, such as Al-Ruwehi, Al-Riami, Al-Mandhry, and Al-Mazrui—both recent immigrants and old residents—became clove cultivators.[24] By 1860, the British consul in Zanzibar, Christopher Rigby, was referring to "Arab landed proprietors" as a "sort of aristocracy." [25] From an experimental venture, the cultivation of cloves had over a period of some forty years grown into a major underpinning of Zanzibar's elite.

Cloves appear to have stimulated migration from Oman, although many Omanis also came to trade and to follow the Sultan's court, with its opportunities for patronage, when it moved to Zanzibar.[26] Estimates—none based on systematic collection of data—of the number of Omanis in Zanzibar vary from 300 in 1776 to 1,000 (including other Arabs) in 1819 and 800 in 1844; while visitors in 1854, 1857, and 1872 all said there were 5,000 Omanis in Zanzibar.[27] Immigration continued into the latter part of the century, and the Omani population undoubtedly rose. In 1877 alone, some 1,000 Arabs emigrated from Oman to Zanzibar.[28]

In the 1840s clove cultivation spread to Pemba, which had the advantage of being wetter than Zanzibar in the growing season and drier during the harvest. Nearly 2,000 frasilas of cloves were produced in Pemba in 1845, 10,000 in 1849. Some of the best properties in Pemba were developed by rich inhabitants of Zanzibar, who left their slaves to work under a trusted overseer, often a slave himself. The older Arab inhabitants of Pemba and the Wapemba themselves also began to plant cloves. Pemba, however, did not fully realize its potential until after 1872, when a disastrous hurricane struck its politically dominant neighbor to the south.[29]

24. MSA 3, 15, 21, 26, 34, 36.

25. C. P. Rigby, "Report on the Zanzibar Dominions, 1 July 1860," reprinted in Mrs. Charles E. B. Russell, ed., *General Rigby, Zanzibar, and the Slave Trade* (London, 1935), p. 328.

26. Gray, *Zanzibar*, p. 167.

27. Morice to de Cossigny, 4 November 1776, in Freeman-Grenville, *French*, p. 79; Albrand, "Extraits," pp. 72–73; Hamerton to Bombay, 2 January 1842, PP 1844, XLVIII, 1, p. 420; Hamerton to Aberdeen, 2 January 1844, FO 54/6; Osgood, p. 35; Burton, *Zanzibar*, 1: 368; Mgr. Gaume, *Voyage à la Côte Orientale d'Afrique pendant l'année 1866 par le R. P. Horner* (Paris, 1872), p. 258.

28. Report of S. B. Miles in "Report of the Persian Gulf Political Residency and Muscat Political Agency for the Year 1877–78," in *Selections from the Records of the Government of India*, no. 152 (Calcutta, 1883), pp. 2, 129. Absentee landlordism was common in Oman, even in good date country, because Omanis preferred to stay in Zanzibar and it was exacerbated by Oman's economic decline after 1860. Landen, *Oman Since 1856*, pp. 127, 414. The first systematic survey of the Zanzibar population was made in 1921, at which time 18,884 Arabs—Omani and Hadrami—lived in Zanzibar and Pemba. Zanzibar Protectorate, "Report on Non-Native Census, 1921" (Zanzibar, 1921).

29. Loarer, O.I., 5/23, notebook 4, and "Ports au Nord de Zanguébar," O.I., 2/10, notebook D; C. Guillain, "Côte de Zanguébar et Mascate, 1841," *Révue Coloniale* 1

Zanzibar's and Pemba's clove industry was not based on a breakthrough in world demand for cloves, such as the new demand for oils that stimulated the palm-oil industry of West Africa in the nineteenth century. Before the development of Zanzibar's plantations, demand for cloves, mainly in India and Arabia, brought producers high prices and profits for their small harvests.[30] Market conditions were revolutionized by changes on the supply side. Zanzibar offered sufficient rainfall, soil of the proper depth and composition for the delicate clove tree, and freedom—except for the freak hurricane of 1872—from the storms that almost literally blew out the clove industry of Bourbon.[31] It also was able to acquire an adequate labor supply. By the 1840s, Zanzibar was producing cloves on a scale that was extraordinary for the spice trade.

As a result, the price of cloves fell from $5-$5½ per frasila in 1840 to $4 in 1845, and to $2-3 in 1856 (see Table 2:4). In the mid-1840s, Seyyid Said began to fear that the clove market was becoming glutted and that his personal properties would depreciate in value. Although no official action was taken to call a halt to clove planting, the pace was reduced because of the fall in price.[32] Clove exports leveled off around 1850, implying that 1845 ended a decade of rapid expansion in new planting.[33]

During the period of growth, investment was above all directed toward slaves.[34] Hamerton wrote in 1844, "The people are growing rich,

---

(1843): 538; Krapf, Journal, 7 March 1844, CMS CA5/016/165; R. L. Playfair, "Report on the Result of the Observations and Enquiries made during a Tour in the Various Countries around Zanzibar, especially those more or less connected with the Slave Trade," *TBGS* 17 (1864): 257; MSA 3, 9, 15, 21; G. E. Tidbury, *The Clove Tree* (London, 1949), pp. 23–24, 27.

30. Sheriff, p. 183.

31. Tidbury, pp. 16–17; Loarer, O.I., 5/23, notebook 4.

32. Loarer suggested to the Sultan that he impose a tax on each new clove tree planted and forbid the destruction of coconut trees, but Seyyid Said replied that the cost of enforcement was too great. Loarer, O.I. 5/23, notebook 4; Guillain, *Documents*, vol. 2/1, p. 145.

33. Although some cloves were shipped in American and European vessels and the Sultan tried sending his own ships to New York and Marseilles, the European and American traders in East Africa were far more interested in ivory. Nicholls, *The Swahili Coast*, pp. 324–75.

34. Slaves were chosen as laborers and Central Africans as slaves mainly because the establishment of slave-trading routes had made them available. The Dutch ethnographer N. J. Nieboer argued that slavery is not likely to arise in a situation of "closed resources," where land is scarce and people are forced to work in order to eat; it is likely to emerge in cases of "open resources," where potential laborers can meet their own subsistence requirements and so would work for others only if compelled. The East African case appears to conform to his schema, for land was more plentiful than people, and it is hard to see how any combination of necessity and inducements could have brought sufficient

and able to buy more slaves to cultivate cloves, the chief article now cultivated, and from which considerable profit is derived in a few years." [35] Anticipating high returns, planters borrowed money from Indian financiers, creating a pattern of indebtedness that was to continue up to recent times (see chap. 4). Although the plantation owners needed much labor for planting, the chief strain on the labor force occurred at harvest time, so that the greatest impact of expanded planting was felt in the last few years of the 1840s. The short jump in slave supplies in 1847 thus came at an auspicious moment for the clove industry. Loarer's contention that too many trees had been planted for the labor force to handle proved wrong, and plantation agriculture was able to establish its prominence securely.[36]

It is difficult to assess the expansion of Zanzibar's slave population with any precision, since even the offhand estimates of visitors are not based on acquaintance with all parts of the island. Table 2:2 summa-

TABLE 2:2

The Population of Zanzibar Island

	Slave Population	Total Population
1811	150,000	200,000
1819	15,000	
1834		50–200,000
1835	100,000	150,000
1844	360,000	450,000
1846	40–150,000	60–200,000
1849	100,000	
1857	200,000	300,000
1860		250,000

SOURCES: Smee, 1811, in Burton, *Zanzibar*, 2:496; Albrand, "Extraits," pp. 72–73; Hart, MS, p. 10; Ruschenberger, p. 46; Hamerton to Aberdeen, 2 January 1844, FO 54/6; Guillain, *Documents*, vol. 2/1, p. 81; Loarer, O.I., 5/23, notebook 4; Burton, *Zanzibar*, 1:312, 462–63; Rigby, "Report," p. 328.

clove pickers to Zanzibar voluntarily. However, Nieboer's theory has limited explanatory power here, for the planters found themselves in a situation of open resources by choice. The difficult question is why they wanted to establish plantations in the first place. Nieboer's theory suggests a direct correlation between the availability of land and the extent of agricultural slavery, and this approach is too mechanical to delve into the complex mixture of ambitions and values that underlie the will to exploit. See H. J. Nieboer, *Slavery as an Industrial System*, rev. ed. (The Hague, 1910). For a critique by an anthropologist, see Bernard J. Siegel, "Some Methodological Considerations for a Comparative Study of Slavery," *American Anthropologist* 47 (1947): 357–92.

35. Hamerton to Aberdeen, 2 January 1884, FO 54/6.

36. On the slave supply around 1850, see Loarer, O.I., 5/23, notebook 4, and Captain Fournier to Ministre de la Marine, 12 July 1854, Réunion, 135/1035.

rizes the estimates that do exist. The lower estimates seem more reasonable than the higher ones. Nevertheless, it is safe to say that Omani
Arabs—under 5,000 in all accounts—were vastly outnumbered by their
slaves.

Whatever the actual figures, observers did notice increased density of
population in clove-growing areas. Toward the beginning of the century, visitors were struck by the sparseness of population and cultivation. In the 1870s, travelers who explored the rural areas reached the
opposite conclusion. One visitor found the countryside near Zanzibar
to be "most densely populated." He saw one village with 2,000 people
and several with 1,000.[37] A British physician, James Christie, a sensitive
observer with many years' experience in Zanzibar, considered the island "densely populated" because of the labor required for clove picking.[38] An expanding slave population helped make it possible to grow
cloves as a plantation crop, while the demands of export agriculture altered the relaxed regime of agricultural slavery described by explorers
in the early nineteenth century (see chap. 5).

The other principal prerequisite of clove growing was land. Whether
Arabs expropriated land for their clove plantations or merely used
vacant land can never be answered definitively. John Middleton has
argued the latter position, citing archeological and genealogical evidence that the Wahadimu, the Swahili people of Zanzibar, have always
lived in the southeastern portion of the island, which is not suitable for
cloves. In addition, the explorers Smee and Albrand noted that the
western portions of the island, which became the centers of clove cultivation, were sparsely cultivated before the advent of cloves. On the
other hand, Sir John Gray, who knew Zanzibar traditions and the land
situation well, stressed the importance of forceful occupation. Arabs, in
his view, obtained some land by clearing jungle, but they also evicted
Wahadimu landowners from their plots and acquired other farms by
fraud, by bribing Wahadimu leaders, or by harassing Wahadimu into
selling land.[39] It is also hard to believe that all the Wahadimu would
have stayed in southeastern Zanzibar, given the poor fertility of that
area in comparison with the north and west.

It is quite possible that Arabs and Wahadimu had different views of
what was taking place. Under local custom, land cannot be alienated

37. Alfred Belleville, "Trip Around the Southern End of Zanzibar Island," *Proceedings
of the RGS* 20 (1875–76): 74.

38. James Christie, *Cholera Epidemics in East Africa* (London, 1876), p. 314. The population of the town also rose substantially, reflecting increased activity in the port. Rigby,
"Report," p. 328.

39. Middleton, pp. 11–12; Gray, *Zanzibar*, pp. 167–68. The explorer Baumann also
believed the expropriation thesis. Oscar Baumann, *Die Insel Sansibar* (Leipzig, 1897), p.
19. Middleton, Gray, and Baumann do not spell out their sources.

permanently, although a foreigner may be granted the right to use land that is lying idle. A scattered Wahadimu population in central or western Zanzibar might therefore have been willing to allow Arabs to use some of their land, perhaps for a token rental. After all, Arabs had lived in the vicinity of the port for a long time without encroaching on the local population. However, the Arabs, accustomed to freehold tenure under Islamic law, may have regarded this transaction as a purchase.[40]

Once the profitability of clove cultivation was clear, less subtle forms of expropriation may have been used to expand plantations—all authorities admit that encroachment along the fringes of clove-growing areas took place.[41] The Sultan undoubtedly supported Omanis in acquiring land, hoping to reward his followers, give Arabs a stake in the Zanzibari economy, and foster agricultural development. Islamic law gave individuals title to land whether it had been obtained by clearing, seizure, or purchase.[42] In any case, a sharp division arose between Arabs cultivating cloves and other tree crops in northern and western Zanzibar, and Wahadimu cultivating subsistence crops supplemented by small-scale cash crops in southern and eastern Zanzibar.[43] This unequal ethnic division of land became a major source of tension in the twentieth century.[44]

In Pemba, however, valleys and ridges penetrate most of the island, and fertile land is more evenly distributed than in Zanzibar. Undoubtedly Arabs acquired much of the good clove-growing land along the ridges by a combination of purchase, clearing of virgin land, appropriation by force, and appropriation by misunderstanding.[45] Arabs and Wapemba ended up interspersed among each other. Unlike Wahadimu, Wapemba became clove cultivators themselves, although on a smaller scale and perhaps at a later date than the Arabs of Pemba. (see below). Living far away from the center of Omani society in Zanzibar, linked to Wapemba by physical proximity, a similar rural life-style, and

40. On land tenure, see Middleton, and Zanzibar Government, "A Review of the System of Land Tenure in the Islands of Zanzibar and Pemba," by W. R. McGeach and W. Addis, 1945. The rental of lands from "Swahili chiefs" for a payment in rice is mentioned by Albrand, pp. 70–71. His visit took place before the rise of clove planting.

41. Gray, *Zanzibar*, pp. 167–68; Middleton, p. 12; McGeach and Addis, p. 7.

42. McGeach suggests that the Sultan gave his fellow Omanis grants of land or permission to clear. McGeach and Addis, p. 7.

43. As a French missionary living in Zanzibar observed, "Wherever the fertile soil begins, there begin the Arab estates." Le P. Horner, letter, 7 December 1865, St. Esprit, 196/B.

44. Michael F. Lofchie, *Zanzibar: Background to Revolution* (Princeton, N.J., 1965).

45. Baumann, *Pemba*, p. 9; Addis, in McGeach and Addis, p. 19; Gray, *Zanzibar*, pp. 172–73; Zanzibar, "Inquiry into certain claims," p. 11.

common participation in clove growing, the Omanis of Pemba developed closer social relations with Wapemba than the Omanis of Zanzibar did with Wahadimu.[46]

The once abundant land of Zanzibar became scarce and relatively expensive after the expansion of the clove industry took place. In 1860 a large estate could be bought for $5,000—a very substantial sum in a country where total government revenue was only $200,000. In 1870 English missionaries looking for land in the clove-growing area not far from the port learned that "There is no great stretch of fertile land which is not already occupied." Having found some land but seeking to expand in 1875, the mission was asked for $3,000 for a large but relatively infertile shamba, and more for a smaller but more fertile one.[47] Even the daughter of the Sultan had trouble acquiring a plantation where she wanted one, because all the land was owned and nobody wanted to rent it.[48] Explorer Joseph Thomson reported in 1879 that so much land had been cleared for clove and coconut trees since Burton's visit in 1857 that the climate had been altered and Burton's meteorological measurements no longer applied.[49] Nevertheless, some observers claimed that the value of an estate was largely determined by the number of slaves one owned. This may be going too far, but it does suggest that while land was no longer abundant, only the combination of land and slaves was economically valuable.[50]

Omanis had come to Zanzibar in pursuit of commerce. By 1850 much of their wealth was coming from agriculture, indeed from a crop that was new to them.[51] This development owes something to the ob-

---

46. There was a political dimension as well: Wapemba had sought the help of Seyyid Said when they wanted to get rid of the overrule of the Mazrui of Mombasa. The Al-Busaidi replaced the Mazrui in 1823 on the basis of an agreement with the Wapemba. In the twentieth century, Arabs had better relations with Wapemba than with the Wahadimu. Gray, *Zanzibar,* pp. 171–73; Lofchie, p. 170.

47. Rigby, "Report," pp. 341, 342; Bishop Steere, Answers to Queries of Sir Bartle Frere, 15 January 1873, PP 1873, LXI, 767, p. 127; Steere to Festing, 2 June 1875, UMCA Archives, Al (III), box 1, fol. 1200. Scattered data on plantation prices contain such figures as $1,100, $1,750, and $14,000 for an immense plantation owned by a Frenchman. See deeds, dated 1879 and 1892, in the papers of Sir John Gray, Cambridge University Library, Box 28, and Donald Mackenzie, "A Report on Slavery and the Slave Trade in Zanzibar, Pemba and the Mainland of the British Protectorate of East Africa," *Anti-Slavery Reporter,* 4th ser. 15 (1895): 73–74.

48. Ruete, p. 258.

49. Joseph Thomson, *To the Central African Lakes and Back* (London, 1881; repr. 1968), 1: 16.

50. Pelly to Forbes, 1 February 1862, Proceedings for May 1862, INA, Reel 2; Hamerton to Bombay, 2 January 1842, PP 1844, XLVIII, 1, p. 419; Christie, *Cholera,* p. 328.

51. A growing body of literature points to the ability of African producers, in a variety of situations, to innovate in respect to crops, farming techniques, and the organization of

scure Omani who apparently brought clove shoots to the island, and more to the ruler who proved that they were profitable. More fundamentally, the process was a response to economic forces: the age-old demand for spices, the extension of communications from Zanzibar to potential sources of labor and markets for produce, the vagaries of the slave trade, the availability of capital, and access to fertile land.

THE PLANTATION SYSTEM AT ITS HEIGHT, 1850–1872

By 1850 the importance of the clove industry was established and its rate of growth had slowed down. The data on clove exports, summarized in Table 2:3, are scanty and sometimes conflicting, but taken as a whole, they show that clove production remained fairly constant through the 1850s.[52] The slowing down of clove planting, beginning around 1845, was a long-term trend that was mainly the result of declining prices. There was less incentive to plant clove trees in the 1850s when the price was $2 per frasila than in 1840, when it was $5. In the 1860s, when the price was still lower, landowners sometimes did not replace dying clove trees.[53]

A secondary cause of stagnation, at least in the 1860s, was the beginning of British antislave trade efforts directed at Zanzibar itself. The 1847 ban on the slave trade to Arabia was not enforced until 1861, when British warships began apprehending slave dhows. Even this failed to stop the slave trade to Arabia and did not directly affect the supply of slaves to the plantations, which remained, until the 1870s, legal and ample.[54] However, the British consul, Rigby, decided to enforce an Indian regulation that prohibited Indians, as British subjects, from engaging in the slave trade or owning slaves. Some 8,000 slaves, including many field hands, were confiscated.[55] This was a small percentage of Zanzibar's slaves but it had a considerable effect on investment. If Indians were unable to own slaves, they would be unable to make use of land in their possession. As they were the principal finan-

---

production, as well as to respond to changing regional and international markets. See Hopkins, *Economic History of West Africa.*

52. Harvests varied greatly, partly because of weather and partly because pickers, in a good harvest, damaged the tree by pulling off stems along with the clove buds, so that the next year the crop was especially bad. G. E. Seward, "Report," Political Consultations, December 1866, INA, Reel 2.

53. J. A. Grant, *A Walk Across Africa* (Edinburgh, 1864), p. 15; Horner to Gaume, 1 July 1869, St. Esprit, 196/xII.

54. If anything, measures against the Arabian slave trade increased the supply at Zanzibar. On the slave trade after 1850, see chapter 4.

55. Rigby, Diary, 3 September 1861, quoted in Russell, *General Rigby*, p. 95; Rigby to Anderson, 21 March 1860, FO 84/1130.

TABLE 2:3

EXPORTS OF CLOVES FROM ZANZIBAR, 1852–1868

Year	Volume (Frasilas)	Amount (M.T. Dollars)	Price ($/fra)
1852–53	128,000		
1853–54	140,000		
1856	142,857		2–3
1859	138,860	250,000	=1.8
	200,000	382,000	=1.9
1859–60		210,000	
1860 *	200,000		
1861–62		175,000	
		201,840	
1862 *	200,000	400,000	=2.0
1862–63		275,000	
		343,000	
		232,087	
1863–64	137,220	155,000	=1.5
		179,498	
		214,000	
		206,498	
1864–65		469,400	
		227,000	
		335,000	
1865 *	100–342,000		
1865–66		304,000	
1866–67		237,000	
1867–68		273,000	
		300,000	
		125,644	
pre-1872 *			1–1.5

SOURCES: Burton, Zanzibar, 1:364–65; Rigby, "Report," p. 343; Playfair, "Report," TBGS, p. 283; Seward, Report on Commerce, 1864–65, Political Consultations, December 1866, INA, Reel 2; Playfair to Russell, 1 January 1865, FO 54/22; Kirk, Report, 1870, FO 84/1344; Hines to Seward, 25 October 1864, Ropes to Seward, 5 October 1865, Ropes to State Dept., 31 December 1865, and Webb to State Dept., 10 March 1869, US Consul, 5; Jablonski to MAE, 28 December 1863, 31 December 1865, 28 May 1866, 31 December 1866, 31 December 1867, 31 December 1868, and Guillois to MAE, 10 December 1873, MAE, 2, 3; Sheriff, p. 186, n. 55.

NOTE: More than one figure for the same year indicates estimates of different observers.

* Estimate of average at this time.

= Calculated from Volume-Amount data.

ciers in Zanzibar and their loans were secured on mortgages on land, this made it less advantageous for Indians to foreclose. As a result, Indians were somewhat reluctant to supply capital for land or slaves. This problem, too, was a temporary phenomenon, for Rigby's successors after 1862 did not enforce his policy. The attack on Indian slaveholding was only resumed in 1874.[56]

The major long-term problem can be seen in Table 2:4. Zanzibar was becoming dependent on India's taste in spices. The demand for cloves, for culinary and medicinal uses, was modest in Europe, and the inability to make large and consistent inroads into a wider market was the major limitation on the growth of the clove industry.

TABLE 2:4

DISTRIBUTION OF CLOVE EXPORTS OF ZANZIBAR

(By Percentage)

Exported to	1859	1864–65	1867–68
Arabia	6	10	3
India	40	63	62
England	4	8	
United States	19	3	22
France	24	9	8
Germany	6	8	5
Totals	99	101	100

SOURCES: Rigby, Report, 1 May 1860, FO 54/17; Jablonski to MAE, 28 May 1866, 31 December 1868, MAE. Vessels often stopped in Muscat or India after Zanzibar, so the European share may be an overestimate.

An important implication of the stabilization of the clove industry was that Zanzibar did not become totally dependent on it. The trend toward the replacement of other crops by clove trees that was noted in the 1840s did not continue. Of greatest importance to the export economy was the coconut tree. Long a popular crop, the coconut palm "almost covered" Zanzibar in 1819. In the 1840s, coconuts were sent to the Red Sea region, Arabia, Madagascar, and India, while about 40,000 frasilas of coconut oil, worth $50,000, were also exported.[57] Because of the eagerness to plant cloves, coconut trees were at one time uprooted, but by the mid-1850s they had regained their former status. In fact,

56. Dériché to MAE, 2 May 1860, MAE, 2; Pelly to Forbes, 12 February 1862, Pelly Papers, FO 800/234; Webb to Cass, 1 September 1860, US Consul, 4, *NEMA*, p. 512; Prideaux, Report, 1873–74, FOCP 2915, p. 80.

57. Albrand to Milius, 1 June 1819, Réunion, 72/472; Loarer, O.I., 5/23, notebooks 3, 5; and "Rapport politique et commerciale sur Zanzibar," by the Captain of *La Syrène*, 9 June 1844, O.I., 15/65.

owing to the declining price of cloves and the ease of caring for coconut trees, the popularity of coconuts continued to increase in the 1860s.[58] Table 2:5 indicates the importance of this industry. The principal foreign customer was France, which bought coconuts or dried coconuts (copra) for conversion into coconut oil. The oil itself was sometimes manufactured by camel-driven presses and exported from Zanzibar. The price fell as the supply increased, but not as drastically as that of cloves. Burton reported that the price was $12.50 per 1,000 coconuts in 1857, and the American consul said it ranged from $6 to $10 in 1864.[59]

TABLE 2:5
Exports of Coconuts and Coconut Products
(In M.T. Dollars)

1859	90,500
1861–62	102,117
1862–63	143,126
1863–64	200,000
1864–65	152,500
1867–68	200,000

Sources: Rigby, Report, 1 May 1860, FO 54/17; Kirk Report, 1870, FO 84/1344; Hines to Seward, 25 October 1864, and Webb to State Dept., 10 March 1869, US Consul, 5; tables compiled from U.S. consular reports in NEMA, p. 553.

Unlike the clove tree, the coconut tree was fully integrated into the local economy. It was a source of oils, beverages, food, building material, and firewood. While cloves were mainly grown on hills or ridges, much of the rest of Zanzibar was a forest of coconut and other fruit trees.[60] The coconut was less of a plantation crop than the clove, although large coconut plantations did exist. An agricultural expert, William Fitzgerald, who toured Zanzibar and Pemba in 1891, found that coconut palms were irregularly planted and the nuts haphazardly collected. Many people had small plots with a variety of trees, of which the

58. Burton, Zanzibar, 1: 218–19; Seward, "Report," INA, Reel 2; Hines to Seward, 25 October 1864, US Consul, 5, NEMA, p. 528; Horner to Gaume, 1 July 1869, St. Esprit, 196/XII.

59. Burton, Zanzibar, 1: 221; Hines to Seward, 25 October 1864, US Consul, 5, NEMA, p. 528; William E. Hines, "Dominions of the Sultan of Muscat—Zanzibar," 1864, United States Commercial Relations, 1865, p. 506.

60. This included the areas occupied by Wahadimu and not just the Arab-dominated areas near town. Rigby, "Report," 1860, p. 327; Speer to Seward, 26 November 1862, US Consul, 4; Belleville, pp. 69–74, Baumann, Sansibar, p. 35, Baumann, Pemba, p. 12.

coconut was one, while large proprietors planted coconut trees near their houses and allowed their slaves to do the same.[61]

Visitors to the countryside of Zanzibar saw a dazzling variety and richness of crops. Orange, mango, banana, lemon, jack fruit, bread fruit, and other trees were plentiful, not only in the plantation areas, but in the less fertile southern and eastern portions of the island as well. Rice, millet, and cassava were grown in Zanzibar and Pemba, while a number of vegetables were also plentiful—all grew on land that was not good for cloves.[62] Before the development of clove plantations, Pemba exported grain. However, by the 1840s Zanzibar had to import wheat, maize, and rice. Between 1860 and 1872 grain imports varied between $48,000 and $175,000 each year. Most came from India, Madagascar, and Mozambique, but the fertile fields of the adjacent mainland also made their contribution.[63] Zanzibar's demand for grain helped stimulate the development of plantations on the mainland, a process discussed in chapter 3.

However, the staple food of the slave population of Zanzibar was a locally grown crop, cassava. Each slave grew his own food on a plot provided him, while slaves—outside of the clove harvest—had time to grow a variety of crops for their masters (see chap. 5). It is possible that the principal reasons why grain was imported were to cater to the preference of the rich for rice and to feed the burgeoning population of Zanzibar town. In fact, rice—the luxury grain—made up the bulk of grain imports.[64] The profits coming from cloves may have made planters lose interest in producing surpluses of food for the city, but plantation slaves were capable of meeting much of the subsistence needs of the plantation.

61. W. W. A. Fitzgerald, *Travels in the Coastlands of British East Africa and the Islands of Zanzibar and Pemba* (London, 1898), p. 523; F. C. McClellan, "Agricultural Resources of the Zanzibar Protectorate," *Bulletin of the Imperial Institute* 12 (1914):420; M. Jablonski, "Notes sur la géographie de l'Ile de Zanzebar," *Bulletin de la Société de Géographie* (Paris), 5th ser. 12 (1866):361.

62. Albrand, "Extraits," p. 69; Ludwig Krapf, "Additional remarks on the island of Zanzibar or Ongoodja," incl. Krapf to Coates, 10 January 1844, CMS CA5/016/25; Guillain, *Documents*, vol. 2/1, pp. 124–25; Burton, *Zanzibar*, 1: 228–48; Browne, pp. 341, 436; Belleville, pp. 69–74; Rigby, "Report," 1860, p. 338; Playfair to Anderson, 15 November 1862, FO 84/1204.

63. Coffee, dried fish, sugar, salt, and sherbert—valued at $63,000 to $82,000—were also imported. Some may have been reexported, and it is impossible to tell who actually consumed these items. Loarer, O.I., 5/23, notebook 3; Guillain, *Documents*, vol. 2/1, pp. 124–25, 145; Rigby, "Report," 1860, p. 339; Speer to Seward, 20 November 1862, US Consul, 4; Kirk, Report, 1870, FO 84/1344; Prideaux, Report, 1873–74, FOCP 2915, pp. 97–100; *NEMA*, p. 553, tables.

64. Rigby, "Report," p. 344; Zanzibar Government, "Statistics of the Zanzibar Protectorate," by R. H. Crofton, 1921, p. 20.

In addition, Zanzibari farmers attempted to grow two other crops for sale. One was chili pepper, whose contribution to Zanzibar's exports rose from $5,000 in 1867–68 to $36,000 in 1880–81. If late nineteenth-century patterns also held true earlier, the principal chili growers were the Wahadimu.[65]

The second crop was sugar. Zanzibaris had long grown and processed sugar cane for local use. Both Seyyid Said and his successor Seyyid Majid tried seriously to establish sugar as a commercial crop, making arrangements with Europeans to develop their plantations. Both failed, owing largely to the incompetence, dishonesty, and ill-health of the European partners, although sugar continued to be grown for local use, and small mills, driven by steam or camels, remained in operation. The attempts, in any case, reveal the desire of two Sultans to develop a second plantation crop.[66]

In 1841, when clove production was still in an early stage of development, Seyyid Said told Hamerton that all the people of Zanzibar could subsist on their little farms.[67] By the 1860s, the Sultan's picture of self-sufficiency was less true. The sources of income and the style of life of Zanzibar's leading citizens depended on an export crop, and the fertile island was importing grain. Nevertheless, the transformation into an export-oriented economy was far from complete. Even on the plantations of the Sultan and the wealthiest Arabs, a great number and variety of fruit trees and other crops remained. Subsistence crops were being grown by slaves on every plantation. The coconut, which brought Zanzibar nearly as much money as the clove in the late 1860s, was not solely a plantation crop. The southern and eastern portions of the island of Zanzibar remained outside the clove economy. In Pemba, much rice was still produced in the valleys, and a variety of tree crops

65. Hines to Seward, 25 October 1864, US Consul, 5, NEMA, p. 528; Kirk, Report, 1870, FO 84/1344; Report of Consul Batchelder, 1881, United States Commercial Relations, 1880–81, p. 396; Baumann, Sansibar, p. 37; Fitzgerald, p. 540.

66. For the major fiasco in Anglo-Zanzibari economic cooperation, see Reginald Coupland, The Exploitation of East Africa 1856–1890: The Slave Trade and the Scramble (London, 1939), pp. 178–81. Some of the other fiascos are described in Waters Papers, Notes, 18 October 1842, Ward to Buchanan, 13 March 1847, US Consul, 2, and Ward to Shepard, 14 December 1848, Ward Papers, in NEMA, pp. 253, 384, 398; Loarer, O.I., 5/23, notebook 5; Extract, Commandant de la Station de Réunion et de Madagascar to Ministre de la Marine, 10 September 1850, O.I., 15/65; Osgood, p. 24; Burton, Zanzibar, 1:222. Zanzibaris' own efforts to grow sugar for local use reduced but did not eliminate the need to import sugar. See Massieu to Ministre de la Marine, 9 October 1822, O.I., 17/89; Albrand, "Extraits," pp. 76–77; Krapf, "Remarks," CMS CA5/o16/25; Kirk, Report, 1870, FO 84/1344; Prideaux, Report, 1873–74, FOCP 2915, p. 99; Belleville, p. 71; Fitzgerald, p. 516.

67. Hamerton to Willoughby, 20 August 1841, FO 54/4.

flourished. The clove plantation, in short, became part of, but did not replace, the earlier agricultural patterns of Zanzibar.[68]

Nor did agriculture come to dominate the export economy of Zanzibar. The port remained an entrepôt, and ivory, gum copal, and other products of the mainland of Africa continued to move through the port on their way to India and Europe, while cloth, brass wire, beads, guns, and other European imports spread from Zanzibar over much of East Africa. Table 2:6 shows the total trade of Zanzibar.

TABLE 2:6
Trade of Zanzibar, 1859–1876
(In M.T. Dollars)

	Value of the Customs Farm *	Imports	Exports
1859	196,000	4,080,000	3,400,000
1861–62	200,000	1,809,185	2,140,080
1862–63	190,000	2,692,430	2,338,970
1863–64	195,000	3,230,384	3,649,761
1864–65	310,000	3,612,180	3,479,874
1867–68	310,000	3,587,754	1,856,000
1870–71	310,000		
1872–73		3,356,959	
1873–74		3,093,150	
1875–76	450,000		

SOURCES: Rigby, Report, 1860, p. 344; Speer to Seward, 26 November 1862, US Consul, 4; Playfair to Bombay, 15 June 1863, FO 54/20; Hines to Seward, 25 October 1864, US Consul, 5; Playfair to Russell, 28 June 1865, FO 84/1295; Ropes to State Department, 5 October 1865, US Consul, 5, NEMA, p. 538; Kirk, Report, 1870, FO 84/1344; Prideaux, Report, 1873–74, FOCP 2915, pp. 97–100; Kirk to Derby, 25 August 1876, FO 84/1454.

* The right to collect and keep duties was rented to an Indian for a negotiated sum.

This period, unlike the previous decades, was not one of impressive growth. In fact trade declined in 1861. The crackdown by Rigby on Indian slaveholding damaged the credit system for traders as well as for plantation owners. Wars in the interior of Africa cut off the supply of export items, while the American Civil War made cotton, the major im-

68. This also aided the clove-planting process. The costs of feeding owners and workers could be covered outside the market nexus, in effect lowering the cost of planting. On the importance of such mechanisms, see Sara S. Berry, *Cocoa, Custom, and Socio-Economic Change in Rural Western Nigeria* (Oxford, 1975).

port, scarce and expensive. These factors were temporary, and trade returned to its former level.[69]

With annual clove exports usually in the $200,000 to $300,000 range, it is clear that Zanzibar's business did not depend solely on that crop. Cloves generally accounted for 10 percent of total exports, although they were the only major export from the islands themselves. The Sultan derived much less revenue from his cloves than from the customs farm.[70]

Omanis, as noted in Chapter I, remained active in commerce, especially in the carrying trade and caravan leadership. Arabs, including poor Omanis and members of leading families of Zanzibar, continued to participate in the slave trade. Some invested their profits in clove plantations, but others still went up country or traded by sea. Tippu Tip, the most successful of all, followed in his father's footsteps as an up-country trader. He gradually became wealthy, acquired clove plantations in Zanzibar, but still ventured up country. As all traders aspired to do, he acquired a large following of slaves and others, so that he was a military, as well as a commercial, figure in parts of Tanzania and the eastern Congo.[71] Other Arabs of Zanzibar, including members of leading families, became powerful and wealthy leaders in such trading centers as Unyanembe, Tabora, and Ujiji. At times, some members of a family resided in Zanzibar, while their relatives stayed up country.[72] Burton, who visited Zanzibar in 1857, could still say, "The Arab noble is still, like those of Meccah in Mohammed's day, a merchant."[73]

TOWARD A PLANTATION SOCIETY

However important trade remained to many Omanis, the plantation had a great impact on the social structure and patterns of daily life. By

69. Jablonski to MAE, 2 February 1862, and 28 December 1863, MAE, 2.

70. Less than 10 percent of the Sultan's income in the 1860s came from the produce of his estates. The customs farm was by far the largest item, and only cloves from Pemba were then subject to taxation. Playfair to Bombay, 15 June 1863, FO 54/20; Kirk, Report, 1870, FO 84/1344.

71. Hines to Seward, 26 October 1864, US Consul, 5; Christie, "Slavery in Zanzibar," p. 35; Memorandum by Sir B. Frere on Connection of British Subjects with East African Slave Trade," 27 August 1872, FOCP 2269, pp. 4–5; Henry M. Stanley, *How I Found Livingston* (London, 1873), p. 13; Elton to Prideaux, 2 March 1874, FOCP 2499, p. 6; Tippu Tip, *Maisha*, pp. 43, 45, 57, 61.

72. For a particularly good study of such a community, in which Zanzibaris played important roles in a complex, ethnically mixed town, see Beverly Bolser Brown, "Ujiji: The History of a Lakeside Town, c. 1800–1914" (Ph.D. diss., Boston University, 1973).

73. Burton, *Zanzibar*, 1: 376.

1860, as noted earlier, officials were referring to Arabs as a landed aristocracy.

As in all plantation societies, not all planters [74] were wealthy aristocrats. A small number possessed slaveholdings that were vast by the standards of any slave society, and first among them was the Sultan. Despite the continual division of property at the death of each Sultan, successors were able to obtain more land and slaves. In 1872–73, Seyyid Bargash was earning some $25,000 per year from his estates. He owned extensive plantations and, according to one source, 4,000 slaves. As late as the 1890s, the Sultan possessed many large plantations run by overseers and worked by an estimated 6,000 slaves.[75] Other close relatives were wealthy, with estates valued at up to $88,000. Seyyid Bargash's sister, Bibi Zem Zem, reputedly owned 500 to 600 slaves. Other members of the Al-Busaidi group were large proprietors, most notably Seyyid Suleiman, who owned over 2,000 slaves.[76]

Other Omani Arabs had large estates. Visitors said that the largest landlords owned 1,000 to 2,000 slaves, although such figures are likely to be inflated.[77] A major shamba could contain 10,000 clove trees, and some planters owned more than one.[78] Tippu Tip at first had no plantation of his own, although his wife owned considerable property. He invested some of the proceeds from his trading in slaves and ivory in land in Zanzibar, and his property was reportedly worth £50,000 at the

74. A planter is a person who has someone else plant for him.

75. Prideaux, Report, 1873–74, FOCP 2915, p. 79; Msgr. R. de Courmont, "Le Sultanat de Zanguébar," *Missions Catholiques* 18 (1886): 384; Fitzgerald, pp. 507, 519, 535–36; Hardinge to Salisbury, 7 December 1895 (telegram), FOCP 6805, p. 148; "Summary of Scheme Submitted by Sir John Kirk," 12 December 1896, FOCP 6838, p. 4.

76. Churchill to Stanley, 19 August 1868, FOCP 4202, p. 154; Germain, "Zanzibar," p. 534; Kirk to Bombay, 30 August 1871, FO 84/1344; Macdonald to Salisbury, 3 March 1888, FO 84/1906; Rashid bin Hassani, "The Story of Rashid bin Hassani of the Bisa Tribe, Northern Rhodesia," in Margery Perham, ed., *Ten Africans* (London, 1963), p. 106. Rashid was a slave of Bibi Zem Zem.

77. Ruschenberger, p. 34; Guillain, *Documents*, vol. 2/1, p. 52; Osgood, p. 51; Burton, *Zanzibar*, 1: 466; Germain, "Zanzibar," p. 533; Christie, "Slavery," p. 31. These figures may simply be the traveler's way of saying that these planters had vast numbers of slaves. They are high even by comparison with Caribbean sugar plantations, where economies of scale and high concentrations of wealth gave rise to the largest slave plantations in the Americas. In the early eighteenth century, a leading planter in the British West Indies had a few hundred slaves. In Jamaica at the end of the century, the average estate possessed 180 slaves. Dunn, *Sugar and Slaves*, pp. 46, 91; Fogel and Engerman, *Time on the Cross*, 1: 22.

78. In 1902, the leading planters of Pemba included Salim bin Ahmed Al-Riami, Saleh bin Ali El-Riami, and Suleiman bin Mbarak, who owned 10,000 trees apiece. Mohamed bin Juma had 5,000 trees. Neither these figures nor the estimated number of slaves possessed by the major planters should be given too much weight. Cave to Lansdowne, 24 September 1902, PP 1903, XLV, 955, pp. 20–21.

end of the century.[79] In 1895, according to Donald Mackenzie, who visited Zanzibar on behalf of the Anti-Slavery Society, one Abdalla bin Salim owned six mashamba and 3,000 slaves, while his wife owned seven small mashamba and 1,600 slaves. Five others owned over 250 slaves each. In Pemba, Mohamed bin Juma bin Said had seven plantations and 2,000 slaves, as well as additional holdings in Zanzibar.[80] His cousin claimed that he owned 500 himself, while a leading official in Pemba was said to own 500.[81] A few landowners from the Hadramaut had vast landholdings; Mohamed bin Abdalla Bakshuwein, for example, had valuable estates in Pemba and Mombasa and smaller ones in Malindi.[82]

These large landowners were a small fraction of the total. The British vice-consul in Pemba thought that the average landlord owned thirty slaves. Mackenzie calculated an average of sixty-seven per shamba in Zanzibar and Pemba by comparing lists of mortgages with an estimate of the total number of slaves.[83] But his estimate of the slave population—266,000—is higher than most, and the mortgage lists are likely to yield a low estimate of plantations. Therefore, Mackenzie's calculation errs in the direction of excess, and the vice-consul's figure of thirty, although a rough estimate, appears to be in the right neighborhood.[84] Mackenzie, believing 15,000 Arabs lived in Zanzibar and

79. Heinrich Brode, *Tippoo Tib: The Story of His Career in Central Africa*, trans. H. Havelock (London, 1907), pp. 48, 248, 253; Robert Nunez Lyne, *An Apostle of Empire Being the Life of Sir Lloyd William Mathews* (London, 1936), pp. 214–15. Mackenzie, pp. 92–93, said he owned seven mashamba and 10,000 slaves, which is a way of saying he owned "many" slaves.

80. Mackenzie, pp. 77, 92–93. Fitzgerald also noted that Mohamed bin Juma owned "plenty of slaves," and Arthur Hardinge singled out Abdalla bin Salim and Tippu Tip as "Great native magnates." Fitzgerald, pp. 594, 602; Hardinge to Salisbury, 23 April 1898, PP 1898, IX, 559, p. 72.

81. Mackenzie, pp. 73, 75. The British vice-consul in Pemba said that the richest Arab there was Ali bin Abdulla El-Thenawi, who owned 500 slaves, while three or four others owned 300 or more. Report by Mr. O'Sullivan upon the Island of Pemba, incl. Hardinge to Salisbury, 18 June 1896, PP 1896, LIX 395, p. 41.

82. Euan-Smith to Derby, 26 February 1875, FOCP 2915, p. 203. For a biography of this unusual man, see Mbarak Ali Hinawy, *Al-Akida and Fort Jesus, Mombasa* (London, 1950).

83. The lists mentioned 3,296 mashamba in Zanzibar and Pemba. Mackenzie added 20 percent for unregistered mortgages and divided it into an estimate made by Seyyid Bargash that there were 266,000 slaves on the islands. Mackenzie, p. 94. An earlier source estimated there were 1,000 mashamba in Pemba—close to Mackenzie's figure—but another visitor thought that 4,000 Arab landed proprietors were in Zanzibar. Holmwood to Kirk, 10 May 1875, FOCP 2915, p. 185; John A. Dougherty, *The East Indies Station; or the Cruise of H. M. S. "Garnet" 1887–90* (Malta, 1892), p. 17.

84. The average figure is thus well below the late eighteenth-century average for Jamaica (180), but is greater than that in most parts of the Southern United States. Fogel and Engerman, 1: 22; Wood, p. 163.

Pemba, calculated that an average of five or six Arabs lived on each shamba.[85] His population estimate is high, and a figure of three or four Arabs plus thirty to forty slaves per shamba is as reasonable a guess for the late nineteenth century as one can make.

On the bottom of the scale was the small-holder. In Pemba in 1875 there were many small patches of cloves worked by one or two slaves.[86] Even citizens of Zanzibar town who acquired a little money bought land and a few slaves. If so inclined, they settled the slaves on the land with orders to bring in the produce, and enjoyed the pleasures of urban life.[87] At a later date, many people owned small plots with all the products of Zanzibar growing on them: cloves, coconuts, mangoes, cassava, and others.[88]

The clove growers of Zanzibar were principally Omani Arabs. Some Hadramis did become plantation owners, but more typically they were temporary residents or town dwellers. Many came as port laborers and invested their earnings in slaves, who in turn worked in the ports for their masters' benefit.[89] Many people from Madagascar, the Comoro Islands, and elsewhere in the Indian Ocean came and went, serving on dhows or engaging in petty trade. Those who settled there generally worked in town as servants to Europeans and supervisors, or else they sailed and fished. The successful ones sometimes bought slaves and hired them out to others.[90] These immigrants formed part of an urban working population, but over the years they tended increasingly to become the owners of workers. Free laborers were marginal to the Zanzibari economy, and on the plantations, virtually all labor consisted of slaves.[91]

85. Mackenzie, p. 94.

86. Holmwood to Kirk, 10 May 1875, FOCP 2915, p. 185.

87. Edward Steere, *Some Account of the Town of Zanzibar* (London, 1869), p. 12. Small-holders, especially town residents, often hired out their slaves for urban labor. See chapter 5.

88. W. W. A. Fitzgerald, "Report on the Spice and Other Cultivations of Zanzibar and Pemba Islands," incl. Portal to Rosebery, 2 October 1892, FOCP 6362, p. 101.

89. During the monsoon there was also a large floating population of sailors and traders from the Hadramaut, as well as Oman, Sur, and India. Rigby to Anderson, 11 February 1860, FO 84/1130; E. Quass, "Die Szuri's, die Kuli's, und die Sclaven in Zanzibar," *Zeitschrift für Allgemeine Erdkunde*, n.s. 9 (1860) 421–26; Constantin-Abel Semanne, *Essai d'une topographie medicale sur l'Ile de Zanzibar* (Paris, 1864), p. 13. On port labor, see also chapter 5.

90. Tozer to UMCA, 24 December 1864, in Gertrude Ward, ed., *Letters of Bishop Tozer* (London, 1902), p. 100; Christie, *Cholera*, p. 332; Germain, "Zanzibar," p. 552; Baumann, *Sansibar*, pp. 32–33; Karl Wilhelm Schmidt, *Sansibar: Ein Ostafrikanisches Culturbild* (Leipzig, 1888), p. 85. A few Africans from the adjacent coast came to Zanzibar to flee from enemies or famine. They fished or became tenants on small mashamba, where they grew subsistence crops. Burton, *Zanzibar*, 1: 344–45.

91. Quass, p. 443; Hamerton to Bidwall, 27 April 1843, FO 54/5; M. S. Nolloth, "Extracts from the Journal of Cap. M. S. Nolloth, H. M. S. *Frolic*," *Nautical Magazine* (1857),

The Wahadimu of Zanzibar participated very little in the clove economy. Whether by choice or because of the loss of their land, they lived on portions of the island which were not suitable for cloves. Some owned slaves, but there was no large-scale agriculture for which to use them. The leader of the Wahadimu, the Mwenye Mkuu, was one of few, if not the only, major slaveowner. Wahadimu shared more or less equally in their limited opportunities, and trade was marginal to an economy based on farming and fishing.[92] The Wapemba, living interspersed among the Arabs of Pemba, embraced clove growing to a greater extent. They generally did so on a smaller scale than their Arab neighbors, although they, too, used slaves. Sometimes Arab men married Wapemba women, an act which gave them access to Wapemba land.[93] In short, most plantation owners, including virtually all the major ones, were Omanis, and almost all the plantation workers were slaves.

In this respect, as chapter 3 makes clear, Zanzibar differed from the rest of the coast, where the older Swahili population fully participated in the development of plantation agriculture. The reasons were largely political: Omanis dominated Zanzibar as they failed to dominate the mainland or even Pemba. Wahadimu either stayed in the relatively infertile lands to the east and south of the town or were pushed farther in those directions. Moreover, Arabs in Zanzibar—unlike mainland planters—grew a crop that had not been grown locally and whose cultivation required obtaining seedlings from previous planters and learning new techniques. Only in the interspersed settlements of Pemba did such communication cross ethnic lines.

Small-holders and large-holders were enmeshed in the international clove economy, and the course it took deeply affected the evolution of rural life in Zanzibar. Accounts of particular plantations are lacking, as are the data needed to calculate average incomes or rates of return on investment. The best one can do is to assume that the major limiting

---

p. 137; Hardinge to Buxton, 26 November 1896, Anti-Slavery Society Papers, Rhodes House, Oxford University, G5. See also chapter 5.

92. Pelly to Forbes, 12 February 1862, Pelly Papers, FO 800/234; Christie, "Slavery," p. 49; Hardinge to Salisbury, 8 September 1897, PP 1898, LX, 559, p. 12; Baumann, *Sansibar*, pp. 35–38; Last to Raikes, 8 February 1903, FOCP 8177, p. 71; Horner, letter, 7 December 1865, St. Esprit, 196/B.

93. Farler to Mathews, 31 January 1899, PP 1899, LXIII, 303, p. 35; Mackenzie, p. 80; Farler to Rogers, 15 August 1904, FOCP 8382, p. 108; Zanzibar, "Inquiry into Claims," p. 5, 30–31. These observations on the connection between ethnicity and clove growing were borne out by later surveys. See Zanzibar Government, "Memorandum on Certain Aspects of the Zanzibar Clove Industry," by G. D. Kirsopp, 1926, p. 6, and Edward Batson, "The Social Survey of Zanzibar," unpublished MS, 1961, vol. 15, copy in the Foreign and Commonwealth Office, London.

factor on clove production was the number of cloves a plantation owner's slaves could pick. Using this crude method, and an estimate from 1900 that five workers were needed to pick 100 clove trees (although ten would have been more desirable), plus a figure of six pounds per tree per year as the average yield, one comes up with the result that thirty slaves could harvest about 100 frasilas of cloves each year.[94] At the prices prevailing in 1839, this would yield $500—an enormous sum by local standards, even allowing for the middleman's share. The market value of thirty slaves was then around $600 to $900, so that slaves could very quickly produce their own value in cloves. However, by 1870 the price was below $2, and the thirty slaves could only produce $200 worth of cloves. This is relatively close to a contemporary estimate by Dr. Christie that the profit per slave was less than $5 per year.[95]

A large income required a truly enormous number of slaves. At 1870 prices, 1,000 slaves could care for 20,000 trees yielding $7,000. That, in the Zanzibari economy, was a very large sum indeed, but only the Sultan, leading followers like Seyyid Suleiman, and unusual entrepreneurs like Tippu Tip could approach it. Islamic laws of inheritance—providing that all sons by wives or concubines receive an equal share, while daughters receive a half share and other relatives varying portions—meant that estates tended to fragment rather than accumulate over the generations.[96]

Once prices fell from their high level of the early 1840s, the average slaveowner had little room for costs that had to be paid in cash. It was essential for planters that slaves provide most of their own and their owner's food and shelter, that technology be kept simple, and that other factors of production be minimized.[97] Zanzibar's richness in fruit,

94. The productivity figure is from O'Sullivan-Beare, Report on Pemba, 1900, Foreign Office, Diplomatic and Consular Series, no. 2653, p. 11. This calculation comes up with gross sales only, neglecting middleman's markup, which is unknown. Nor is it possible to estimate, even roughly, the cost of land, credit, or other costs. The productivity estimate, however, is low, since not all clove trees ripened simultaneously, and the harvest could be spread out a little. On some large mashamba in 1902, there were anything from 17 to 200 trees per laborer. Cave to Lansdowne, 24 September 1902, PP 1903, XLV, 955, pp. 20–21.

95. Christie, "Slavery," p. 32.

96. On inheritance in Zanzibar, see Peter A. Lienhardt, "Family Waqf in Zanzibar," East African Institute for Social Research, Conference Paper, 1968. For example, the estate of Seyyid Said, valued at $425,363, was divided among his sons, who received $57,917 each, and his daughters, each of whom got $28,958. The son was thus much less wealthy than the father. Coghlan, "Proceedings," Ind. Off., L/P&S/5/145, p. 113.

97. Much more work needs to be done on the structure of the Zanzibari economy, particularly its linkages with Indian Ocean and European commercial spheres. However, it is clear that Zanzibar could not have achieved the specialized plantation economy of Carib-

cassava, and other crops therefore was crucial to the viability of the plantation economy. If the planter wanted to eat imported rice or to purchase luxury goods, he could devote most of his cash income to that purpose or he could borrow against his estate. But if times were bad, he could rely on the produce of the plantation itself.[98] Only because plantations were capable of producing the necessities of daily life were they able to survive the periods of adversity described in chapter 4.

Buying more slaves—to replenish or expand the labor force—was the principal difficulty. Given the small revenue, it is not surprising that much of Zanzibar's land came to be mortgaged.[99]

High clove prices made plantation development desirable; declining prices made rural self-sufficiency a necessity for all but the wealthiest. These developments brought about a deep change in the urban, commercial life characteristic of Omanis at the beginning of the century. For some, plantation ownership was at first nothing more than an investment, and the plantation could be left in the charge of slaves. In the 1840s, Guillain and Loarer wrote that relatively few plantation owners actually lived on their estates. They came to their plantations at harvest time to ensure that a sufficient supply of cloves was picked.[100] The Sultan, however, was already setting a new model for plantation life. Seyyid Said spent four days each week in his big house on one of his plantations. On Mondays and Fridays, he held court in Zanzibar town, while many visitors were received at his country estate. He spent much time at his other plantations as well. According to one of his daughters, two plantations had palaces for his use, and six or eight had villas.[101] Seyyid Said was not just a rich Sultan exploiting his slaves and land but a landlord enjoying life on his estates.

Others followed his example, building residences on their lands and

---

bean sugar islands, which imported many staples for masters and slaves alike. Plantations in the Southern United States were more self-sufficient. Richard B. Sheridan, *Sugar and Slavery: An Economic History of the British West Indies, 1623–1775* (Baltimore, 1974), pp. 314–15.

98. Travelers' impressions of rural life and self-sufficiency are discussed later in this chapter.

99. A plantation owner with thirty slaves and a 10 percent attrition rate (birth and death rates are not known), or one seeking to expand by 10 percent, would have to pay $60 to $90 for the slaves, not counting interest, the cost of raising young slaves, etc. This would absorb a high percentage of the total income. However, slaves in Zanzibar cost vastly less than slaves in the United States, where prices could be as high as $800 in 1850. Fogel and Engerman, 1: 76. On mortgages, see chapter 4.

100. Guillain, *Documents*, vol. 2/1, p. 81; Loarer, O.I., 5/23, notebook 4.

101. Loarer, O.I., 5/23, notebook 1; Farsy, pp. 57, 59, 61–62; Ward to State Department, 21 February 1846, US Consul, 2; Guillain, *Documents*, vol. 2/1, p. 30; Ruete, p. 87.

spending more and more time at a "country seat." Rigby, in 1860, visited a number of country residences, while the American consul in 1862 noted that Arab shamba owners were taking their families with them to their estates and living there throughout the few months of the picking season.[102]

By the 1870s some Arabs still resided in town and left their estates to their slaves, with a landless Arab or a trusted slave as overseer. Others preferred to "lead a quiet retired life on their estates, and only visit the town to dispose of their produce, transact business, and visit their friends." [103] Many retained "large handsome houses" in Zanzibar town but came to town only for a visit, a ceremony, or a call on the Sultan on his twice-weekly court sessions. As Sir Bartle Frere wrote after his visit to Zanzibar in 1873:

> Their time is for the most part passed at their 'shambas,' estates in the country, where they live a life of indolent ease, surrounded by slaves, borrowing money with facility from Indian traders if their estates are flourishing, doing without it if the estate is in difficulties. At the worst, the poorest estate in this rich island will always yield enough food and shelter for them and their slaves, however numerous, and it is one of the peculiarities of the Arab character that, with great capacity for luxurious enjoyment, the Arab seems never to lose his power of living content and respected on the most frugal supply of the base necessities of life.[104]

Skeptical as one must be about English views of Arab indolence, Frere's comment reveals a shift to a more rural life-style. The explanation for what Frere observed was not the laziness of the Arab character but the fact that the Zanzibari economy provided subsistence even when it failed to provide cash: Arabs could afford not to succeed. High clove prices in the 1840s encouraged development of the rural areas, while declining prices thereafter strengthened rural self-sufficiency.[105]

Frere not only says that Omanis could always survive on what their plantations produced, but that they could live a "respected" life even in hard times. Omani values had not come to identify respectability with

102. Rigby, "Report," 1960, p. 327; Speer to Seward, 26 November 1862, US Consul, 4; Richard Waters, Journal, 3 June 1838, *NEMA,* p. 208.

103. Christie, "Slavery," p. 31, and *Cholera,* pp. 312–13.

104. Sir Bartle Frere, "Memorandum on the Position and Authority of the Sultan of Zanzibar," incl. Frere to Granville, 7 May 1873, PP 1873, LXI, 767, p. 112. Later, Baumann noted the importance of the rural life and the constant movement back and forth between city and country. *Sansibar,* p. 32.

105. This was even truer of Pemba, for there no urban centers to distract from plantation life. The importance of living in the countryside to Arab life in parts of East Africa was explained to me by Ahmed Abdalla Al-Mazrui, MSA 4.

income. Wealth was very much an attribute of status, but not the dominant attribute.

Nevertheless, consumer goods became important for personal use, enjoyment, and display. The major import—cotton cloth—became, thanks to decades of trade, a necessity for a large portion of the population. As wealth from trade and agriculture fell into Omani hands and as a greater variety of foreign goods entered the port, Arabs acquired a taste for European furniture, mirrors, and china.[106] At weddings and other ceremonies, women showed off their clothes, jewels, and personal servants.[107] Modest amounts were spent on imported carpets, crockery, gold lace, and perfume.[108]

Yet the quiet opulence of the plantation mansion of the Old South or the overindulgence of the West Indian sugar planter did not become part of life in Zanzibar. Some of the foreign consuls, interested in selling more of their countries' produce, found the Arabs' new interest in such items to be distressingly modest. As the French consul wrote:

> The very restrained needs of the inhabitants, the simplicity, and I would say, the originality of their taste will for a long time be an obstacle to the introduction in these regions of French products, which in general are little sought after.[109]

The Arabs selected only those items they wanted from the luxuries Europe had for sale. A few mirrors, carpets, pictures, and some old china were sufficient for a homeowner to give an impression of luxury. Otherwise, houses were simply furnished.[110]

In addition to the new fancy for European products, two older items were particularly valued as symbols of wealth: doors and daggers. As the visitor to Zanzibar can still observe, Zanzibari houses are designed around their elaborate and often beautifully carved doors. These are the work of local craftsmen, including slaves, and are in many houses

---

106. Rigby, Report, 1860, p. 332; Horner, letter, 24 June 1864, St. Esprit, 196/B; Alfred Grandidier, *Notice sur l'île de Zanzibar* (St. Denis, Réunion, 1868), p. 10. Cloth imports—for transshipment and local use—were over $1,000,000 annually. Prideaux, Report, 1873–74, FOCP 2915, pp. 97, 99.

107. Steere, p. 14; Guillain, *Documents*, vol. 2/1, pp. 86–87; Burton, *Zanzibar*, 1:386–88. Precisely because avenues of display were limited, these ceremonies were very important indicators of wealth and status. Margaret Strobel. "Women's Wedding Celebrations in Mombasa, Kenya," *The African Studies Review* 18 (1975): 35–45.

108. Prideaux, Report, 1873–74, FOCP 2915, pp. 97–100. The largest such item was crockery—valued at $27,000 in 1873–74.

109. Cochet to MAE, 15 January 1857, MAE, 2.

110. India Government, *A Medico-Topographical Report on Zanzibar*, by John Robb (Calcutta, 1879), p. 5; Browne, pp. 435, 438–40; Horner, letter, 8 October 1868, St. Esprit, 196/B; Cochet to MAE, 2 January 1857, AN, Af. Etr., BIII/438.

the one external mark of distinction.[111] The respectable Arab rarely ventured outside his door without his sword or dagger, preferably an ornamented silver one.[112]

This ability to be content with a minimum of luxuries was one reason why so many European writers asserted that Arabs were lazy. Hamerton wrote that as soon as Arabs were producing sufficient cloves "to enable them to sleep away their lives and procure women for their harems," they would turn over their mashamba to an overseer and "appear to care little how matters are carried on." An American consul felt that Arabs were content with the "quiet enjoyment of their shambas, slaves and seraglios." More harshly, a French visitor claimed that most Arab landowners led "an idle life." [113] Seyyid Majid himself observed to the American consul that "My subjects are indolent and do not know how to make business." [114] All missed the point. It was not a question of indolence so much as a social system that placed relatively little value on work and wealth for their own sake.

In Zanzibar, as well as Oman, the religious element of life remained important, even as business became a more central occupation. Arabs spent much time in the daily prayers prescribed by their religion.[115] A recent study by B. G. Martin has demonstrated that a community of Islamic scholars developed in Zanzibar. Some of these scholars traveled to Arabia and the Middle East to make the pilgrimage to Mecca or to study. All based their scholarship and teaching on texts by scholars throughout the Muslim world, and some produced original work of their own. The most famous had pupils from many places in East Africa and other parts of the Indian Ocean region. They and their pupils played essential roles in the government, serving as kadis (judges) and as advisors to the Sultan.[116] They were among the most

111. On slaves as artisans, see chapter 5. Door-carvers were also observed by Baumann, *Sansibar*, p. 42.

112. Burton, *Zanzibar*, 1:384–86; Guillain, *Documents*, vol. 2/1, p. 88; Schmidt, p. 37.

113. Hamerton to Bombay, 13 July 1841, copy in Gray Papers, Cambridge University Library, box 1; Speer to Seward, 26 November 1862, US Consul, 4; Courmont, p. 393. See also Krapf, Journal, 7 March 1844, CMS CA5/016/165, and Germain, "Zanzibar," pp. 552–53.

114. Speer to Seward, 26 November 1862, US Consul, 4.

115. Steere, pp. 12–13; Burton, *Zanzibar*, 1: 388–90; Guillain, *Documents*, vol. 2/1, p. 95. Etienne Marras, "L'Isle de Zanzibar," *Bulletin de la Société de Géographie de Marseille* 5 (1881): 195.

116. B. G. Martin, "Notes on Some Members of the Learned Classes of Zanzibar and East Africa in the Nineteenth Century," *African Historical Studies* 4 (1971): 525–45; Abdalla Saleh Al-Farsy, *Terehe ya Imam Shafi na Wanavyuoni Wakubwa wa Mashariki ya Africa* (Zanzibar, 1944), pp. 76–77. Many of the leading scholars were Hadramis, but Seyyid Bargash encouraged Ibadi scholarship and brought about the publication in Zanzibar of important Ibadi works. Joseph Schacht, "Bibliothèques et manuscrits abadites," *Revue Africaine* 50 (1956): 375–98.

respected men of Zanzibar, and some were remembered long after their deaths.[117]

Some of the families that furnished the leading scholars were notably successful in business, and it is likely that economic success contributed to the creation of a society that could afford the time needed for a scholarly life. The Al-Ruwehi family supplied Zanzibar with some of its leading Ibadi scholars, and this family also owned extensive clove plantations. Several of the leading Sunni scholars came from active trading families.[118]

That these families chose to take success in business as an opportunity to pursue a scholarly life, and that Zanzibaris in general continued to enjoy a life of limited material extravagance, point to the enduring quality of the Omanis' social values. Nevertheless, by 1870 the clove plantation had become important both as an investment and as a way of life. Money was earned and enjoyed; businessmen and planters altered their investments in response to price changes; traders went on arduous and risky journeys in search of gain; and farmers experimented with new crops.

This was not a confrontation between new economic incentives and an archaic ideology. Even in Oman, Ibadi asceticism had not prevented Omanis from enjoying the fruits of commercial success. Perhaps a continuation of high clove prices over several decades would have submerged old communal rivalries beneath common economic interests and would have made economic success a more important component of ideology. But by the 1850s, overproduction was forcing the price down. Instead of an export-economy dominated by high price incentives—like the Caribbean sugar economy at its peak—Zanzibar developed plantations as integrated units, capable of providing both subsistence and cash income. Nor did agricultural development lead to further transformation of the economy. As chapter 4 will suggest, Omanis became increasingly hemmed in after 1872 by the structural weaknesses of the plantation economy: lack of control over marketing and finance as well as low clove prices and a threatened slave supply.

The new economic conditions did not force wealthy planters and traders to reformulate the ideology that justified their superior position. Economic success per se did not define their high status, although it was an important component of it. What defined the upper stratum of society is best expressed by a term still used by Arabs and Swahili today, *heshima*—meaning, literally, "respect." It implied sufficient

117. See the biographies of some of these scholars in Farsy, *Terehe*, which he wrote for the benefit of Zanzibaris in 1944.

118. Joseph Schacht, "Notes on Islam in East Africa," *Studia Islamica* 23 (1965): 121; MSA 34; Martin, pp. 531–41.

wealth to have a decent home and wear decent attire and to purchase the few luxury goods that were valued. It implied being able to provide guests with hospitality.[119] In both Oman and Zanzibar, *heshima* meant having a retinue of slaves, and that was expensive. *Heshima* also meant coming from a good family and from an Omani communal group whose power and place in society were recognized. It required an "aristocratic appearance and behavior." To be respected, one also had to be a good Muslim, learned as well as pious. Wealth was part of this picture, but it was not equated with personal worth.[120] There were substantial incentives to make profits, but less pressure to maximize them, either for display or investment.

The process of plantation development transformed, rather than overthrew, the connection between slaves and status in the scale of Omani values. Having dependent followers had long been an important component of power and prestige. The increasing economic importance of slaves was added to their social value. As a German visitor wrote, "The number of slaves one owns is still a criterion of power and reputation." [121] Yet it was the ownership of slaves—not just the income they produced—that was valued. Whether the clove industry prospered or stagnated, the slaves' labor helped provide subsistence while their presence conveyed prestige.

If the growing economic value of slaves did not end their social meaning, neither did it end their political importance. To be sure, Zanzibar was more peaceful than Oman and if the Sultan's control over outlying areas of the islands and over the mainland was weak, at least he had a better grip on the port with its all-important customs house, plus his own vast plantations.[122] Still, feuds between communal groups

119. On the importance of hospitality and visiting to Zanzibari society, see Steere, pp. 12–13; Guillain, *Documents*, vol. 2/1, pp. 32–33; Burton, *Zanzibar*, 1: 388–90; Henry Stanley Newman, *Banani: The Transition from Slavery to Freedom in Zanzibar and Pemba* (London, 1898), p. 62; Pearce, pp. 217, 230; Robert Nunez Lyne, *Zanzibar in Contemporary Times* (London, 1905), pp. 216–17.

120. Note the sentiment expressed in the Swahili proverb: "Kupata si kwa werevu; na kukosa si ujinga" (Getting is not of cunning and lacking is not stupidity). W. E. Taylor, *African Aphorisms or Saws from Swahili-Land* (London, 1891), nos. 191, 192. See also the observations of the German visitor Schmidt, pp. 30, 39, and the discussion of values in Jan Knappert, "Social and Moral Concepts in Swahili Islamic Literature," *Africa* 40 (1970): 35.

121. Schmidt, p. 46. Similar views are expressed in Hamerton to Bombay, 2 January 1842, PP 1844, XLVIII, 1, p. 419; Pelly to Forbes, 1 February 1862, Proceedings for May 1862, INA, Reel 2; Christie, *Cholera*, p. 328.

122. There is as yet no adequate analysis of Zanzibari politics in the nineteenth century, but it would appear that the distribution of power and relations among communal groups were neither static nor radically altered from the time of Seyyid Said's arrival until the 1870s. See Gray, *History of Zanzibar;* Sheriff; and Andreas Birken, "Das Sultanat Zanzibar im 19 Jahrhundert," (Ph.D. diss., Eberthard-Karls-Universität zu Tübingen, 1971).

and between individuals continued to erupt, and slaveowners—including the Sultan and his rivals—occasionally had to mobilize their slaves and other followers (see chap. 5).

The balance among the tasks and functions of slaves was changing, but what still counted most was their presence. A dependent plantation labor force could be assimilated into older notions of "the following." By 1872, slaves had become a part of plantation life—most of them lived on the plantations, taking care of themselves, working for their masters, but above all *there*. Slaves' productivity had become, for the first time, a major consideration, but it was not the only consideration.

The slaveowners were, for the most part, planters. However, they were not a planter class: a class whose dominant material basis is the income generated by plantations and whose status is primarily determined by the social fact of plantation ownership. It was not simply that communal differences inhibited planters from coalescing as a class, but a question of the economic and social significance of the plantation. Commerce, including that in items unrelated to plantations, was also important to a large segment of the Omani elite, while the ownership of land and slaves, as well as the income derived from them, were elements, but not dominant elements, of social status. Political power, moreover, was a matter of personal followers, communal affiliations and alliances, and dynastic conflicts—not a derivative of plantation ownership. The ruling family incorporated cloves into its other, more lucrative sources of wealth—commerce, taxes, and tribute. Plantation agriculture had changed the way Omanis and their slaves worked and lived, but it did not overwhelm Zanzibar as it did the Southern United States, the Caribbean, and Brazil. Older social structures and values remained a vital part of Zanzibari society throughout the nineteenth century.

3 Arab and African Slaveowners on the Mainland Coast

The mainland coast was part of the same Indian Ocean trading system as Zanzibar and was buffeted by the same winds of change in the nineteenth century. Trade between coastal cities and the interior was expanding, and the scale of agricultural production was increasing. While Zanzibar profited from a valuable new crop, the coast found its role in the Indian Ocean network by producing old ones, grain and coconuts. Not only did the scale of agricultural production increase vastly from the 1820s, but in parts of the coast—most strikingly Malindi—new ways of organizing production were developed. The characteristic coastal farming unit—a family supplemented perhaps by a few slaves working alongside it—gave way to plantations, large-scale operations based on closely supervised slave labor.[1]

The same extension of trading networks that had stimulated the clove industry of Zanzibar linked food-poor areas in Arabia and the Horn of Africa with the fertile mainland coast, while the wealth that Arabs of Oman and the Hadramaut were obtaining from their trading activities made them able to import more foodstuffs. Meanwhile, Zanzibar itself began to import grain. Millet was much in demand in Arabia and Zanzibar, while coconuts and sesame—a seed from which oil was extracted—fed an expanding market in Arabia as well as the eagerness of French traders in Zanzibar to obtain oil-producing crops.[2] Mainland farmers found the means to meet these demands through the slave-trading infrastructure that developed in the late eighteenth

1. A fine discussion of Swahili agriculture may be found in Janet Bujra, "An Anthropological Study of Political Action in a Bajuni Village, Kenya" (Ph.D. diss., University of London, 1968). It is hard to prove that the type of agriculture described by Bujra existed before the mid-nineteenth century, for no detailed descriptions exist. The predominance of small-scale agriculture is inferred from the observations of Lieutenant Emery in Mombasa in 1824–26, which are discussed below. The use of slaves along the coast was mentioned, but not described, by Don Francisco d'Almeida in 1505 and Monsieur Morice in 1776. (Documents reprinted in Freeman-Grenville, ed., *The East African Coast*, pp. 106, 109, and *The French at Kilwa Island*, p. 107.) Outside of the plantation context, nineteenth-century Swahili agriculture was not very different from that practiced by hinterland peoples. See Ylvisaker, "Lamu Archipelago," and Spear, "The Kaya Complex."

2. On the demand for grain and sesame, see Capt. Loarer, "Ile de Zanguebar," O.I., 5/23, notebooks 2 and 3; Guillain, *Documents*, vol. 2/2, pp. 313–16, 336–37; Ladislas-Cochet to MAE, 15 January 1857, MAE, 2.

century, extended, at times, by slaves dumped on the coastal market due to fluctuations in the export trade.

This chapter will examine agriculture in two parts of the northern coast, Mombasa and Malindi. Mombasa, long a small-scale grain-producing area, extended its fields farther into its hinterland in the 1840s. Malindi developed rapidly in the 1860s and 1870s to become the leading grain-growing area of the entire coast. These two places embrace the most important variations in response to the changing economic situation. Malindi was a new settlement, founded solely for the purpose of exploiting its rich and largely unoccupied lands. Mombasa was an old city, dominated by a trading community with long traditions of urban life. This chapter will show the different ways that the economy and society of these towns were affected by the expansion of agriculture, and part 2 will examine the impact of these changes on the organization of agricultural labor and the day-to-day lives of the slaves.[3]

MALINDI: THE GROWTH OF A PLANTATION TOWN

In the 1850s, Malindi was an abandoned ruin, visited occasionally by passing dhows and by Galla hunters and pastoralists who lived in its hinterland.[4] In Portuguese times it had been a center for the cultivation of fruit and other products as well as a trading port of some significance, but as Mombasa became the focus of Portuguese interests, Malindi declined. It was finished off in the late eighteenth century, as Galla nomads moved south, sacking whatever was in their path. However, by mid-nineteenth century, fortunes were changing once again. The power of the Galla, besieged from the north by Somali, was declining.[5]

There are as many different versions of the refounding of Malindi as there are ethnic groups in the town, but all of them stress the arrival of people by sea in search of agricultural land. The most definite evidence available comes from two Europeans, the German von der Decken and the American Thornton, who, in November 1861, saw the stone houses

3. Agriculture in other parts of the coast generally fits between these two extremes, although local geographical and political conditions heavily influenced the way farming was done and labor utilized. See Ylvisaker; McKay, "Southern Kenya Coast"; and a forthcoming dissertation of Takaungu for the University of Wisconsin by Peter Koffsky.

4. William Owen of the British navy and the missionary Krapf both saw the ruins in the early nineteenth century. Owen, *Narrative of Voyages*, 1:402; Ludwig Krapf, *Travels, Researches and Missionary Labours during an Eighteen Years' Residence in Eastern Africa* (Boston, 1860), pp. 124–25.

5. For a general introduction to Malindi, see Esmond Bradley Martin, *The History of Malindi: A Geographical Analysis of an East African Coastal Town from the Portuguese Period to the Present* (Nairobi, 1973). Much new material on the Galla may be found in Ylvisaker.

Map 3: The Coast of Kenya

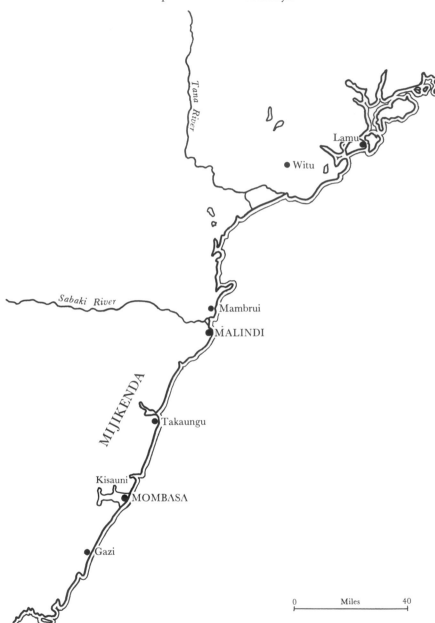

of the town being rebuilt by 50 settlers, 150 Baluchi soldiers, and 1,000 slaves sent by the Sultan of Zanzibar.[6]

Today, four distinct ethnic groups exist in Malindi and Mambrui, a sister village about twelve miles up the coast. These are the Washella (Swahili from a town on Lamu island farther up the coast), Bajuni (Swahili from elsewhere in the Lamu Archipelago), Omani Arabs, and Hadrami Arabs. Most Washella and Bajuni informants believe that their ancestors had begun farming in the Malindi-Mambrui area, without settling permanently, before the Sultan sent the expedition observed by the explorers. This was an extension of farming patterns in the Lamu region, where the largely island-dwelling Swahili population could only grow coconut trees on the islands and so crossed to the mainland to grow grain.[7] The part of Malindi where the Washella supposedly built their temporary huts is to this day known as Shella. However, the Galla were still in the area and attacked or kidnapped anyone who went alone to get water from the Sabaki River. Most Washella informants say that for this reason the Washella sought the protection of the Sultan, who sent the Baluchi soldiers, a governor, and Arab settlers to help.[8] According to the Washella—and other groups agree—the different peoples who had come to Malindi concentrated in their own respective quarters of the town but lived in relative harmony. Most Bajuni gravitated to Mambrui.[9]

Most Omani Arabs, on the other hand, claim that Malindi was refounded by order of the Sultan of Zanzibar. Seeking to expand cultivation in his dominions, he sent some of his fellow Omanis from Muscat and Zanzibar, along with Baluchis to protect them from the Galla. Once the area was pacified, other settlers of various origins came and began to farm.[10] Hadrami Arabs most often went to Mambrui and

6. Otto Kersten, *Baron Carl von der Decken's Reisen in Ost Afrika* (Leipzig, 1871), 2: 419; Richard Thornton, diary, 1 November 1861, in H. A. Fosbrooke, "Richard Thornton in East Africa," *Tanganyika Notes and Records*, no. 58–59 (1962), p. 54.

7. MAL 1, 66. Farming patterns in the Lamu area are discussed at length by Bujra and Ylvisaker.

8. MAL 1, 9, 17, 27. Thornton noticed that the recently arrived Baluchis were stationed along the route to the Sabaki River because slaves had been killed by Gallas while fetching water. Diary, 2 November 1861. This portion of the diary is not in Rhodes House, Oxford, and I was shown a copy by Peter Koffsky, who obtained it from H. A. Fosbrooke.

9. MAL 4, 17, 26, 27, 36, 41, 45, 46. Consul Kirk and Vice-Consul Gissing both noted the establishment of farms north of Mambrui by people from Lamu. Kirk to Derby, 4 April 1877, PP 1878, LXVII, 495, p. 305; Gissing to Kirk, 14 September 1884, FOCP 5165, p. 243.

10. MAL 18, 28, 56, 59. A person of slave origin, brought up in an Omani household, gave the same version as his owner's people, while someone whose ancestors were slaves of an Mshella gave the Washella version. MAL 30, 31.

Omanis to Malindi, although all four communal groups were well represented in each village.[11]

There is no way to make a certain choice between these two versions.[12] But both acknowledge the most important elements of the other's stories: the Arabs admit that the Washella and Bajuni came on their own to Malindi seeking land, while the Washella and Bajuni admit that Omanis and Hadramis came for the same purpose and that the Sultan sent troops and a governor to protect and control the settlement.[13] So began an ethnically diverse plantation town.

Whether a remarkable first crop or the result of several years of farming, much grain had already been harvested by November 1861.[14] Malindi was soon sending grain to Arabia, produced by "some thousands of slaves." [15]

When Frederic Holmwood of the British Consulate at Zanzibar visited Malindi in 1874, he saw "fine farms well stocked with slaves extending for miles in every direction." Areas that had been uncleared bush at the time of his visit the previous year were now under cultivation. Between Malindi and Mambrui, plantations extended up to six hours' marching time inland. Consul Kirk estimated grain exports to be around $150,000 in 1873.[16] Each year thirty dhows left Malindi with

11. Charles New, who visited Mambrui in May 1866, was told by the governor, Hemed bin Said Al-Busaidi, that he had founded the town seven months previously. Charles New, "Journal, 1 May-8 June 1866," *United Methodist Free Church Magazine* 10 (1867): 500. A similar version of the founding of Mambrui was given by the grandson of the alleged founder, MAL 28. Some Hadrami Arabs in Mambrui say that Hemed bin Said founded the city; others say it was Bajuni. MAL 40, 44.

12. The Washella-Bajuni version has the advantage of being consistent with these peoples' habit of seeking mainland farms for grain, whereas the Omani version postulates a specific expedition to develop an area that they had not used for generations. British officials in Zanzibar were well aware of the Sultan's expedition to build Dar es Salaam, but there is no mention of a similar venture in Malindi.

13. A Baluchi informant descended from one of the original soldiers stressed the role of the Baluchis in pacifying the area, without which a viable agricultural settlement would have been impossible. He did admit that Washella may have come earlier to farm, suffering greatly from the Galla. MAL 5. No informants mentioned that the governor initially paid the local Galla $450 a year to keep quiet. Frederic Holmwood, Report, incl. Prideaux to Derby, 24 November 1874, FOCP 2915, p. 16–17.

14. Thornton and von der Decken were told that a British antislave trade patrol had recently entered Malindi harbor and burned three dhows, one of which contained 5,000 bags of grain. Thornton Diary, 1 November 1861. The dhow-burning incident is also described by W. C. Devereux, *A Cruise in the "Gorgon"* (London, 1869; repr. 1968), pp. 137–38, and by two informants, MAL 59, 60.

15. Rebmann to CMS, 28 April 1862, CMS CA5/M3; New, "Journal," p. 504. New wrote that Malindi had a population of 10–15,000 in the 1860s, which is an exaggeration. Charles New, *Life, Wanderings and Labours in Eastern Africa* (London, 1873), p. 166.

16. Holmwood, FOCP 2915, p. 7; Kirk to Granville, 6 November 1873, PP 1874, LXII, 749, pp. 101–02. A Frenchman estimated that grain exports were between $80,000 and

millet, destined principally for the Hadramaut, while fifteen to twenty took away sesame. Other dhows carried grain to Zanzibar.[17]

Malindi had become, in Kirk's words, "the granary of Eastern Africa." Among Swahili, the town became known as *Mtama,* "Millet." As the intense cultivation near the sea exhausted the soil, the fields were allowed to lie fallow and cultivation was extended inland. The plantations reached 10 to 15 miles inland by 1877, while behind Mambrui the whole area was "one extensive field." [18]

The 1880s were the height of Malindi's prosperity. A visitor called it "a vast sea of *mtama.*" Vice-Consul Gissing, a British official touring the area in 1884, found the soil "rich and very carefully cultivated." Although the area being farmed was still increasing, the "available extent of land for increase is practically without limit." [19] Agricultural exports, as Table 3:1 shows, were large and growing. Meanwhile, coconut trees were being planted in large numbers, and mangoes and other fruit trees were planted as well. By 1890, there were "forests" of coconut, mango, orange, and other trees, although the fruit was mainly consumed locally.[20]

Most of the grain was carried away by big dhows owned by people

TABLE 3:1
EXPORTS OF MALINDI AND MAMBRUI

| | 1884 | 1887 | |
	Frasilas	Frasilas	M.T. Dollars
Millet	500,000	500,000	150,000
Sesame	120,000	250,000	150,000
Beans	120,000	200,000	80,000
Other	20,000	3,000	1,800
Total Value	$275,000		$381,800

SOURCES: Gissing to Kirk, 16 September 1884, FOCP 5165, p. 247; Frederic Holmwood, "Estimates of Present Customs Duty upon the Trade of His Highness the Sultan's Dominions between Wanga to Kipini inclusive," 6 May 1887, in Sir William Mackinnon Papers, Africa, IBEA, no. 943, School of Oriental and African Studies, University of London.

$120,000 each year. H. Greffulhe, "Voyage de Lamoo à Zanzibar," *Bulletin de la Société de Géographie et d'Etudes Coloniales de Marseille,* 2 (1878): 338.

17. Holmwood, Report, filed with Prideaux, Administrative Report on Zanzibar, 1873–74, FOCP 2915, pp. 86–87. See also Guillois to MAE, 10 December 1873, MAE 3.

18. Kirk to Derby, 4 April 1877, FOCP 3686, pp. 562–63; MAL 9, 26, 28, 36.

19. Frederick Jackson, *Early Days in East Africa* (London, 1930), p. 51; Gissing to Kirk, 16 September 1884, FOCP 5165, p. 247.

20. Gissing, FOCP 5165, p. 247; Alexandre Le Roy, "Au Zanguébar Anglais," *Missions Catholiques* 22 (1890): 606; W. W. A. Fitzgerald, "Report on the Native Cultivation, Products and Capabilities of the Coast Lands of the Malindi District," 1891, copy in Royal Commonwealth Society Library.

from Arabia and the Persian Gulf, which came down each year with the monsoon winds. Smaller dhows, owned by Lamu people and occasionally by Malindi people, also took grain to the arid coast of Somalia. Local dhows brought grain to Zanzibar as well. The export of grain was handled by firms in Malindi and Mambrui. Most were Indian—with connections with merchants in Mombasa or Zanzibar—but a few were Hadrami. Grain was brought to Malindi on the heads of slaves or on donkeys and sold to the grain merchants, who then sold it or consigned it to the dhows.[21]

Malindi's expansion owed much to the relative solidity of the grain market. Grain prices rose in the 1870s and remained relatively stable. Millet sold for $.30 per frasila in 1884 and the same in 1891, although sesame fell from $.50 to $.30.[22] Although it is impossible to calculate yields or productivity, Kirk estimated in 1873 that a slave could produce $42 worth of grain and sesame in one year, which was close to his purchase price at that time. If Kirk's estimate of 4,000 to 5,000 field slaves is accurate, they would in theory be able to produce $168,000 to $210,000 worth of grain, a figure that is consistent with available export data.[23]

If Kirk's estimates are even close, the rate of return on slave capital must have been much higher in Malindi than in Zanzibar, at least after clove prices declined. I have been told that a man could become rich in one season, and the life histories discussed below suggest that this may have been only a modest exaggeration.[24] Once established, a planter could do very well indeed. One of the biggest, Suleiman bin Abdalla Al-Mauli, was at one time paying an export *duty* of $940 on his crop. This would correspond to sales of $7,500 of millet.[25]

Malindi's extraordinary development from an abandoned town to the granary of East Africa had much to do with a factor common to most plantation areas: low population density and the political weakness of the previous inhabitants. The Galla could be held off by Baluchis and appeased by a small payment until they could be ignored, and the northward migrations of Mijikenda agriculturalists who lived in the coastal hinterland south of Malindi were not a factor there until

21. Holmwood, FOCP 2915, pp. 86–87; Greffulhe, p. 340; MAL 8, 10, 18, 26, 27, 42.
22. Kirk to Derby, 4 April 1877, FOCP 3686, p. 563; Gissing, FOCP 5165, p. 246; Fitzgerald, Report on Malindi, p. 4.
23. Kirk's estimate of productivity sounds high, but his estimate of the number of slaves may be low. Kirk to Granville, 6 November 1873, PP 1874, LXII, 749, pp. 101–02. Compare the calculated exports with the actual figures in Table 3:1.
24. MAL 44.
25. Bell Smith, Report on Malindi-Takaungu Districts, December 1892, incl. IBEA Co. to FO, 18 March 1893, FO 2/57.

around 1890, by which time Arab and Swahili settlers were firmly in control of the rich coastal plain.[26]

The evidence of Holmwood, Gissing, and others suggests that land was available for those who could clear the bush in the 1870s and 1880s.[27] Most informants agree that new land was claimed simply by being cleared. Applications for land titles during the early colonial era frequently claimed land on the grounds that it was "cleared by myself" or "cleared by my slaves." [28] Once cleared, land was generally used for one to three years and then allowed to revert to bush and restore itself. The original owner retained title under Islamic law but went on to clear a new shamba.[29]

The size of plantations, therefore, was mainly determined by the number of slaves one owned. As one informant put it, "nguvu ni watumwa," "strength is slaves." [30] Some settlers came to Malindi with their slaves; others came as relatively poor people and bought slaves with the proceeds of their own labor.[31] In 1866, 217 of the slaves legally exported from Zanzibar were consigned to Malindi, but they were undoubtedly supplemented by others who avoided the duty at Zanzibar.[32]

26. By 1874, the number of soldiers was down to thirty, and shortly thereafter payments ceased. Holmwood, FOCP 2915, pp. 15–16; Weaver to Craufurd, 23 July 1896, CP/1/75/46. Galla, as well as Sanye, remained in the vicinity until Mijikenda agriculturalists occupied the area behind the coastal plain, and occasional conflicts continued to erupt. The Mijikenda migrations reached the Sabaki River about 1890, as noted by Le Roy, p. 607; Binns to Lang, 28 January, 19 February, and 26 March 1890, CMS G3/A5/o/1890/33, 49, 157. For more on the Mijikenda, see Spear.

27. Holmwood, FOCP 2915, p. 7; Gissing to Kirk, 16 September 1884, FOCP 5165, p. 247. A British official in 1896 wrote that 75,000 of the 160,000 acres of fertile land in the Malindi-Mambrui area were unappropriated. He probably misunderstood the Muslim law on abandonment, but is right in finding little pressure on land. Weaver to Craufurd, 23 July 1896, CP/1/75/46.

28. Muslim law makes no distinction between land that is seized by force and land that is purchased—both are property and can be used, sold, or mortgaged in much the same way as under English law. Charles Hamilton, *The Hedaya, or Guide* (London, 1791), 4: 129–32; Testimony of Sheikh Mohamed bin Omar Bakar, former chief kadi of Kenya, 12 July 1934, hearing re a/c 2WS of 1919, Lamu; Interview, current chief kadi, Abdalla Saleh Al-Farsy, MSA 21. On the situation in Malindi, see Gissing, FOCP 5165, p. 243; a/c, *passim;* MAL 5, 9, 17, 26, 36, 40.

29. W. W. A. Fitzgerald, Report, incl. IBEA to FO, 15 October 1891, FO 84/2176; Weaver to Craufurd, 23 July 1896, CP/1/75/46; testimony of slaves of Abdulla bin Abdulla Hussein, a/c 23D 1914; MAL 35, 40, 44, 58.

30. MAL 40. The same point is made in the report by Fitzgerald, as cited above, and by other informants, MAL 44, 52, 59.

31. MAL 12, 27, 28, 30, 31, 36.

32. Memorandum by Seward on the Slave Traffic in the Port of Zanzibar, n.d. [1866], FO 84/1279. Some slaves were obtained from the Galla, probably by purchase. Kirk to Granville, 27 June 1871, FO 84/1344.

In 1873 Kirk estimated that Malindi was importing 600 slaves per year just to maintain its stock of 6,000 slaves.[33]

Malindi's growth occurred in a time of trouble for slave traders. The slave trade by sea was harassed by British warships in the 1860s and outlawed in 1873 (see Appendix 2 and chapter 4). By making exports to Arabia more difficult, these measures may have contributed to the expansion of slave plantations in Malindi, although it was only after 1873 that the Arabian trade was effectively curtailed. Even after 1873, slaves continued to arrive from distant parts of East Africa, although they had to be marched along the coast from Kilwa instead of being sent by sea. In 1874, Holmwood estimated that Malindi was absorbing 1,000 slaves per year from the land route—the same number as Mombasa, which had a larger free population, absorbed. Kirk noted in 1877 that Malindi had an "immense" demand for slaves, but that it "has in one way or another been supplied." [34] Only in the mid-1880s did the supply run low.

The scattered and unreliable estimates of population suggest that Malindi and Mambrui together had 5,000 to 10,000 slaves and over 1,000 Arabs and Swahili. There were about 500 mashamba held by these groups in 1912–15, so that the average number of slaves per shamba was in the range of ten to twenty.[35] The rich, however, owned more than one shamba; a few individuals owned over ten.

Local people say that many slaveowners had only two or three slaves, while someone whom they would consider a very big slaveowner had 100 to 150. Some concrete figures come from records of the confiscation of slaves of some planters who ran afoul of the British in the early 1890s. Suleiman bin Abdalla Al-Mauli, one of the richest slaveowners in the entire area, had 261 slaves, working on over 1,000 acres of land plus several coconut mashamba. Another Omani had 120, while two of his kinsmen had 32 and 24.[36] These figures hint that considerable concentration of wealth in slaves and land may have existed.

33. Kirk to Granville, 6 November 1873, PP 1874, LXII, 799, p. 102. This corresponds to a 10% attrition rate, which is plausible.

34. Holmwood, FOCP 2915, p. 8; Kirk to Derby, 4 April 1877, FOCP 3686, p. 563. In 1877, Malindi was second only to Pemba in slave imports.

35. Estimates run from 4,000 to 5,000 field slaves plus 1,000 supervisors and domestics in Malindi (Kirk, 1873), to 6,000 to 7,000 slaves in town (Greffulhe, 1874), to 5,000 total population in Malindi and 500 to 600 in Mambrui (Holmwood, 1874), to 3,000 in Mambrui (Gissing, 1884). The estimate of the number of mashamba is from a/c, Malindi and Mambrui. For the population figures, see Kirk to Granville, 6 November 1873, PP 1874, LXII, 749, pp. 101–02; Greffulhe, p. 340; Prideaux, Report, 1873–74, FOCP 2915, p. 86; Gissing, FOCP 5165, p. 242.

36. MAL 17, 35, 45, 52; Bell Smith to de Winton, 5 January 1891, incl. Sultan of Zanzibar to Euan-Smith, 30 January 1891, FO 84/2146; Macdougall to Craufurd, 28 April 1897, CP/1/75/46; Acting District Commissioner, Malindi, to District Commissioner, Mombasa, 24 March 1914, CP/1/11/66.

The size of plantations also varied greatly. The Coast Land Settlement, conducted in 1912–15 in Malindi and summarized in Table 3:2, gives a rough idea of the varying degrees to which different individuals and communal groups acquired land.[37]

Landholdings, in general, were large—much larger than those near Mombasa, as comparison with Table 3:5 (p. 103) shows. Substantial planters owned several mashamba (as many as ten or twenty), but the average size of an individual shamba was still 61 acres. This scale of operations was the key to the success of Malindi's planters: it compensated for the low value of grain per acre and allowed planters to translate the well-organized labor structure they developed into profits.

At first glance, Table 3:2 suggests that Omanis were predominant in the plantation economy. Their ability to gain control over land is not surprising, since their commercial experience would have provided them with more capital with which to buy the slaves needed to clear

TABLE 3:2

LANDOWNERS IN MALINDI AND MAMBRUI

	NUMBER OF OWNERS FROM EACH COMMUNAL GROUP				
Acres owned	Omani	Hadrami	Shella	Bajun	Total
9 or less	10	9	4	11	34
10–49	18	27	16	21	82
50–99	12	11	9	7	39
100–499	15	8	3	8	34
500–999	2	3	1	1	7
1,000 or more	3	2	1	0	6
Total owners	60	60	34	48	202
Total acres	14,478	8,178	4,603	3,628	30,887
Average acres per owner	241	136	135	76	153

SOURCE: Calculated from a/c, Malindi and Mambrui. Where communal affiliation was not given in the transcript, the information was obtained from informants. People from other communal groups are not included in this table, although the only one with significant holdings in the 1800s are the Baluchis, with 1,054 acres.

37. The main distortion from the nineteenth-century situation comes from one man: Salim bin Khalfan Al-Busaidi (with a little help from his sons) was buying up land to expand his already large landholdings. A modest redistribution of land took place in the early colonial period, not to Omanis in general, but to him in particular. Indians and Europeans also bought land. However, the data on sales from 1903 onward (Reg., Mal), plus internal evidence in the a/c transcripts, indicate that land sales came from all communal groups and did not affect their relative shares—except for Salim bin Khalfan and sons. All the other large holdings in Table 3:2 were obtained wholly or mostly by inheritance, and so reflect land accumulation in the nineteenth century.

bush, while strong connections in Zanzibar would have facilitated business. However, further examination reveals that much of the imbalance
in communal landownership is attributable to Salim bin Khalfan Al-
Busaidi, who owned 5,228 acres, and his sons Ali and Seif, who owned
1,499—nearly half the entire Omani share.[38]

In fact, land was highly concentrated, but in the hands of a diverse
elite. The top thirteen landholders—those with over 500 acres—came
from all four communal groups. Together, this elite owned 56 percent
of the land retained by the original groups. Among the Washella, the
descendants of Abdulla Hussein and his brother Abubakar owned over
half that group's land. Two Hadrami accounted for 41 percent of the
Hadrami share, and the two leading Bajuni planters controlled 27 percent of their group's land.[39] The Omani advantage is still apparent, but
members of all groups were able to acquire vast tracts of land.

It is worth pausing to look at some of the small number of families
that owned most of the land of Malindi and Mambrui. The richest of
all was Salim bin Khalfan. He came to Malindi from Muscat, probably
before 1870, as a man of modest means, although from the same communal group as the Sultan of Zanzibar. One informant said that Salim
worked alongside his slaves in the fields when he first arrived.[40] Much
of his land was obtained by clearing forest, but as time went on he
purchased land from others, often for a few pieces of cloth or for
dates.[41] He became governor of Malindi sometime around 1870, and
from 1885 to 1887, and again from 1891 until his death in 1920, he
was governor of Mombasa.[42] As an official, it was natural that people in
financial distress should turn to him—he became a leading money-

38. If this family is given credit for only the lands they claimed by virtue of having
cleared them—1,000 acres—the average acreage held by Omanis dips to 148, much
closer to the Hadrami and Shella averages. It is impossible to tell how much of the land
that Salim, Ali, and Seif purchased was bought before the colonial period. This was virtually the only Omani family in Malindi that was as successful under the new regime as
under the old.

39. Separate figures for Malindi and Mambrui (broken down by plot, not owner) are
given in Cooper, "Plantation Slavery," tables 13 and 14, pp. 184, 186. The major Hadrami landowners were concentrated in Mambrui, where they owned over half the total
of the four groups. There were fewer Bajuni in Mambrui than Malindi, but they had bigger holdings. Most Washella lived in Malindi, as did most Omanis. Few planters had
holdings in both areas.

40. MAL 17.

41. MAL 12, 28. In 1890 he bought a plot in Malindi for $1,000 and sold it a week
later for a 14% profit. 31A 1893, Reg., Msa.

42. A report from 1874 says that when his nephew was acting governor of Mombasa,
he looked to his uncle for advice, which suggests that he was an experienced official by
then. Holmwood, FOCP 2915, pp. 15–16. For his tenure in Mombasa, see Berg, "Mombasa under the Busaidi Sultanate," pp. 334–36.

lender, as the Mombasa records attest. He is not remembered as a harsh usurer, even among rival groups, but informants do state that much of his land came from mortgages that had not been repaid.[43] Salim continued to buy or otherwise acquire both urban and rural land, and he became the largest Arab landowner in the Mombasa area as well as in Malindi. As Mombasa developed from a modest trading center to a major port, he was able to rent or sell this land for enormous sums. By the time of his death at the age of over eighty, his property was worth £175,000, a sum that no other Arab could approach.[44]

Suleiman bin Abdalla Al-Mauli, although one of the wealthiest men in Malindi, retained the fierce independence of his Omani forebears. He did not merely acquire vast lands near Mambrui and many slaves—over 1,000 acres and 261 slaves—but made himself into a local potentate. Known as Suleiman Kimenya (from *kumenya*, to beat or thrash), he is still remembered for his pugnaciousness and refusal to accept Al-Busaidi rule. He armed his own slaves and did not hesitate to use them for fighting. In 1890, Suleiman sided with the Sultan of Witu in an armed conflict against the Sultan of Zanzibar and his British backers. For this unsuccessful revolt he was executed and his lands confiscated.[45]

If Suleiman exemplified the Omani value of the independence of a chieftain and his personal followers, Bi Salima binti Masudi Al-Hasibi typified the values of paternalism. Born in Muscat, she came to Malindi by way of Zanzibar. Her first husband died and her second left Malindi to become governor of Mombasa.[46] With a strong personal interest in her own slaves and land, she ignored Islamic principles regarding the seclusion of women. She would go to her land from her house in town

43. MSA 12, 14, 25. Informants also stress the fact that he bought land very cheaply at a time when most people did not think it had significant monetary value. MSA 3, 14; MAI. 3, 12, 17. There is a record of foreclosure by Salim bin Khalfan in Mombasa. 61A 1893, Reg., Msa.

44. The tremendous appreciation of his urban property in Mombasa accounted for most of his fortune at the time of his death. By value, 81% of his landed property was in Mombasa, less than 3% in Malindi and Mambrui, even though he was by far the biggest landowner there. His property at his death is listed and assessed in Probate and Administration Cause 114 of 1920, on file in the High Court, Nairobi. The deed registers in Mombasa contain many land purchases and mortgages made by him.

45. Bell Smith to de Winton, 7 January 1891, incl. Sultan of Zanzibar to Euan-Smith, 30 January 1891, FO 84/2146; J. M. McGuhaie to Euan-Smith, 7 November 1890, incl. Euan-Smith to Salisbury, 8 November 1890, FO 84/2066; MAL 18, 26, 30, 44. For his activities in Witu, see Ylvisaker, pp. 253–54, 265–66. His land does not figure in Table 3:2.

46. She apparently completed the mosque which her second husband had started. Some call it the mosque of Ali bin Nassir; some, the mosque of Bi Salima. Official documents indicate that she made two houses into waqf for the benefit of this mosque. List of property made over to mosques in Malindi, filed in MAL/2/1.ADM 7/1, KNA.

on a donkey, carrying a gun and a machete, to supervise her slaves, of which she had at least sixty-four.[47] Today, old people say she was "hodari sana" (very skillful), or "mkali sana," (very fierce), but informants of slave origin, including one raised in her house, claim she was a kind slaveowner who treated her slaves well and never had problems with runaways. Herself childless, she brought up a number of slave-children in her house and gave them a Koranic education. She was much admired in town for sending food to the mosques each evening during Ramadan. She died shortly after 1900, leaving several enormous mashamba to a kinsman from Arabia.[48]

Hadramis had an important place in Mambrui, thanks in part to Islam bin Ali Al-Kathiri. The Al-Busaidi governor of Mambrui, Hemed bin Said, retained more of the old clannish fighting spirit than most. When Islam—a Hadrami who had been a trader in Lamu—settled in Mambrui, built a modest house of wood and mud, and began to farm, Hemed had no objections. But when Islam prospered, acquired more slaves and land, and—finally—started to build a stone house not far from the governor's own, Hemed refused him permission to build in stone. Islam then went to Zanzibar and obtained permission from Seyyid Bargash to build as large a house as he wished. He returned to Mambrui with a letter from the Sultan, as well as guns and slaves who knew how to use them. Islam refused to honor the governor's summons to his court, and instead sent him the Sultan's letter while preparing to fight. An uneasy standoff ensued, and Islam proceeded to build his house. With high stone walls, gun ports on the top floor, an interior well, and an interior garden, the house was actually a fort. Hemed decided it would not be prudent to intervene, and Islam continued his life as a prosperous farmer, helping other Hadrami Arabs to get started.[49]

Less important as a defender of Hadramis' place in Mambrui, but more important as a landowner and trader, was Ali bin Salim Bashara-

47. In 1886 she bought 64 slaves from Ali bin Nassir and mortgaged them to Abdalla Hussein. 124A 1894 Reg., Msa.

48. Her heir received six plots with 440 acres, while another plot of 330 acres registered by Salim bin Khalfan had been bought from her. The best-informed persons on her life were a man of slave descent raised in her household, Awade bin Maktub, MAL 18, and a kinsman, MAL 59. Other valuable observations came from MAL 24, 26, 27, 38, and 60.

49. The most detailed narrative of these events comes from the grandson of Islam bin Ali Al-Kathiri, MAL 40. It is confirmed in its essential details by others of various origins: MAL 36, 37, 44, 45. The best evidence of all is the fortified house of Islam bin Ali, still standing and occupied by his grandson. His sons owned seven mashamba with over 568 acres (acreage figures for one of them are missing), and the Islam bin Ali mosque in Mambrui had been given an additional seven mashamba of 344 acres.

hil. Born in the Hadramaut, he came to Mambrui, while his brother
Ahmed went to Lamu. They worked together as grain exporters.
Ahmed owned two dhows, while Ali operated a camel-driven sesame-
oil mill and a large warehouse and store in Mambrui. The oil, sesame,
millet, as well as goats and skins, were sent to Arabia and India. Meanwhile, Ali farmed. The heirs of the two brothers later received title to
twelve mashamba with 1,689 acres, the largest totals in the Mambrui
area.[50]

Swahili farmers were included among this wealthy elite. Lali Hadaa,
a Bajuni from north of Lamu, gave up seafaring to settle in Malindi.
He cleared many mashamba, installing a slave-supervisor on each and
using three more slaves to keep an eye on all of them. His descendants
ended up with ten mashamba totaling 472 acres.[51]

Abdulla Hussein was in still another class. Born in Shella, Lamu, he
was one of the original Washella settlers in Malindi. He was considered
a leader of his community, the man to whom Washella turned to settle
disputes or to support them in the informal workings of local politics.
He also acquired numerous slaves and much land. As of 1912–15, his
heirs (principally his grandchildren) owned 1,929 acres of land.[52] Even
as substantial an Omani planter as Bi Salima once borrowed $7,000
from Abdulla Hussein, for which she mortgaged sixty-four slaves and
some land. The slaves and the land later passed into Abdulla Hussein's
possession.[53] His brother Abubakar was also an early settler and a large
landowner.[54]

Not surprisingly, the agricultural prosperity of Malindi attracted Indian merchants. In 1870, there were 21 trading houses in Malindi and
two in Mambrui. The Indian population was then all male and limited
to the Bohora community. In 1874, there were 49 houses, and other
Indians from Mombasa visited Malindi during the millet and sesame
harvests. By 1887, the Indian community had apparently become more

50. Interview with grandson of Ali bin Salim Basharahil, MAL 43. Another informant's grandfather brought produce to Ali bin Salim's warehouse on a camel. MAL 37.
An old Indian trader in Mambrui was also well-informed about this family, MAL 42.

51. The principal sources are a kinsman, MAL 26, and MAL 24, 31.

52. According to testimony in 1914, two mashamba were cleared by his slaves forty
years previously (ca. 1874). On one shamba he had forty slaves. A/c 7D, 23D, 38D 1914.

53. The transfer of property to Abdulla Hussein took place in 1886. 1A 1894, Reg.,
Msa. The leading Bajuni planter, Lali Hadaa, also borrowed $3,603, and at one time
the governor of Mambrui owed Abdulla Hussein's daughter Rs 500, for which he
mortgaged a shamba. Reg., Msa., 13A 1894, and Reg., Mal., 2B 1903.

54. Abubakar's heirs received nine mashamba of 403 acres in Malindi and two with
306 acres in Mambrui, while a 324-acre shamba was sold before the title allocation. The
account of the two brothers is based on information from the leading Mshella elder, Abdalla Seif, MAL 17, two descendants of slaves of Abdulla Hussein, MAL 24 and 31, and
other knowledgeable old men, MAL 12, 18, 26.

stable, for there were 34 women and 49 children living in Malindi and Mambrui, in addition to 54 adult males. Aside from a few Khojas and one Hindu, all were Bohoras—communal ties were important to setting up a trading group.[55]

The most successful Indian firm in Malindi was that of a Bohora named Jivanji Mamuji. He left India for Mombasa as an adult and then went to Malindi, where he opened a store in a part of town that later became known as Kwa Jiwa, the place of Jivanji. He bought maize, millet, and sesame from the local planters and sent it to Mombasa, Zanzibar, and Arabia, where agents disposed of it. He also brought goods from Mombasa to Malindi to be sold at his store. His son Gulamhussein later became a grain exporter in partnership with his younger brother Abdulhussein, who took care of the Mombasa end of the business. The firm of Abdulhussein-Gulamhussein owned four or five dhows, but much of their grain exports were sent by the Arabian dhows that came during the season for grain. They invested in property, both in town and in the country, and were among the leading money-lenders of Malindi. Their property was never developed, but some of it was later sold at a profit.[56] These successful traders and financiers preferred not to become planters themselves.

A number of common features emerge from these brief biographies. Malindi was built up in a generation. The elite consisted of immigrants, with no local roots but with connections in their places of origin— Lamu, Muscat, the Hadramaut, and Zanzibar. Their wealth was based entirely on the rapid growth of agriculture and on trade in agricultural produce.[57] Some, particularly Omanis, came with capital; others made a fortune from humble beginnings. Malindi's elite were essentially nouveaux riches, but among them were people who still sought to maintain their political independence, their religious values, and paternalistic relations with their dependents.

As in other plantation societies, a few planters owned most of the land, while others owned small plots—and most fell between the two extremes. The landowners of Malindi differed from planters in most

55. John Kirk, Administrative Report, 1870, FO 84/1344; Holmwood, FOCP 2915, p. 86; Kirk to Granville, 6 November 1873, PP 1874, LXII, 749, pp. 101–02; Census of British Indian Subjects, August, 1887, incl., MacDonald to FO, 19 December 1887, FO 84/1854.

56. As of 1912–14, they owned eight mashamba with 453 acres. The grandson of Jivanji Mamuji was most informative, as was another Bohora. MAL 10, 81.

57. Trade in nonagricultural products was small-scale, and only in the 1890s did Mijikenda grain become important as a trade good. Holmwood, FOCP 2915, p. 86; Gissing, FOCP 5165, p. 243.

areas of the New World by their ethnic diversity.[58] They came from different places and kept close ties among themselves but still managed to live in relative harmony. Informants so relish tales about the exceptions to this generalization—the activities of Suleiman bin Abdalla and Islam bin Ali, for example—that one can be confident it is accurate. After all, Malindi was no more the ancestral home of one group than another, and all could make a living from the abundant land and the toils of slaves brought in from outside.

When conflict did erupt, people like Islam bin Ali and Suleiman bin Abdalla relied above all on the fighting potential of their personal slaves. Power—whenever someone chose to exercise it—required a dependent following. Islam's actions also had the effect of bolstering the Hadramis' collective position in Mambrui. Through the master, slaves contributed to the strength of the communal group.

Even if overt communal conflict was rare, the four groups remained distinct, and people even to this day are conscious of their communal affiliation and of the traditions of their group.[59] In the nineteenth century, the groups maintained a degree of political solidarity. Each had a structure of leadership and turned to respected men to settle internal problems.[60] The governor of Malindi, an Omani appointed by the Sultan of Zanzibar, had only thirty troops in 1874, and could hardly rule without the acquiescence of the communal groups.[61] Group identity thus coexisted with relative harmony in the town, growing out of common residence and common economic activities.[62]

As the town became established as a center for grain exports and as a home for planters, stone houses were built. An explorer saw twenty of

58. This diversity was not simply a matter of different origins but of variations in culture as well. Recent immigrants from Oman spoke Arabic as a first language and Swahili only as a second. They practiced the Ibadi version of Islam rather than the Sunni version followed by Swahili. They differed in habits of dress, in the intricacies of kinships systems, and in other matters. They have since moved toward greater cultural similarity, more on the terms of the Swahili than on those of the Arabs.

59. Narrower kinship groups, such as lineages, were of little political importance and were not the focus of loyalty. Since everyone was an immigrant, there was not enough time to build up these kinship networks, and only the broader affinities of common origins and culture were a meaningful basis for association. The vagueness of Swahili kinship groups has also been noted in a study of Lamu. Prins, *Sailing from Lamu*, p. 269.

60. People mentioned by informants as leaders in the old days turn out to be among the original settlers of the town as well as, in general, successful planters.

61. Holmwood, FOCP 2915, p. 15.

62. The importance of village solidarity to Swahili communities—over and above the communal cleavages that exist within them—is stressed by G.E.T. Wijeyewardene, "Some Aspects of Village Solidarity in Ki-Swahili Speaking Communities of Kenya and Tangan-

them in 1874. The less fortunate Arabs and Swahili lived in houses made from mud on wooden frames.[63] The rich were the most likely to live in town, where they could enjoy their homes and rely on slaves to bring them their food and take care of the farms.[64] Visitors, however, were not impressed by the appearance of Malindi town, in contrast to that of the lush fields around it.[65] The desire to turn a town residence into a mark of status—evident in the elaborately carved doors of Zanzibar—was lacking in Malindi. Some planters had second houses on their estates, where they sometimes stayed, especially during busy periods in the agricultural cycle. Others lived permanently on their estates.[66] Today, some people stay on their mashamba all week and come to Malindi on Friday for prayers. Even town-dwellers generally walked or rode a donkey to their fields each morning, returning to town in the evening.[67]

One of the town's most important functions was as a place to pray, and gestures of display and generosity were often focused on religion. Successful planters, like Salim bin Khalfan, Bi Salima, and Abdulla Hussein, had mosques built at their expense and in their names. A kadi appointed by the Sultan of Zanzibar, was in charge of enforcing Islamic law, although no local scholarly tradition evolved.[68]

Looking at the lives of its elite and the social structure of the town only reinforces the basic fact that Malindi was a plantation town. Its settlers came in search of profit and they lived modestly. The plantations were even more self-sufficient than those of Zanzibar. The local people did not develop the taste their sophisticated urban compatriots had for rice, although they grew some of it, and mostly consumed the same product they sold, millet.[69] Oil was made locally from sesame or

---

yika" (Ph.D. diss., Cambridge University, 1961). One of the villages he studied was Mambrui.

63. Greffulhe, "Voyage," p. 340; MacDougall, Quarterly Report, last quarter, 1900, incl. Eliot to Lansdowne, 22 February 1901, FO 2/445.

64. MAL 17.

65. For an early view, see Devereux, *Cruise*, pp. 403–04, and for a later one, Gissing, FOCP 5165, p. 241. The lack of an urban orientation distinguished this plantation town from other Swahili towns. Allen, "Swahili Culture Reconsidered," p. 132.

66. MAL 1, 30, 34, 58; LeRoy, p. 606.

67. MAL 1, 17, 18, 37, 45; A. G. Smith to Lang, 24 January 1891, CMS G3/A5/o/1891/61.

68. The kadi in the late nineteenth century was the son of an Omani planter. He later became kadi of Zanzibar, an indication of the lack of scope for an able Islamic jurist in Malindi. This man was Ali bin Mselem Al-Khalasi, son of the husband of bi Salima binti Masudi by a previous wife. MAL 59, 60. The building of mosques by members of Malindi's planter community was mentioned by MAL 17, 18, 26, 44.

69. MSA 14.

coconuts. Fish was plentiful and goats and chickens were kept. Several informants have told me that in the old days there was little on which to spend money. Profits were reinvested in land and, above all, in slaves.[70]

Yet the planters developed a strong attachment to Malindi and especially to its fertile land.[71] A diverse group of people had created a new town and an agricultural enterprise whose scale and organization went beyond anything they had experienced before.

MOMBASA: AGRICULTURE IN A PORT CITY

Mombasa also participated in the expansion of agriculture on the East African coast, but not so dramatically as Malindi. Lacking vast stretches of unoccupied land, the opportunities for expansion were less, while extensive and growing trade with the interior provided alternative sources of income, and the urban environment offered a different style of life from that of an agricultural outpost.

Mombasa, like Malindi, was growing farm produce as far back as Portuguese times. Nevertheless, when the British established their short-lived protectorate in Mombasa in 1824, they did not find agriculture in a very advanced state. Mombasa was even importing grain.[72] Still, the people of Mombasa worked hard in their fields. Lieutenant Emery, who lived there for two years, often noted in his diary: "Most of the inhabitants at their shambas," "Most of the inhabitants employed at the shambas on the main," "the natives are to the Northward collecting their grain." They grew grain and sesame, which they brought across the narrow space of water separating the island of Mombasa, where

70. MAL 40, 44, 52, 59. Import duties collected at Malindi and Mambrui in the 1890s were very low. "Report by Sir A. Hardinge on the Condition and Progress of the East Africa Protectorate from its Establishment to the 20th of July, 1897," PP 1898, LX, 199, p. 11.

71. There is much continuity in the Arab-Swahili population of Malindi. A few, notably Salim bin Khalfan, earned a fortune in Malindi and went on to fulfill higher political and business aspirations; some returned to their ancestral homes; but most remained in Malindi. This attachment to the town was mentioned by almost every informant.

72. Lieutenant Emery often noted in his diary that dhows with grain were arriving from Pemba, Lamu, Faza, or simply "the North." Not all was for local use, for Mombasa was a regional distribution center. Lieut. James B. Emery, "Journal of the British Establishment of Mombasa and Remarks on Mombas," with Master's Log of H.M.S. *Barracouta*, 1824–26, ADM 52/3940, entries for 28–29 September, 4, 5, 27 October, 25 November 1824; 29 January, 3, 14, 30, 31 March, 25 April, 12 September, 28 October 1825; 18 April, 5 July 1826; and others. See also Thomas Boteler, *Narrative of a Voyage of Discovery to Africa and Arabia Performed by His Majesty's Ships Levin and Barracouta from 1821 to 1826* (London, 1835), 1: 375–77.

most people lived, from the more fertile mainland.[73] Emery's account suggests that if slaves were used on the mashamba of the people of Mombasa, they worked alongside, and not in place of, their masters.

Trade was more developed than agriculture. Although lacking direct trade routes into the deep interior, the people of Mombasa obtained ivory, as well as gum copal, honey, beeswax, rhino horn, skins, cattle, and other such products from their Kamba and Mijikenda neighbors.[74] According to Emery, an average of 150 vessels entered Mombasa each year, paying duties of $11,000 in cash and $5,000 in kind. There was a sizable trade with Bombay, Cutch, and Surat, and many Indians were attracted by that trade to settle in Mombasa.[75]

The farmers and traders of Mombasa were mostly Arabs of Omani origin or local Swahili. The Swahili included people from various parts of the coast. Migrants from different places have formed distinct groups, known as the Twelve Tribes, although all Swahili groups have been open to absorbing migrants from different areas and the ties of common origin are largely mythical. Sons remained members of their father's tribe. By the nineteenth century, these tribes had formed two confederations, the Nine Tribes and the Three Tribes. Each tribe was both a collection of kinship groups and a political body united to promote the interests of its members.[76] A small number of Omani Arabs had also settled in Mombasa long ago. Members of the Al-Mandhry communal group, for example, have resided there since at least the sixteenth century.[77] Numerically predominant, the Swahili have also dominated the cultural life of the town, and Omanis gradually adapted eating habits, dress, house style, dances, and other aspects of culture from their Swahili neighbors. The common practice of Omani men marrying Swahili women no doubt accelerated this process. Most Omanis in Mombasa eventually went over to the Sunni version of Islam observed

73. Emery, Journal, 14 September, 3 October 1824; 28 April, 3, 7 May, 1, 6, 22 June 1826; Emery to Cooley, November 1833, and Emery to Cooley, 18 December 1835, Emery Papers, RGS, London.

74. Emery to Christian, 22 July 1826, ADM 1/70; Emery to Cooley, November 1833, and 20 December 1833, Emery Papers, RGS. Alpers argues that the creation of these trading relationships with the immediate hinterland accounted for the rise of Mombasa in the late fifteenth century. Alpers, *Ivory and Slaves*, p. 45.

75. Emery to Cooley, 19 May 1835, Emery Papers; William Owen, Replies of Prince Membarrok, incl. Cole to Bathurst, 19 June 1824, CO 167/72; Emery to Christian, 22 July 1826, ADM 1/70. See also Sir John Gray, *The British in Mombasa 1824–1826* (London, 1957).

76. F. J. Berg, "The Swahili Community of Mombasa, 1500–1900," *Journal of African History* 9 (1968): 40. Actual kinship groups, as opposed to these communal groups, had minimal political significance. Ibid., pp. 40–42.

77. F. J. Berg and B. J. Walter, "Mosques, Population and Urban Development in Mombasa," in B. A. Ogot, ed., *Hadith 1* (Nairobi, 1968), p. 60.

by the Swahili, while in places like Malindi and Zanzibar, which lacked a numerically and culturally dominant Swahili population, Omanis held onto their Ibadi creed.[78]

The political history of Mombasa is characterized by intrigue and factionalism, as well as by the tenacity with which communal groups clung to their independence. Rarely, however, did political factions divide along Arab-Swahili lines. More often, certain of the Twelve Tribes allied with certain Arab tribes to oppose similar combinations, while both sides tried to form alliances with the Mijikenda peoples living in the hinterland. All groups, however, sought the support of the Sultan of Oman to throw out the Portuguese from Mombasa in 1698 and again to re-expel them when they returned briefly three decades later. Their victory left Mombasa with an Omani governor. However, when the Al-Busaidi dynasty came into power in Muscat, the governor, from the Al-Mazrui communal group, did not recognize the new regime. He established a Mazrui dynasty, which received much support from Swahili. Not until 1837 did Seyyid Said finally dislodge the Mazrui, and he only did so when a substantial portion of the Swahili came over to his side. The defeated Mazrui were allowed to settle in Takaungu and Gazi, but many of them never lost their desire to regain hegemony over Mombasa, and were periodically assisted in their uprisings by a number of Twelve Tribes leaders. Meanwhile, the Al-Busaidi generally ruled Mombasa with a gentle hand allowing the leaders of the Twelve Tribes to administer most of their internal affairs.[79] In short, the society of Mombasa was far from homogeneous, and loyalties to particular communal groups—more so than vague ethnic categories like Arab or Swahili—were strong.

After the Al-Busaidi victory in 1837, trade increased in Mombasa, more as a result of the general pattern of penetration inland than because of the policies of Seyyid Said. The trading area behind Mombasa was only a minor slave-trading zone, but the tempo of trade in ivory and other such items with the Mijikenda and Kamba was stepped up, and later Swahili and Arab traders began to venture from Mombasa deep into the interior of East Africa.[80]

78. These points were explained to me by MSA 9, 14, 19. There is also much to be learned about Arab-Swahili interaction from Margaret Ann Strobel, "Muslim Women in Mombasa, Kenya, 1890–1973," (Ph.D. diss., University of California at Los Angeles, 1975).

79. Berg, "Swahili Community," pp. 35–56.

80. Trade with the Mijikenda and Kamba in the late 1840s and 1850s is described by Guillain, *Documents*, vol. 2/2, pp. 265–66, 273, 382–83; Burton, *Zanzibar*, 2: 45–46; and Krapf, *Travels*, pp. 99, 105. See also Berg, "Mombasa"; John Lamphear, "The Kamba and the Northern Mrima," in Gray and Birmingham, eds., *Pre-Colonial African Trade*, pp. 75–102; and Spear, pp. 119–24, 135–49.

At about the same time, agriculture in Mombasa broke away from the small scale described by Emery. The missionary Ludwig Krapf observed in 1844 that the Muslims of Mombasa were settling inland toward the hills behind the coast. He was surprised how "systematically the Mahomedans encroach upon the Wanica [Mijikenda] land in this direction." They erected small hamlets along the hills and peopled them with their slaves, who were set to work growing rice and maize. They gave trifling presents to the Mijikenda and traded with them. The more land the Muslims got, the more slaves they wanted, and the more land they could then clear. Krapf termed the increase in the number of slaves "fearful." [81] This expansion was part of a long-term and coast-wide process of economic development, but it was aided in 1847 and 1848 by a temporary abundance of slaves resulting from the impact of the treaty banning the slave trade to Arabia.[82]

French visitors in the late 1840s also found a different situation from that described by Emery. Boats came from Zanzibar to buy maize, and Mombasa was exporting about 3,000 tons of grain. Some of this was obtained by traders from the Mijikenda, but the rest was grown by slaves. Sesame was also being grown at Mombasa, and some oil was being processed locally.[83]

In the 1860s, authorities in Zanzibar became aware of Mombasa's expanding grain output, while the occasional visitors to the Mombasa hinterland saw "thriving plantations" with grain, coconuts, and fruit trees. The land was "very fertile" and "well cultivated." [84] More slaves were being brought in from Kilwa—720 by sea in 1866, as many as 1,000 by land in 1874. This slave labor, wrote Holmwood in 1874, was being used on plantations near the island to grow millet.[85]

Statistics collected in 1884, summarized in Table 3:3, show that Mombasa had become a major center for the production and export of

81. Krapf to Coates, 25 September 1844, CMS CA5/o16/28; Krapf, "East Africa Mission from letters, September 1844," *Church Missionary Record* 17 (1846): 3; Krapf, Journal, 29 December 1848, CMS CA5/o16/172.

82. See Appendix 2. Krapf specifically mentions the abundance of slaves in Mombasa. Krapf to Venn, 16 November 1848, CMS CA5/o16/74. Most came from Kilwa, but some came from Chagga country in northern Tanzania, which was experiencing internal warfare. Ibid., 20 November 1846, CA5/o16/64; Guillain, *Documents*, vol. 2/2, p. 267.

83. Loarer, "Ports au Nord de Zanguebar," O.I., 2/10, notebook D; Guillain, *Documents*, vol. 2/2, pp. 261, 315–16, 336.

84. Righy to Anderson, 11 February 1860, FO 84/1130; Richard Thornton, Journals, entry for 10 June 1861, Rhodes House, Oxford University, MSSAfr. s49, vol. 3; New, *Life*, pp. 52–54.

85. Seward, Memorandum, 1866, FO 84/1279; Holmwood, FOCP 2915, pp. 8, 85; The continued importance of Kilwa as the source of Mombasa's slaves is also stressed in Burton, *Zanzibar*, 2: 46; and Euan-Smith to Derby, 26 July 1875, FOCP 2915, p. 204. On the slave supply after 1873, see chapter 4.

grain and coconut products. Agricultural produce accounted for about half of Mombasa's exports, ivory for most of the rest. The largest portion of the agricultural produce came from the "coast districts." Gissing was most impressed by the cultivation in the area north of Mtwapa Creek, especially Kurwitu and Takaungu, rather than the area closer to Mombasa.[86]

TABLE 3:3

THE EXPORTS OF MOMBASA, 1884

	Quantity (Frasilas)	Value (Dollars)
Millet	100,000	$ 30,000
Maize	200,000	40,000
Beans	3,000	1,500
Sesame	20,000	10,000
Copra	13,000	13,000
Coconuts	100,000 nuts	1,000
		$ 95,500
Nonagricultural items (e.g. ivory)		92,150
Total exports		$187,650

SOURCE: Gissing to Kirk, 16 September 1884, FOCP 5165, p. 246.

Gissing's observation is in line with the opinion of other Europeans and local informants that the people of Mombasa, although they had vastly extended their farming since 1840, still did not carry out cultivation as intensively as the inhabitants of Takaungu or Malindi.[87] With a larger population than Malindi in 1884, Mombasa exported one-fifth as much millet as Malindi and one-sixth as much sesame. Its overall agricultural exports were worth just over one-third of Malindi's.[88] This difference was mainly the result of differing economic opportunities.

On the positive side, Mombasa remained a trading center, exporting ivory, gum copal, and other produce gathered by the African peoples of the interior, as well as maize grown by the Mijikenda. Interior trade grew after the 1840s and accounted for half of Mombasa's exports in 1884, compared with none of Malindi's.[89] In a collection of deeds from

86. Gissing, FOCP 5165, pp. 246–47.
87. A. C. Hollis, "Report on the Rights of the Natives at the Coast between the Tana River and Mombasa," 30 September 1907, incl. Sadler to Elgin, 22 October 1907, CO 533/32; MSA 14, 20, 26, 37.
88. Compare Tables 3:1 and 3:3.
89. The active state of the caravan trade was also noted by Kirk to Granville, 6 November 1873, PP 1874, LXII, 749, p. 101. Swahili activism in trade cut down the role of Kamba and Mijikenda middlemen. Berg, "Mombasa," p. 102; Spear, p. 221.

the 1890s, 173 transactions involved ivory.[90] As Table 3:4 illustrates, all communal groups were active in this trade. Arabs and Swahili were also active in up-country caravans and the dhow trade, while Indians were concentrated—but not to the exclusion of Arabs—in import-export businesses and finance.[91] The wealthiest Arab and Swahili families generally owed their affluence to a combination of trade and agriculture (see below).

TABLE 3:4

PARTICIPANTS IN CREDIT TRANSACTIONS INVOLVING IVORY,
1893–1899
(By Percentage)

	Debtor	Creditor
Omani	12	21
Twelve Tribes	31	7
Arab-Swahili name, ethnic group not known	19	4
Slave origin	14	1
Indian	1	40
Baluchi	10	19
Other, not known	12	8
Totals (173 cases)	99	100

SOURCE: Reg. Msa, B-series.

NOTE: In these deeds, the debtor was engaged in trading ivory, being financed by the creditor. It cannot be ascertained which transactions involved up-country purchases and which, trade in Mombasa itself.

On the negative side was the absence of vast stretches of land suitable for grain cultivation, the key to the success of Malindi. The most striking data come from the Coast Lands Settlement during the colonial period and give a rough indication of the distribution of land in the late nineteenth century.[92] Table 3:5 shows the size of land holdings in

90. Reg., Msa, B-series. This file contains 566 deeds from the period 1892–99, excluding those that did not involve some kind of sale or loan. In a 20% sample of the A-series, a file of deeds involving land sales or mortgages, 18 debts of ivory, with land or houses as collateral, were recorded. The total size of this sample was 547 deeds.

91. In 1887 there were 483 Indians in Mombasa, compared with 82 in Malindi. Macdonald to FO, 19 December 1887, FO 84/1853. For more on trade, see Berg, "Mombasa," esp. pp. 198–208.

92. These figures underestimate somewhat the Twelve Tribes share in the nineteenth century. Preliminary analysis of shamba sales from 1891 to 1905 shows that sales exceeded purchases from the Twelve Tribes and were near-even for Omanis. More work is being done on this data, but it does not effect the present point: land-holdings were small, even for Omanis.

Kisauni, one of the principal agricultural areas of the mainland adjacent to Mombasa. The average shamba in Kisauni was only 6.9 acres, one-ninth of the average in Malindi. The difference in the average landholding was greater still, for Malindi's planters frequently owned several mashamba: 8.5 acres per owner in Kisauni, 151 in Malindi. Only three of Kisauni's planters owned over 100 acres; six of Malindi's owned over 1,000.

TABLE 3:5
LANDOWNERS IN KISAUNI

	NUMBER OF OWNERS FROM EACH COMMUNAL GROUP					
Acres owned	Omani	Hadrami	Three Tribes	Nine Tribes	Arab-Swahili *	Total
9 or less	37	12	29	46	181	305
10–49	16	6	5	15	25	67
50–99	5	0	0	0	0	6
100–499	2	0	0	0	1	3
Total owners	60	18	34	61	208	381
Total acres	1,227	153	184	412	1,276	3,252
Average acres per owner	20	8.5	5.4	6.8	6.1	8.5

SOURCE: Calculated from a/c, Mainland North. Other communal groups are not included, notably Europeans and Indians, most of whom acquired land recently.

* "Arab-Swahili" refers to a recognizable Arab or Swahili name for which no communal affiliation could be obtained.

Malindi's grain economy was based on extensive land and intensive labor. Mombasa did not offer such opportunities. Agriculture—as evidence taken in court in the early 1900s and oral data gathered in 1972–73 confirms—was built around the small farm. Some planters had two slaves, some six. One of the wealthiest Swahili landowners of all reputedly had forty. This compares with known, and probably conservative, figures of 120 and 261 for two Malindi landowners.[93]

Local sources insist that on the small mashamba that predominated, it was more profitable to sell coconuts and copra than grain. Some of the land surrounding Mombasa was also better suited to tree crops than grain.[94] Besides providing $14,000 worth of exports in 1884, co-

93. See the testimony of Farsiri bin Aziz and Ahmed bin Matano in the case of Abdullah bin Sheikh bin Yunus, on behalf of the *Thelatha Thaifa* vs. *Wakf Commission* vs. *Government of East Africa*, Land Registration Court, Mombasa, 1912, a/c 15N of 1912 (hereafter referred to as Three Tribes Case); testimony of Mwinyi Amadi, Civil Case 928 of 1898, District Court, Mombasa; MSA 9, 29, 31, 32.

94. MSA 3, 14, 35.

conuts were used extensively by local people for cooking and oil, while the leaves served as roofing and the wood as fuel. More of an urban center than Malindi, Mombasa had a more substantial local market. Other fruits were important parts of the diet. Gissing wrote that the availability of fruit, even if the grain crop failed, made Mombasa "the paradise of the poor."[95] Trees—as in Zanzibar but unlike in Malindi— acquired a monetary value independent of the land on which they were planted.[96] The small size of plots, the modest level of grain production, the degree of urbanization, and the importance of fruit trees, all shaped the way in which slave labor was utilized in Mombasa.

The small size of farms resulted from Mombasa's size, setting, and age. There were only a few hundred Arabs in Mombasa, as in Malindi, but there were several thousand Swahili in Mombasa and fewer in Malindi.[97] Moreover, Mombasa—unlike Malindi—was surrounded by a fairly dense population of agriculturalists. Expansion in the 1840s had meant encroachment on Mijikenda lands: Yet the Mijikenda were themselves expanding northward and could muster considerable strength. They limited Mombasa's potential expansion; while in outlying areas, Swahili and Mijikenda farms were interspersed.[98] Finally, Islamic law provides for the division of property among all the deceased's children and, under some circumstances, a wider group of heirs, so that in an area which had been occupied for generations, land ownership was likely to become highly fragmented.[99]

With many people of diverse origins desiring access to land, land ownership and use became intricate problems. As more Arabs settled in Mombasa in the early nineteenth century, they sent slaves to the ad-

95. Gissing to Kirk, 14 September 1884, FOCP 5165, p. 238.

96 . See deeds for sales of trees in Reg., Msa, 305A 1907, 306A 1907, and the deeds filed with a/c 229N 1916. On Zanzibar, see Middleton, *Land Tenure in Zanzibar.*

97. It is impossible to be more precise than this owing to the absence of population statistics and to the fact that the observers whose offhand estimates we do have were often unable to distinguish slaves from Swahili. Guillain in 1847 estimated that the city of Mombasa had a population of 3,000 and the surrounding countryside, 6,000, of whom 220–30 were Arabs and three-fourths, slaves. Burton in 1857 gave the population as 8–9,000, including 350 Arabs, while Holmwood in 1874 said the population was 12,000, most of whom were Swahili. A population count at the end of the century in the city (not the district as a whole) found 496 Arabs and 14,574 free Swahili plus 2,667 slaves. Guillain, *Documents,* vol. 2/2, pp. 235–37; Burton, *Zanzibar,* 2: 75; Holmwood, FOCP 2915, p. 85; Hardinge, "Report," PP 1898, LX, 199, p. 8.

98. Guillain, *Documents,* vol. 2/2, p. 239; Krapf, in *Church Missionary Record,* 1846, p. 3; MSA 31, 32. Spear also emphasizes that Mombasans were eager to establish stable trading relations with Mijikenda. They had at various times needed Mijikenda military allies. Mombasa therefore had to tread carefully. Spear, pp. 128–31.

99. J. N. D. Anderson, *Islamic Law in the Modern World* (New York, 1959), p. 79; MSA 3, 11, 14.

jacent mainland to cultivate for them.[100] However, the two confederations of Swahili in Mombasa claimed different spheres of interest in
these areas. The Three Tribes claimed land on the southern part of the
island and on the adjacent mainland to the south and west. The mashamba of the Nine Tribes were mainly located in Kisauni, to the
north. In several bitterly argued land cases of the early twentieth century, the elders of both confederations asserted that they had the right
to all land in their spheres of interest. The Swahili used to clear this
land collectively, but once cleared it was divided into individual plots,
which were held as freehold under Islamic law.[101] In the land cases,
Swahili leaders claimed that an individual could sell land to an outsider
provided he obtained the consent of the elders of his confederation,
but this claim may be the result of a new interest in selling land at a
time when its market value was increasing. It is likely that, as in the
Wahadimu areas of Zanzibar, the use but not the ownership of land
could be granted to an outsider.[102] It is also likely that Arabs regarded
as a sale what Swahili thought to be only a rental.[103]

Whatever the case, Arabs, Baluchis, and others acquired tracts of
land in the nineteenth century. The Swahili did not dispute the testimony at the land hearings that these non-Swahili had in practice cultivated land for many decades in the areas over which the Swahili
claimed hegemony.[104] The British rejected communal claims to land,

100. Richard Thornton, Journals, 8 June 1861, Rhodes House; Price to Hutchinson,
27 February 1875, CMS CA5/023/15; MSA 31. Many claimants for land based their
claims on the assertion that their slaves had cleared the land. See the testimony of
Ahmed bin Matano, Farsiri bin Aziz, Ali bin Mohamed Hinawi, and Shariff Mohamed
Nur Balawi, Three Tribes Case; Khamis bin Khalfan, Hamed Tahir, and Said Abdulrah-
man, a/c 42N 1918 (Nine Tribes Case); Mwana Khashi binti Bahari, a/c 94N 1917.

101. Khamis bin Khalfan, Nine Tribes Case; Abdalla bin Sheikh Mtangana and Abdulrehman bin Gulam Mchangamwe, Three Tribes Case; Mwijahi bin Sudi Mchangamwe
in *Charlesworth and Marsden* vs. *Salim bin Khalfan*, Civil Case 37 of 1913, High Court,
Mombasa. Collective clearing of land was described to me by MSA 9, 22, 24. Numerous
files in the Coast Province series, KNA, also pertain to disputes over land claimed by the
Twelve Tribes.

102. Abdalla bin Sheikh Mtangana and Mzee Mohamed bin Matano Mkilindini, Three
Tribes Case; Said Abdulrehman, Nine Tribes Case. On Zanzibar, see Middleton.

103. This misunderstanding, deliberate or otherwise, is still a source of bitterness on
the coast. In interviews conducted by a reporter with elders in a Swahili village near
Mombasa, Swahili admitted that they had allowed Arabs to borrow land, but vigorously
insisted that the Arabs had taken the land from them. See Neta Peal, "Mwakirunge—Site
with Historic Past," *Daily Nation* (Nairobi), 17 April 1970. Arabs denied that the Swahili
had any right to this land, and asserted that plots were the freehold property of whoever
cleared them. Testimony of Ali bin Salim Al-Busaidi and Rashid bin Sud Shikeli, Nine
Tribes Case.

104. Seif bin Salim Al-Busaidi, Ali bin Salim Al-Busaidi, and Rashid bin Sud Al-
Shikeli, Nine Tribes Case; Shariff Mohamed Nur Balawi, Three Tribes Case.

and the Kisauni land settlement summarized in Table 3:5 reflects allotments on the basis of evidence of long occupation or purchase by individual Swahili and non-Swahili alike.[105] Plots owned by Swahili, Omani Arabs, Hadrami Arabs, Muslim Mijikenda, Baluchi, ex-slaves, and others, were interspersed throughout the area claimed by the Nine Tribes. Omanis, whether justly or not, were awarded the largest share, while the Three Tribes actually had significant land holdings in the sphere of the Nine Tribes.[106]

The Swahili also practiced shifting cultivation, so that portions of land were left fallow (remaining the property of their owner) while the owner or user cultivated elsewhere.[107] Much land was therefore vacant at any given time. Paradoxically, land was sometimes not fully utilized, perhaps because it was only available in parcels that were too small to make grain cultivation worth while.[108] These complications reflect a flexible attitude toward land. It was used for subsistence and for income, but only exceptional landowners could derive from it a great deal of wealth. Only during the colonial period did land itself become a highly valued commodity.

The small-holder predominated in Mombasa, just as the large landholder predominated in Malindi. Nevertheless, some families acquired considerable wealth, through both land and trade. A look at one of the oldest Omani groups in Mombasa, the Mandhry, illustrates this combination. Resident in Mombasa since at least Portuguese times, the Mandhry built their houses not far from Fort Jesus and farmed chiefly on the northern mainland. Said bin Rashid Al-Mandhry was a major landowner in Kisauni, receiving title to four mashamba with a total of

105. The procedures in these cases favored anyone with a written deed or who could easily round up neighbors to testify that he had been cultivating that particular plot. It discriminated against those who cultivated irregularly. These procedures favored Omanis more than Swahili, and in particular the members of leading families. Its net effect was to rigidify a system of rights in land that had in fact been flexible.

106. Some of the land owned by members of the Three Tribes was inherited by the children of Three Tribes males and Nine Tribes females, who belonged to their father's communal group. This was even more true of Arabs and other outsiders, who married into a Swahili group to obtain access to land. Hamis Salim Jeneby, Ali Mohamed Hinawi, Three Tribes Case; Seif bin Salim Al-Busaidi, Nine Tribes case; MSA 9.

107. New, Life, p. 62; Seif bin Salim Al-Busaidi and Said Abdulrehman, Nine Tribes Case; MSA 19, 22.

108. In the 1870s, the Church Missionary Society, looking for land for a mission station in Kisauni, found relatively sparse cultivation except near villages. The land they purchased in 1878–79 was described in many deeds as wasteland, and it was bought for $2 to $5 per shamba from Swahili and others who retained rights of ownership. Africans connected with the mission were later able to use this land. Yet elsewhere in the vicinity, visitors noted well-cultivated mashamba. Price to Hutchinson, 27 February 1875, CMS CA5/023/15; Lamb to Wright, 30 November 1876, CMS CA5/M4; deeds filed with a/c 101N 1915; Gissing to Kirk, 14 September 1884, FOCP 5165, p. 238; Holmwood, FOCP 2915, p. 86; New, Life, p. 54.

78 acres. He also was a leading trader and a money-lender, sometimes working in partnership with his relatives. A deed, for example, dating from 1895, shows him consigning trade goods worth $2,000 to Rashid bin Khamis Al-Mandhry, who was to exchange these goods for others and hand over two-thirds of his profits to Said. Other deeds involve loans against property and financing of trade, as well as the buying and selling of land.[109] Ali bin Salim bin Ali Al-Mandhry was a land specula-tor in the late nineteenth century and thereafter. He was also at one time a trader.[110] Majid bin Ali Al-Mandhry was an up-country trader, dhow owner, money-lender, and landowner as well. Other kinsmen were also landowners and traders.[111] The wealthiest members of the other leading Omani groups in Mombasa—Mazrui, Shikeli, and Mu-hashami—had similarly diversified interests.[112] One of the best-known Hadrami families of Mombasa, the Shatry, also owned land in Kisauni while engaging extensively in trade.[113]

Such prosperity was not limited to Arabs. Swahili were the most numerous groups among the ivory traders, as Table 2:4 reveals, and several Swahili were leading up-country traders.[114] Others were among

109. Reg., Msa, 94B 1895; see also Reg., Msa, 120B 1894, 181, 216, 25A 1894, 131, 201A 1896. MSA 14. His wife also owned several mashamba and houses. Probate and Administration Case no. 40 of 1938, High Court, Nairobi.

110. He eventually became embroiled in a major land case, when he sold an Indian land he had bought from members of the Jibana tribe, which they had no right to sell. Jibana Tribe vs. Abdulrasol Alidina Visram, Civil Case 60 of 1913, copy in CP/1/25/271. His children received 64 acres in Kisauni. He also had land in Malindi. a/c 73D 1915, MSA 27.

111. In the 20% sample of deeds involving land, 1891–99, the size of transac-tions—sales and mortgages—were substantially larger for the Mandhry than for the gen-eral populace. Thirty-nine percent of the Mandhry's transactions involved property worth over Rs 500 ($235), as opposed to 18% of Omanis in general, and 15% for Swahili. They lent out nearly Rs 8000 without collateral, and lent more on mortgages. Various Mandhry's left large estates—including mashamba, urban land, houses, and uncollected loans. See Probate cases no. 201 of 1919, no. 4 of 1932, and no. 40 of 1938, High Court, Nairobi. The individuals mentioned in the text also frequently appear in the deed regis-ters, and I have learned much about them from Al-Amin bin Said Al-Mandhry and Said bin Mohamed bin Ali Al-Mandhry, MSA 14 and 15.

112. The largest holding in Kisauni—227 acres—belonged to Rashid bin Sud Al-Shikeli. Salim bin Kassim Al-Mazrui traded upcountry when young, owned dhows, and later became an exporter of agricultural produce. Mohamed bin Kramis Muhashami ex-ported agricultural products in addition to owning over seventy acres of land in Kisauni. These names frequently appear in the deed registers and are also mentioned by infor-mants as being among the wealthiest. MSA 3, 9, 12. See also Probate case no. 92 of 1910.

113. Kisauni land records indicated that members of this family had six mashamba there, the largest being 22 acres. Information on the family comes from two descendants, MSA 16 and 17.

114. Jackson, Early Days, p. 190; MSA 19; McKay, pp. 175, 183. The deed files contain eleven ivory transactions involving the children of Khamis bin Shaibu Al-Kilifi (one of the Nine Tribes).

the most extensive landowners and slaveowners in Mombasa. A missionary claimed that Khamis bin Kombo Al-Mutafi, a leader of the Nine Tribes, owned five hundred slaves. This is an exaggeration, but he definitely was a wealthy slaveowner. When his property was confiscated as punishment for joining the Mazrui in a rebellion in 1895, he owned three mashamba worth $1,643, a stone house in Mombasa worth $376, and a clove plantation in Pemba worth $469.[115] Juma bin Muhunzi Al-Changamwe was a trader and slaveowner around the middle of the nineteenth century. His sons came to possess extensive urban property, as well as mashamba and trading interests: one raised a loan of $1,520 on a house, and another obtained credit for a deal involving eighteen frasilas of ivory by mortgaging seven plots and a shamba.[116] Swahili prosperity is also underscored by the fact that Swahili founded five mosques between 1837 and 1895, while Arabs founded four and restored three others.[117]

It is still fair to argue that, as a whole, Omanis prospered more than Swahili in the nineteenth century. Table 3:5, even allowing for an underestimate of Swahili control of land, indicates that Swahili, as a whole, owned less than their share of farmland and that a larger percentage of Swahili than Arabs were small-holders. Their transactions—sales and mortgages—on both urban and rural property also tended to involve more modest amounts than those of Omanis.[118] Swahili were, by and large, small-holders, but a few were among the wealthiest men in Mombasa.

The difference between Mombasa and Malindi was not just the difference between small plots and large ones, or between a trading elite

115. Shaw to Lang, 4 June 1887, CMS G3/A5/o/1887/222; Mackenzie to Sanderson, 21 January 1896, FO 107/65; Minute to Sadler to Secretary of State for Colonies, 2 December 1907, CP/1/63/76.

116. 266A 1892, 191A 1894, Reg., Msa. Other deeds involving them include 6A 1892, 246A 1897, 301A 1900, 166A 1902, 651A 1903, 746A 1903, and 711A 1905. According to an informant, Juma himself contributed to the building of the Mwijabu mosque, dated 1868. MSA 28. Other Swahili landowners of major importance included Shafi bin Matano Al-Tangana, Mwijabu bin Isa Al-Changamwe, and Mohamed bin Juma Al-Mutafi. In fact, one of the leading Omani families in Mombasa reputedly owed much of its fortune to a wise marriage to an heiress of the last-named Swahili. Interview with Shamsa binti Mohamed Muhashamy by Margaret Strobel, 25, 31 January 1973; deeds of sale from the estate of Shafi bin Matano, 469–70A 1905; sale of property by the children of Mohamed bin Juma Al-Mutafi, 381, 386, 571A 1897, 81A 1899, 381A 1898, 276, 376A 1902; list of property made over to the Mosque of Mwijabu bin Isa in a letter shown to me by Mohamed Umeya; MSA 25, 28, 37.

117. Berg and Walter, p. 86.

118. 36% of the deeds by which Swahili sold or mortgaged land were for less than 100 rupees ($47). For Omanis, 22% of such transactions were for less than 100 rupees. Reg., Msa, A-series, 1891–99. See also Berg and Walter, p. 86.

and a planter elite. There was a difference in the ambiance and social life of the two towns. People lived in Mombasa because it was their home and their parents' home. Malindi, founded around 1860, was inhabited by people who were motivated to give up, at least temporarily, their accustomed life and live in a frontier boom town. Social life and leisure were more valued in Mombasa, as they were in Zanzibar. Two French missionaries in the 1880s described the importance of visiting and companionship to the people of Mombasa:

> At any hour of the day one encounters them, visitors or visited, seated in front of their houses, on stone benches known under the name of *baraza,* wetting their lips with their small cups of coffee, speaking of the bad weather or saying nothing, but always looking serious.[119]

One of these visitors commented elsewhere on the slow pace of life, of the pleasures of walking slowly, saying "a few words in passing," or stopping at the door of friends before going to the mosque or returning home.[120] Such visitors tended to ascribe such behavior to lethargy, but they failed to understand a culture that valued social relationships more than profit.

Mombasa was also a center of religious scholarship and Swahili poetry. The Mazrui, in particular, included a number of the leading Islamic scholars of the area.[121] Several poets achieved local fame and helped contribute to the development of this art form.[122] Such activities are by no means imcompatible with the pursuit of wealth, but they do suggest a more cultured, genteel style of life than was possible in Malindi.

Being a member of an old, recognized family was an important source of prestige in Mombasa. People are still highly conscious of family origins and take pride in proclaiming the number of generations

119. A. Le Roy and R. de Courmont, "Mombase (Afrique Orientale)," *Missions Catholiques* 19 (1887): 535. Ludwig Krapf made a similar observation. "Memoire on the East African Slave Trade," 1853, CMS CA5/016/179, p. 49.

120. A. Le Roy, "Au Zanguebar anglais," p. 465. The importance of such a life-style to Arabs and Swahili is also emphasized in a fascinating description of Swahili life by a British official in the early colonial period. Mervyn Beech, MS on Swahili Life, in the library of Fort Jesus, Mombasa.

121. Several of them came from the Mazrui family. They are mentioned in Al-Amin bin Ali, "History of the Mazru'i Dynasty of Mombasa," trans. James M. Ritchie, copy in History Department Archives, University of Nairobi.

122. Several Swahili poets of Mombasa are mentioned in an account of the participation of one of them in political intrigue in the 1870s published by Mbarak Ali Hinawy, who includes a long poem by Abdalla bin Masud Al-Mazrui. Mbarak Ali Hinawy, *Al-Akida and Fort Jesus.* See also Jan Knappert, *Traditional Swahili Poetry* (Leiden, 1967).

they have lived there.[123] In Mombasa, there was more stress on heshima, a quality of respectability that attached to persons of good family, pious conduct, and at least a reasonable income, while in Malindi there was no established elite against which to measure one's position.

Although the Twelve Tribes and the various Omani and Hadrami groups were all accepted as part of Mombasa society, and although members of all these groups shared in agricultural expansion, the groups retained their individual sense of identity and internal structures. Politics in Mombasa remained contentious, and occasional incidents caused the groups to mobilize their members, as well as to seek allies among other Arab and Swahili groups.[124] Such incidents made it clear that the man of power still needed followers to support him in his political struggles, even if he now needed laborers to pick his coconuts.

COASTAL AGRICULTURE: SOME COMPARISONS

Mombasa and Malindi, along with Zanzibar, shared in the development of a commercialized and differentiated agricultural organization, but the forces for change and continuity affected each area to a different degree. In Malindi, the impact of the plantation on the prosperity of the elite, on social values, and—as chapter 5 will show—on the organization of labor, was greatest. The town was a new one, with no established upper class, no traditions of urban life and scholarship, and no trade to diversify economic interests. Malindi's fertile soil could support several harvests of different crops each year, while the enormous quantity of available land, in relation to a small free population and simple farming technology, meant that the main limit on production was the number of slaves one owned and the intensity with which they worked.

If Malindi was the Alabama of East Africa, Mombasa was the Virginia. Cultivation was extended after the 1840s, and leading Arab and Swahili families derived a substantial portion of their income from their lands and slaves. However, agricultural opportunities were limited by the shortage of land, while trade provided alternative sources of income. Grain production was limited, and the coconut tree did not create the same demands for an efficient form of labor organization as did the large grain fields of Malindi. Meanwhile, the established urban

123. This has been clear from many of my interviews. See also Strobel, "Muslim Women," and Peter Lienhardt, "Introduction" to *The Medicine Man: Swifa ya Nguvumali* (Oxford, 1968), p. 19.

124. Such a pattern of internal unity and external intrigue was evident in the Al-Akida incident of 1874. See Mbarak Ali Hinawy. The continued importance of the communal groups is stressed by Berg, "Swahili Community," pp. 52–55.

society of Mombasa felt the impact of the new wealth from agriculture less than Malindi did. In comparison with Malindi, the forces of the new plantation economy were weaker and the strength of the old social norms, greater.[125]

Zanzibar's situation lay between the two mainland towns. The clove industry was wholly new and extensive, a vital basis of the wealth of the Omani elite. However, especially near Zanzibar town, the politics of the court, Islamic scholarship and prayer, and urban society, distracted people from their plantations, while trade remained a source of income for many Zanzibaris. Farther away, rural society—as in Malindi—was more important. Above all, the pervasive influence of plantation agriculture did not continue to build up after mid-century. The decline of clove prices discouraged more intensive cultivation of cloves and preserved Zanzibar's rich and varied agricultural economy from the ravages of comparative advantage. Moreover, as shown in chapter 5, the clove tree did not require the continuous labor that grain production did. Zanzibar's plantations became largely self-supporting economic and social units rather than specialized commodity-producing organizations.

In all these areas, the dominance of large-scale, export agriculture over the economy and the society remained less pronounced than in even the most "seigneurial" of New World plantation societies.[126] Students of North American slavery have debated whether the plantation economy should be considered a capitalist or precapitalist institution. On the one hand, plantations produced for a world market and their owners—imbued with the profit motive—sought to make farming an efficient enterprise. The plantation could be a factory in the fields.[127] On the other hand, within the plantation itself, almost all legal authority and social bonds were centered on the master. He was the lord of a dependent following. The slaveholder's values and ideology, Genovese argues, were more aristocratic than bourgeois.[128]

Whatever the balance between capitalist and precapitalist elements in the Southern United States, the society of the coast leaned more in the precapitalist direction. It was not that a commercial spirit was lacking among Omani and Swahili planters, or that plantation develop-

125. The south coast of Kenya and the northern part of the coast of Tanganyika faced an even greater population pressure and intermingling of Mijikenda and Swahili agriculturalists than Mombasa, while conflict among local groups was more continuous and intense. Plantation development was thus even more limited than in Mombasa, and coastal agriculture was less differentiated from Mijikenda modes of production. See McKay, chapter 5.

126. Genovese, *The World the Slaveholders Made*.

127. Fogel and Engerman, *Time on the Cross*, esp. 1: 129.

128. Genovese, *The Political Economy of Slavery*.

ment did not reveal a pattern of rational responses to market incentives. Compared with Oman earlier in the nineteenth century, the East African coast appeared to be moving in the *direction* of a capitalist economy.[129] But in Zanzibar the forces pushing it that way weakened around mid-century with the fall in clove prices, while in Mombasa land-shortage and other factors constrained the movement toward capitalistic agriculture. In Malindi, as the following two chapters explain, slave shortages slowed expansion in the 1880s, while the difficulties of controlling slaves helped to limit the extent of exploitation and to reinforce older paternalistic norms. In all parts of East Africa, people had rather limited interest in imported consumer goods, and the items which traders provided were not sufficient to change their minds. Opportunities for expansion and innovation were less in the Indian Ocean system than in the more dynamic Atlantic economy.

The fact that East Africa was not pushed steadily along the road to capitalism was not simply due to the weakness of new economic forces but also to the strength of older social structures and values. The government of the Sultanate of Zanzibar was weak, and the political as well as social roles of communal groups were great. Swahili groups like the Twelve Tribes in Mombasa and the Washella in Malindi, and Arab groups such as the Al-Mandhry and Al-Harthi, were held together by common experiences and a sense of common identity as well as by the need for political unity. Whenever conflict broke out, each group mobilized its followers, slaves included. Individuals like Suleiman bin Abdalla, seeking to expand their own power, relied on personal followers. In these instances, society divided along vertical lines rather than along class or racial divisions. The continued political importance of such ties between lord and servants was a countervailing force working against the tendency of slaves in a productive economy to be relegated to the role of laborers.

The type of plantation agriculture that developed on the East African coast transformed, and in some ways strengthened, these personal ties. From an urban phenomenon in most Islamic societies, slavery became a predominantly rural one. More isolated than the urban household, the plantation was a social unit in itself.[130] Especially in remote

129. Polly Hill has astutely shown that capitalist elements in African economies do not exclusively derive from contact with Europe. Nevertheless, capitalist elements or capitalist tendencies are not the same thing as a full-fledged capitalist economy, let alone a capitalist society. See Polly Hill, *Studies in Rural Capitalism in West Africa* (Cambridge, 1970).

130. Richard Wade contrasts the city in the United States South, where people of all classes could mingle, with the "semi-isolation" of the plantation, where most contacts were within the confines of the estate. *Slavery in the Cities: The South 1820–1860* (New York, 1964), p. 56.

areas like Malindi and Pemba, relations among those dwelling on a plantation could be intimate, and the self-sufficiency of a shamba enhanced its solidarity. Although the growth of export agriculture tended to undermine vertical social ties by placing slaves in a unique and menial role, it simultaneously had the reverse effect—the creation of a new type of social unit in rural areas. Part 2 will look at the effects of changing economic and social conditions on the lives of masters and slaves, and on the ties that bound them together.

4 The Slave Supply and the Plantation Economy, 1860–1890

The slaveowners of East Africa, like their counterparts in other regions of the world, relied on distant sources of labor. The development of a slave-trading network made possible the growth of the plantation economy. The long land and sea routes remained vital, not only for further expansion, but to replace the manpower losses from death, desertion, manumission, and mobility.[1]

These routes became issues in a European controversy based on political and moral arguments that meant little to the Arabs and Swahili of East Africa. The motives behind the British attack on the East African slave trade—a continuation of their assault on the Atlantic trade—are beyond the scope of this study, as are the details of the campaign itself.[2] The central question of this chapter is whether the slaveowners, in the face of British action, were able to obtain the supplies of slaves they needed in order to maintain their economic and social position.

In the 1860s, the Zanzibar-centered slave-trading system was effectively performing its function of supplying both the plantations and the external slave trade. After 1873, traders and planters had to adjust to the British attempts to cut the supply routes. However, to assess the impact of these actions on plantation agriculture, it is necessary to look beyond the question of the slave supply to a broader set of problems that coastal planters shared with plantation owners in other parts of the world: commitment to a particular economic structure, the uncertain-

1. None of these factors is quantifiable, but all were significant. In the New World, only the Southern United States had a self-sustaining slave population, and that took generations to attain. Mortality was bound to be high among immigrants to a tropical region, while coastal slaveholders lacked the repressive capacity to curtail desertion and could not avoid using manumission and mobility as elements of social control. See chapter 6.

2. For an overview of a century of British policy and actions, see Suzanne Miers, *Britain and the Ending of the Slave Trade* (London, 1975). Coupland, *Exploitation of East Africa*, is very Eurocentric, but the much-needed revisionist analyses have been inadequately researched and argued. Richard D. Wolff, *The Economics of Colonialism: Britain and Kenya 1870–1930* (New Haven, Conn., 1974), pp. 30–46, and R. M. A. van Zwanenberg, "Anti-Slavery, the Ideology of 19th Century Imperialism in East Africa," in B. A. Ogot, ed., *Hadith 5* (Nairobi, 1975), pp. 108–27. See also Francois Renault, *Lavigerie, l'esclavage africain et l'Europe* (Paris, 1971).

ties of international markets, lack of control over marketing and finance, and a narrow base of taxation.

Export agriculture did not continue its impressive expansion, and it did not lead to a wider development of the coastal economy. Nevertheless, the plantation economy did not collapse, and it even survived the early years of colonial rule. It survived, in part, because of its limited development: slaveowners had not become totally dependent—for food and status—on the vagaries of faraway markets.

CONTINUITIES IN THE SLAVE TRADE, 1860–1873

The mixture of trade and agriculture in the Zanzibari economy depended on a slave supply that could support both. Recovering rapidly from the dip in the export trade to Arabia in 1847, hardly pausing when British cruisers began to burn slave dhows in 1861, the slave traders were able to supply slaves to old markets in Arabia and the Persian Gulf and respond to the stimulus of the expanding plantation economy within East Africa. The links between the markets of East Africa and Arabia, the slave merchants and financiers of the coast, and Arab and African slave traders deep inside Africa, were functioning efficiently, tying the destinies of thousands of people from a variety of societies to the coastal economy.

A conservative idea of the extent of the trade can be seen in Table 4:1, which summarizes records of slaves paying duty at Kilwa for shipment to Zanzibar as well as permits issued for exports from Zanzibar. In addition, Zanzibar received between 400 and 3,000 slaves each year from the mainland coast directly opposite the island, plus slaves brought in by the Sultan's family, who did not have to pay duty, and by smugglers, who chose not to do so. Most likely, between 15,000 and 20,000 slaves entered Zanzibar each year. Some 3,000 to 5,000 were sent from Kilwa directly to ports along the northern mainland or—in violation of the treaties—to Arabia.[3] Altogether, the slave trade of the northern section of the East African coast was in the neighborhood of 20,000 to 25,000 slaves per year in the 1860s. Not until the eighteenth century had the Atlantic slave trade—drawing from a wider area and exporting to a more dynamic economic system—surpassed this magnitude.[4] Slave trading was a major business; the slaves entering Zanzibar were worth $100,000 to $270,000 annually.[5]

3. See the sources for Table 4:1. Sir Bartle Frere noted that slave-trade statistics based on customs figures were underestimates because of laxity in the collection of duty and smuggling. Frere to Granville, 29 May 1873, PP 1873, LXI, 767, p. 147.

4. Curtin, *The Atlantic Slave Trade*, p. 266.

5. Rigby to Anderson, 27 August 1860, Fort William Proceedings for April, 1861, INA, Reel 2; Kirk Report, 1870, FO 84/1344; *NEMA*, Table E, p. 553.

TABLE 4:1
THE SLAVE TRADE OF ZANZIBAR, 1859–1872

| Year | Legal Imports from Kilwa | Legal Exports from Zanzibar to: | | | | Total Exports |
		Pemba	Mombasa-Malindi	Lamu	Other	
1859	19,000					
1862–63	13,000					
1863–64	14,000					
1864–65	13,821					
1865–66	18,344					
1866		2,389	937	5,044	338	8,708
1866–67	17,538					
1867						7,819
1868						7,855
1868–69	11,944					
1869						5,009
1870		1,060	624	2,637	151	4,472
1871	14,392					8,462
1872	14,721					9,381

SOURCES: Memorandum by Seward on the Slave Traffic in the Port of Zanzibar, n.d. [1866], FO 84/1279; Kirk to Clarendon, 1 February 1870, FO 84/1325; Report of the Select Committee on the East African Slave Trade, PP 1871, XII, 1, p. v; Kirk to Granville, 27 June 1871, FO 84/1344; same to same, 25 January 1872, FOCP 4206, p. 3; Rear-Adm. Cummings to Admiralty, 10 January 1873, FOCP 4207, p. 226.

NOTE: Low figures for 1869 and 1870 reflect the cholera epidemic, which affected slaves at Kilwa and en route.

The East African subjects of the Sultan were legally permitted to transport slaves within the Sultan's East African dominions up to 1873. The export of slaves to Arabia and any slave trading by residents of Arabia were illegal (see Appendix 2). The vast legal trade described above was thus the work of Zanzibaris and other peoples—such as Swahili and Comorians—resident on the coast. British sources often claimed that "lower classes" of Swahili and Zanzibar Arabs, as well as "Northern Arabs" (residents of Oman) operating in violation of the law were the perpetrators of the trade. However, some of the slave dhows investigated by British cruisers turned out to belong to leading Omanis of Zanzibar, including the Sultan's son, sister, brother, and nephew, as well as the prime minister and his daughter. Rigby asserted that both the Al-Busaidi and the rival Al-Harthi families sold slaves.[6] Omanis had

6. Ludwig Krapf, Memorandum on the East African Slave Trade, 1853, CMS CA5/016/179, p. 30; Hamerton to Malet, 29 August 1851, Ind. Off., R/15/1/0/121; Elton to Prideaux, 2 March 1874, FOCP 2499, p. 7; Rigby, diary, 3 August 1861, in Russell, General Rigby, pp. 93–94; Rigby to Bombay, 4 April 1859, encl. to secret letter no. 57 of 23 May 1859, Ind. Off., L/P&S/5/140; Ludwig Krapf, "Journal," in Church Mission Intelligencer 1 (1850): 232; Krapf, "Additional Remarks on the Island of Zanzibar or Ongoodja,"

not completed the transition from adventurers and slave traders to genteel estate owners.

Because of the distinction made between the legal and illegal slave trades, it is virtually impossible to account for the distribution of slaves between the local and export markets. Although exports were not effectively curtailed before 1873, British ships began searching dhows in 1861, and passes were required for shipments within the legal slave-trading zone. The exports from Zanzibar cited in Table 4:1 thus omit the large—but unquantifiable—number of slaves who were sold illicitly in Zanzibar or else were kidnapped by slave dealers. Moreover, slave traders often sent slaves to Arabia under passes to Pemba and—most often—Lamu.[7] Pemba, before it filled the gap left by the devastation of the hurricane of 1872 in Zanzibar, had only a modest need for slaves; Lamu hardly needed more slaves than the Mombasa-Malindi region. The re-export statistics of Table 4:1 thus conceal a substantial export trade to Somalia, Arabia, and the Persian Gulf. The figures suggest that in many years less than half of Zanzibar's imports stayed there; in reality the number was even less.

The growing mainland settlements got much of their slaves from this same trading network, either from the entrepôt in Zanzibar or from Kilwa, illegally avoiding the customs house at Zanzibar. Few came from the nearby hinterland.[8]

Whatever the exact distribution of slaves, local officials and naval officers agree that the export trade to Arabia was flourishing in the decade before 1873, while the plantations of the islands and mainland coast remained amply supplied.[9] Rigby wrote in 1860 that the supply of slaves in Zanzibar was "abundant." His successor as British consul believed that the supply exceeded the demand. A decade later, Sir Bartle Frere, reporting on the slave trade for the British government, found that this was still the case. Bishop Steere, a missionary resident in Zanzibar since 1866, agreed.[10] Their conclusions are supported by data on

incl. Krapf to Coates, 10 June 1844, CMS CA5/016/25; Rigby to Anderson, 14 May 1861, FO 84/1146; Rigby to Pelly, 4 September 1861, Pelly Papers, FO 800/234; Kirk to Granville, 29 May 1873, FOCP 4207, p. 55.

7. Report of the Special Committee on the East African Slave Trade, PP 1871, XII, 1, p. vi; Testimony of Bishop Steere, ibid., p. 73; Kirk to Granville, 22 February 1871, FO 84/1344. On slave-trade suppression and techniques of evasion, see Coupland, pp. 152–81, and Kelly, *Britain and the Persian Gulf,* pp. 576–637.

8. Burton, *Zanzibar,* 2: 46; Holmwood, Report, 1874, FOCP 2915, p. 85. On the avoidance of local sources before the 1880s see below.

9. Official views on the trade to Arabia are summarized in Committee Report, PP 1871, XII, 1, pp. iii–x. For a view from Arabia, see Palgrave, *Narrative,* 2: 362.

10. Rigby, Report, 1860, p. 342; Consul Pelly, Memorandum submitted to the Government of Bombay, 12 November 1862, copy in Pelly Papers, FO 800/234; Frere to Granville, 29 May 1873, PP 1873, LXI, 767, p. 149; Testimony of Bishop Steere, PP 1871, XII, 1, p. 75.

prices. Estimates of prices of field hands or male slaves between 1860 and 1873 are in the range of $10 to $30, roughly on the order of, or slightly less than, the prices prevailing in the early 1840s.[11] On the mainland, observers also found slave supplies adequate in a time of plantation development.[12] The vast demand for slave labor to pick the continuing large clove harvests and to sow the expanding grain crops was being met.[13]

These reports conceal a serious conflict among Omanis that reflects the extent to which the economy of the coast had become differentiated from that of Oman. Zanzibar had become the center of the old Omani trading network as well as an agricultural center, while the commercial economy of Oman had not developed beyond its eighteenth-century bounds. By mid-nineteenth century, Oman was in decline, unable to maintain the eastern end of its trade routes in the face of steamships and Indian competition on the trade routes within the Persian Gulf and to India. Omani seamen depended increasingly on slave trading and piracy, while British actions against Persian Gulf pirates encouraged those in search of illicit profits to turn southward.[14]

Even before 1850, Northern Arabs come to Zanzibar in search of slaves by purchase or kidnapping had proved bothersome.[15] The situation grew worse after the death of Seyyid Said in 1856. His territory in Oman passed under his will to his son Seyyid Thuwain, while Zanzibar and the parts of the coast which he claimed, were inherited by another son, Seyyid Majid. The division was far from equitable, and Thuwain sent an expedition to Zanzibar to try to seize the heart of his father's commercial empire. Only British intervention prevented a war between Oman and Zanzibar, but the peace agreement—by which Zanzibar paid Oman an annual subsidy of $40,000—did little to ease the bitter conflict.[16]

11. Germain, "Zanzibar," p. 546; H. M.'s Commissioner's (Cape of Good Hope) to Russell, 19 May 1864, PP 1865, LVI, 1, p. 66; Speer to Seward, 26 November 1862, US Consul, 4; Christie, "Slavery," p. 32; Burton, *The Lake Regions*, 2: 376; Captain Colomb, *Slave Catching in the Indian Ocean* (London, 1873), pp. 56–57; Kirk to Granville, 22 July 1873, FOCP 4207, p. 126; Playfair to Russell, 30 May 1865, FO 84/1245.

12. Kirk to Granville, 6 November, 1873, PP 1874, LXII, 749, p. 102; Holmwood, FOCP 2915, p. 8; Kirk to Derby, 4 April 1877, FOCP 3686, p. 563. See also chapter 3.

13. The slave traders were able to adjust to such calamities as a cholera epidemic that swept across East Africa in 1869–70, hitting the slave population of Zanzibar as well as slaves then en route, and the hurricane that hit Zanzibar's clove trees in 1872 and caused an increased demand for slaves in Pemba, which had escaped the storm, and a decreased one in Zanzibar. Only temporary dislocations were caused by these problems. Christie, *Cholera*, pp. 415–16; Kirk to Granville, 25 January, 22 May 1872, FOCP 4206, pp. 2–3, 55.

14. Landen, *Oman*, pp. 148–151.

15. Letters from Hamerton, 1849, 1851, cited in Gray, *Zanzibar*, p. 252.

16. Coghlan, "Proceedings," Ind. Off. L/P&S/5/145.

Thereafter, Omani slave trading took on an increasingly predatory tone. In 1860 and 1861 the Northern Arabs were in "great force" in Zanzibar town, kidnapping slaves from their local owners, terrorizing the servants of foreigners, and clashing with the Sultan's troops. They raided Pemba and Mombasa as well. Each year after that, the monsoons brought Northern Arabs and a wave of kidnapping to Zanzibar. John Kirk, then the British consul, estimated in 1870 that they stole 2,000 slaves a year. Others were sold to them.[17]

While many Zanzibaris undoubtedly profited from the sale of slaves to Northern slave dealers, the fragile power of the Sultan could not ensure that order would be maintained or that the kidnapping would not threaten the local slave supply. These dangers helped induce Seyyid Majid to cede increasing power to the British navy to accomplish what he could not do—restrain the Northern Arabs. In March 1861, he requested a British warship to clear the port of piratical dhows. Two British vessels also began for the first time to enforce the treaty banning exports of slaves to Arabia, burning dhows accused of smuggling.[18] These measures did not end the slave trade to Arabia or the depredations of the Northern Arabs, but they did remove a threat to the Zanzibari regime. The vulnerability of the system was exposed. Seyyid Said had built a large commercial empire on shifting political sands.[19] His control over the African peoples of the East African coast, and even over Omanis was limited. He lacked a significant military force. His son had to turn to the British to hold off his brother Thuwain and to combat the Northern Arabs, as well as to defeat a rebellion in his own backyard by his brother Bargash. When the formerly rebellious Bargash succeeded Majid in 1870, he was not in control of the international situation. Zanzibar could not hope to thwart the wishes of the world's most industrialized nation any more than the sugar colonies

17. Rigby to Anderson, 28 March 1860, FO 84/1130; Rigby, diary, 8 March 1861, in Russell, p. 90; Devereux, *A Cruise in the Gorgon*, pp. 109–10; Pelly to Forbes, 12 February 1862, Pelly Papers, FO 800/234; Seward to Bedingfed, 27 November 1866, FOCP 4201, p. 71; Cap. Bowden to Com. Montresor, 30 June 1865, FOCP 4199, p. 153; Ibrahim bin Sultan to Sultan of Zanzibar, 7 January 1869, PP 1870, LXI, 701, p. 46; Hines to Seward, 31 March 1864, US Consul, 5, *NEMA*, p. 525; de Vienne to MAE, 19 August 1869, MAE, 3; Frere, Memorandum on the Position and Authority of the Sultan of Zanzibar, incl. Frere to Granville, 7 May 1873, PP 1873, LXI, 767, p. 116; Kirk to Clarendon, 1 February 1870, FO 84/1325.

18. The Sultan and his government, wrote Consul Pelly in 1862, "earnestly desire the destruction of the northern slave trade." Pelly to Forbes, 12 February 1862, Pelly Papers, FO 800/234. See also Devereux, p. 366; Rigby, quoted in Coghlan, "Proceedings," p. 98; Statement of Claims and Grievances presented by Seyyid Majid, 14 October 1860, in ibid., p. 119; Testimony of Rigby, PP 1871, XII, 1, p. 44; Rear-Adm. Walker to Com. Dupré, 27 November 1861, and Walker to Admiralty, 19 December 1861, FOCP 4196, p. 263.

19. This problem is treated effectively by Sheriff, "Rise of a Commercial Empire."

which England had herself spawned could resist changing English views on the morality of slavery. Zanzibar's slave economy was vulnerable at its most exposed position, the supply routes.

Nevertheless, during their long years of effective operation, these routes had brought people of diverse origins into Zanzibari society. By the time Zanzibar had begun to retain a high proportion of its imports of slaves, Kilwa was its leading supplier. Its prominence continued until the British interfered with shipments of slaves by sea in 1873. In 1860 about 75 percent of Zanzibar's slaves came from Kilwa; in 1866 the figure was nearly 95 percent.[20] Kilwa, with a substantial community of Arab and Swahili traders and Indian financiers, drew its slaves from a wide area, most notably the region of Lake Nyasa and the northern part of what is now Mozambique. Slaves of Makua, Makonde, Ngindo, and Yao origins were mentioned as early as 1811. Yao and Ngindo slaves remained numerous throughout the history of slavery, although Makonde and Makua diminished somewhat.[21]

By the 1840s, the importance of slaves from near Lake Nyasa was increasing. So numerous were they during the period when the slave trade was at its height, that *Wanyasa* became a generic term for people of slave origin.[22] Various peoples in the interior of Tanzania, notably the Nyamwezi, also made their contribution to the coastal population.[23] Zigua and other peoples living behind the Mrima, the mainland coast adjacent to Zanzibar, were very important in the early nineteenth century, but were being eclipsed by 1860 by slaves from the deep interior who came to Zanzibar via Kilwa. They again increased in importance in the 1880s, as slave traders adjusted once again to new conditions.[24]

Notable by their absence were slaves from the nearby peoples, such as the Wahadimu of Zanzibar, or the Mijikenda, who lived behind the

20. Rigby, "Report," p. 333; Sheriff, p. 440.
21. Smee, log, 7 April 1811, Ind. Off., L/MAR/c/586; list of slaves captured in 1810 by a naval vessel, cited by Sheriff, pp. 79–80; Guillain, "Rapport Commercial," O.I., 2/10; Burton, *Zanzibar*, 1: 112; statistics on origins of slaves freed in 1901, incl. Last to Raikes, 5 February 1902, PP 1903, XLV, 955, p. 8. On the slave trade routes to Kilwa and the people affected, see Alpers, esp. chapter 7.
22. Guillain, "Rapport"; Loarer, O. I., 5/23, notebook 5; Rigby, "Report," p. 333; Germain, "Zanzibar," p. 545; Report, PP 1871, XII, 1, pp. iii, iv. Wanyasa were the most common among the slaves freed in 1901. Last, p. 8. The significance of the local use of the term *Wanyasa* is discussed in chapter 6. See also Alpers, pp. 239–43.
23. Guillain, *Documents*, vol. 2/2, p. 305; Holmwood to Granville, 8 September 1881, FOCP 4626, p. 339; Last, p. 8.
24. Lt. Hardy, Report, 1811, Ind. Off., L/MAR/c/586, pp. 188–90; Guillain, *Documents*, vol. 2/2, p. 305; Rigby to Anderson, 21 March 1860, FO 84/1130; Rigby, "Report," p. 333; Charles Pickering, *The Races of Man and their Geographical Distribution* (London, 1849), pp. 197–98. See also Feierman, *The Shambaa Kingdom*, p. 137.

Map 4 : Sources of Slaves

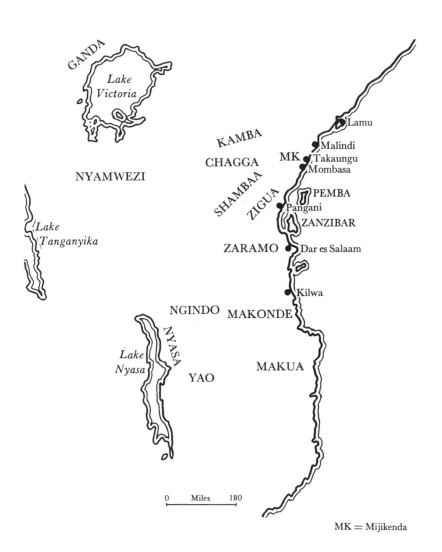

GANDA

Lake
Victoria

KAMBA

CHAGGA

NYAMWEZI

SHAMBAA

ZIGUA

MK

Lamu

Malindi

Takaungu
Mombasa

PEMBA

Pangani

ZANZIBAR

Lake
Tanganyika

ZARAMO

Dar es Salaam

Kilwa

NGINDO   MAKONDE

NYASA

Lake
Nyasa

YAO

MAKUA

0   Miles   180

MK = Mijikenda

plantation areas of the Kenyan coast.[25] Living close to the plantations, these peoples were too much of a threat to be antagonized by slave raids and could escape home too easily.[26] It was more prudent for the coastal inhabitants to obtain slaves from peoples deep in the interior. However, internal conflict sometimes shook nearby societies, and the coastal people were not above using or exporting the prisoners of war.[27]

In the 1860s, a centralized slave-trading mechanism was in full operation, gathering slaves from a wide area of the interior of East Central Africa, funneling them through Kilwa, and then, most often, through Zanzibar, for distribution to local clove plantations, the grain and coconut plantations of the northern mainland, and the external slave trade.

RESTRICTIONS ON THE SLAVE TRADE, 1873–1890

When the British finally pressured the Sultan of Zanzibar, Seyyid Bargash, to issue a decree banning all trade in slaves by sea in 1873, they were extending a policy that had begun a half-century earlier. It was only to reach its logical conclusion when slavery itself was abolished in 1897 on the islands of Zanzibar and Pemba, and in 1907 in Kenya. This record of gradual restriction of the slave trade is summarized in Appendix 2.

Yet the earlier measures against the external slave trade had been ineffective, and the transport of slaves to East African plantations was legal. Once all seaborne slave trading, regardless of destination, was made illegal, the British navy was able to keep cruisers in the waters off Zanzibar, blocking the sea routes in the relatively narrow passage between the mainland and the islands.[28] The slave traders responded to

25. Rigby, "Report," p. 333; Germain, "Zanzibar," p. 545; W. Christopher, "Commanding H.M.S. *Tigris* in the East Coast of Africa," *Journal of the RGS* 14 (1844): 102; Grandidier, *Notice sur l'île de Zanzibar*, pp. 11–12.

26. For similar reasons, American slaveholders soon learned that African slavery was safer and more economical than Indian slavery. Wood, *Black Majority*, p. 39.

27. For example, fighting between Galla and Somali in the late 1860s and early 1870s produced many slaves in the Lamu hinterland, most of whom were sent to Somalia and other northern areas. Ylvisaker, "Lamu Archipelago," pp. 198–203. Wars among the Digo and other peoples in the area south of Mombasa supplied many of the labor needs of that portion of the coast, at least in the late nineteenth century. McKay, "Southern Kenya Coast," pp. 117–18.

28. On the 1873 treaty, see Coupland, pp. 182–216, and R. J. Gavin, "The Bartle Frere Mission to Zanzibar," *Historical Journal* 5 (1962): 122–48. A revealing new step toward understanding the mechanisms of the illegal slave trade and the political implications of its suppression is currently being undertaken by Carla Glassman of Boston University in a quantitative analysis of data on captured dhows from 1873 to 1904.

this threat with their usual imagination. As before, there was at first a period of uncertainty during which supplies were held up at Kilwa and prices fell. Then the traders began to move slaves by land through Dar es Salaam, Bagamoyo, Pangani, Mombasa, Malindi, and north as far as Somalia. Although long and grueling, the trek by land was legal. Mainland plantations had little trouble obtaining the slaves they wanted. Vice-Counsul Holmwood's estimates of the number of slaves sent by the land route in 1874, shown in Table 4:2, are probably high, but there is no doubt that large caravans were regularly making their way to the coastal towns.[29] In fact, prices on the mainland fell, and Holmwood found that cultivation was being extended.[30]

TABLE 4:2
SLAVES SUPPLIED TO MAINLAND SETTLEMENTS, 1874

	Number	Price
Pangani, Tanga	1,000	$20–25
Mombasa and region	1,000	25–30
Takaungu	5,000	25–30
Malindi	1,000	30–35
Lamu and region	2,200	35–40
Somalia	Unknown	35–45

SOURCE: Frederic Holmwood, Report, incl. Prideaux to Derby, 24 November 1874, FOCP 2915, p. 8.

Supplying the islands was a more serious problem. The demand was greatest in Pemba, where clove plantations were expanding rapidly in response to the high prices following the hurricane of 1872. Instead of shipping large cargoes of slaves from ports like Kilwa, the slave traders marched slaves to the mainland opposite Pemba and then slipped them into the island at night in canoes or small dhows.[31] It was difficult for

29. Frederic Holmwood, Report, incl. Prideaux to Derby, 24 November 1874, FOCP 2915, p. 8. Holmwood apparently extrapolated his figures from counting slaves that passed during a high point in the trade. Prideaux to Derby, 9 March 1875, FOCP 2915, p. 121; Kirk to Derby, 9 April 1875, ibid., p. 139. For other accounts of the land traffic, see Frederic Elton, *Travels and Researches among the Lakes and Mountains of Eastern and Central Africa*, ed. H. B. Cotterill (London, 1879), pp. 94, 104; Rev. W. S. Price, "Pictures from East Africa—Notes by the Rev. W. S. Price," *Church Mission Gleaner* 2 (1875): 42; Greffulhe, "Voyage de Lamoo à Zanzibar," p. 335.

30. Holmwood's price estimate of $30 to $35 at Malindi may be compared with Kirk's estimate of $40 to $55 the previous year. Holmwood, FOCP 2915, pp. 7, 8; Kirk to Granville, 6 November 1873, PP 1874, LXII, 749, p. 102.

31. See the following consular dispatches, all from FOCP 2915: Prideaux to Derby, 27 February, 9 March, 1875, p. 113, 121; Holmwood, cited in same to same, 9 March 1875, pp. 124–25; Kirk to Derby, 9 April 1875 and 12 November 1875, pp. 139, 260; Holm-

the British to capture small vessels at night, but slaveowners had to give up the efficiency of larger dhows.

British officials believed that they had effectively stopped the large-scale export of slaves to Arabia, but they admitted that they had failed to stop the trade to Pemba. Slaves were being smuggled illegally across the water from the damaged plantations of Zanzibar to the productive ones of Pemba, while fresh slaves were arriving from the mainland. Some dhows and canoes were captured, but both naval officers and consular officials believed that more got by.[32] Holmwood, after inspecting Pemba, concluded that as early as 1874 the island had met its special demand for slaves. Slaves from a variety of mainland areas, as well as older slaves, were plentiful on the clove plantations of Pemba.[33]

When the slave trade by land was abolished in 1876, the pattern of temporary dislocation followed by new techniques of evasion was once again repeated. However, it was now possible for Arab officials in coastal towns—acting on orders of the Sultan, who was in turn pressured by the British—to arrest slave dealers. The traders could no longer claim that their slaves were intended for the legal branches of the slave trade—there were no such branches any more. The governors and soldiers of the Sultan arrested slave dealers and freed slaves in such coastal ports as Windi, Lindi, and in the Bagamoyo-Pangani area, from which slaves had been shipped to Pemba.[34] In Kilwa, long the principal slave-trading port, the slave trade ceased at the time of the 1876 decree, revived when the governor connived in it, and ceased again when he was removed by the Sultan.[35] Caravans began to avoid

---

wood to Kirk, 10 May 1875, p. 185. Comparison of figures on the number of slaves per dhow in 1866, when exports to Pemba were legal, and the number of slaves in dhows caught off Pemba after 1873, indicate a marked drop in large cargoes. Memorandum by Consul Seward on the Slave Traffic in the Port of Zanzibar, n.d. [1866], FO 84/1279; MacDonald to Admiralty, 28 May 1877, FOCP 3686, pp. 727–28; Adm. Corbett to Admiralty, 8 August 1879, FOCP 4286, pp. 638–39.

32. Kirk to Granville, 27 May 1873, FOCP 4207, p. 54; Vice-Admiral MacDonald to Admiralty, 28 May 1877, FOCP 3686, p. 724; Holmwood to Kirk, 10 May 1875, FOCP 2915, p. 185; Euan-Smith to Mackinnon, private letter, 1 July 1875, Mackinnon Papers, School of Oriental and African Studies, London; Kirk to Derby, 1 May 1876, FO 84/1453. The view from Zanzibar, that the Arabian slave trade was substantially ended, is confirmed in the Annual Reports of the Persian Gulf Political Residency and Muscat Political Agency, 1875–76 (p. 77) and 1876–77 (p. 78), in Selections from the Records of the Government of India, nos. 128, 138, Ind. Off.

33. Holmwood, memorandum, incl. Prideaux to Derby, 9 March 1875, FOCP 2915, p. 125; Holmwood to Kirk, 10 May 1875, incl. Kirk to Derby, 17 June 1875, ibid., p. 185.

34. Kirk to Derby, 1 May 1877, FOCP 3686, p. 598; same to same, 6 April 1877, ibid., p. 564; Capt. Tracey to Kirk, 6 March 1878, FOCP 3928, p. 358; Holmwood to Kirk, 30 January 1880, FOCP 4498, p. 430; Kirk to Granville, 3 May 1881, FOCP 4626, p. 253.

35. Kirk to Derby, 11 December 1876, 5 February 1877, FOCP 3686, p. 487, 520–21.

Kilwa and other coastal ports, moving farther inland to avoid the Sultan's soldiers.[36]

The effort of the British navy to blockade Pemba continued, while the Sultan's soldiers sometimes captured slaves newly landed on the islands. Between 1876 and 1884 the number of captures was smaller than officials expected. They concluded, probably correctly, that this reflected at least some decline in the slave trade to Zanzibar and Pemba.[37] In addition, many of the slaves caught near Pemba turned out to be experienced slaves being moved from Zanzibar.[38]

Slave traders also seemed to be obtaining slaves from sources closer to Pemba instead of relying solely on the long and dangerous routes to the deep interior. People such as the Shambaa and Zigua, living inland from the coast opposite Pemba, were torn by wars. The wars produced captives and were in turn exacerbated by the guns and trade goods which local leaders could obtain for slaves. Such slaves could be taken from concealed inlets on the nearby coast to Pemba.[39] However, similar conflicts in the far interior—including the regions of Lake Nyasa, Uganda, and the eastern Congo—also produced slaves, and substantial numbers of them were brought to the coast in defiance of the risks of interception.[40] At times, these slaves were kept near the coast until they

36. Kirk to Derby, 22 June 1876, FO 84/1453; Vice-Admiral MacDonald to Admiralty, 28 May 1877, FOCP 3686, pp. 724–35; Kirk to Salisbury, 18 June 1878, FOCP 3928, p. 413; Kirk to Granville, 3 September 1881, FOCP 4626, p. 315. Slave traders at Kilwa also sold off slaves to nearby Africans, including the Makonde, who had previously been among the most frequent victims of the trade. Cultivation and rubber collection in the southern coast expanded. Kirk to Derby, 11 December 1876, FOCP 3686, p. 487; letter of Chauncy Maples, missionary in Masasi, reprinted in *Anti-Slavery Reporter*, 4th ser. 3 (1883): 229–30; Holmwood to Kirk, 30 January 1880, FOCP 4498, p. 428.

37. Kirk to Derby, 28 June 1877, FOCP 3686, p. 629; Kirk to Derby, 4 January 1878, Capt. Sulivan to Rear-Adm. Corbett, 20 June 1878, Rear-Adm. Corbett to Admiralty, 28 June 1878, all in FOCP 3928, pp. 305, 530–31, 535; Kirk to Granville, 24 November 1883, FOCP 4914, p. 219. The reports of foreign consuls and visitors generally confirm the British viewpoint. Consul Cheney, Report, 1883–84, incl. Cheney to State Department, 1 July 1884, US Consul, 7; LeP. Charmetant, *D'Alger à Zanzibar* (Paris, 1882), p. 148; Joseph Thomson, *To the Central African Lakes and Back* (London, 1881, repr. 1968), 2: 272.

38. The proportion of experienced slaves among those captured increased from 7% in 1876 to 80% in 1879 and indicates the efficacy of the measures on land. Kirk to Salisbury, 23 February 1880, FOCP 4498, p. 415.

39. Rear-Adm. Corbett to Admiralty, 8 August 1879, FOCP 4286, p. 634; Kirk to Derby, 3 May 1881, FOCP 4626, p. 254. On conflict in the interior, see Feierman, esp. pp. 169–70, and Roberts, *Tanzania*, passim.

40. At the time of abolition, the peoples that had long provided the greatest number of slaves, the Yao and the Nyasa, were still the most numerous, but Manyema from the Congo, Zaramo from near the coast, and Nyamwezi from the middle of Tanzania were common as well, and a smaller number of slaves from Buganda made it as far as the islands. Last to Mathews, 10 January 1901 PP 1901, XLVIII, 173, p. 29; and Last to Raikes,

learned Swahili and could therefore be passed off as domestic slaves in case they were caught while en route to a plantation.[41] As these efforts to decrease risk were being made, the old land route from Kilwa to the coast opposite Pemba and north to Mombasa and Malindi was relatively quiet, and by 1878 large caravans were no longer reaching Malindi.[42] Many slaves were diverted to southern markets, notably Madagascar.[43]

The machinations of the slave traders suggest that they were having trouble getting slaves to purchasers on the islands and the plantations of the northern mainland. The scanty data on prices support this conclusion. A visitor to Zanzibar in 1882 found that slaves cost $60 to $100, while Vice-Consul C. S. Smith wrote that in 1884 prices in Pemba varied from $50 to $80.[44] These prices are two or three times greater than those before the crackdown. Nevertheless, the continual captures made by the navy indicate that it was still worthwhile to try to smuggle slaves.

Then, in 1884, a substantial revival of the slave trade took place. It lasted for four or five years, until the European takeover of Africa. The revival stemmed from three factors. On the demand side, the ample supply of slaves that observers noted in 1874 had worn thin. Prices were up and, as shall be seen in the next sections, there is some evidence of shortages of labor in the fields. On the supply side, a devastating famine—still remembered today—struck the mainland from Tanganyika to Kenya. People were desperate enough to sell their neighbors, their children, and even themselves in order to survive. Wars also continued in the coastal hinterland and in the far interior. Famine and wars made slaves available relatively close to the coast of

5 February 1902, PP 1903, XLV, 955, pp. 8–9. On the slave trade in the far interior, see C. F. Holmes, "Zanzibari Influence at the Southern End of Lake Victoria: The Lake Route," *African Historical Studies* 4 (1971): 477–503.

41. C. S. Smith to Kirk, 5 July 1884, FOCP 4165, pp. 219–21; S. Tristram Pruen, *The Arab and the African: Experiences in Eastern Equatorial Africa During a Residence of Three Years* (London, 1891), p. 223. Evidence from slave autobiographies confirms this. Many stayed for long periods near the coast before being shipped to Zanzibar. See A. C. Madan, ed., *Kiungani or Story and History from Central Africa* (London, 1887), pp. 71–72; story of Persis Chimwai, Swahili MS 178, Swahili Collection, University of Dar es Salaam; P. L. Jones-Bateman, ed., *The Autobiography of an African Slave-Boy* (London, 1891), pp. 21–23.

42. The views of the missionaries were cited by Kirk to Derby, 8 January 1878, FOCP 3928, p. 304. See also Kirk to Granville, 16 March 1884, FOCP 5165, p. 161; and Greffulhe, p. 335.

43. Miles to Granville, 23 June 1883, FOCP 4914, pp. 154–55.

44. Capitaine Storms, "L'esclavage entre le Tanganika et la côte est," *Le Mouvement Antiesclavagiste* 1 (1888–89): 17; Report by Lieut. Smith, incl. Kirk to Granville, 13 March 1884, FOCP 5165, p. 160; Kirk to Derby, 22 June 1876, FO 84/1453; Rear-Adm. Corbett to Admiralty, 8 August 1879, PP 1880, LXIX, 313, p. 315. Schmidt gives a lower figure, but notes that the price had recently doubled. *Sansibar*, p. 46.

Kenya and to the mainland adjacent to Zanzibar, making it possible to avoid the risks of the march from Kilwa north. Finally, the British cruisers were having their attention diverted by the exigencies of imperial rivalries.

The increase in the slave trade in 1884 was noted by most observers on the scene. In October 1884, Consul Kirk reported a large increase in slaves coming from Zaramo territory in famine-stricken Tanganyika. Other witnesses in Zanzibar and the mainland noted the increase in caravan movements.[45] In 1886, Kirk wrote that the slave trade was greater still, while others found that the export of slaves from the mainland to Pemba was well organized and "more or less continuous throughout the year." [46] The navy was soon making more captures than before, but these were only a small percentage of the illicit traffic.[47] The Arabs, wrote a missionary in 1889, had recently "stocked their plantations with slaves." [48]

The plantation owners of Mombasa, Malindi, and other plantation zones to the north were also diversifying their sources of slaves. Caravans, avoiding Kilwa, came by more direct routes from the interior. Slaves of Chagga origin from the region near Mt. Kilimanjaro came to Mombasa through the Teita hills.[49] Shambaa slaves were sent via the Teita region to Malindi and other coastal areas.[50] From the interior of Kenya came some slaves of Masai, Kikuyu, and Kamba origin. Most of these slaves were brought by traders of coastal origin, but Kamba some-

45. Reports include Kirk to Granville, 24 October 1884, FOCP 5165, p. 250; Ledoulx to MAE, 18 December 1884, MAE, 5; letter of J. A. Williams, missionary with the UMCA, in *Anti-Slavery Reporter*, 4th ser. 6 (1886): 130; Smith to Kirk, 5 July 1884, incl. Kirk to Granville, 25 July 1884; Bishop Smythies, cited by C. S. Smith, "Explorations in Zanzibar Dominions," *RGS Supplementary Papers* 2 (1889): 104.

46. The purchaser absorbed the risk and paid the shipper a commission. Leading slaveowners in Pemba relied on clients, trusted slaves or ex-slaves, and others with whom they had a personal relationship to bring them slaves. Kirk to Rosebery, 1 July 1886, FOCP 5459, pp. 321–22; Rear-Adm. Richards to Macgregor, 30 August 1886, PP 1887, LXXVIII, 313, p. 21; C. S. Smith to Kirk, 5 July 1884, incl. Kirk to Granville, 25 July 1884, FO 84/1678; Dougherty, *East Indies Station*, pp. 43–44, 59–60; Fremantle to Admiralty, 23 October 1888, PP 1888, LXIV, 255, p. 101; Les R. P. Baur et LeRoy, *A Travers le Zanguebar* (Tours, France, 1887), p. 109. Relations among shamba owners, dhow owners, and dhow captains emerge from Glassman's study of captured slavers.

47. Smith to Kirk, 5 July 1884, incl. Kirk to Granville, 25 July 1884, FO 84/1678; Kirk to FO, 20 August 1889, FOCP 6010, p. 39–40. On dhow captures, see the annual volumes on the slave trade in the Parliamentary Papers and Glassman.

48. Memorandum by Horace Waller, 1889, in UMCA Archives, Box D4.

49. Gissing to Kirk, 26 June 1884, FOCP 5165, p. 216; Kirk to Granville, 21 May 1885, FO 84/1725. Some informants mentioned Kamba, Teita, and Chagga slaves (MAL 44, MSA 28), but most refer to slaves and ex-slaves as "Wanyasa," which suggests the preponderance of slaves from the distant interior.

50. Henry Binns to CMS, 29 September 1879, CMS CA5/031/11.

times assisted them. Behind Malindi, the Sabaki River was used by slave caravans as a route between the interior of Kenya and the richest plantation area of the coast.[51]

These sources had been used to only a limited extent before the impact of the 1876 treaty was felt. Likewise, few slaves had come from the neighboring Mijikenda.[52] However, faced with starvation in 1884,[53] large numbers of Mijikenda pawned themselves or their children for grain to the coastal plantation owners, who had been spared the drought afflicting the immediate hinterland. Most likely the Mijikenda expected that such people could be redeemed, but this rarely happened.[54] Such sales were frequent throughout the famine, but as soon as it ended in 1885, they stopped.[55]

As in many parts of East and Central Africa, captives taken in local fighting among the Mijikenda subgroups were often sold as slaves.[56] However, not until the late nineteenth century is there substantial evidence of slave raids by coastal Arabs. Such raids may have had something to do with short supplies after 1876 and with Arab perceptions of

51. Smith to Kirk, 18 June 1885, PP 1886, LXII, 515, p. 124; William Astor Chanler, *Through Jungle and Desert* (London, 1896), p. 489; John Ainsworth, Report on Machakos District, 1893, incl. IBEA Co. to FO, 31 August 1893, FO 2/59; J. R. L. MacDonald, *Soldiering and Surveying in British East Africa 1891–1894* (London, 1897), p. 44; Fitzgerald, *Travels*, p. 157.

52. Greffulhe, p. 335, claims that the land route to Malindi was effective until 1878, when the actions of the Sultan's governors along the way blocked the movement of caravans. On the primacy of Kilwa as a source of slaves before that time, see above and chapter 3.

53. A similar process had occurred during a severe famine in the late 1830s. Some children obtained as pawns had been sent to Zanzibar and Arabia. In retaliation, some Mijikenda broke off relations with coastal rulers and stole cattle. Ludwig Krapf, Memoir on the East African Slave Trade, 1853, CMS CA5/016/179; Guillain, vol. 2/2, pp. 267–68; R. L. Playfair, "Visit to the Wanika Country in the Vicinity of Mombassa and the Progress made by the Christian Missionaries at that place," *TBGS* 17 (1864): 274; Pickering, p. 192. For a Mijikenda perspective, see Spear, "The Kaya Complex," p. 171.

54. Haggard to Kirk, 8 September 1884, FOCP 5165, p. 233; Kirk to Granville, 23 September 1884, ibid., p. 227; Rev. Binns, cited by J. Duckworth in *Anti-Slavery Reporter*, 4th Ser. 22 (1902): 24–25; Euan-Smith to Salisbury, 30 May 1888, PP 1888, LXXIV, 255, p. 18; Hardinge, Report, PP 1898, LX, 199, p. 61. On pawnship among one Mijikenda group, see H. M. T. Kayamba, "Notes on the Wadigo," *Tanganyika Notes and Records* 23 (1947): 96.

55. Kirk to Granville, 14 February 1885, PP 1886, LXII, 515, p. 106.

56. Letter of J. Erhardt, 27 October 1854, *Church Mission Intelligencer* 6 (1885): 96; Kirk to Granville, 31 May 1873, PP 1874, LXII, 749, p. 21; Bishop Steere to Penney, 30 June 1881, UMCA, A1 (III), box 1, fol. 348; Smith to Kirk, 18 March 1885, PP 1886, LXII, 515, p. 122. On the southern Kenyan coast in the late nineteenth century, the leading source of slaves was the immediate hinterland; after that, war-torn northern Tanzania. McKay, "Southern Kenya Coast" p. 117.

Mijikenda weakness after the famine of 1884.[57] A number of Giriama—the Mijikenda group living now behind Malindi—claim that Arabs often raided Mijikenda villages for slaves. Although Mijikenda traded with the coastal towns, it was dangerous for them to go there alone for fear of being kidnapped.[58] When questioned about the exact identity of the slave raiders and kidnappers, they most frequently mentioned the Mazrui followers of Mbaruk bin Rashid.[59] He had developed a personal following capable of military action, which he used against the Al-Busaidi in Mombasa as well as against Mijikenda. Missionaries also reported fighting between Mijikenda and Mazrui in 1879, and with greater intensity in 1881–82 and 1884–85. In April 1884, the Giriama repulsed a heavy attack by the Mazrui.[60] Mijikenda fighting ability was undoubtedly the main reason why more extensive slave raids did not take place.[61] The balance of power fluctuated, but the Mijikenda remained a secondary source of slaves for the coastal plantations.[62]

The various techniques for obtaining slaves were ultimately negated by the takeover of East Africa by European powers. In 1888 the Germans moved into Tanganyika, and a British-chartered company took over coastal Kenya. Zanzibar became a British protectorate in 1890 and officials kept watch for any slave smuggling. Cases of slave trading were uncovered in all these areas throughout the 1890s, but the advent of

57. This possibility was suggested by Vice-Consul Haggard to Kirk, 8 September 1884, FOCP 5165, pp. 232–33. See also Spear, p. 222, and Berg, "Mombasa under the Busaidi Sultanate," p. 230.

58. MAL 16, 48, 49, 62. A person from another Mijikenda group, the Ribe, made similar points. MSA 8.

59. MSA 8. MAL 72, 65. An informant of slave descent mentioned the Mazrui raids, and added that Suleiman bin Abdalla Al-Mauli, another man with an independent military following, also was involved in slave raids. MAL 30.

60. George David to CMS, 28 February 1879, CMS CA5/06/3; Handford to Lang, 16, 19 April, 17 May 1884, CMS G3/A5/o/1884/48, 57, 66; same to same, 18 February 1885, CMS G3/A5/o/1885/29. Peter Koffsky, in a dissertation he is completing for the University of Wisconsin, suggests that the conflict of 1881–82 was in part brought about by Mijikenda reactions to Mazrui slave raids.

61. It was also risky to keep Mijikenda slaves, since it was easy for them to run away. An Arab of Mambrui said that slaveowners would not want Giriama slaves "even for free" because they would run away. MSA 44.

62. In a list of 379 slaves claimed by Rashid bin Salim Al-Mazrui, eleven were Mijikenda and 193 Wanyasa. Most of the rest were wazalia. List, included in Rashid's claim for compensation, 1908, CP/1/62/46. The thirty slaves of a Swahili woman of Mombasa, around 1900, reflected the effects of the famine: it included eleven Mijikenda, some of whom had been pawned. Most informants of slave origin in Malindi said that there were few Mijikenda among their fellow slaves. Margaret Strobel, "The Interaction of Slave and Freeborn Members of a Swahili Domestic Unit," Paper presented to the American Historical Association, Atlanta, Ga., 28 December 1975, p. 7; MAL 24, 31, 34, 35, 38.

imperial rule meant the end of that form of commerce on a large scale.[63]

The success of slave traders in preserving their business between 1876 and 1890 is difficult to assess. As with most clandestine activities, quantitative information is unavailable. By the late 1870s, the large-scale, centralized slave-trade system was at an end. It is hard to imagine that secret canoe voyages, petty kidnappings, and clandestine caravans were able to achieve the same results as the supply mechanism of the 1860s. At the very least, slaves became more expensive: prices in Pemba were in the $50 to $100 range in the early 1880s, fell in 1884, and were back to $100 in 1890.[64] However, it is even more difficult to argue that the measures of 1873 and 1876 effectively curtailed the supply of slaves to the plantations of the islands and mainland. Continued British efforts at interception revealed continued attempts at evasion. An organized supply system—although frequently operating on a small scale—continued to function, and it responded effectively to changing conditions. Slaves from the deep interior continued to reach the coast, while increased efforts were made to exploit the areas nearer the plantations. The numbers of slaves who arrived were probably less than the vast numbers who reached Zanzibar and the Kenyan coast before the late 1870s, but higher prices also reduced the incentives to send slaves on the vulnerable sea route to Arabia. Available supplies were concentrated on the plantations.

AGRICULTURAL PRODUCTION, 1873–1890

The real test of Zanzibar's and Pemba's manpower was the ability of slaves to pick the cloves. In the 1860s, with slaves readily available, good harvests varied between 150,000 and 300,000 frasilas—worth $200,000 to $300,000—and were more likely to be near the lower figure. After the hurricane of 1872, prices rose sharply, and slaveowners transferred slaves to Pemba to ensure that all trees would be thoroughly picked. Many planted new trees there instead of, or in addition to, rebuilding their old plantations in Zanzibar. Having even

63. Rear-Adm. Kennedy to Admiralty, 29 January 1894, PP 1895, LXXI, 143, p. 23; Rennell Rodd to Rosebery, 31 December 1893, ibid., pp. 17–18. Lists of captured dhows and reports by officials for this period may be found in Documents relatifs à la repression de la traite des esclaves publiées en execution des articles LXXXI et suivants de l'acte général de Bruxelles (Brussels, 1892——).

64. Fitzgerald, Travels, p. 610; Fremantle to Admiralty, 25 February 1891, PP 1890–91, LVII, 1057, p. 2, Ledoulx to MAE, 18 December 1884, MAE, 5. In a rare bill of sale from the Lamu area, dated 1889, 16 slaves were valued at an average of $103 each. Document filed with Mohamed b. Abubakar vs. Secretary of State for the Colonies, Civil Appeal 68 of 1908, High Court, Mombasa.

more fertile soil than Zanzibar, Pemba became the leading clove production area. A clove tree takes at least six years to reach maturity and more to attain maximum productivity, so the real burden fell on the slaves around 1880. Table 4:3 shows what they produced.

TABLE 4:3

CLOVE EXPORTS FROM ZANZIBAR AND PEMBA, 1867–1892

	Exports (Frasilas)	Exports (M.T. Dollars)	Price ($/fra)
1867–68		$200–300,000	$1–2
1872–73	=50–60,000 P *	500,000 P	9
1873–74	=20,000 P	200,000 P	
1875–79			9 (av.) †
1876–77	=100,000	900,000	
1877–78	=122,000	1,100,000	
1878–79	=85,000	765,000	
1880–81	140,000	1,260,000	
1883–84	300,000	1,050,000	3.75
1884–85	185,000	630,000 (av.)	=3.3
1885–86	159,000		
1886–87	130,000		
	130,000	=455,000	3.3–3.7
1889	285,000 (av.)		
1890	509,862		
1891	393,640		
	378,000	1,134,720	=3.0
1892	357,669	=895,000	2.5–2.75

SOURCES: Prideaux, Report on Zanzibar, 1873–74, FOCP 2915, p. 82; Guillois to MAE, 10 December 1873, MAE, 3; Consul W. H. Hathorne, *United States Commercial Relations*, 1879, p. 238. Consul Batchelder, Report on Zanzibar, *United States Commercial Relations*, 1880–81, p. 396; Miles to Granville, 1 February 1883, FOCP 4914, p. 112; Trade Report on Zanzibar, 1883–84, incl. Cheney to State Department, 1 July 1884, US Consul, 7; Consul Pratt, *United States Commercial Relations*, 1887, p. 838; Frederic Holmwood, Memorandum on the Clove Trade of Zanzibar, 4 February 1888, FO 84/1915; H. Greffulhe, note annexed to Lacau to MAE, 16 March 1889, MAE, 6; Report on Zanzibar, Foreign Office, Diplomatic and Consular Series, no. 991, 1891, supplement 1, pp. 6–14; ibid., 1892, p. 9; "Clove Industry of Zanzibar," *Kew Bulletin* (1893), p. 20; Fitzgerald, *Travels*, p. 560.

* = calculated from other data in this table. P means exports of Pemba only; Zanzibar production very small.

† av. means source indicates this is an average figure for that time.

These figures clearly show the results of the maturation of the clove trees planted after 1872.[65] A further large increase occurred in 1889

65. This point is also emphasized by the American consul, Batchelder, in his trade report in *United States Commercial Relations*, 1880–81, p. 396.

and 1890. Possibly this increase reflects better reporting, but it may also result from continued planting in Pemba once that island proved its worth in the early harvests. In the 1890s, Pemba was providing two-thirds to three-fourths of the cloves shipped from Zanzibar harbor.[66] It may also be that the revival of the slave trade in 1884 provided slaves to increase picking. What is certain, however, is that the largest clove crops in the history of Zanzibar and Pemba were being gathered in the early 1890s.

Planters made some attempts to hire Wapemba during the harvest or to allow squatters on their land in exchange for labor during the picking season, but nonslave labor remained of minor importance.[67] One visitor claimed that in the 1880s slaves were made to work harder because of the labor shortage, but other sources fail to confirm this.[68] No technological innovations occurred. It is possible that labor was shifted from other pursuits to cloves, but the increased activities of Europeans in East Africa were diverting urban slaves to caravan porterage.[69] Whatever adjustments were made, the slave supply of Zanzibar and Pemba must have been sufficient to perform its most exacting task.[70]

In view of the fifteen-odd years of measures against the slave trade, an explanation of productivity must fall back on two possibilities: slaves were reproducing themselves and/or new slaves were being imported. The former possibility goes against the opinions of most observers, who believed that the birth rate among slaves was low and the death rate high. The latter implies that the British blockade of Zanzibar and Pemba failed to stop slave imports to those islands. Most likely, both factors helped to maintain the slave population. Of slaves freed in Zanzibar in 1900–01, 31 percent were locally born and the rest came from

66. Fitzgerald, p. 560.

67. Pemba lacked the market in slaves for hire that existed in Zanzibar town. It would be possible to hire slaves from neighboring plantations if the period of the harvest was not uniform, and limited numbers of Wapemba were employed around 1890. Fitzgerald, pp. 539, 549–50; Report by Lieutenant Smith on Pemba, incl. Kirk to Granville, 13 March 1884, PP 1884–85, LXXIII, 385, p. 50; Vice-Adm. Macdonald to Admiralty, 28 May 1877, FOCP 3686, p. 725.

68. G. A. Fischer, *Mehr Licht im Dunklen Weltteil* (Hamburg, 1885), p. 68. See also chapter 5.

69. Portal to Salisbury, 12 September 1891, PP 1892, LXXIV, 499, pp. 4–6; Euan-Smith to Salisbury, 1 November 1888, FOCP 5896, pp. 433–34; Fischer, p. 70.

70. Finding new sources of labor after abolition required the resources of the British bureaucracy, the help of the governments of Kenya and Tanganyika, and economic changes that forced or encouraged many Africans to work for wages. Such resources were not at the disposal of the sultanate. There is no adequate study of postabolition Zanzibar, but see L. W. Hollingsworth, *Zanzibar under the Foreign Office 1890–1913* (London, 1953).

the mainland.[71] The opinions of observers, untrained in demography, about birth and death rates were probably exaggerated, while large numbers of slaves were smuggled into the islands.[72] The available evidence does not permit a more complete or certain explanation, but sufficient numbers must have been present on the clove plantations of Zanzibar and Pemba.

The reports of visitors to clove-growing areas suggest that the expanding harvests were not gathered without difficulty. Before 1884, expanding clove production coincided with the most effective enforcement of the prohibitions against the slave trade. In 1880, when the first trees planted after the hurricane were bearing, Kirk noted that the demand for slaves was high.[73] However, in 1882–83—by which time expanded harvests had driven down the price of cloves—Consul Miles found that the demand for slaves in Pemba had fallen. In Zanzibar, "The Arab shambas have been pretty well stocked." [74] Miles may have gone too far, for one year later Vice-Consul Smith, touring Pemba, saw underbrush growing among clove trees and land that had once been tilled reverting to bush; he attributed the deterioration in agriculture to a lack of slave labor.[75] Indeed, his visit coincided with the low point of the slave trade. It may well be that the slaves brought to Pemba after the famine of 1884 helped to postpone the decline of the labor force.

Fitzgerald, in 1891, presented a mixed picture.[76] He saw many uncultivated fields and neglected clove plantations, and blamed this undercultivation on the scarcity of slave labor. One plantation he visisted had half the complement of slaves that was needed. Some attempts were being made to hire clove pickers or to acquire tenants, but only a few free laborers were hired in the picking season, and year-round cul-

71. Those born on the mainland had either survived twenty-seven years in Zanzibar, which must have been close to the average life-span for Zanzibaris, slave or free, or else had been smuggled in illegally after 1873. The figures are from Last to Mathews, 10 January 1901, PP 1901, XLVIII, 173, pp. 29–30; and Last to Raikes, 5 February 1902, PP 1903, XLV, 955, pp. 8–9.

72. The data do not permit any conclusive analysis of demographic trends, but the question of reproduction by slaves is discussed in chapter 6, as are manumission and mobility.

73. Kirk to Salisbury, 23 February 1880, FOCP 4498, p. 413.

74. Miles to Granville, 15 December 1882, and 23 June 1883, FOCP 4914, pp. 93, 154–55. A French visitor in 1881 noted that the export of slaves had ceased but that proprietors still had slaves. Charles Courret, A l'est et à l'ouest dans l'Ocean Indien (Paris, 1884), p. 133.

75. Smith, PP 1884–85, LXXIII, 385, p. 49, 50. However, Smith noted that Arabs were planting rice to supplement their income from cloves.

76. In the interim Arab plantation owners were complaining about shortages of slaves. Vice-Consul Berkeley to Euan-Smith, 14 June 1888, FOCP 5896, p. 283; Lacau to MAE, 3 May 1888, MAE, 5. See also Fischer, p. 68.

tivation was done entirely by slaves. At the same time, Fitzgerald saw other plantations that were well cared for. In fact, he saw many young clove plants—an indication that planters had enough confidence to go through the arduous process of planting new trees—and at one point he observed that the cultivation of cloves in Pemba seemed to be increasing.[77] After 1890, the Protectorate Government and new decrees (see Appendix 2) tightened the net on the slave trade still further. Throughout the decade, officials commented on the steadily dwindling supply of slave labor. They, like their predecessors, were probably exaggerating, for clove harvests remained large.[78]

Observers may well have overestimated the extent of decline by neglecting to note that land was often deliberately allowed to revert to bush. The instances of neglected plantations—in the midst of others which were flourishing—also suggest that some owners were able to master the intricacies of clandestine slave buying better than others, and that some plantations had higher attrition rates of slaves than others. Finally, the extent of clove cultivation, especially in Pemba, had expanded greatly during a period of high prices when Zanzibar's plantations were temporarily out of production. The subsequent decline in the price would discourage intensive cultivation of the expanded plantations. The fact that cloves were a glut on the world market is as reasonable an explanation for undercultivation as lack of labor.[79] The evidence indicates that, as of 1890, the labor supply to clove plantations was a problem, and one that undoubtedly resulted in hardship for many slaveowners. But it does not point to an economic crisis. Cloves were still being grown on the plantations of the Arabs of Zanzibar and Pemba.

The mainland was not affected by declining slave imports until a later date, largely because it had done so well after 1873, when sea traffic was being curtailed more effectively than land caravans. When the

77. Fitzgerald, *Travels*, pp. 525, 539, 549–50, 606–07. See also Schmidt, pp. 151–52, and Baumann, *Die Insel Sansibar*, p. 28.

78. The consul in 1892 estimated that one-fourth to one-third of the clove crop would remain unpicked for lack of labor, but failed to note that even this harvest was a glut on the market. Portal to Rosebery, 2 October 1892, FO 84/2233. See also Hardinge to Kimberley, 20 February 1895, PP 1895, LXXI, 143, p. 32; and Hardinge to Salisbury, 10 January 1896, PP 1896, LIX, 395, p. 23. On the continuing large clove harvests in the 1890s, see Zanzibar Government, *Statistics*, 1931, pp. 15–17.

79. Kirk noted in 1883 that the incentive to import slaves into Pemba was low because of the fall in the price of cloves. Kirk to Granville, 24 November 1883, PP 1884, LXXV, 353, p. 129. Another source even suggested that prices fell so low by the 1890s that planters kept cultivating cloves only to keep their slaves busy! O. Warburg, "Vegetationsbilder aus Deutsch-Ostafrika. Gewüznelkonplantage in Sansibar," *Deutsche Kolonialzeitung* 8 (1895):242.

slave supply began to diminish in the 1880s, the mainland was reaching its peak as a grain-producing area. In fact, Malindi's exports increased in value by 38 percent between 1884 and 1887.[80]

After the land routes between Kilwa and the Kenya coast became hazardous, the Malindi area—which had the greatest demand for slaves—experienced some of the same difficulties as the islands. Vice-Consul Gissing visited Malindi and Mambrui in 1884 and wrote that the number of slaves there was declining.[81] However, the severe famine occurred that year, and it is possible—although a direct causal link cannot be established—that the reopening of the slave trade enabled Malindi to expand its agricultural output between 1884 and 1887.

Yet the renewed slave trade was not on the scale of former days, and in 1888 the Imperial British East Africa Company stationed representatives in Malindi to keep an eye on illicit activities.[82] When Fitzgerald came to Malindi in 1891, he found that few new slaves were arriving and slaves were growing scarcer. He blamed the extent of abandoned land he saw on the lack of labor. Nevertheless, in his thorough tours of the Malindi area, he also saw many areas of extensive cultivation. He was impressed by the care with which crops were raised on many plantations. In Mambrui, he found the country "rich and fertile" and wrote that "a great deal" of millet and sesame was being produced.[83]

The French missionary LeRoy, who visited Malindi in 1890, also observed extensive cultivation of grains and fruit and saw dhows taking these products to distant lands. In 1892, Malindi and Takaungu had a "very fruitful" grain harvest, so much so that it exceeded the shipping capacity of the local vessels to export it.[84] Although little was done to provide alternatives to slave labor in the 1890s, several government officials in those years were still impressed by the "carefully cultivated shambas" and "splendid crops" of the coast between Mombasa and Malindi.[85] The main effect may have been to constrain further expansion. Grain cultivation—especially clearing new land—is highly labor-

80. See chapter 3, Table 3:1.

81. Gissing, FOCP 5165, p. 247.

82. However, as late as 1891 Fitzgerald heard reports that slave caravans were still coming down the Sabaki River to Mambrui. *Travels*, p. 157.

83. Ibid., pp. 18, 22, 206; Report, September–October 1891, p. 5, copy in Commonwealth Office Library, London.

84. LeRoy, "Au Zanguebar Anglais," 22: 606; *Gazette for Zanzibar and East Africa*, no. 16, 18 May 1892.

85. Weaver to Craufurd, 24 July 1896, and Taubman to Weaver, 1 July 1896, incl. Weaver to Craufurd, 25 July 1896, CP/1/75/46; Macdougall, Quarterly Report on Malindi District, 8 April 1901, incl. Eliot to Lansdowne, 5 May 1901, FOCP 7823, p. 168; Marsden to Eliot, 24 December 1901, FOCP 7946, p. 127; "Report by Mr. A. Whyte on his Recent Travels along the Sea-Coast Belt of the British East Africa Protectorate," PP 1903, XLV, 759, pp. 3–7.

intensive. Labor shortages were undoubtedly a problem along the coast, hurting some slaveowners more than others, but visitors' reports do not convey a sense of a drastically deteriorating grain and fruit economy.[86]

PROBLEMS OF A PLANTATION ECONOMY

The vulnerability of the slave supply was but one of the structural weaknesses that limited the planters' control over economic life and their ability to adjust to new situations. As Gavin Wright said of the cotton economy of the Old South, such weaknesses were: "typical of many economies in history based essentially on extractive resource-intensive exports, which expand rapidly during a period of rising external demand, but which do not lay the institutional foundations for sustained growth once this era has passed."[87] Plantation agriculture has made men rich; it has left plantation regions poor.

Specialization was a key to the planters' success—and to their undoing. Trading networks, capital investments, and forms of labor organization were all geared to production for export. When demand faltered, so did the economy.

In slave economies, some scholars argue, the heavy capital investment in labor made planters incapable of responding rapidly to changes in external demand. At the same time, the relationship of a master to his dependents reintroduced archaic values into a commercialized economy. Attachment to plantation life committed planters to a particular social system, so that they sought to maintain a dependent labor force even when the plantation economy was no longer viable. The idea of owning slaves could be so important to the slaveowning class that nonplantation economic activities—including commerce and finance—appeared vulgar and grasping. If in good times planters acquired large fortunes, they left much of the profits to more enterprising middlemen and were ill-equipped to cope with change.[88]

86. Fitzgerald's reports of undercultivation may have been influenced by the fact that most of his time was spent on the plantation that had been confiscated from Suleiman bin Abdalla Al-Mauli. A masterless slave plantation would be especially prone to undercultivation.

87. Gavin Wright, "Prosperity, Progress, and American Slavery," in Paul A. David, Herbert G. Gutman, Richard Sutch, Peter Temin, and Gavin Wright, *Reckoning with Slavery* (New York, 1976), p. 304.

88. This view is emphasized in Genovese, *Political Economy of Slavery*. See also Harold D. Woodman, *King Cotton and His Retainers: Financing and Marketing the Cotton Crop of the South, 1800–1925* (Lexington, Ky., 1968), and Paul A. David, "Slavery: The Progressive Institution?" in David et al., pp. 165–230. For an opposed view, see Fogel and Engerman, *Time on the Cross*. For divergent views of the economics of West Indian slavery, see Williams, *Capitalism and Slavery;* Sheridan, *Sugar and Slavery;* and Richard Pares, *Merchants and Planters* (Cambridge, 1960).

Some economists stress that many of the structural weaknesses of plantation economies apply even in the absence of slave labor. Linkages to the outside were stronger than linkages within the local economy— except when it came to labor. At best, plantations competed with other sectors of the economy for land and low-paid labor; at worst, the entire system was structured to provide low-paid, unskilled labor.[89] Even high prices for plantation commodities did not lead to the development of other sectors of the local economy.

On the coast of East Africa, the slave plantation helped make some Omanis, Hadramis, and Swahili rich. But its very success tied the planters to the trading networks that had made the economy's expansion possible. To be sure, the coastal economy was not as bound up in export agriculture as the Old South was in cotton, but it was one of few sources of cash income. Meanwhile, rural self-sufficiency reinforced older notions of dependency and made planters increasingly committed to plantation life and their role as slaveholders. As in parts of the Americas, outsiders dominated certain vital parts of the economy, further restricting the planters' ability to adjust to external forces.

These problems were most acute in Zanzibar and Pemba, and their impact became most severe as the price of slaves mounted after the late 1870s. The major problem was the price of cloves. After the high prices that had stimulated the rapid expansion of the clove industry declined, the rate of growth fell substantially in the 1850s and 1860s. A second cycle began in 1872, when the hurricane destroyed over half of Zanzibar's clove trees. Prices rose from $2 per frasila to about $9, leading to the rapid development of Pemba, which had been spared the storm. As production increased in the early 1880s, prices once more began to decline, again hitting $2.

The crux of the problem was limited demand. Zanzibar was producing for a less dynamic market than were the sugar, cotton, and coffee plantations of the Americas. India remained the dominant importer. Between 1877 and 1889, over 60 percent of Zanzibar's clove exports were sent there. Some were reexported to other countries in Southeast Asia or to Europe, but India itself was consuming nearly 40 percent of Zanzibar's production.[90]

89. George L. Beckford, *Persistent Poverty: Underdevelopment in Plantation Economies of the Third World* (New York, 1972); Lloyd Best, "Outlines of a Model of a Pure Plantation Economy," *Social and Economic Studies* 17 (1968): 283–324; Jay R. Mandle, *The Plantation Economy: Population and Economic Change in Guyana 1838–1960* (Philadelphia, 1973). The importance of nonmarket mechanisms for recruiting and controlling low-paid labor in plantation economies is stressed by Mandle and Willemina Kloosterboer, *Involuntary Labour Since the Abolition of Slavery* (Leiden, 1960).

90. Calculated from "Trade of British India with British Possessions and Foreign Countries," PP 1881, LXXXVIII, 1, pp. 215, 292; PP 1886, XLIX, 549, pp. 25, 86; PP 1890–91, LVIII, 693, pp. 48, 238–39; and from Table 4:3. Despite India's purchases, the

Plantation production undermined the basis of the lucrative spice trade—extreme scarcity.[91] Clove plantations, as argued in chapter 2, had small profit margins. By the 1880s, planters were caught between rising prices for slaves and falling prices for the commodities they produced.

They tried again with the one crop that they knew buyers wanted and which was already widespread in Zanzibar, coconuts. Coconut and copra exports fell during the post-hurricane period, but as clove prices fell, coconut exports rose. By the 1890s they were back to roughly the same level as the 1860s, an earlier period of low clove prices—that is, $200,000 to $300,000 per year.[92] This was still well below what cloves brought in, and Zanzibar faced competition from many parts of the world—including her mainland dominions—and from other sources of vegetable oils.[93]

The squeeze on income was further tightened by a tax structure which itself reflected the narrowness of the state's financial options and the variability of export agriculture. Before the 1870s, the only tax on cloves had been the standard five-percent import duty charged on cloves sent to Zanzibar harbor from Pemba for sale abroad. When prices rose after 1872, a duty of $2.50 per frasila was added, bringing the total tax on cloves from Pemba to over 30 percent of the current price. In the 1880s, with prices falling, taxes were adjusted and eventually applied to Zanzibar as well, but they remained at 25 to 35 percent of the export price. This tax was paid by the merchant who brought the cloves to the customs house, but he in turn deducted it from the price paid to the grower.[94]

The Sultan probably had little alternative to taxing his major local

---

large harvests of the early 1890s were a glut on the London clove market. Strickland to Mathews, 31 January 1894, FOCP 6526, and Warburg, p. 242. See also Tidbury, *Clove Tree*, pp. 13, 196–206.

91. Cloves were thus a very different product from sugar. Sugar plantations suffered from competition, low profit margins, and soil exhaustion, rather than from lack of demand. See E. J. Hobsbawm, "The Seventeenth Century in the Development of Capitalism," in Genovese, *Slave Economies*, 1: 151.

92. Zanzibar, *Statistics*, 1931, p. 19; Fitzgerald, *Travels*, p. 564. An American consul noted that the renewed interest in coconut trees was a response to low clove prices. Report of Consul Pratt, *United States Commercial Relations*, 1887, p. 838.

93. France was the principal buyer of coconut products. Foreign Office, Diplomatic and Consular Report on Zanzibar, no. 1194, 1892, table D and p. 9; Trade Report on Zanzibar, 1886–87, incl. Pratt to U.S. State Department, 20 September 1887, US Consul, 8. On the oil market, see Hopkins, *Economic History of West Africa*, pp. 125–28, 131–32.

94. Kirk to Wedderburn, 27 January 1872, FOCP 4206, pp. 6–7; Prideaux to Derby, 31 July 1874, FO 84/1399; Miles to Granville, 1 February 1883, FOCP 4914, p. 112; Smith, PP 1884–85, LXXIII, 385, p. 49; Greffulhe, note annexed to Lacau to MAE, 16 March 1889, MAE, 6; Hardinge to Salisbury, 4 May 1896, PP 1896, LIX, 395, p. 37.

asset, and his British successors failed to come up with anything new until the 1920s. The other possible source of revenue was taxing trade. Not only did treaties with European powers fix certain duties, but Zanzibar was used by merchants for its convenience as an entrepôt rather than for its own products, so that the Sultan did not dare to tax trade heavily. The tax on cloves was indeed, as a foreign observer put it, a "crushing" burden on the clove growers.[95]

Omani planters could not control external markets or the slave supply routes. They also depended on outsiders to market their produce and supply the credit they needed to buy slaves and other items. These two functions—sources of control over the clove industry as well as profits—were largely filled by Indians. Slaves sometimes carried the produce of their masters' estates on their heads to Zanzibar town, where it was sold to a broker, who was likely to be an Indian.[96] However, Indians managed to obtain a role for themselves as middlemen, buying directly from the producer, arranging for transportation, and selling to a clove broker in the town. Their presence in clove-growing areas so annoyed Seyyid Bargash, who claimed that they bought cloves directly from the slaves without ever paying the master, that he issued an order in 1870 banning Indians from the clove-growing areas. He did not—and probably could not—enforce it.[97] In the 1890s, an official complained that Indians in Pemba were acting as a "ring," acting together to set the terms under which they bought the clove crop.[98]

The role of middleman could be lucrative. Tharia Topan, who became the wealthiest Indian in East Africa, started his career as a clove carrier. According to a biography written by his son, Tharia came from India as a penniless young man. He went to work for the customs master, Jairam Sewji (who was a Hindu, while Tharia was an Ismaili), but did not like the job. He was able to borrow two donkeys and carts and hired a servant to help him go to distant plantations to collect cloves. He purchased as many cloves as the donkeys could carry, returned to town, and sold them to a broker for a large profit. Taking advantage of the rapid decline in the price of cloves the farther the distance from the town, Tharia allegedly made over $1,000 the first season and over $4,000 the second. He got to know the plantation owners and made ar-

95. Lacau to MAE, 3 May 1888, MAE, 5.

96. Christie, "Slavery," p. 35; Kirk to Wedderburn, 27 January 1872, FOCP 4206, pp. 6–7.

97. Seyyid Bargash to Churchill, 31 October 1870, and Churchill to Bombay, 17 November 1870, FO 84/1325; Kirk to Bombay, 25 March 1871, FO 84/1344.

98. Hardinge to Salisbury, 10 January 1896, PP 1896, LIX, 395, p. 26. Not only was the planters' bargaining position against middlemen weak, but it was also weak against outside buyers. And unlike colonial planters, those of Zanzibar had no political influence in consumer countries with which to obtain favorable duties or price supports.

rangements to ensure a regular supply. Living simply, he was able to buy several slaves and set them to work with the carts. Meanwhile, he invested in the import business and in his own clove plantations. He also traveled to India and made agreements with Ismaili firms to purchase cloves. Eventually, he reached the stage where he could keep cloves in his own warehouse and wait for an advantageous price. Tharia's biographer claims, undoubtedly with much exaggeration, that he bought and sold one-half of the clove crop of Zanzibar.[99]

Tharia Topan's story reads like a homily to the virtues of the self-made man. More fundamentally, the story indicates how badly clove producers had neglected marketing problems, as well as the importance to the middleman of building an integrated firm—linking the clove plantations with the market in India, while controlling trade in imports as well. Topan's tactics were typical of the successful Indian firms, who paid close attention to their links with both producers and customers.[100] Omanis ignored these avenues to profit.

One indication of the limitations of Omani aspirations in business, plus the constraints of personal and communal rivalry among Omanis, was the fact that the Sultan chose to farm out the job of collecting customs to an Indian for a rental rather than to entrust the job to his own people. Jairam Sewji was customs master for many years, followed in 1876 by Tharia Topan. The customs master was not only able to collect vastly more in duties than he paid for the privilege, but he was able to use his position to establish close contacts with merchants for his personal business. Jairam Sewji and his agent Ludda Damji realized a fortune of between £1 and £2 million and invested £434,000 in loans and mortgages to Arabs, Indians, and Europeans. Tharia Topan was probably the wealthiest man in all of East Africa when he died in 1891.[101]

Arab dependence on Indians was most important in the field of fi-

99. Topan, "Biography of Sir Tharia Topan," MS, pp. 55–90, 154, 167. On the Indian role in clove marketing, see also Ward to Buchanan, 7 March 1847, US Consul, 2, *NEMA*, p. 375; O'Sullivan, Report on Pemba, PP 1895, LIX, 395, p. 40.

100. Rigby, Report, 1860, p. 329; Ward to Buchanan, 7 March 1847, *NEMA*, p. 375; Hamerton to Willoughby, 28 September 1841, FO 54/4. An interesting picture of the relationship between Tharia Topan and a leading foreign merchant emerges from the latter's letters, published in Norman R. Bennett, ed., *The Zanzibar Letters of Edward D. Ropes, Jr., 1882–1892* (Boston: African Studies Center, Boston University, 1973). For an important analysis of commerce at Zanzibar, see Sheriff.

101. Kirk to FO, 8 October 1871, incl. Kirk to Ind. Off., 8 October 1871, Ind. Off., L/P&S/9/49; Memorandum by Sir Bartle Frere respecting Banians or Natives of India in East Africa, 1873, PP 1873, LXI, 767, p. 102. List of properties in the estate of Tharia Topan prepared in accordance with decrees of High Court of Bombay, 1893, and Consent Decree of 1901. Filed with 25B and 74B of 1904, Reg., Msa.

nance. However much Omanis could rely on their plantations for the necessities of daily life, their desire for luxury goods, and above all their need to buy slaves, often induced them to borrow. Given that field hands cost $20 to $30—even more after 1873—that it took years for clove trees to mature, and that income was modest, expanding a plantation almost certainly required credit. Some Arabs and Swahili lent money on landed security at interest rates of 15–20 percent per year, evading or ignoring the Koranic prohibitions on usury.[102] But as early as 1843 British officials began to note that Arab plantations were being mortgaged to Indians. By 1861, Consul Rigby feared that Arab property would pass into the hands of their Indian creditors.[103]

Actually, officials went on making such predictions until the 1930s—without their coming true.[104] The Omanis did not lose their land, but they did continue to become heavily indebted. An official who served in Zanzibar in the 1870s and 1880s estimated that two-thirds of the property in Zanzibar and Pemba was mortgaged to Indians.[105] Mackenzie, who visited Zanzibar in 1891, also claimed that the great majority of mashamba were encumbered. He saw records of 2,350 shamba mortgages in Zanzibar, for an average of $580 per shamba, plus 946, averaging $876 each, in Pemba.[106]

Even Zanzibar's most progressive businessman and most extensive landlord, the Sultan, turned to Indians to raise funds. Seyyid Said took a year's advance in revenue from Jairam Sewji, and his son Majid was deeply in debt to Jairam as well. The debt had to be deducted from the customs farm.[107]

102. Burton, *Zanzibar*, 2: 407. Some Arabs financed traders headed to the interior, including the two most important up-country traders, Tippu Tip and Rumalyza. Tharia Topan later became the principal creditor of Tippu Tip. Tippu Tip, *Maisha*, p. 91.

103. Hamerton to Willoughby, 9 October 1843, Political Consultations for 8 June 1844, INA, Reel 1; Rigby to Anderson, 14 May 1861, FO 84/1146.

104. See, for example, Memorandum by Frere on Banians, PP 1873, LXI, 707, p. 102, Zanzibar Government, "Report on the Indebtedness of the Agricultural Classes, 1933," by C. A. Bartlett and J. S. Last, 1934, and "A Note on Agricultural Indebtedness in the Zanzibar Protectorate," by Sir Ernest M. Dowson, 1936.

105. Memorandum by Fredric Holmwood on the Clove Trade of Zanzibar, 4 February 1888, FO 84/1915. Similar views may be found in Guillois to MAE, 15 October 1873, MAE, 3; Macdonald to Salisbury, 3 March 1888, FO 84/1906; Baumann, *Sansibar*, p. 27, and *Pemba*, p. 12; Fitzgerald, *Travels*, p. 611.

106. Mackenzie, p. 94. The surveys conducted by the colonial government confirmed the extent of indebtedness to Indians, although a more detailed study of mortgage records might yield a more nuanced picture. Bartlett and Last, Dowson.

107. Webb to Ward, 27 September 1851, Ward Papers, *NEMA*, p. 488; Churchill to Bombay, 4 March 1868, FOCP 4207, p. 137; Prideaux, Report, 1873–74, FOCP 2915, p. 79.

The efficacy of Indian finance for slave plantations was severely shaken in 1874—just when Pemba needed capital to stock its plantations. Kirk began, repeating Rigby's brief efforts of 1860–61, to enforce a law which forbade Indians, as British subjects, from possessing slaves.[108] Indians could no longer accept the most valuable capital good—slaves—as security, nor could they obtain the labor needed to make use of the second most valuable capital asset—land.[109] In the aftermath of Kirk's actions, plantation owners in Pemba found it difficult to obtain credit at all, and the best risks had to pay high interest rates—often 15 or 25 percent. Mortgages on land remained the dominant form of credit, at a continued high cost.[110]

The constraints on creditors was the major reason why massive mortgaging of plantations did not lead to massive transfers of land, even when clove prices fell once again and slave prices rose. Then too, Indian specialization in commerce and finance was profitable, and many were reluctant to become planters or estate managers.[111] Often, an Indian creditor would rewrite a debt when the debtor defaulted. Thereafter the creditor could collect as much of the interest as the debtor could afford, while maintaining financial control over his property. As interest payments kept mounting, the debtor stood little chance of ever being able to redeem his property.[112]

This arrangement was to an extent mutually beneficial—the debtor did not lose his plantation or his status and the creditor received payments, even if they were less than he was entitled to receive, without losing financial control over the property. This control could be used to

108. Kirk's actions are summarized by Coupland, *Exploitation,* p. 219. Tharia Topan, who had gone deeply into clove production, had to free hundreds of slaves. According to his biography, he gave his freed slaves huts and hired many as wage laborers.

109. Under some circumstances, the loan was made on the clove crop. Euan-Smith to Derby, 31 July 1876, FOCP 2915, p. 209.

110. Guillois to MAE, 15 October 1873, MAE, 3; Smith, Report on Pemba, PP 1885, LXXIII, 390, p. 50. High interest rates continued. Hardinge to Salisbury, 10 January 1896, PP 1896, LIX, 395, pp. 25–26; Fitzgerald, *Travels,* p. 611.

111. This tendency was still evident after abolition, putting Indians and Arabs on the same footing in the competition for labor. Even when Indians foreclosed, the former owner often remained on the plantation, legally a tenant. Zanzibar, Annual Report, 1913, cited by Zanzibar, "Agricultural Indebtedness," pp. 3–4; Zanzibar Government, "Zanzibar: The Land and Its Mortgage Debt," by C. F. Strickland, 1932, p. 4; Christie, "Slavery," p. 50. Indians, like Omanis, stuck to certain roles in the economy, and Arabs continued their domination of plantation ownership, especially of the larger units. Zanzibar, "Zanzibar Clove Industry," p. 5, and Batson, "Social Survey,'" MS, vol. 15.

112. Smith, PP 1884–85, LXXIII, 385, p. 50; Zanzibar, "Indebtedness of the Agricultural Classes," p. 6; O'Sullivan, Report on Pemba, PP 1896, LIX, 395, p. 44.

force the owner to sell cloves to him.[113] Such arrangements enabled the plantation system to go on, even when the ability to foreclose, normally considered an essential part of finance, was severely curtailed. It was not conducive, however, to encouraging landowners to develop their properties further, since they would only be making foreclosure more inviting. Nor did financial failure result in the transfer of property to more efficient landlords.

The system therefore had a fragile stability: squeezed between low prices for cloves and high prices for slaves, compounded by high interest rates, Arab estate owners maintained their position as the proprietors of land and slaves.[114]

A full explanation for Indian predominance as merchants and money-lenders must await further study of the Indian Ocean commercial system and the Indian communities.[115] What can be said here is that it was part of a more general problem: factors and creditors in other plantation economies formed a distinct group from planters and siphoned off much of the profits. Part of the explanation may lie in access to credit in economic centers. The factor in the Southern United States could himself get credit from the North or from Europe and was in a position to control its distribution to planters.[116] The Indian firms in Zanzibar, although they did not necessarily come from India with trading capital of their own, could channel it through the complex Indian Ocean system, thanks to their widespread networks. Similarly, marketing required a chain of contacts, in India as well as Zanzibar.

113. O'Sullivan, p. 43, and Hardinge to Salisbury, 10 January 1896, PP 1896, LIX, 395, p. 26.

114. In a survey of clove-tree holdings done in 1922, 1,218 Arabs owned 1,869 mashamba with an average of 394 trees each on the island of Zanzibar, while 2,973 Arabs owned 6,819 mashamba with an average of 130 trees on Pemba. The next largest category of clove-tree owners were Swahili, who generally owned small mashamba. Indians and others constituted only 3.1% of the clove growers. The Arab owner of a large estate was still the dominant factor in the clove economy, although the African smallholder had become more important since abolition. Zanzibar, "Memorandum on the Zanzibar Clove Industry," p. 6.

115. One explanation that is clearly incorrect is that the Islamic religion was the cause of Omanis' lack of entrepreneurial vigor. Many of the Indians in Zanzibar, Tharia Topan included, were Muslim, and Islamic jurists have developed numerous ways of avoiding the Koranic restrictions on usury. Any explanation for what Muslims did and did not do must rest on analyses of particular Muslim groups in specific economic and social situations. See Rodinson, *Islam and Capitalism*.

116. Woodman, passim. See also Pares, pp. 38–50, and Stein, *Vassouras*, pp. 17–19, 30. Sheridan notes how West Indian capital was drained off to England, but shows that, unlike the case of Zanzibar, there was a close connection between planters and merchant-factors. Sheridan, pp. 262–305.

Such networks were especially likely to follow ethnic or communal lines in preindustrial societies—where impersonal institutions to enforce contracts were weak, where economic information was disseminated slowly and narrowly, and where commodity markets took the form of personal contacts. Relationships of trust and cooperation based on kinship or common origins could be mobilized for economic purposes. Close relations among a trading community discouraged outsiders from cheating or attacking it. In other words, ethnic specialization was not the result of the idiosyncratic preferences of different peoples, but was an effective way of organizing economic activity.[117]

Omani specialization in plantation agriculture was also socially rational. As in many societies that were heavily involved in slavery, the fact of slaveownership was a source of prestige which other, more individualistic, endeavors failed to provide. In addition to plantation agriculture, the commercial activities in which Omanis did best—the dhow and caravan trades—relied for their success not just on personal acumen, but on the supervision of dependent followers: slaves, clients, and others. The most successful traders, such as Tippu Tip, were in fact chieftains commanding immense personal followings. Values are never fixed, but the slave plantation—as a social as well as an economic unit—and older Omani social values, were mutually reinforcing.

External forces and internal weaknesses meant that the rapid expansion of the clove industry in Zanzibar and Pemba did not lead to the further development of the Zanzibari economy. The incentives for growth in the clove industry diminished when prices fell, and while the size of harvests did pick up in the late 1880s—possibly as a response to declining incomes, possibly as a result of improved labor supplies after 1884—income from clove exports was no higher than it was in the late 1870s. Nor did planters have much opportunity to diversify their interests. Clove trees were long-term investments, and much capital had been committed to the slave-labor force. Labor could be shifted to coconuts, but they provided only a little help. Most important, planters—squeezed by high slave prices, high taxes, and heavy indebtedness to Indians—had little capital. And Indian capital was heavily tied up in mortgages that they could not readily liquidate, although they had investments in other sectors of the Indian Ocean commercial system.

The planters of Zanzibar maintained their position largely because

117. The competitive advantage of Indians would lie in the centrality of India to the regional commercial system and the fact that their diaspora followed the lines of that system. Abner Cohen, "Cultural Strategies in the Organization of African Trading Diasporas," in Claude Meillassoux, ed., *The Development of Indigenous Trade and Markets in West Africa* (London, 1971), pp. 266–84.

their commitment to export agriculture was not total. Some had trading interests, and all could benefit from the rich variety of Zanzibar's food crops. The trend toward the rural life that began in the 1840s continued; the increasing orientation toward export agriculture did not.

The problems facing the planters of Malindi and Mombasa were of the same nature, but not of the same magnitude. Then again, the scale of their economy was also more modest. In 1884 the sales of agricultural produce from Mombasa and Malindi combined came to less than half of Zanzibar's clove exports. As a trading center, Mombasa's stature was secondary; Malindi's was nonexistent.

The slave supply of the mainland coast suffered after 1876, but it was in a better position than the islands to benefit from the upsurge after 1884. Just as important was the stability of grain prices. In the peak years between 1884 and 1887, prices for millet at Mombasa stayed at $.30 per frasila, maize rose from $.20 to $.25, and sesame from $.50 to $.60. Grain prices remained constant through 1891, although sesame fell to $.30.[118] Nevertheless, the markets for grain, mainly Somalia and Arabia, were not themselves developing, and the prospects for expanding exports still further were not bright, even if the labor to clear new land had been available. Nor was the dhow trade growing, and it might not have been able to handle a breakthrough in exports had one occurred.[119]

Ethnic specialization affected the mainland coast as well as the islands. Indian firms, like that of Jivanji Mamuji in Malindi, were the most important exporters of plantation produce, although Hadramis, such as Ali bin Salim Basharahil, were active in this line as well.[120] In Malindi, Omanis, Washella, and Bajuni stuck to farming, but in Mombasa, virtually all communal groups participated in the active up-

118. Gissing to Kirk, 16 September 1884, FOCP 5165, p. 246; Holmwood, "Estimates of Present Customs Duty upon the trade of His Highness the Sultan's Dominions between Wanga to Kipini Inclusive," 6 May 1887, in Sir William Mackinnon Papers, Africa, IBEA, no. 943, School of Oriental and African Studies, University of London; Fitzgerald, "Report on the Native Cultivation, Products, and Capabilities of the Coast Lands of the Malindi District," 1891, copy in Royal Commonwealth Society, p. 4.

119. The economic decline of Oman after the mid-nineteenth century is discussed by Landen, *Oman since 1856*. On the dhow trade, see *Gazette for Zanzibar and East Africa*, no. 16, 18 May 1892.

120. See the brief biographies in chapter 3. In addition to Jivanji Mamuji and his sons, two other Bohoras, Mohammedbhai Taibji in Malindi and Taibji Waliji in Mambrui, were important traders, as well as money-lenders. MAL 10, 42.

country trade. The port's import-export houses, however, were probably dominated by Indians, plus a few Hadrami firms.[121]

The Indian role in supplying credit was substantial, but the problem of extensive mortgaging of plantations to Indians that is reported in Zanzibar did not beset the mainland coast. To be sure, leading planters often borrowed heavily. Suleiman bin Abdalla Al-Mauli, one of Malindi's biggest, fell short of cash at one point and borrowed from a Swahili family of Lamu. Unable to pay them back, he obtained a loan from Tharia Topan, the leading Indian financier of Zanzibar. To pay back Tharia Topan, he mortgaged his land to Salim bin Khalfan Al-Busaidi. He was also in debt to Islam bin Ali Al-Kathiri, a Hadrami from nearby Mambrui. When the British confiscated his plantations because he had fought against Zanzibari authority on the coast, he was $15,000 in debt, while the nominal value of his land and slaves was $25,000.[122]

This example suggests that wealthy individuals from many communal groups were involved in money-lending. Although records are lacking from the period when credit was primarily needed to buy slaves, the deed files from the period before the abolition of slavery—a difficult time for landowners—bear this out. Salim bin Khalfan lent out more money against more mashamba than anybody in Mombasa, and he was active in Malindi too. Although few Swahili in Mombasa were money-lenders, in Malindi, Abdulla Hussein, the wealthy Mshella, lent large sums of money to rich members of other communal groups.[123] Baluchis were particularly important in financing the ivory trade in Mombasa.[124]

Overall, the Malindi land records from 1903 to 1906 contain only 15 mortgages on mashamba by Arabs or Swahili, compared with 24 mortgages of town plots or houses. Of the mortgages on mashamba, half were to Indians, and most of these occurred just before abolition.[125] Similarly, in Mombasa, deeds from 1891 to 1905 contain twice

121. Macdonald to FO, 19 December 1887, FO 84/1853; MSA 16, 17, 18; Berg, "Mombasa," pp. 198–208.

122. Another confiscated estate, valued at $2,100, was encumbered by debts of $4,000. Bell Smith to de Winton, 5 January 1891, FO 84/2146; Statement of Ali bin Salim Al-Busaidi, 24 December 1908, Ali bin Salim to Provincial Commissioner, Coast, 16 July 1908, Minute by C. R. W. Lane, 15 August 1904, on petition of Raya binti Suleiman bin Abdalla, 18 June 1904—all in CP/1/62/48. See also chapter 3.

123. Abdulla Hussein lent $7,000 to Bi Salima and $3,603 to Lali Hadaa. See his biography in chapter 3. Data on Mombasa come from a computer analysis of the 20% sample of Reg., Msa, A-series.

124. See Table 3:4. Abdulrehman bin Mirza was notable among the Baluchi financiers and traders, as his many recorded loans indicate. A-series, B-series, and MSA 11.

125. A-series, Malindi. Fourteen of twenty-four urban properties were mortgaged to Indians.

as many mortgages of urban property as of mashamba. Indian creditors accounted for 47 percent of farmland mortgages, 56 percent of
urban mortgages, 43 percent of debts involving ivory, and 60 percent
of loans without collateral.[126] While an unsure guide to the nineteenth
century, these records suggest that shamba land may have been second
in importance to urban property as collateral for loans, and that Indians had an important—but not exclusive—role in finance.

For the people of the mainland coast, grain proved a steadier source
of income than spice did for the people of Zanzibar. Its planters were
not so tightly squeezed by falling prices and heavy indebtedness, and
the plantation economy was more self-sufficient.[127] Yet, constrained by
the shortage of slaves and the lack of a dynamic market for its produce,
there was little opportunity for further, large-scale expansion. Grain
did not have the same effect on Malindi as sugar did on Cuba.

The problems of the plantation economy of the islands and mainland
cannot be attributed solely to the measures taken by the British against
the slave trade between 1873 and 1890. Stagnation and dependence affected plantation economies in many parts of the world and in many
eras. But despite the scarcity and high price of slaves, the uncertainties
of international markets, the lack of control over marketing and finance, and (in Zanzibar) overtaxation, the plantation economy was not
collapsing. The slaves continued to provide for the plantation residents, as they raised and harvested vast export crops.

The Arab and Swahili landowning and slaveowning elites still dominated Zanzibar and the mainland coast when slavery was abolished in
the early colonial era. To a large extent, they even survived abolition—
poorer than before, but with their status in the society of the coast
largely intact. The ownership of slaves had put them in a position of
privilege, but the ownership of land kept them there. As in other plantation societies, landowners tried to retain a dependent labor force—
although more expensive and less well-disciplined than before—by
transforming slaves (and others) into tenants. But in this situation the
planters of Zanzibar prospered more than those of the coast of Kenya,
a change in fortunes that points to the crucial role of coercion—in one
guise or another—in plantation economies. The British rulers of Zanzibar, fearing social change and depending on clove exports for gov-

126. A-series sample, Mombasa (162 mortgages), and B-series, Mombasa, 1892–99.

127. The mainland coast of Kenya was also not overburdened by taxation. In Malindi
in 1887, duties were about 11% of the value of exports. This was partly the result of price
stability, but more important, it was the result of politics. In the East African dominions
of the Sultan of Zanzibar, the nearer a port was to the seat of power, the higher the duties. See Sheriff, "Rise of a Commercial Empire."

ernment revenues, helped the old landowners obtain cheap labor through the enforcement of the ex-slaveowners' land rights, taxation, forced labor, assisted migration of labor, vagrancy laws, and a variety of court-enforced tenancy systems. In Kenya, such labor supply mechanisms served white farmers, especially in the Highlands of central Kenya. Lacking the political and economic power to make their tenants work, coastal planters could only enjoy the social rewards of having dependents on their land. In the one case, the colonial economy absorbed the older plantation economy; in the other, colonialism subordinated it to a new group of farmers. Economic success depended on power over labor—to obtain and control it—as it had in the nineteenth century.[128]

CONCLUSIONS

The period from 1873 to 1890 was an eventful one in East Africa, but on the plantations surprisingly little was changed. The islands were legally cut off from their slave supply in 1873, the mainland in 1876. Slaveowners were forced to devise new ways of obtaining slaves. They partially succeeded, but by 1880 slaves had ceased to be the abundant and cheap item that had made possible the rapid expansion of the plantation economy. Yet the slaves' work was getting done: clove and grain exports were higher at the end of this period than ever before.

This was the era of decisive European intervention in Africa. There is no denying the economic impact of Europe on the Indian Ocean commercial system, but plantation crops were of decidedly secondary concern to the imperial powers in this period.[129] Even the early years of colonial rule affected the plantations mainly by completing what was supposed to have been done before 1890—cutting off the slave supply.

But the threat to the slave-trade routes and the other dimensions of coastal involvement in an international economic system had a great effect on the continued evolution of the plantation economy. In Zanzibar, declining prices in the 1850s slowed the earlier pace of plantation growth even though slaves were abundant, while a sudden price rise in 1872 led to the development of Pemba's clove plantations despite the prohibition on importing slaves and a crisis in the credit system. But the export economy and the income of the planters were severely ham-

128. I intend to follow up this study with a sequel comparing the effects of abolition on agriculture and agricultural labor in Zanzibar and the Kenyan coast.

129. A full understanding of the indirect effects of European capitalism's involvement in the Indian Ocean commercial system upon the plantation economy—through changes in credit and marketing—awaits a study which treats that system as a totality.

pered by declining clove prices, rising slave prices, high interest rates, and overtaxation.

On the mainland, plantation development was steadier. Mombasa's expansion after the 1840s was limited by the lack of land and the complexity of its urban setting, but Malindi became the center of immense grain plantations that continued to flourish in the 1870s and 1880s. In Malindi, the shortage and high price of labor, particularly in the early and late years of the 1880s, may well have restrained further expansion.

As in most plantation economies, expansion did not lead to a further transformation of the economy. The profits to finance economic change were probably the highest in Malindi, but its assets as a plantation center made the development of a strong local economy unlikely: relative isolation, abundant land, a small number of planters with large numbers of slaves. Zanzibar had a more substantial population and was the focal point of a regional trading network, but its planters were constrained by falling incomes, heavy debts and the loss of the profits of marketing and finance into a wider commercial system.

Had the profits of the plantation economy been greater or more lasting, or had they led to diverse new forms of investment and consumption, the imperatives of productivity might have had even more influence on the lives of masters and slaves than they did. But the earlier trends toward increasingly commercialized agriculture did not continue, and its influence on social organization and values did not become pervasive. Instead, the development of a more rural, more self-sufficient economy left Zanzibar and the mainland with a land- and slaveowning elite that had limited incentives to intensify production and also a cushion against the failure of the export sector. Slaves were still part of their master's following, and their presence was valued even when the income they generated fell. That following was now part of plantation society, and slaves had become an important means of production.

Part 2

The Treatment of Slaves

5 Slaves at Work

The most obvious question to ask about slavery is "How harshly were slaves treated?" Scholars in the Americas initially tried to decide which slave systems were harsher than others. Their attempts have revealed more about the scholars than about anything the slaves actually experienced. Harshness certainly includes a material element: the hours the slaves worked, the way they were punished, the amount and quality of food they received, and the quality of housing in which they lived. By such standards, the treatment of slaves in the United States compares favorably with, for example, Jamaica.

However, it is possible to argue that, psychologically and socially, the Old South had a more deleterious impact on its slaves than did Jamaica. North American slaveowners provided their slaves with more food, but Jamaican slaves—working their own small plots on their own time—achieved a measure of self-reliance as well as nourishment. Jamaican masters' indifference to the lives of their slaves may have given slaves more scope to develop their own social and cultural practices, thus preserving themselves from their masters' notions of superiority.[1]

To declare a slave system "good," "bad," "harsh," or "mild" is to say very little at all. Slavery is fundamentally a form of subordination and the problem is to analyze the dimensions which that subordination takes. No matter what the master wanted from his slaves, he had to make them bend to his will.

Control required more than a whip. The act of violence that underlay social control in all slave societies was the enslavement process itself. Stanley Elkins was correct to emphasize the dehumanizing tendencies inherent in capture, the Middle Passage, and the slave market, although he underestimated human resilience in the face of them.[2] This process did not turn slaves into children or strip them of the cul-

1. Among the best treatments of these methodological problems are Eugene D. Genovese, "The Treatment of Slaves in Different Countries: Problems in the Applications of the Comparative Method," in Foner and Genovese, *Slavery in the New World*, pp. 202–10; Sidney W. Mintz, "Slavery and Emergent Capitalisms," in ibid., pp. 27—37; Davis, *The Problem of Slavery in Western Culture*, esp. pp. 54–58, 223–61; Genovese, *The World the Slaveholders Made;* and Lombardi, "Comparative Slave Systems in the Americas," pp. 156–74.

2. Elkins, *Slavery;* Ann J. Lane, ed., *The Debate over Slavery: Stanley Elkins and His Critics* (Urbana, Ill., 1971).

ture of their homelands, but it did cut slaves loose from social institutions, taking away the context in which the culture had meaning.

The slaves' acute needs for protection, access to land, understanding of a new society, and the opportunity to develop social relationships could themselves allow slaveowners to set the conditions under which slaves became part of the society they were forced to enter. Slaveowners could, in some circumstances, make loyal followers out of people they had bought, but only by actually meeting the needs the slaves had of them and by ensuring that the personal ties of superior to inferior were closer than those among the slaves themselves.

In other cases, above all where most slaveowners were absentee landlords, coercion was the predominant element of control. With society sharply polarized into the owners and the owned, the power of the state and substantial unity among the slaveowners were both needed to repress collective action by the slave class.

In the Southern United States, the state played an essential role in maintaining slavery, but Eugene D. Genovese has stressed the dynamic role of the plantation itself. For planters who made the plantation a way of life, the intimacy of day-to-day existence left them little choice but to confront their slaves' humanity and create a social order out of an agricultural enterprise.

To argue that a paternalistic social order developed in the Old South, as Genovese makes clear, is not to minimize the extent of economic exploitation, brutality, or intimidation.[3] All these were part of the relations of subordination in a plantation economy. However, the slave was not a worker who performed a specific function for a limited portion of each day, but a dependent person, under the master's authority.

Paternalism is often seen only from above, as the benevolence of a superior person toward his inferiors. That was the image the slaveowners were trying to create.[4] Genovese stresses reciprocity. What to the slaveowners appeared as generosity, appeared to the slaves as an obligation. If he did not fulfill it, the master might still have his whip, but not his authority.

Violence was part of paternalism. Without it, the awe that slaveholders tried to instill lacked substance; but without the sense of awe,

3. Genovese, *Roll, Jordan, Roll.* Genovese does not explain the way paternalism developed, and his analysis of the contradictions in Southern society and ideology raises many questions. I will take up the question of how fully the concept of paternalism explains differing patterns of class rule in my Conclusions.

4. E. P. Thompson writes that in eighteenth-century England, "paternalism was as much theater and gesture as effective responsibility." It was "a studied technique of rule." "Patrician Society, Plebian Culture," *Journal of Social History* 7 (1974): 397.

force had to be applied continuously. A slaveowner who punished judi-
ciously—in terms he himself defined—might get his slaves to acknowledge, however grudgingly, that their conduct was limited by certain
rules, that they had certain obligations.

The reciprocal obligations between masters and slaves were worked
out by continual testing before they acquired the status of customs; and
even then, the tacit understandings that emerged regarding the work
load, personal rights of slaves, and punishments were continuously
stretched by both groups. Obviously, the master had more effective
sanctions, but precisely because the master wanted obedient subordi-
nates, not just unwilling laborers, slaves did have ways to influence the
system, to "transform paternalism into a doctrine of protection of their
own rights." [5] They could stage slowdowns, damage property, withhold
the respect the master desired, and—if conditions were desperate
enough—attempt to escape or rebel. Seeing paternalism as an interac-
tive process, a "subtle equilibrium," allows us to understand the contradictions of plantation life: the coexistence of obedience and resistance
on the part of the slaves, and kindness and brutality on the part of the
masters.[6]

Paternalism was also an ideology, an attempt by slaveowners to justify
the social order, not only to themselves, but to those whom they wished
to control.[7] The planters' hegemony depended, in large part, on their
ability to manipulate cultural and legal norms. Their position had to
appear as a matter of superiority—be it cultural, social, or racial—and
not just as a matter of force.

That was why the life the slaves built for themselves was so important. The combination of physical power and cultural control was formidable, but it was not all-powerful. For slaves, acts of resistance that
appear to us merely symbolic and futile could be attempts to attack the
edifice of ideological and cultural domination. They chipped away at
the awe with which the slaveowner tried to surround himself; they denied that the planter's law was justice; and they refused to believe in
the slaveowner's superiority.[8] By developing a culture of their own—
with its own values, beliefs, and forms of expression—they were deny-

5. Genovese, *Roll,* p. 49.

6. Gerald W. Mullin, *Flight and Rebellion: Slave Resistance in Eighteenth-Century Virginia*
(New York, 1972), p. 72.

7. Genovese is arguing that paternalism was a social reality, although he is aware of the
hypocrisy and contradiction that entailed. Others stress paternalism as a myth. William R.
Taylor, *Cavalier and Yankee: The Old South and the American National Character* (New York,
1961).

8. Thompson writes of a plebian "countertheater" that confronted the theater of the
patricians. Plebian culture deliberately blasphemed the deferential culture of paternalism. Thompson, esp. p. 402.

ing that they were nothing but inferior members of their master's society. They had to understand and use the ways of their owners' society, but at the same time they could deny their superiority. To create a social life in the slave quarters was not easy, but it proved to be the best defense Southern slaves had against their dependent position in a paternalistic order.

The development of paternalism in the Southern United States was a movement in the opposite direction from the currents of European and American history, toward a more organic social organization within a culture that was becoming increasingly market-oriented and individualistic. The process led to deep contradictions between the relationships and values engendered by the plantation and the political, economic, and cultural structures of the wider society.

On the coast of East Africa, the historical process was different: the agricultural roles of slaves grew out of a form of slavery that had emphasized the relationship between leaders and followers, within a society characterized by closely knit communal groups and patriarchal relationships. In the one case, paternalism grew out of the plantation; in the other, the plantation grew out of paternalism.

SLAVES AND CLOVES

A British visitor to Zanzibar in the period of the clove industry's most rapid expansion observed, "Since the recent introduction of profitable articles of cultivation, slavery in Zanzibar has assumed a form more resembling its condition in America." [9] However imprecise the comparison, the direction of change in Zanzibar was apparent: the lives of Zanzibar's slaves—swelled by new imports from the interior of East Africa—were altered by the demands of plantation agriculture.

The clove tree has very particular demands. It requires concentrated labor for several months of the year, the picking season. There are ordinarily two clove harvests each year, a large one around November or December and a small one in July to September. The clove—a bud that grows from the tips of the branches of the tree—must be broken off together with the stem but without injuring the branches. A careless picker is likely to damage the delicate branches of the clove tree. It is necessary to go over the same tree several times, carefully picking the cloves as they ripen. If not harvested promptly, cloves are likely to spoil. In Zanzibar the rainy season often coincides with the large harvest, making conditions for the pickers unpleasant and drying a difficult chore.[10]

9. Pickering, *The Races of Man*, p. 190.
10. Tidbury, *The Clove Tree*, pp. 26–27, 113–14; Warburg, "Vegetationsbilder aus Deutsch-Ostafrika," p. 242.

Slaves harvested cloves under the supervision of older, trusted slaves. A supervisor kept track of the number of baskets a slave picked, and a lax slave could be beaten or deprived of a holiday. Female slaves were mainly responsible for separating the buds from the stems and for spreading them out on mats to dry. Cloves were taken in each night and during rain. The drying process took six to seven days—longer in the event of bad weather.[11] Once dried, cloves were packed in gunny sacks and carried to Zanzibar town by the slaves, or else sold to an enterprising middleman, like the young Tharia Topan, who would take them to the Indian clove brokers in town or, in Pemba, ship them to Zanzibar.[12]

The principal demand for slave labor thus occurred at the time of the harvest. Dr. Christie, who lived in Zanzibar in the early 1870s, said that labor could not be found beyond the estate. Others, however, said that it was possible to supplement the labor of the slaves attached to the plantation by employing *vibarua*—slaves who were hired out by their masters for day-labor.[13] Some landlords, however, did not like to do this, believing that only their own slaves would take proper care of the trees. In addition, most vibarua were concentrated in Zanzibar town, far away from most plantations, so that the demands of the clove harvest essentially determined the number of slaves a landowner had to own.[14]

During the harvest, these slaves had to work very hard. They picked cloves eight or nine hours a day, seven days a week, instead of the customary five days of labor. However, two Englishmen with long experience in Zanzibar and Pemba indicate that slaves were paid for the two extra days of work, one saying that they were given one-third to one-half of the cloves picked, and the other saying they were paid four pice (about three cents) for every *pishi* (about one-half gallon).[15]

The work was not only intensive but skilled. A French visitor in the

---

11. Loarer, O.I., 5/23, notebook 4; Guillain, *Documents*, vol. 2/1, pp. 145–46; Fitzgerald, *Travels*, p. 559; Hardinge to Salisbury, 10 January 1896, PP 1896, LIX, 395, p. 25.

12. Clove marketing is described in chapter 4.

13. Christie, *Cholera Epidemics in East Africa*, p. 314; Quass, "Die Szuri's, die Kuli's und die Sclaven in Zanzibar," p. 443; Vice Adm. Macdonald to Admiralty, 28 May 1887, FOCP 3686, p. 725; Lieut. Smith, Report on Pemba, 1884, PP 1884–85, LXXIII, 385, p. 50; Fitzgerald, "Report on the Spice and Other Cultivation of Zanzibar and Pemba Islands," incl. Portal to Rosebery, 2 October 1892, FOCP 6362, p. 100.

14. Fitzgerald, *Travels*, pp. 539, 549–50, 601–02. A limited number of Wapemba and other laborers were paid to assist in harvests. Smith, PP 1884–85, LXXIII, 385, p. 50.

15. Christie, "Slavery in Zanzibar As It Is," p. 34; Hardinge to Salisbury, 10 January 1896, and "Report by Mr. O'Sullivan upon the Island of Pemba," incl. Hardinge to Salisbury, 18 June 1896, PP 1896, LIX, 395, pp. 25, 42; O'Sullivan to Hardinge, 26 September 1895, Zanzibar Archives, copy in papers of Sir John Gray, Cambridge University Library, box 27.

early days of large-scale clove growing thought the slaves were careless and broke many branches unless carefully watched. But others were impressed by the slaves' expertise and noted the trust that plantation owners placed in the skill of their own slaves.[16]

The delicacy of the harvesting process most likely accounts for the custom of paying slaves for piece-work. Zanzibari planters did not make such payments for other, less precise, agricultural tasks; and in Malindi, where careless harvesting of the annual crops could cause no permanent damage, no such payments were made. In the United States South, positive incentives often supplemented punishment, but these were generally occasional gifts or races and prizes rather than a system of regular payments.[17] Nevertheless, in Zanzibar a difficult job had to be done and the slaves had no choice but to do it. Compared to some other slaves, the delicacy of their duties gave them a *relatively* strong bargaining position to obtain customary payments and set customary limits on work; but they were still slaves.

Clove trees are not sugarcane—and the difference had much to do with the working lives of slaves. In the sugar industry, economies of scale were considerable, and West Indian plantations were usually very large. Harvesting involved more back-breaking labor and less care than picking cloves. Highly skilled slaves were required in processing, but for most the work was heavy and dangerous. Round-the-clock operations during the harvest were not unusual.[18] Market conditions and values shaped the organization of labor, but in itself the clove tree was a weaker force than sugar in pushing slaves toward a life of nearly unbearable labor.[19]

16. Loarer, O. I., 5/23, notebook 4; Fitzgerald, *Travels*, pp. 601–02; McClellan, "Agricultural Resources of the Zanzibar Protectorate," p. 415.

17. Fogel and Engerman, 1: 148–50, 206, emphasize positive incentives, but they appear to have exaggerated both the regularity of payments and rewards and the chances slaves had for upward mobility within the plantation hierarchy. See Gutman, *Slavery and the Numbers Game*, pp. 42–88. See also Genovese, *Roll*, pp. 313–14; Kenneth Stampp, *The Peculiar Institution* (New York, 1956), p. 151; and Robert S. Starobin, *Industrial Slavery in the Old South* (New York, 1970), pp. 99–106.

18. The brutal similarity of sugar plantations, regardless of the cultural background of their owners, is emphasized by Knight, *Slave Society in Cuba*. This and other studies stress the impersonal structure, heavy workload, and reliance on physical punishment, rather than positive incentives, to ensure discipline for all but the most skilled slaves. Ibid., p. 73; Dunn, *Sugar and Slaves*, pp. 190–98; Patterson, *The Sociology of Slavery*, pp. 65–69; and Elsa Goveia, *Slave Society in the British Leeward Islands at the End of the Eighteenth Century* (New Haven, Conn., 1965), pp. 130–31.

19. That crop requirements did not completely determine labor utilization is clear from the fact that West Indian planters deliberately stuck to inefficient farming techniques in order to keep the labor force occupied all year round. Dunn, p. 200. In eighteenth-century Cuba, coffee growing did not lead to heavy overwork for slaves; in nineteenth-century Brazil it did. Knight, Stein, *Vassouras*, pp. 135–37.

Outside of the clove-picking season work still had to be done. The most exacting task, also demanding skill and care, was planting new clove trees on an expanding shamba. Cloves were grown from seedlings, which were first planted in a special shaded nursery. After nine to twelve months in the nursery and a one- or two-month exposure to sunlight, they were planted. Slaves dug a series of holes, kept in line by a rope, each of which consisted of a four-foot-deep hole to serve as a catch-drain and a further hole one foot deeper to receive the plant. Young trees had to be watered, and the ground around them had to be weeded.[20] Once planted, the clove tree needed little attention and, according to most observers, received even less. Weeding was done with short-handled hoes made by local blacksmiths.[21] Visitors to clove plantations in the nineteenth century found that weeding was not done thoroughly and that the trees were rarely pruned.[22]

This work—and the task of growing grain, fruit, coconuts, and other items—occupied the slaves all year round. The customary work-week for both men and women was five days. Slaves had Thursdays and Fridays off, the former to cultivate for their own subsistence and the latter to observe the Muslim sabbath.[23] According to Consul Kirk, this custom broke down to some extent after the ruin of Zanzibar's clove trees in the hurricane of 1872 and the extraordinarily high demand for slaves in Pemba, but even in Pemba the two days became customary free time again.[24]

Daily assignments varied. Christie claimed that slaves sometimes worked from daybreak until 4:00 P.M., but more typically they quit by

20. Tidbury, p. 46; Fitzgerald, *Travels,* pp. 554–58.

21. Speer to Seward, 26 November 1862, US Consul, 4; Osgood, *Notes of Travel,* p. 26; Lyne, *Zanzibar in Contemporary Times,* p. 268; Hardinge to Salisbury, 10 January 1896, PP, 1896, LIX, 395, p. 25.

22. Portal to Chappel, no. 17, n.d. [1892], Portal Papers, Rhodes House, Oxford University, s108; R. L. Playfair, "Extract from the Administrative Report . . . ," p. 282; Hines to Seward, 25 October 1864, US Consul, 5, *NEMA,* p. 527; Burton, *Zanzibar,* 1: 362; William E. Hines, Report, *United States Commercial Relations,* 1865, p. 505; Warburg, p. 242.

23. Ruschenberger, *A Voyage Round the World,* pp. 34–35; Speer to Seward, 26 November 1862, US Consul, 4; Burton, *Zanzibar,* 1: 466; Rigby, "Report," 1860, reprinted in Russell, *General Rigby,* p. 334; Ludwig Krapf, "Additional Remarks on the Island of Zanzibar or Ongoodja," incl. Krapf to Coates, 10 June 1844, CMS CA5/016/25; Gaume, *Voyage à la Côte orientale,* p. 258; Colomb, *Slave Catching in the Indian Ocean;* pp. 373–74; Kirk to Derby, 1 May 1876, FO 84/1453; Rashid bin Hassani, "The Story of Rashid bin Hassani," p. 99; MSA 21.

24. Kirk to Derby, 1 May 1876, FO 84/1453; O'Sullivan, "Report 1896," pp. 41–42. When the British set up machinery, in connection with the decree of 1897 abolishing slavery, to receive the complaints of slaves, one of the most common ones in Pemba was denial of the customary two days off. "Report by Vice-Consul O'Sullivan on the Island of Pemba, 1896–97," PP 1898, LX, 361, p. 6.

noon. On many visits to the shamba areas during the day, he only saw slaves working on their own plots.[25]

How hard did slaves work? The opinions of observers are bound up in their own cultures' prejudices about work. They should not be taken literally, but their judgment is accurate enough to confirm that nothing like a Caribbean work routine befell Zanzibar's slaves. Rigby felt that the "Arab is too indolent and apathetic to make his slaves exert themselves." [26] An American wrote that slaves "do less work, on the average, in a month than a Mississippi slave does in a week," a situation he attributed to a climate that made it possible to raise crops with little effort. Another American asserted that Arabs generally owned more slaves than they could keep profitably employed, an observation that may reflect the relative slackness outside the harvest season.[27]

It would be valuable to see if the labor regime changed in response to fluctuations in clove prices and the labor supply, but the data are not systematic enough. Observations like those cited above are vague, but they span the 1840s and 1850s, when high clove prices and expanding plantations put a premium on productivity, as well as the 1860s, when expansion had slowed. However, G. A. Fischer, a German with long experience in Zanzibar, argued that the slave shortage of the 1880s, by forcing planters to rely on fewer slaves to pick the same quantity of cloves, resulted in heavy overwork.[28] His argument is logical, but planters also had to consider that increased rates of mortality, desertion, and resistance would reduce the slave supply still further.[29] Indeed, another contemporary, Consul Miles, felt that conditions had improved and the mortality rate fallen as a consequence of the higher price of slaves.[30]

25. Christie, "Slavery," pp. 34–35.

26. Rigby, "Report," p. 334. The same view is expressed in Pelly to Forbes, 12 February 1862, Pelly Papers, FO 800/234; and Grandidier, *Notice sur l'isle de Zanzibar*, p. 13.

27. Browne, *Etchings of a Whaling Cruise*, pp. 434–35; Osgood, p. 51. Similar views were expressed by Speer to Seward, 26 November 1862, US Consul, 4; Loarer, O.I., 5/23, notebook 5; and Journal of Lieut. Christopher, entry for 18 July 1843, incl. Bombay to Secret Commission, no. 54, Ind. Off., L/P&S/60.

28. Fischer, *Mehr Licht*, p. 68. He could have added that falling clove prices, by making it necessary to pick more cloves to maintain a steady income, might have exacerbated the situation.

29. An economist has argued that working slaves to death is in fact an economically rational response to certain circumstances, including low supplies with high interest rates. Nathaniel H. Leff, "Long-Term Viability of Slavery in a Backward Closed Economy," *Journal of Interdisciplinary History* 5 (1974): 103–08. Fischer's observations, it should be said, came in the context of a criticism of British antislave trade policy.

30. Miles to Granville, 1 March 1883, FOCP 4914, p. 124. He claims that the annual death rate was 8–12%, compared with an estimate of 22–33% by Hamerton in 1844. Neither estimate is based on demographic data, and a lowering of the death rate could also

The evidence is inconclusive. However, no matter how responsive planters were to changing incentives, the structure of the plantation economy tended to soften fluctuations in income. The economic downturn of the 1850s had discouraged a trend toward a high-incentive export economy. That the plantation was integrated into a social system which stressed dependency by no means implied that owners would not try to extract more labor from their slaves when they needed it, but it does make it unlikely that they would sacrifice the continuity of plantation life altogether. Nevertheless, such labor "regulations" as the five-day week should not be seen as inviolable rules, but as customs which slaveowners might try to bend without undermining the social structure, and which slaves might try to alter if they could.

However long or hard slaves worked, the essence of plantation labor was supervision. Plantations depended on a chain of command. On large estates, there were three levels of supervisors, called *msimamizi*, *nokoa*, and *kadamu*. The latter two, almost always slaves, dealt directly with the field hands. On a larger shamba, the *msimamizi* was often an Arab, a poor relative of the master, or another landless person. On a smaller estate, he was more likely to be a slave or a freed slave. Other individuals were put in charge of specific tasks. Locally born slaves, termed *wazalia*, were preferred for these leadership roles, and they received certain privileges. The master could come and go as he pleased. As indicated in chapter 2, some slaveowners in Zanzibar preferred an urban life, leaving the supervision of the estate to the *msimamizi*, while others lived continually on the plantation, especially in areas—notably Pemba—that were far from town. Even resident landlords had to delegate responsibility, for the wealthy often owned more than one plantation.[31]

For Muslim slaveowners, the provision of food, shelter, clothing, and medicine was a religious and legal obligation. More important, in order to integrate slaves into the Zanzibari plantation economy, their attachment to the estate had to be firmly secured, while they had to be settled

be explained by arguing that disease would take a heavier toll during a period of heavy new imports than during a low point in the slave trade. Later reports by consuls in Zanzibar provide no evidence of increased workloads, although the vice-consul in Pemba called the Arab "a stern and exacting task-master, often a cruel one as well." Hardinge to Salisbury, 4 May 1896, PP 1896, LIX, 395, p. 37; C. S. Smith, "Slavery," in A. E. M. Anderson-Morshead, *The History of the Universities' Mission to Central Africa 1859–1909* (London, 1909), pp. 406–07; O'Sullivan, "Report, 1896," pp. 41–42.

31. Christie, "Slavery," pp. 31–32; Hardinge to Salisbury, 10 January 1896, PP 1896, LIX, 395, p. 25; Fritz Weidner, *Die Haussklaverei in OstAfrika* (Jena, Germany, 1915), p. 33; Fitzgerald, *Travels*, pp. 588–604; MSA 4, 21, 34. On privileges accorded supervisers, see chapter 6.

in such a way that they would not constitute a burden on their owners. The concentration of land in clove-growing areas in the hands of a moderate number of Omani planters helped give them the ability to create these ties of economic dependence. In virtually all cases, a land-owner provided each slave or slave family with a plot from his estate upon which to grow food and build a hut. The master had to feed new slaves until their crops came up.[32] The attachment of slaves to the master could be further strengthened by the distribution of fish or meat to supplement their diet. Tharia Topan, for example, reportedly gave his slaves fish once a week and beef or camel curry on occasional Fridays.[33]

But most of the slaves' food came from the small plots their owners gave them and which they worked on their own time. Cassava, a root crop that is the staple in many parts of Africa, was the basic element of the slaves' diet. Although dependable and requiring little labor, cassava has a lower protein content than grains and other crops.[34] Slaves cared for their cassava, as well as some fruit and vegetables, on Thursdays and Fridays, and presumably during whatever free time was available on other days. They were often able to produce a marketable surplus of small crops.[35] According to Christie, slaves were allowed to cultivate as much land as they could in the time given them, and they kept goats and fowl as well. Masters, he felt, encouraged slaves to raise their own crops and animals to create an attachment to the estate.[36]

Since only certain parts of a plantation were usually suitable for growing cloves, the master had little to lose and much to gain by foster-ing this kind of dependence. From the master's point of view, depen-dence meant attachment to the estate; from the slaves', a chance to plant what they wanted, to farm at their own pace without the regimen-tation of collective labor, and to feel that they were providing for them-selves. Neither the demands of the economy nor the values of the owner required that all aspects of life be governed by plantation dis-cipline. Here Zanzibar paternalism diverged from that of the United

32. Hamerton to Bombay, 2 January 1842, PP 1844, XLVIII, 1, p. 419; Christie, "Slav-ery," pp. 33–34; India Government, *A Medico-Topographical Report on Zanzibar*, by Robb, p. 16.

33. Topan, "Biography," MS, p. 136.

34. William O. Jones, *Manioc in Africa* (Stanford, Calif., 1959), pp. 6–9, 20–23.

35. Ruschenberger, pp. 34–35; Loarer, O.I., 5/23, notebook 5; Krapf, "Additional Remarks"; Rigby, "Report," p. 334; Capt. H. A. Fraser, "Zanzibar and the Slave Trade," in Steere, *Slave Trade*, p. 17; Burton, *Zanzibar*, 1: 466; Devereux, *A Cruise in the "Gorgon,"* p. 107; Colomb, pp. 373–74; Kirk to Derby, 1 May 1896, FO 84/1453; Fitzgerald, *Travels*, p. 516; Baumann, *Sansibar*, p. 29; Grandidier, p. 13.

36. Christie, "Slavery," p. 33. This system was also used in the British West Indies, but it tended to break down when sugar demanded more land and labor. In the Leeward Islands, planters in the eighteenth century relied increasingly on imported food. Goveia, pp. 136–37; Patterson, pp. 216–23.

States South, where most food was produced by group labor under supervision and supplied to slaves by the master, and where gardens were only supplementary. In this sense, Zanzibari slaves had more personal control over the rhythm of their daily lives.[37]

The extent of slaves' personal control over farming also derived from their ability to take advantage of the opportunities offered. Doubtless, slaves could have learned how to care for a garden, but all the peoples who contributed to the slave population of Zanzibar were already agriculturalists, and most consumed the principal crop of Zanzibari slaves—cassava—as well as other important foods like maize and millet.[38]

Slaves lived together as families in a hut near their gardens. Masters supplied slaves with the modest materials—mainly wooden poles to be used as a frame for mud, and dried coconut leaves—to build a house. Observers generally found the huts were "good sized" and reasonably clean.[39] Scattered among the fields, with building materials readily available and labor supplied by slaves themselves, housing was basically similar to that of free Africans in Zanzibar and the mainland. As with food, slaves largely provided for themselves.

Masters were supposed to supply slaves with clothing, although slaves apparently wore little of it. According to Hardinge, the customary allotment was a shirt or gown every six months for males and two pieces of cloth for females.[40] However, some sources claim that slaves did not receive clothing and were forced to purchase it with the modest earnings of their plots.[41]

Islamic law required the master to care for slaves regardless of their ability to work.[42] Hardinge reported that Zanzibari slaveowners were indeed obliged by law to provide for sick slaves.[43] Another official

37. Genovese, "Treatment," in Foner and Genovese, p. 203. Wood notes that the plots which slaves in South Carolina had during the early days of the colony were taken away from them as the intensity of rice cultivation increased and the level of repression mounted. *Black Majority*, p. 139.

38. George P. Murdock, *Africa: Its Peoples and Their Culture History* (New York; 1959), pp. 295–313. The importance of slaves' prior experiences with agriculture and cattle-raising to life on the plantations is emphasized by Wood, pp. 35–62. He raises the possibility that slaves taught their masters how to grow rice.

39. Rigby, "Report," p. 334; Christie, "Slavery," pp. 32–33; Devereux, p. 107; Grandidier, p. 18; H. A. Fraser, p. 17.

40. Hardinge to Kimberley, 26 February 1895, PP 1895, LXXI, 143, p. 29; Guillain, *Documents*, vol. 2/1, pp. 82–84; Mackenzie, "Report on Slavery and the Slave-Trade in Zanzibar, Pemba, and the Mainland," p. 88; Grandidier, p. 8.

41. O'Sullivan, "Report, 1896," p. 41; Gaume, p. 258; Baumann, *Sansibar*, p. 22.

42. Hamilton, *The Hedaya*, 1: 418; Richard Niese, *Das Personen- und Familienrecht der Suaheli* (Berlin, 1902), p. 44.

43. It was considered disgraceful to evade this obligation by freeing a slave who was unable to support himself. Hardinge to Kimberley, 26 February 1895, PP 1895, LXXI, 143, p. 29; Cave to Grey, 18 June 1906 (telegram), FOCP 8932, p. 771.

claimed that slaves freed by the British sometimes refused to accept the deed of freedom because then no one would support them when they were sick or old.[44] An old slave could be supported by the gift of a portion of the estate to cultivate for his own use while remaining free of obligations to work for the master.[45] There is contradictory evidence from missionaries, however. Bishop Steere claimed that "masters turn out their sick slaves to die or get well as they may, only if they get well they claim them again." Others witnessed several instances of the abandonment of sick slaves.[46] Some masters lived up to the standards of Islamic ethics; others found the cost and trouble too great.

The Prophet Muhammed said that masters should forgive their slaves seventy times each day. The master who beat a slave was warned that he could then only find redemption by freeing that slave. The most serious transgressions of slaves should be punished by the kadi, not the master, for such acts—including theft, illegal intercourse, and apostasy—were crimes against Allah. Crimes such as murder were covered by retaliation or the payment of blood money. If a slave should be killed, the master was protected against property loss, but a master who killed his own slave did not pay blood money: he had destroyed his own property.[47]

But the Koran offered little guidance on the punishment of breaches of plantation discipline. Certain points of jurisdiction had to be worked out between the masters and kadis. The courts tended to leave matters such as failure to finish assigned tasks and running away, to the masters—provided that they did not inflict overly severe punishment.[48] In a letter to the governor of Mombasa, the Sultan of Zanzibar in 1881 defined the jurisdictions: no slave should be given more than ten lashes, and if a slave's crime could not be adequately punished that way, then the case should go to the authorities. In cases of cruelty, the master should be punished and the slave confiscated.[49] Hardinge wrote

44. Rodd to Rosebery, 31 December 1893, PP 1895, LXXI, 143, p. 17; Fischer, *Mehr Licht,* p. 67. An early colonial official wrote that he knew of an upper-class Arab who took a job with the government because he had inherited many old slaves and was obliged to support them. W. P. James Fawcus, "Experience in Zanzibar and East Africa," *Manchester Geographical Society Journal* 24 (1908): 7–8.

45. Mackenzie, p. 77.

46. Steere to Robins, 27 July 1878, UMCA Archives, A1 (III), box 2, fol. 482; Letter of J. P. Farler, 4 July 1895, reprinted in *Anti-Slavery Reporter,* 4th ser. 16 (1896): 49; O'Sullivan, "Report, 1896," p. 42; Le R. P. Horner, letter, 31 October 1877, St. Esprit, 196/XII.

47. Muhammad Kasim Mazrui, *Historia Ya Utumwa Katika Uislamu na Dini Nyengine* (Nairobi, 1970), p. 5; Hamilton, *Hedaya,* 2: 12, 13; Brunschvig, " 'Abd," 1: 29; Joseph Schacht, *An Introduction to Islamic Law* (London, 1964), p. 177, 182, 186–87.

48. The jurisdictional problem was explained to me by the former and present chief Kadi of Kenya. MSA 21, 26.

49. Kirk to Granville, 28 March 1881, FOCP 4626, p. 236.

in 1895 that the maximum penalty a master could inflict on his slave was nineteen lashes or a short imprisonment. A slave could complain to the kadi if excessively beaten, and if the master committed this offense twice, the kadi could force the master to sell the slave.[50]

Other observers claimed that most punishment was inflicted judicially and harsh measures were seldom used by slaveowners.[51] Witnesses, in fact, saw slaves being punished by government officials. For such crimes as escape and theft, they were put in chains and assigned tasks on public works or thrown into prison until reclaimed by their masters. Eleven of the thirty-six prisoners a missionary saw in a Pemba prison in 1897 were slaves jailed for refusing to work, running away, and threatening or quarreling with their masters.[52]

However, other visitors saw stocks on plantations or in towns used to punish slaves personally.[53] It is difficult to tell what went on in parts of Zanzibar and Pemba far from the eyes of kadis and visitors, but such experienced observers as Hamerton, Rigby, Burton, and Christie believed that whipping was not routinely used and cruel punishments were rare.[54] O'Sullivan, however, said that flogging for small offenses was frequent on Pemba, and occasional cases of extreme brutality did occur. Governmental authority was particularly weak on that island, and masters tended to whip slaves themselves, turning slaves over to the government mainly for imprisonment.[55] The government's willingness to handle the masters' problems of controlling slaves hardly meant that the slaves' offenses were studied impartially, but at least it reduced some of the personal element in the punishment of slaves.

Should a master excessively punish his slave in violation of Islamic law or Zanzibari customs, the slave had limited recourse. Hamerton said that if a slave could escape to the Sultan, he would be protected and his evidence against his master received at law. A kadi could order a master to sell a slave if the slave complained of cruelty.[56] According to Hardinge, masters who killed their slaves had to pay one-half the

50. Hardinge to Kimberley, 26 February 1895, PP 1895, LXXI, 143, p. 28.

51. Playfair, "Report on the Result of the Observations and Enquiries," p. 263; Christie, "Slavery," p. 36.

52. Rigby, "Report," p. 331; Devereux, pp. 106–07; Mackenzie, p. 73; Jerome Becker, La Vie En Afrique ou Trois Ans Dans l'Afrique Centrale (Paris-Brussels, 1887), 1: 27; Quass, p. 446; Grandidier, pp. 16–17; Farler to Burtt, 7 November 1897, Friends Archives, London, PZ(F)/3.

53. Miss Allen, "Glimpses of Harem Life," Central Africa 1 (1883): 147–48; J. E. E. Craster, Pemba, The Spice Island of Zanzibar (London; 1913), p. 212.

54. Hamerton to Bombay, 2 January 1842, PP 1844, XLVIII, 1, p. 419; Rigby, Testimony, PP 1871, XII, 1, p. 47; Burton, The Lake Regions, 2: 375; Christie, "Slavery," p. 43.

55. O'Sullivan, "Report, 1896," p. 42.

56. Hamerton to Aberdeen, 2 January 1844, FO 54/6, and Christie, "Slavery," p. 47. See also Joseph Thomson, To the Central African Lakes and Back, 1: 17.

blood money for a free person into the public treasury and were subject to imprisonment at the Sultan's pleasure.[57] However, Donald
Mackenzie, who visited Zanzibar and Pemba on behalf of the British
Anti-Slavery Society, claimed that the authorities, being themselves
slaveholders, did nothing to check abuses, and that slaves were in fact
subject to arbitrary punishments. After the abolition act of 1897, British officals charged with enforcing it received frequent complaints of
unfair punishment from the slaves.[58]

As in all slave societies, the practical limits of enforcing laws and
group norms on individual slaveowners were considerable. Zanzibar,
moreover, lacked a police force and a bureaucracy even if its rulers had
wanted to maintain standards of conduct. In areas most distant from the
seat of government, especially Pemba, the influence of Islamic jurists
was especially weak, and there is some evidence that cruel abuse of
slaves was more common there than in Zanzibar.[59] Nearer the capital,
slaves had some chance to complain if the customs of Zanzibar and the
laws of Islam were violated, but as in most societies, judges came from
among the powerful, not the weak. The desire to increase productivity,
plus the heat of anger at a slave, could counter the norms regarding
punishment. Still, it is important to be aware of Zanzibari notions of
which punishments were right, even if Zanzibaris often did what was
wrong.

Governmental weakness had another meaning, however. In most
American plantation areas where slaves, as in Zanzibar, vastly outnumbered their owners, and even in the Southern United States, where
slaves were most often a minority, police forces, militias, and slave patrols were important instruments of social control. They could catch
runaways and back up the master who was unable to maintain order
himself. Soldiers did imprison or return runaways, but Zanzibari masters could not rely on such reserves: armed forces existed mainly in
Zanzibar town and were not exactly awesome.[60] Divided as they were,
Omanis could not count on mutual support unless the entire system
were threatened.[61] Such considerations would not have deterred a

57. Hardinge to Kimberley, 26 February 1895, PP 1895, LXXI, 143, p. 29.
58. Mackenzie, p. 79; PP 1898, LX, 361, p. 61.
59. O'Sullivan, "Report, 1896," pp. 41–52; Hardinge to Salisbury, 10 January 1896, PP
1896, LIX, 395, p. 24.
60. Newman, p. 185; Burton, *Zanzibar*, 1: 265–66; Adrien Germain, "Nôte sur Zanzibar," pp. 542–43. On the mechanisms of social control in the Americas, see, for example, Dunn, esp. pp. 256–62; Patterson, pp. 31–33, 281–82; Genovese, *Roll*, pp. 22,
594; and Wood, pp. 271–84.
61. The one major slave revolt that is documented was put down with the help of
Hadrami mercenaries (see below). In general, American planter societies were relatively
homogeneous in ethnic terms, while class and other divisions were most often set aside

slaveowner from punishing an individual slave, but for a master to terrorize systematically his entire work force would have been a risky course of action.

In their overall assessments of slavery in Zanzibar, European officials and visitors made it clear that they had not observed overwork and brutality of the sort evident in accounts of West Indian slavery. Similar opinions come from people with different prejudices and experiences, and cover good and bad periods of the Zanzibari economy. These opinions do reflect personal biases and incomplete understanding of a foreign society, but some reveal the insights of sensitive observers.

Hamerton, the British consul during the expansion of clove cultivation in the 1840s, wrote that "the Slave is well fed in general, and ill-treatment or cruelty on the part of the master is of very rare occurrence." So little coercion was used that "the master has little control over his slaves." [62] Rigby, the most vigorous of the official opponents of the slave trade, acknowledged that Arabs were "not cruel to their slaves." [63] Hardinge was struck by the ways in which Zanzibari customs provided "relaxations and indulgences" not found in Islamic law. Limitations on the amount of work required were generally adhered to, while food, clothing, shelter, and medical care were provided.[64]

The one official who felt otherwise was the vice-consul in Pemba during the 1890s, O'Sullivan, who wrote that Arabs were "often cruel" and took no interest in their slaves' welfare other than to provide them with land for their own use. He singled out the case of Ali bin Abdulla Al-Thenawi, who punished a slave who had tried to run away by flogging him and then keeping him tied to a tree on his plantation for seven months. However, other slaveowners in Pemba disapproved of Ali, and O'Sullivan admitted that he knew of other masters whose slaves "appear to be happy and contented with their lot." [65] Conditions may in

---

when it came to controlling slaves. Genovese, *Roll*, p. 24; Patterson, p. 282; Genovese, *World*, pp. 98–102.

62. Hamerton to Aberdeen, 2 January 1844, FO 54/6, reprinted in *Anti-Slavery Reporter*, 4th ser. 14 (1894): 55; Hamerton to Bombay Secretary, 2 January 1842, PP 1844, XLVIII, 1, p. 419.

63. Rigby, Testimony, PP 1871, XII, 1, p. 47. Other consuls held similar opinions. Playfair to Russell, 30 May 1865, FO 84/1245; Rodd to Rosebery, 31 December 1893, PP 1895, LXXI, 143, pp. 16–17; Smith, "Slavery," pp. 406–07; Hardinge to Kimberley, 26 February 1895, PP 1895, LXXI, 143, p. 29.

64. Hardinge, p. 29. Hardinge is wrong in calling the provision of food, clothing, etc., customary rather than legal. Providing food was a Koranic requirement, although the way of implementing it was customary.

65. Hardinge to Salisbury, 10 January 1896, PP 1896, LIX, 395, p. 24; O'Sullivan, "Report, 1896," p. 42.

fact have been worse on Pemba than in Zanzibar. Nevertheless, O'Sullivan's reports should serve as a reminder that paternalistic norms in
East Africa, as in other slave societies, could be forgotten and slaves
subjected to rigid discipline or wanton abuses.

The fact that missionaries shared the opinions about the mildness of
slavery is significant in view of their opposition to both slavery and
Islam and their experience with freed or escaped slaves. Bishop Steere
said, "There are all kinds of masters; some starve their slaves, and some
beat them; but, as a rule, they fare well." [66] David Livingstone described the cruelties of the slave trade in great detail but felt that slaves
who survived the journey to Zanzibar had a better fate in store for
them: "The Arabs are said to treat their slaves kindly, and this may be
said of native masters; the reason is, master and slave partake of the
general indolence." As civilization progressed, he believed, the wants of
the masters would multiply and slaves would be driven harder.[67] Livingstone's last point shows considerable perception—the treatment of
slaves depends less on the race of their owners than on the extent to
which the social and economic system provides incentives to increase
productivity. Such incentives were much stronger in 1870 than in 1810,
but they were still limited by the weakness of the clove economy and
the restricted importance of wealth to Zanzibari society.

Other visitors to and residents in Zanzibar made similar points.
Loarer, a dispassionate Frenchman studying Zanzibar's commerce in
the late 1840s, wrote that slaves suffered greatly en route, but once in
Zanzibar experienced "moral and material well-being." [68] The British
explorer John Speke felt that the material conditions of slaves were better than those of free Africans in the interior, and that the burden of
slavery lay in social degradation and separation from kinsmen.[69]

A few observers were able to see the condition of the slave within the
context of a social system. Captain Colomb, a British naval officer stationed in Zanzibar, thought that the good condition of slaves derived
not only from the "gentle indolence" of their Arab masters, but from
the fact that the Arab was the "feudal chief of his dependents, and

66. Bishop Steere, Testimony, PP 1871, XII, 1, p. 76.

67. David Livingstone, *The Last Journals of David Livingstone, in Central Africa, from 1865
to his Death* (London; 1874), 1: 7. For a similar argument, see Quass, p. 442.

68. Captain Loarer, O.I., 5/23, notebook 5. An American merchant who was also
there in the 1840s had similar views. Michael Shepard, MS log of *Star*, 1844, *NEMA*,
p. 262.

69. John H. Speke, *Journal of the Discovery of the Source of the Nile* (London; 1863),
p. xxvi. Another explorer, Richard Burton, who was particularly acute, also felt that
Arabs generally treated their slaves well. *Zanzibar*, 1: 463–64, and *Lakes*, 1: 370. For some
American viewpoints, see Speer to Seward, 26 November 1862, US Consul, 4; W. G.
Webb to State Department, 11 May 1861, US Consul, 4, *NEMA*, pp. 517–18.

offers them the protection we understand by the term." [70] James Christie, the physician, found the social and moral conditions of slaves in the town, where relationships were impersonal, to be inferior to those in the countryside, where slaves were more like family members. In rural areas, masters and slaves came to a tacit understanding of what they could expect from one another:

> The masters, knowing the latent power they have to control, manage their slaves with great prudence and tact, and never have the least fear of a servile revolt.
>
> The slave knows very well that there are certain orders that he must obey, and that he must do a certain amount of work for his master, but he knows equally well that the master dare not and would not transgress the understood privileges and acknowledged rights of their slaves.[71]

Christie's remarks—coming from a trained and perceptive social observer—suggest that Arabs in the 1870s retained a sense of the slave-owner's role as provider and patron. They used force as the ultimate means of discipline, but did so sparingly. This paternalism contains reflections of Islamic ideals and Omani practices of a previous era, but its continued viability in the 1870s was also the result of the particular form which economic change took. Clove cultivation and plantation life demanded intensive labor for part of the year and dependence for the rest. As a result, the ideology and practice of paternalism was not so much eroded as transformed. A rural landlord, surrounded by dependents who must work for him when he required their help and farm their own small plots when he did not need them, was the new ideal.

The portrait of Zanzibari slavery that emerges from the accounts of foreigners hardly suggests that the Arabs of Zanzibar were kinder people or more indulgent task-masters than slaveowners in other parts of the world. Instead, they point to an adaptation of the master-slave relationship to the rhythms of clove cultivation and rural life. Slave life included much hard work and the constant threat of punishment, but social control also depended on the slaves' attachment to their masters' land and positive incentives. Islamic law and—more important—Zanzibari customs, laid out a set of norms governing the amount of work a master could expect from his slaves, his obligations toward them, and the means he could use to discipline them; but the slaves' means of enforcing these norms on the master were weaker than the master's means of coercing his slaves. Those who might confuse paternalism with benevolence on the part of the masters and submissiveness on the

70. Colomb, pp. 312, 374.
71. Christie, "Slavery," pp. 42–43.

part of the slaves should note that slaves ran away with considerable frequency and that at least one major slave revolt took place, a topic I shall take up later on. Resistance was not merely symptomatic of the oppression inherent in slavery, but it was the major weapon slaves could wield to preserve whatever rights they had. Its prevalence testifies to the uneasiness of the confrontation between the demands of the master for labor and deference, and the desire of his dependents to live their own lives. That visitors to Zanzibar did not find a scene of unmitigated exploitation even in a time when labor was increasingly needed, points to the partial success of this effort on the part of the slaves, not just the limited requirements of the masters.[72]

Grain, Coconuts, and Slave Labor in Malindi and Mombasa

As in Zanzibar, the expanding agricultural economy of the Sultan's mainland dominions created a need for new forms of labor organization appropriate to the scale of production, the particular crops being grown, and local conditions. In Mombasa, where the incentives to increase productivity were least, slaveowners were often content with loose supervision; but in Malindi, where efficient labor led to the greatest returns, slaveowners developed a form of gang labor under constant surveillance.

Kirk, visiting Malindi in the 1870s, observed "gangs of field labourers" at work on the Malindi mashamba.[73] Fitzgerald, the agricultural expert sent in 1891 to manage the confiscated slave plantation of a rich Malindi landowner, described gang labor in some detail. Slaves worked in groups of five to twenty under a headman who was also a slave. When cultivating, slaves worked from 8:00 A.M. to 5:00 P.M. When sowing grain, they began work at dawn. The clearing of new land was done on a task basis—each slave had to clear a fixed area of bush, 100 by 4 yards, each day. Similarly, an area of 200 by 4 yards was

---

72. That slaves in other African societies had even greater rights may have had something to do with their owners' greater weakness. In trying to find why slaves in the West African kingdom of Gyaman were freed of most of their labor obligations after the first generation, Emmanuel Terray rejects the argument that this society had a relatively great need to assimilate new members via enslavement. However, locally born slaves—unlike new slaves imported from diverse areas—were all too likely to unite in the face of heavy burdens. It was safer to allow the children of slaves to advance beyond their parents, where they might be useful in preventing rebellion among a new batch of imports. Slaves in Zanzibar had to face slaveowners who were less threatened from outside than those of Gyaman, but who lacked the strength and solidarity of New World planter classes. Emmanuel Terray, "La captivité dans le royaume abron du Gyaman," in Meillassoux, L'esclavage en Afrique précoloniale, pp. 437–48.

73. Kirk to Derby, 4 April 1877, FOCP 3686, p. 563.

the daily assignment for hoeing.[74] The only tools were a billhook for clearing bush and a short-handled hoe for digging, planting, and weeding—field labor was indeed arduous.[75]

Most informants in Malindi, including descendants of both slaves and slaveowners, also describe this relatively rigid organization of labor. All slaves worked, men and women alike.[76] Slaves usually had to clear one *ngwe*, named after the length of rope used to estimate the size of the plot to be cleared, each day. After that, their required work was done. Informants of slave descent (*wazalia*) generally said that this task took all day, while descendants of free people (*waungwana*) more often, but not always, claimed that an ngwe of ground could be cleared in a morning.[77]

Judging by the wide agreement among different types of informants, the customary limits on workloads were deeply ingrained. In any slave system, there is a point beyond which slaves cannot be driven, and in most cases tacit agreements between master and slave about the limits of the system emerge. Even Jamaica had customary limits on the workload. Yet these limits were very high—up to eighteen hours a day during peak seasons. The United States South—despite its patriarchal tendencies—was part of a competitive society, and even the most genteel slaveowners had little choice but to use their slaves efficiently or face bankruptcy. By custom, slaves had at least one day off per week plus certain holidays, but during peak periods the workweek could average 70 to 75 hours.[78] In Malindi, the pressure on *everybody* to work with such intensity was less, even though Malindi was more oriented toward efficient production than Mombasa or even Zanzibar. The workweek, in the most critical accounts, could not have exceeded 40 to 50 hours, and according to others was considerably less. Work in the grain fields of Malindi was regimented and difficult, but the customary work load was less arduous than on most sugar or cotton estates of the New World.

A second difference between Malindi and many Western plantations

74. Fitzgerald, *Travels,* pp. 28, 31. Later, European planters near Malindi required similar tasks of their "free" laborers. Malindi District, *Annual Report,* 1908–09, KNA.

75. Fitzgerald, "Report," in FO 84/2176.

76. MAL 17, 25, 35, 46. One informant, however, said that female slaves only worked on their husbands' plots, and one said they worked in the home. MAL 12, 52.

77. Wazalia sources on this point are: MAL 24, 31, 34, 35, 51. One mzalia said slaves were made to work even after completing an ngwe; another said they might be given household tasks. MAL 30, 35. Waungwana informants include MAL 17, 18, 37, 40, 44, 46.

78. Patterson, pp. 44, 66–68; Knight, pp. 68, 72–84; Goveia, pp. 111, 123–25, 130–33; Fogel and Engerman, 1: 208; Genovese, *Roll,* pp. 314–15; Stampp, pp. 43, 77–85; John Blassingame, *The Slave Community* (New York, 1972), p. 155.

was the status of supervisory personnel. Although Malindi's planters tended to keep a personal eye on their plantations, the supervision of the gangs of slaves was left to the *nokoa,* a slave headman. Selected from among a master's experienced slaves on the basis of ability and loyalty, the nokoa pointed out to slaves what land they were to clear and kept track of their performance. Rich landowners generally owned more than one shamba and relied on trusted slaves to exercise overall supervision when they were not present.[79] Only once, in oral or written sources, did I hear of an overseer who was not a slave.[80]

Slave supervision was essential to plantations in the Southern United States as well, but a slave-supervisor was generally only a driver, not the overseer, who along with the owner was in overall charge of the estate. In parts of the British Caribbean, where absenteeism was rampant, estates were commonly left in the hands of white managers.[81] Often a young, landless man eager to enter the world of the planters, the overseer lacked the master's long-term interest in the welfare of his slaves and stood to gain by showing short-term profits. Overseers were the most hated figures on the plantation. Of course, slave supervisors had to impress their masters to gain privileges, but with years of close contact with their fellow slaves and with opportunities for mobility only within the bounds allowed for slaves, the slave driver had strong emotional and practical reasons for not pushing the slaves too hard. If he was the representative of the master to the slaves, he was also the spokesman for the slaves to the master.[82] The absence of an overseer from a different racial and social group was a load off the backs of Malindi's slaves.

Informants in Malindi rarely mentioned any of the less rigid ways of organizing labor that were found elsewhere on the coast. However,

79. One planter had an overseer on each of his fourteen mashamba and three manokoa supervising them all. MAL 26. Other sources include the son of a nokoa of a leading planter, MAL 35, and MAL 5, 17, 27, 28, and 44.

80. This overseer was an Omani who supervised the other manokoa on an enormous plantation belonging to Malindi's largest landowner, Salim bin Khalfan. This information comes from the overseer's grandson, MAL 32, and the son of a slave on that plantation, MAL 34.

81. Many plantations in the Old South were relatively small and supervised directly by the owner. Gutman claims that about 3% of slave men held managerial positions in the agricultural sector and that nearly all were drivers. He is critical of Fogel and Engerman's higher estimates. See Gutman, pp. 66–69; Fogel and Engerman, 1: 200–02, 210–12, 2: 151–52; and also Stampp, pp. 36–44. On Caribbean absenteeism, see Carl and Roberta Bridenbaugh, *No Peace Beyond the Line: The English in the Caribbean 1624–1690* (New York, 1972), p. 304; Douglas Hall, "Absentee-Proprietorship in the British West Indies, to about 1850," in Lambros Comitas and David Lowenthal; eds., *Slaves, Free Men, Citizens: West Indian Perspectives* (Garden City; N.Y., 1973), pp. 105–36.

82. Stampp, pp. 82–83; Blassingame, pp. 173–77; Patterson, p. 93; Goveia, *Slave Society,* p. 110; Genovese, *Roll,* pp. 12–14, 378–88.

some sources indicate that on coconut mashamba, slaves received a share of the harvest to encourage them to work.[83] There are also a few recorded instances of slaves farming on their own and providing their masters with regular payments in kind or cash.[84] Occasionally, a single master had some of his slaves working in gangs, some on coconut fields with incentive payments, and some on their own.[85]

Where gang labor prevailed, slaves were given their own plots to cultivate for their subsistence. Their size, according to Fitzgerald, varied from 200 by 10 yards to 200 by 50 yards. Slaves kept all the produce of these plots, as well as any poultry or domestic animals they raised. During the dry season, slaves were given Thursdays and Fridays to tend their own plots. In the wet season, they only had Fridays off but were given a ration of grain each day.[86] Oral sources confirm Fitzgerald's observations, but they do not agree on whether slaves had Thursdays off as well as Fridays.[87] Most informants claimed that masters provided slaves with a daily ration of food and that the produce of the slaves' own plots was a supplement to this.[88] Masters were also expected to provide their slaves with clothes.[89]

The same types of sources that describe gang labor in Malindi present a different picture of Mombasa. Arabs and Swahili did use

---

83. W. J. Monson, "Report on Slavery and Free Labour," PP 1903, XIV, 745, p. 3; MAL 47. However, most wazalia informants said that the master took the whole harvest. MAL 24, 34, 38.

84. Slaves on a large block of land confiscated by Sultan Bargash in 1877 from an Arab farmed in this way, paying the governor, who represented the Sultan as owner of the land and the slaves, a sum called in the records *dachili* (correct form = *dakili*, meaning income from a shamba). a/c 2D of 1912. Such a payment to a civilian was mentioned in the case of *Secretary of State for the Colonies* vs. *Madina binti Jemedar*, Civil Appeal 121 of 1908, High Court, Mombasa.

85. a/c 2D of 1912.

86. Fitzgerald, *Travels*, pp. 31–32; Kirk to Granville, 6 November 1873, PP 1874, LXII, 749, p. 102; statement of Kenneth MacDougall, District Officer in Malindi in the 1890s, to H. S. Newman, reported in letter of Newman, 18 January 1897, *Anti-Slavery Reporter*, 4th ser. 17 (1897): 15.

87. This discrepancy actually confirms Fitzgerald's view that the number of days off varied with the season. Informants have simplified this. The different versions and their sources are: only Fridays off—MAL 5, 24, 30, 35, 37; Thursday afternoons and Fridays off—MAL 17, 34; Thursdays and Fridays off—MAL 18, 26, 27, 38, 44. Wazalia advocated all three of these positions, but most believed slaves only had Fridays off. Slaves working on the specialized task of tapping coconut trees for palm wine got no free days, but could keep and sell whatever palm wine they drew on Fridays. Fitzgerald, "Report," p. 7.

88. MAL 5, 12, 18, 26, 28, 44. One mzalia and one Arab said that slaves did not have their own plots, and the master provided 1 to 1½ *ratili* of grain per day. A *ratili* is about one pound. MAL 34, 37.

89. MAL 5, 12, 28, 46.

slaves on their mashamba.[90] In the 1840s, Krapf observed the Mombasa Arabs settling their slaves in "hamlets" outside of the town.[91] New, in the 1860s, described a "settlement of Mombassian slaves" north of the town.[92] Hardinge, in the 1890s, gave a more detailed description of slave villages. Slaves, not all necessarily belonging to the same master, lived in villages of fifty to three hundred people. They worked their masters' nearby fields on their own, but set aside a certain quantity of grain for their town-dwelling owners, who came to collect it periodically. According to Hardinge,

> the coast Arab shows little energy in protecting his interests, and very rarely visits his land to claim his share of the crop, or to ascertain that his slaves are not keeping it back or selling it on their own account, a practice which I have reason to suspect is by no means unfrequent among them. He is content if a certain number of bags of coconuts or of grain, which he sells to the Indian traders, are sent down to him.[93]

The slave village, with its lax supervision on a daily basis, was in fact one of several ways of organizing slave labor in the Mombasa area. Some slaves worked on their own and paid their masters a monthly or annual sum known as *ijara*.[94] On at least some coconut plantations, slaves were allowed to keep a certain percentage of the nuts.[95]

On some of the bigger mashamba on the outskirts of Mombasa, the demands of agriculture could be similar to that of Malindi. One of the forty slaves of Mwijabu bin Isa El-Changamwe, among the richest Swa-

90. See the testimony of many ex-slaves in the cases brought by the Three Tribes and Nine Tribes of the Mombasa Swahili to obtain title for land. a/c 42N of 1918 and a/c 15N of 1912.

91. Krapf to Coates, 25 September 1844, CMS CA5/016/28.

92. Charles New, "Missionary Notices," *United Methodist Free Church Magazine* 10 (1867): 570.

93. It is clear from the context that Hardinge meant his remarks to apply to Mombasa but not Malindi. Arthur Hardinge, "Report," PP 1898, LX, 199, p. 61. The tendency of masters to stay in the city, leaving their slaves in the country, is also noted by Le Roy, "Zanguebar," p. 465.

94. A judge who heard the testimony of many slaves being freed under the 1907 abolition act described the ijara system as one of the two variants of coastal slavery, the other being the requirement of five days' labor on the masters' fields. Mervyn W. H. Beech, "Slavery on the East Coast of Africa," *Journal of the Africa Society* 15 (1916): 147–48. Specific instances of the payment of ijara are mentioned in testimony, in *Juma bin Farjalla* vs. *Abdulla bin Mohamed*, Civil Case 348 of 1911, Town Magistrate's Court, Mombasa, and *Ali bin Abdulrehman* vs. *Secretary of State for the Colonies*, Civil Appeal 13 of 1909, High Court, Mombasa. The amount of ijara in these cases varied from Rs 2 to Rs 5 per month. An apparent case of ijara is also mentioned in Reg., Msa, 167A 1907.

95. Monson, "Report," PP 1903, XLV, 745, p. 3.

hili of Mombasa, told a land court that the slaves would clear bush and then plant millet. The harvest occurred five months later. In the third year, new ground had to be cleared again.[96] Other evidence indicated that many masters had only two or three slaves working on the relatively small plots that were most characteristic of Mombasa.[97]

The written sources, then, suggest that agricultural labor in Mombasa was organized in a variety of ways but in general supervision was more lax than in Malindi. Oral sources differ considerably. Some claim that Mombasa Swahili owned few slaves and that these worked together with their masters on the mashamba.[98] Another informant said that a few slaves worked on their own and paid their masters an annual rent (one or two bags of maize out of every ten), but most worked under a nokoa on their masters' mashamba. They worked for part of each day, six days a week, but were not assigned fixed tasks.[99] Others claimed that slaves were settled on their masters' land, generally cultivated for their own use, and worked for their masters mainly when a special task requiring collective labor arose.[100] Finally, some informants said that slaves, as in Malindi, worked under a nokoa, each being assigned an ngwe to cultivate each day.[101]

These different ways of using labor reflect the variety of agricultural units in the Mombasa area. The slave villages which observers saw on the fringes of the region probably correspond to what local people call *makonde* (singular *konde*), which are large farms for the cultivation of grain.[102] There, slaves worked on their own or under a nokoa, depending on the town-dwelling master's concern for discipline and productivity. However, such large makonde were unusual in the vicinity of Mombasa, for land was relatively scarce and plots smaller than in Malindi.[103]

The smaller gardens, usually closer to or inside the town and devoted to coconut trees, subsistence crops, and vegetables, are known as *viunga* (singular *kiunga*). Only a few slaves could work a kiunga, and on

96. a/c 15N of 1912, testimony of Farsiri bin Aziz. See also Monson, p. 3.

97. Testimony of Razi binti Rashid El-Jeneby, in case of *Charlesworth and Arsden* vs. *Ebrahimji Allibhai*, Civil Case 35 of 1913, High Court, Mombasa; Musa bin Khamis to Craufurd, 1315 A.H. (= 1897 A.D.), CP/1/67/14; Reg., Msa, 150A 1894; MSA 29, 31, 32; Krapf, Memoir on the East African Slave Trade, 1853, CMS CA5/016/179.

98. MSA 9, 22, 37.

99. MSA 14.

100. MSA 12. Testimony in a land case indicated that the property in that case was divided into twelve pieces, one for each of the slaves. a/c 21N of 1917.

101. MSA 22, 29, 31. Krapf wrote that some slaves were given a daily ration of corn while others were allowed one or two days off each week. "Memoir," CMS CA5/016/179.

102. MSA 3, 14, 29, 22.

103. MSA 17, 19, 35, 37. Oral evidence thus confirms the analysis of plot sizes in the Mombasa area, which showed that large plots, needed for makonde, were rare. See Table 3:5.

this type of farm any of the several informal labor arrangements de-scribed by informants and visitors was likely to prevail.[104] The opera-tion was too small and the potential profits too meager to provide in-centives for a more rigid organization of labor.

The labor requirements of particular crops affected the utilization of labor as well. Much less grain was grown than in Malindi, while co-conuts—which could be profitable even on a small scale—were a major crop. Fortunately for Mombasa's slaves, the coconut tree required even less labor than the clove tree. If slaves kept the area beneath the trees clear of bush, they were doing almost all the year-round labor that their master needed for his cash crop. One informant claimed that a single slave could care for two hundred coconut trees.[105] Coconuts required care at planting and skilled work by tree climbers at harvest. Sometimes the latter task was done by specialists in tree climbing hired in the town and paid a percentage of the nuts. At other times, the plan-tation slaves did this work, but even then, acording to some informants, only certain slaves had to climb trees, and they were given compensa-tion.[106] Whatever the arrangement of the harvest, slaves on coconut mashamba did not face the continuous drudgery of their brethren on the large grain estates of Malindi.

The differences in slavery between Mombasa and Malindi were pri-marily in the size of slaveholdings, the regimentation of labor, and the closeness of supervision. In Mombasa, which had more people and less land, there was less use for large holdings of slaves and less reason to squeeze extra work out of the slaves one had. The economic elite of Mombasa had trading interests as well as farms, and urban life offered attractions which Malindi lacked. Finally, its principal crop required less labor than that of Malindi. The need to develop new ways to orga-nize agricultural labor efficiently was stronger in Malindi than in Mom-basa.

One would expect that slaves would be subject to more coercion in Malindi. However, most foreign visitors did not exclude Malindi from

104. MSA 3, 14, 35. A similar distinction between grain makonde (on the adjacent mainland) and coconut mashamba (on the islands) was made at Lamu. Ylvisaker, "The Lamu Archipelago," pp. 73–74.

105. MSA 32. See also, Kirk to Granville, 22 May 1872, FOCP 4206, p. 55; Hines to Seward, 25 October 1864, US Consul, 5; Monson, "Report," p. 3. In Monson's estimate, three slaves would be needed for 200 coconut trees, which is a good-sized plantation by Mombasa standards. See also the Report on Bagamoyo Mission in Bulletin de la Congrega-tion du Saint Esprit 6 (1886): 1016.

106. MSA 3, 9, 13, 14, 26, 28, 29, 32, 35. The provision of payments for a task re-quiring special skill is consistent with practices in the clove harvest in Zanzibar. There were also specialists in tree climbing in Lamu. Ylvisaker, p. 103.

their observations that coastal slaveowners generally did not resort to force. The most negative view of coastal slavery comes from the missionary Charles New, who visited Malindi in the mid-1860s, precisely the time of its most rapid expansion. He stated that, "The treatment of the slaves was to the last degree heartless and cruel; it was indeed a reign of terror." He claimed to have witnessed slaves being beaten and placed in stocks under the harsh sun, while others were chained or collared with wooden beams.[107] Yet even he admitted that slaves were "not so hard driven in East Africa as they were, say, in America, simply because there is less pressure." Slaves were often treated "with humanity, upon the same principle that many men treat their horses kindly." [108]

Another missionary, Krapf, who lived in the hinterland of Mombasa, emphasized the drudgery and compulsion of slave labor during the period of agricultural expansion. Muslim masters, he wrote, were harder and less pleasant than Mijikenda of Kamba slaveowners, because the latter lived and worked along with their slaves, while the Swahili had their slaves work for them. Slaves worked "under compulsion, lazily, unwillingly, and mechnically." [109] Krapf saw distinctions between different slaveowners in terms of religion and tribal identity, but his own remarks indicate that the crucial difference was between situations where close personal relations and similarity of life-style between masters and slaves prevailed, and situations where a more systematic, less personal organization of labor was dominant.

Other European observers had a more benign view of slavery on the coast. Kirk found mainland slavery, even in Malindi, milder than it was in Zanzibar and Pemba, largely because it was easier for the slaves to escape.[110] The Reverend Henry K. Binns, a missionary with long experience in East Africa, said that cases of cruel treatment were rare, while Mervyn Beech, who judged many slavery compensation cases after 1907, described the life of slaves—obviously with exaggeration—as a "comfortable existence." [111] Hardinge believed that masters did not

107. New Life, Wanderings and Labours in Eastern Africa, p. 166. Greffulhe had a harsh view of slavery in Lamu, comparing it unfavorably with conditions elsewhere in East Africa. Greffulhe, "Voyage de Lamoo à Zanzibar," p. 215.

108. One of the incidents which New described turned out to be the punishment of a convicted thief. New, Life, p. 500; Thomas Wakefield, "Rev. Thomas Wakefield's Fourth Journey to the Southern Galla Country in 1877," Proceedings of the RGS 4 (1882): 371.

109. Krapf, "Memoir," CMS CA5/016/179. See also his Travels.

110. Kirk to Salisbury, 23 February 1880, FOCP 4498, p. 414. He found slaves in Malindi "well fed and seemingly well cared for." Kirk to Derby, 4 April 1877, FOCP 3686, p. 563. See also Gissing to Kirk, 14 September 1884, FOCP 5165, pp. 242–43.

111. Rev. Harry K. Binns, "Slavery in British East Africa," Church Missionary Intelligencer, n.s. 23 (1897): 462; and Beech, p. 145.

supervise their slaves closely and contrasted the coast, except for Malindi, with Zanzibar and Pemba. This laxity stemmed "less from good nature or even Oriental indolence than from a knowledge that the master's hold upon his slaves is too slight to enable him to be grasping in his dealings with them." [112] Fitzgerald, who knew Malindi intimately, made much the same point:

> It is entirely against an owner's interest to ill-treat or overwork them, for if ill-used or harshly dealt with in any way, they invariably escape to the various runaway-slave settlements up the Sabaki and elsewhere in the bush.[113]

More will be said about runaway slaves, but the remarks of witnesses like Kirk, Hardinge, and Fitzgerald make it clear that the balance of strength between masters and slaves—unequal as it was—had much to do with forming the customs and patterns of behavior that governed plantation life.

It is difficult to get beyond these general remarks to specific information about punishment. Hardinge claimed that slaves were rarely punished because they would take this as reason to run off.[114] However, other observers, mainly missionaries, have recorded acts of severe punishment which they themselves saw. Most of them involved slaves placed in heavy chains that barely allowed them to walk or with yokes placed around their necks. One slave boy in Mombasa reportedly was flogged and hung by his thumbs for infractions of discipline. Two others claimed they had been kept in irons for seven months and were suffering from sores caused by the fetters.[115]

Whatever the attitudes of the slaveholders, it is not clear that they

112. Hardinge, "Report," PP 1898, LX, p. 61. Hardinge's ability to distinguish between the conditions of slaves in different social and economic environments within East Africa make his testimony especially valuable.

113. Fitzgerald, Travels, p. 32.

114. Hardinge to Salisbury, 10 January 1896, PP 1896, LIX, 395, pp. 24–25. Another British official said that runaways were not returned to their masters for punishment, but were made over to the Arab governor, and the master was required to sell them if the slave wished to change masters. George Mackenzie to Euan-Smith, 19 October 1888, FO 84/1910.

115. William Yates, Dado; or Stories of Native Life in Central Africa (London, 1886), pp. 22–23; Price to Hutchinson, 29 May 1875, CMS CA5/023/26; Price, Journal, 21 May 1876, CMS CA5/023/76; Menzies to Hutchinson, 31 January 1881, CMS G3/A5/0/1881/24. A recently purchased woman in Malindi was put in chains to prevent her return to Mombasa, where she came from; but she escaped anyway, walking 80 miles to Mombasa in her chains. Russell to Lay Secretary, 7 November 1877, CMS CA5/M5; Price, Journal, 19 February 1889, reprinted in W. Salter Price, My Third Campaign in East Africa (London, 1891), pp. 310–11.

had the means to go beyond this level of oppression. Should a slaveowner in Malindi fail to control his slaves himself—and some owned as many as 250—he could call on only thirty soldiers stationed in the town. At this time—1874—Mambrui had a garrison of 10 and Mombasa 180, mostly to guard the fort.[116] As in Zanzibar, the instruments of coercion were relatively weak and mainly effective against individuals. It is impossible to compare quantitatively to extent to which slaveholders in different societies relied on force and the threat of force to "break" their slaves. But East African slaveowners had less leeway in the use of coercion than their American counterparts. The impressionistic data we have, suggest that, however brutally certain slaves were treated, the routine use of physical punishment to intimidate the labor force was less important than in the more paternalistic American slave societies, let alone the West Indies.[117]

Nevertheless, the stick did make an impression on the slaves. Much as informants descended from planters and slaves agreed on the specifics of labor organization, they diverged on the question of severity of treatment. As one might expect, descendants of slaveowners universally claim that slaves were treated kindly, in accordance with Islamic norms. They do admit that slaves were sometimes punished, however, mainly by beatings with a cane, for disobedience or running away, and most say that only the master himself, not the nokoa, could punish a slave.[118] Descendants of slaves agree that beating was the main form of punishment, but add—as New saw in 1865—that slaves were sometimes put in stocks. Most agree that the nokoa could only refer disciplinary cases to the master for punishment. Slaves were punished for not working hard enough—failing to complete an ngwe in a day for example—but also for running away and for disobedience.[119]

However, the wazalia assert that punishment was severe, using phrases like "adhabu kubwa kabisa," or "adhabu sana" (very big punishment, much punishment). Masters were "kali kabisa" (very fierce).

116. Frederic Holmwood, Report, incl. Prideaux to Derby, 24 November 1874, FOCP 2915, p. 15.

117. The best source on discipline in the Southern United States remains Stampp. Fogel and Engerman try to argue against Stampp's view by relying on a diary kept by one plantation owner, which reveals that the average slave was whipped only 0.7 times per year. However, as Gutman points out, their own data indicate that *a* slave on this plantation was whipped every 4.6 days—a potent lesson for all to see. Systematic intimidation of a plantation labor force is a much better measure of the use of "negative incentives" than the frequency with which any one slave felt the whip. Fogel and Engerman, 1: 145; Gutman, pp. 17–41.

118. MAL 17, 26, 44, 46. Only the last of these informants admitted that punishment could be severe.

119. MAL 30, 31, 34, 35, 61.

When I mentioned that I had been told that masters and slaves used to live together in friendship, an mzalia angrily exclaimed, "Urongo!" ("A lie").[120] Wazalia, however, did distinguish between good masters and bad ones. The better ones treated slaves like members of the family and did not punish them. Salim bin Khalfan and Bi Salima binti Masudi were mentioned more than once as having been kind or gentle ("mpole") masters, and others were graded as "mpole kidogo" (somewhat gentle). Others were judged particularly bad.[121] Against a bad master, slaves had little recourse except escape, for the officials to whom a slave might complain were Arabs and slaveowners too, and would support the master.[122] Some sixty-five years after the abolition of slavery, the memory of cruel masters could still excite strong feelings among the sons of Malindi's slaves.[123]

For the slaves of East Africa, the significance of plantation agriculture was not simply that they had to work longer and harder than free farmers or slaves on small units where their labor was merely supplementary. The plantation—a large, internally structured unit—brought about fundamental changes in the conditions of labor and the meaning of labor-time. Outside of the plantation, small-scale Swahili agriculture made use of collective labor for certain tasks, such as clearing bush, but most cultivation was performed by an individual or a narrow kinship group.[124] Gang labor in Malindi was an entirely different matter: it was done on command, not out of cooperation, and as part of a work group that was unique to the plantation. Whatever the positive incentives in slave labor, discipline came more from the plantation hierarchy than from the laborers' own needs and aspirations.[125]

The work rhythms of the plantation slave were also different from those of the small-scale farmer, slave or free. As E. P. Thompson has argued, the concept of working for fixed periods of time was alien to preindustrial peoples. As hard as agriculturalists labored, their work rhythms generally followed seasonal changes and the requirements of subsistence. The fixed pace and rigid workday of the factory represent

120. MAL 30, 34, 35.

121. MAL 30, 34, 35, 38.

122. MAL 30.

123. This legacy of bitterness can be compared to the narratives of ex-slaves from the Southern United States collected in the 1930s by the Works Progress Administration. See George Rawick, ed., *The American Slave: A Composite Autobiography* (Westport, Conn., 1972).

124. Ylvisaker, pp. 85–86. See also Bujra, "Political Action in a Bajuni Village."

125. Likewise, the development of gang labor was the most important change in older patterns of European slavery, and it was the most hated feature of slave life. After Abolition in the United States, slaves struggled to avoid any form of farm work that resembled the gang system. Joel Williamson, *After Slavery: The Negro in South Carolina During Reconstruction, 1861–1877* (Chapel Hill, N.C., 1965), p. 126; Genovese, *Roll,* p. 323.

an altogether different concept of time, while American plantations were "a halfway house for Africans between their agricultural past and their imposed industrial future." [126] Working from "sunup to sundown," bound to the pace of the slave gang, slaves learned that labor had more to do with their master's dictates than with nature or local needs. Yet the rural setting and seasonal flow of tasks made plantation labor very different from factory work.[127]

In this respect, the plantations of the East African coast occupied an intermediate position between societies where the slaves originated and American plantations. Especially in Malindi, where several enormous harvests were produced each year, slaves did not work according to the seasonal pattern of the peasant—they worked continuously. Still, important phases of the agricultural cycle were performed on a task basis: completing the ngwe, not the maintenance of steady work rhythms, was what mattered. In Zanzibar, seasonal work patterns were more important, for the labor requirements of the principal marketable crop fluctuated so greatly over the course of a year. But a customary work-week developed, even if a customary workday did not. The work rhythms of Mombasa's slaves also followed the cycle of a tree crop, and slaveowners lacked the incentives to develop grain cultivation into a continuous process. But in all cases, the pattern of work was largely determined by the slaveowner's crops and the slaveowner's needs.

It was the predominance of the plantation, then, that set coastal slavery in the second half of the nineteenth century apart from forms of slavery in nearby African societies and from earlier forms of slavery on the coast itself. The Mijikenda, for example, also bought slaves in the nineteenth century, used them in agriculture, and exported maize through Mombasa and other coastal ports. But the scale of export agriculture never approached that on the coast, and plantations did not come into being. Slaves were added onto existing Mijikenda subgroups, and their labor supplemented that of their owner's kinsmen and free followers.[128]

126. As Thompson and Genovese make clear, task-oriented time, as opposed to clock-oriented time, was characteristic of preindustrial cultures throughout the world. E. P. Thompson, "Time, Work Discipline and Industrial Capitalism," *Past and Present* 38 (1967): 56–97, and Genovese, *Roll,* pp. 285–324. The quotation is from p. 292.

127. Clock-time was most important to the gang system, while the task system used in certain circumstances allowed slaves to follow, to a greater extent, their own work rhythms. Most slaves had experience with both systems, and everywhere the work load was such that work rhythms were always brisk. Stampp, pp. 54–55; Genovese, *Roll,* pp. 291–94.

128. Spear, "The Kaya Complex," pp. 162–63, 168–71. Slaves, in the changing Mijikenda society of the nineteenth century, were among the followers of the "new men" who came to power. Like free followers, they contributed in diverse ways to the power of their owners.

Because of the plantation, the organization of slave labor on the coast bore a greater resemblance to labor systems in New World slave societies than to those of the coast's immediate neighbors. However, in some other parts of Africa, the complexity of regional economies or the extent of external demand for agricultural commodities created similar incentives. At times, slaves worked under similar conditions to free people. In other situations, they were settled in slave villages, like those of Mombasa, while in areas where levels of production were high and a small elite was able to gain control over large quantities of slave labor, the plantation system became an important part of economic and social organization.[129]

OLD ROLES IN A CHANGING SOCIETY

Agricultural development throughout the East African coast meant that the role of field hand became predominant over the diverse roles that slaves had long filled in terms of both numbers and contribution to the economy. Nevertheless, slaves continued to perform a great variety of tasks in nineteenth-century East Africa. Although a minority of them [130] were soldiers, domestics, artisans, all-purpose laborers, and concubines, these functions were important to maintaining older conceptions of what a slave was, and to avoiding the confusion of the status of slave with work on the plantations.

As in all slave societies, domestic servants not only did such household tasks as cooking, cleaning, and fetching water, but they were also marks of social status. In Zanzibar, according to Hardinge, nearly every free household had slaves to cook and watch the house. In Mombasa as well, the many small-scale slaveowners employed their slaves in the household as well as in the fields. The wealthy could afford a special corps of household slaves, and these servants were a principal means of conspicuous consumption. Christie wrote that the size of the domestic retinues of Zanzibari Arabs—selected from the owner's locally born slaves—was out of proportion to the work they did in the house.[131] Visitors to Zanzibar saw such sights as a veiled Arab princess going down

129. See my Introduction and "Studying Slavery in Africa." Slave villages seem to have been best suited to situations where, as in Mombasa, masters wanted to enjoy the fruits of slave labor but where incentives were not great enough for them to organize and control it as tightly as possible. In addition, slave villages were means of establishing a protective buffer around a society or colonizing new land.

130. No quantitative breakdown of slave occupations is possible, but the highest estimates of the number of urban laborers in Zanzibar is 10,000 to 15,000 (and the lowest, 1,000 to 2,000), while the total number of slaves was well over 100,000.

131. See Hardinge to Kimberley, 26 February 1895, PP 1895, LXXI, 143, pp. 32–33; Christie, "Slavery," p. 36; Thomson, *Central African* 2: 75; Quass, p. 443, on Zanzibar;

the street on a donkey followed by a half-dozen slave attendants, and "crowds of household slaves" in Arab homes.[132] The Sultan had a vast number of domestic slaves, who attended him in his palace and formed an enormous caravan whenever he went to one of his country estates.[133]

Some slaves were given positions of trust in the management of household and business affairs. There was even a category of slaves known as *watumwa wa shauri*, "advice-giving slaves." Such slaves were likely to be wazalia, locally born and raised within the master's household. The wealthiest Arabs preferred Nubian or Ethiopian slaves for positions of trust, and these Causasian-featured slaves commanded a higher price than field hands.[134]

Since the importance of domestic slaves lay largely in their presence, they probably led a less strenuous existence than agricultural laborers. Even the wealthy lived relatively modestly. As a visitor remarked, "it would severely tax the modest brain of a town Arab to devise hard work for his household attendants, so simple is his mode of living." [135] As in the Southern United States, living in the master's house—as many domestics did—gave slaves more comfortable living quarters and better food than field hands, as well as more intimate personal relations with the master.[136]

---

and Monson, "Report," p. 3; Beech, "Slavery," p. 148; and New, *Life*, p. 499, on Mombasa. A Swahili household studied by Margaret Strobel included four female slaves who did the marketing, cooking, and caring for children, plus two concubines. "The Interaction of Slave and Freeborn Members of a Swahili Domestic Unit," p. 9.

132. Speer to Seward, 26 November 1862, US Consul, 4; Christie, "Slavery," p. 36; Mrs. Wakefield, *Memoirs of Mrs. Rebecca Wakefield, Wife of the Rev. T. Wakefield* (London, 1879), diary entry for 9 December 1870, p. 143.

133. Ruschenberger, p. 52; R. O. Hume, "Extracts from the Journal of Mr. Hume," *Missionary Herald* 36 (1840): 60–62; L'Abbé Fava, letter, 25 July 1861, St. Esprit, 195/11. The many services of the Sultan's domestic retinue are described in Ruete's account of her life as a Princess.

134. Kirk to Derby, 1 May 1876, FO 84/1453; Burton, *Zanzibar*, 1: 467–68; Weidner, p. 33. Various categories of trusted and special-purpose slaves are listed in a pamphlet by a Zanzibari that summarizes informally collected traditions. Abdul Aziz Lodhi, "The Institution of Slavery in Zanzibar and Pemba," *Research Report No. 16*, The Scandanavian Institute of African Studies (Uppsala, Sweden, 1973), p. 6.

135. Nolloth, p. 139; Quass, p. 443; Baumann, *Sansibar*, p. 22; Monson, "Report," p. 3.

136. Mwana Kupona's warning to Swahili wives, "Do not associate with slaves/Except during household affairs," suggests that they did in fact associate quite closely. *The Advice of Mwana Kupona upon the Wifely Duty*, trans. and ed. Alice Werner and William Hichens (Medstead, Eng., 1934), p. 45. The intimacy of free and slave women within the household is also noted by Margaret Strobel, "Muslim Women in Mombasa," p. 323. Male informants also remember the close relations with house servants, even though some admit that relations with field hands were impersonal. MSA 11, 20, 25, 37. For more on house servants, see Kirk to Derby, 1 May 1876, FO 84/1453; Burton, *Lakes*, 2: 369–71; Farler to

This intimacy could have a negative side to it, as Genovese has noted in the case of the Southern United States. It often deprived domestic slaves of life in the slave quarters—their one chance to be out of the sight of whites and to behave in their own way.[137] It is impossible to tell if East African slaves felt this same ambivalence. Yet being part of a household had a different meaning in an Islamic or African society than in a Western one. A person's identity was defined less in terms of his individuality and more in terms of the social group to which he belonged. A household was not just a residence but a social and political unit, and belonging to it carried meaningful rewards.[138]

If domestic servants had the closest relations with their masters, town laborers had the most independence. The demand for laborers in a variety of guises was greatest in Zanzibar, for its growth as an entrepôt in the late eighteenth century created a need for port workers and service employees. Mombasa, a lesser port, had similar but more modest demands for such labor, while Malindi had minimal need of nonagricultural labor.[139] European and Indian firms, which needed workers to load and unload vessels, were legally barred from owning slaves, so that a regular business of hiring out slaves developed. Some free labor was available in the port as well, especially recently arrived Arabs from the Hadramaut. However, Hadramis invested their earnings in slaves, and by the 1870s a large portion of Hadrami port workers had become labor contractors.[140] They would hire out slaves on contracts with provisions like the following: the owner agreed to supply the hirer, an Indian, with twelve slaves for five-and-a-half years for $300. The owner had to replace slaves who ran away or died.[141]

By the 1870s a clear distinction was made between two types of port workers: *hamali* (plural *mahamali*) and *kibarua* (plural *vibarua*). Maha-

Mathews, 26 January 1900, PP 1901, XLVIII, 173, p. 12; Baumann, *Sansibar*, p. 22; Fischer, *Mehr Licht*, p. 67.

137. Genovese, *Roll*, pp. 327–65.

138. Hardinge claimed that the domestic slaves of wealthier Arabs were the least likely to claim freedom when the 1897 law in Zanzibar allowed them to do so, largely because of the amenities that were allowed them in the household. Hardinge to Salisbury, 23 April 1898, PP 1898, LX, 559, pp. 72–73. See also Fischer, p. 67.

139. Hardinge to Salisbury, 12 April 1896, PP 1896, LIX, 41, p. 91; MAL 18, 26.

140. Rigby to Anderson, 11 February 1860, Fort William Proceedings for May 1860, INA, Reel 2; Christie, "Slavery," p. 40; Kirk to Derby, 9 January 1878, FOCP 3928, p. 307; Germain, p. 552. Hadramis did continue to arrive in Zanzibar from their homeland, so that some Hadramis continued to work in the port. Mackenzie, p. 90; Quass, pp. 427–29.

141. Sample contracts included in Kirk to Granville, 27 May 1871, FO 84/1344.

mali were the top porters who did the heaviest work in loading and unloading ships. The master was paid directly, but the actual supervision was done by the merchants' employees. In 1895 there were a few hundred mahamali. The ownership of these workers was concentrated in the hands of a few Hadrami Arabs.[142] The mahamali worked hard, but they were apparently better fed and provided for than other town slaves. Some lived in their own huts, others with their master. The latter might even eat with their owner. If they performed work not required by their master or worked overtime, they were allowed to keep the proceeds. Mahamali, wrote Christie, "form a very distinct class, and look upon themselves as superior to the country slaves and ordinary day labourers." [143]

Vibarua worked on a daily basis, doing any of the various jobs that had to be done in the port or around town—cleaning copra, carrying loads, doing construction work, carrying water, and the like. Slave women, as well as men, did such tasks. The vibarua usually appeared in the early morning at businesses that needed labor, or at the Customs House. The slaves were paid directly by the employer in the evening, who left them to make their own arrangements with their masters.[144] The demand for such workers was high. Christie in 1871 estimated their number in Zanzibar at 10,000 to 15,000, which seems excessive, while Hardinge in 1895 said it was 1,000 to 2,000, which seems low.[145] The hiring out of slaves was a way for a relatively poor, landless person—even a slave—to supplement other earnings and eventually improve his economic position. A slave, wrote Bartle Frere, was a "safe, easy, and profitable investment" for the lower classes. It was possible to buy a slave or two and hire them out, giving the slave part of the wages for his subsistence and taking the rest.[146]

142. Christie, "Slavery," p. 40; Fraser to Egerton, 14 August 1867, PP 1867–68, LXIV, 657, p. 120; Mackenzie, p. 90; Hardinge to Kimberley, 13 March 1895, PP 1895, LXXI, 143, p. 39.

143. Christie, "Slavery," pp. 39–41; Kirk to Derby, 9 January 1878, FOCP 3928, p. 306; Weidner, pp. 30–31; Christie, Cholera, pp. 329–30.

144. Christie, "Slavery," p. 38; W. H. Beehler, The Cruise of the "Brooklyn" (Philadelphia, 1885), p. 174. Burton claimed that shamba slaves were sent to do day labor during the slack season, but all other descriptions of plantation labor indicate that slaves remained on the land. In any case, only slaves living near Zanzibar town would be able to perform both field and town labor. Burton, Zanzibar, 1: 466–67.

145. Christie, "Slavery," p. 37; Hardinge to Kimberley, 13 March 1895, PP 1895, LXXI, 143, p. 39. For other observations on vibarua, see Colomb, pp. 362–63, and J. Frederic Elton, Travels and Researches, p. 46.

146. Frere to Granville, 29 May 1873, PP 1873, LXI, 767, p. 149. Ludwig Krapf, "Memoir on the East African Slave Trade," 1853, CMS CA5/016/179; Rigby, "Report," p. 334; Grandidier, p. 13; Fraser, p. 15; Kirk to Derby, 1 May 1876, FO 84/1453; letter from correspondent, 11 June 1889, Anti-Slavery Reporter, 4th ser. 9 (1889): 124. On

The vibarua received between eight pice per day (128 pice = $1) for young children and fourteen to twenty for youths and adults. The master's share was often one-half, generally more if he also supplied the slave with food and lodging. If the slave was out of work, his master was responsible for his welfare.[147] Most of the time, masters could count on earning $1 to $2 per month from a slave. A slave who cost $30 could work off his purchase price in about two years.[148]

As in cities in the Americas, this type of slavery could lapse into an arrangement that gave the slave almost complete independence on a day-to-day basis.[149] In such cases, slaves paid their masters a fixed sum—often around $2 per month—or else a percentage of their earnings. They lived on their own and sought work by themselves, but custom dictated that masters should care for these slaves when they became sick or aged.[150]

The most independent slaves in many societies were skilled artisans, for the kind of work they performed did not lend itself to close supervision and they were too valuable for masters to risk making excessive demands on them.[151] Slaves performed all kinds of skilled labor—carpentry, masonry, sewing, metal work, door-carving, and boat-building. Masters often insisted on having first claim to the services of their skilled slaves, but allowed them to work for others when not needed and to keep a share of the proceeds. Besides having some choice in determining their working conditions, these slaves earned higher wages

---

vibarua in Mombasa, see Hardinge to Salisbury, 12 April 1896, PP 1896, LIX, 41, p. 91, and W. Salter Price, journal entries for 16 March and 24 December 1875, CMS CA5/023/61, 70. In the household studied by Strobel, female slaves were hired out to Indians to work as cooks, and a deed from 1898 mentions that one Zehra, slave of a Shirazi, was hired to an Indian at the rate of Rs 4 per month for fifteen months. In this case, the master was apparently paid directly by the employer. Strobel, "Interaction," and Reg., Msa, 104B 1898.

147. Hardinge to Kimberley, 26 February, and 13 March 1895, PP 1895, LXXI, 143, pp. 29, 39; Christie, "Slavery," pp. 37–39; Fraser, p. 15; Rigby, "Report," p. 334; Quass, p. 443; Burton, *Zanzibar*, 1: 466–67; Gaume, p. 258.

148. Figuring on the maximum wage of 20 pice per day, the employer would pay just over $3 in the course of twenty working days. If the master was taking half, he would get $1.50 per month. Fischer (*Mehr Licht*, p. 66) gave even more optimistic figures.

149. Wade, *Slavery in the Cities*, p. 48; Mary Karasch, "From Porterage to Proprietorship: African Occupations in Rio de Janeiro, 1808–1850," in Stanley L. Engerman and Eugene D. Genovese, eds., *Race and Slavery in the Western Hemisphere: Quantitative Studies* (Princeton, N.J., 1975), p. 377.

150. Steere, *Town of Zanzibar*, p. 10; Rodd to Rosebery, 31 December 1893, PP 1895, LXXI, 143, p. 17; Thomson, *Central African*, 1: 17; Ernest Cambrier, extracts from his journal of a trip to Zanzibar with the Belgian expedition, 1877–78, reprinted in Becker, 1: 404. On Mombasa, see Beech, "Slavery," p. 148, who refers to such payments as *ijara*.

151. Mullin, p. 83; Fogel and Engerman, 1: 56.

than ordinary vibarua.[152] Testimony in a court case in Mombasa provides a rare glimpse into the life of a skilled slave. Fundi Kheri was born near Lake Nyasa around 1865, and eventually was bought by a Mombasan for $85, a high price. He worked as a silversmith, paying his master about $2 per month regardless of what he earned. He continued to work and pay his master for over a year after the legal abolition of slavery in Kenya and then left to go to Pemba.[153]

Just as slavery was adapted to fit the needs of the urban labor market, so it was flexible enough to supply the requirements of the caravan trade. Although many of the goods from the African interior were brought by African peoples like the Nyamwezi and the Yao, coastal caravans also went inland, especially after mid-nineteenth century. Later in the century, European explorers, missionaries, and—in the 1890s—government officials, required many porters.[154] There was a pool of porters in Zanzibar for hire, who came to be known as "Zanzibaris." Many of them were slaves. The master generally received half of the slave's wage, part of which was paid in advance and the rest at the conclusion of the journey.[155] Kirk estimated that a slaveowner could make a profit of $30 per year from a slave hired out as a porter.[156]

152. Christie, "Slavery," p. 41; Last to Mathews, 22 February 1900, PP 1901, XLVIII, 173, p. 6; Beech, "Slavery," p. 148; Thomas Wakefield, "East Africa," *The Missionary Echo* 1 (1894): 156; "Pictures from East Africa," *Church Missionary Gleaner* 4 (1877): 64; Monson, "Report," p. 4; Hardinge to Salisbury, 12 April 1896, PP 1896, LIX, 41, p. 91.

153. Testimony of Abdulla bin Ritwani re Application of the Administrator General, administering the estate of Bakari bin Marwan, for compensation for his slave Fundi Kheri, case No. 211 of 1909, Town Magistrate's Court, Mombasa. The father of one informant was a door-maker in Malindi, and the father of another, a halva-maker. The one's family was fed by the master, and he received none of his earnings, while the other subsisted from a plot which he and his wife farmed. MAL 24, MSA 37.

154. At one time the British consul complained that 1,900 porters had recently left on British caravans, not counting the larger Arab and German expeditions. Officials feared that the island would be "rapidly denuded of adult male labor." Portal to Salisbury, 12 September 1891, PP 1892, LXXIV, 499, pp. 4–6; Euan-Smith to Salisbury, 1 November 1888, FOCP 5896, pp. 433–34.

155. Colomb, p. 387; Thomson, *Central African,* 1: 67–68; Mackenzie, p. 89; Allen to Salisbury, 16 February 1892, PP 1892, LXXIV, 499, p. 6; Hardinge to Buxton, 26 November 1896, Anti-Slavery Papers, Rhodes House, Oxford University, G. 5; Lord Lugard, *Rise of Our East African Empire* (Edinburgh, 1893), p. 447. As with vibarua, not all of the "Zanzibaris" were slaves. Freed slaves and, on the mainland, local Africans served alongside slaves on the caravans. Cambrier, in Becker, 1: 413; Burton, *Zanzibar,* 2: 111–12; Steere to Robins, 27 July 1878, UMCA Archives, A1 (III), box 2, fol. 479. Porters were also recruited in Mombasa. Jackson, *Early Days in East Africa,* pp. 137–38; Hardinge, "Report," pp. 52–53; Richard Thornton, Journal, Rhodes House, MSSAfr. s49, vol. 3, entry for 23 June 1861; Bi Kaje, interview by Strobel, 17 April 1973.

156. Kirk to Granville, 22 September 1871, FO 84/1344.

Arabs also took their own slaves with them on trading expeditions. Slaves, usually wazalia who had served their master for a long time and acquired his trust, were even put in charge of caravans carrying goods worth many times their own market value.[157] Similarly, slaves often served as sailors on Arab or Indian dhows, and the captain himself was sometimes a slave.[158] Ironically, one of the most important tasks such slaves performed was trading in slaves.[159]

The uses of slaves as servants and laborers illustrate the diverse ways in which slaveowners responded to economic and social incentives. Masters and domestic servants had close contact, while masters and slaves they hired out frequently did not. A master who sent his slave on an expedition to the interior was placing great faith in the bonds of loyalty between master and slave, while the master who hired out his slave as a porter was receiving money but leaving the supervision of the slave to someone with no personal interest in him. Many porters and vibarua were living and working among freed slaves and some free laborers, such as Hadramis and Comorians.[160]

Slaveowners in the cities of the Southern United States faced similar conflicts between the impersonal demands of the economy and the personal nature of the master's control. The ways in which slaves were allocated to urban jobs, industry, and agricultural labor as economic conditions varied suggests that masters were very responsive to market forces.[161] Yet other evidence suggests that Southerners had severe misgivings about a process which "has weakened the close connection of master and servant." To allow slaves to live and work on their own was in most cases illegal, although widely practiced. Such laws and many

157. Osgood, p. 51; Hines to Seward, 25 October 1864, US Consul, 5, *NEMA*, p. 532; Speke, p. xxvi; Christie, "Slavery," p. 35. The explorer William Astor Chanler encountered a caravan in the interior of Kenya that consisted entirely of Zanzibaris who were the slaves of several Arabs. Each Arab furnished six to eight slaves and borrowed trade goods from Indians. The slaves banded together for protection, and the most experienced one served as leader. Each group of slaves traded on their master's behalf. They were poorly paid but could live well once out of sight of their masters. This caravan had thirty men, all armed with rifles, and had been gone five months. *Through Jungle and Desert*, pp. 214–17.

158. Speer to Seward, 26 November 1862, US Consul, 4; Captain Bedingfield, 1 December 1866, FOCP 4201, p. 70; Miles to Granville, 16 October 1882, FOCP 4777, p. 261; Kirk to Granville, 18 September 1880, FO 84/1575; Christie, "Slavery," p. 42; Colomb, p. 59; Krapf, *Travels*, pp. 127–28. Ex-slaves are still among dhow crews on the Kenya coast. Prins, *Sailing from Lamu*, pp. 212–14.

159. Osgood, p. 51; Prideaux to Derby, 19 September 1874, PP 1875, LXXI, 759, p. 67.

160. On freed slaves in cities, see chapter 6; and on Hadramis and Comorians, see Burton, *Zanzibar*, 1: 342, and Quass, pp. 427–31.

161. Fogel and Engerman, 1: 55–57, 101–02; Starobin, pp. 135–37. On Rio, see Karasch, pp. 377–89.

opinions expressed in newspaper editorials and elsewhere suggest the fear that social control would break down outside the context of the plantation.[162]

In Zanzibar, practices were not strikingly different, but there is no evidence of this fear of the masterless slave.[163] While there was a certain anonymity in the quarter of Zanzibar where vibarua and others lived, it was a small city, where slaveowners were likely to have many relatives who knew their slaves, where the Sultan's authority was strongest, and where the available jobs were concentrated in the port and Indian and European areas. Slaves were likely to be located and disciplined if they failed to meet their obligations or threatened the social order, but, on a daily basis, they worked and lived without the owners' supervision. Perhaps masters had less fear of their slaves' independence in day-to-day life because they had more confidence in the reality of dependence—a point to which I shall return.

What did this independence mean for the mahamali, vibarua, and artisans? Employers lacked a long-term interest in the slave's welfare, but slaves did have some choice of employers. According to Christie, most employers of vibarua did not treat them harshly, precisely because they would refuse to work for a bad employer.[164] Some officials believed that slaves enjoyed the chance to manage their own affairs and preferred working in town to life in the clove fields.[165] On the other hand, the work was hard. Conditions were worst on caravans, for the slaves could not change employers in the middle of a trek and so had little influence over their own treatment. Loads were heavy, the pace rapid, and the discipline of the caravan leaders severe.[166] Despite the risks, slaves had some choice over when they worked and got to keep

---

162. Wade, pp. 45–54. The phrase quoted is from the *New Orleans Daily Picayune* in Wade, p. 51. Wade's evidence of fears and misgivings about urban slavery is persuasive, but his argument that this in fact led to a decline in urban slavery by 1850 is controversial. See Fogel and Engerman, 1: 98–102, and papers by Claudia Dale Goldin and Harold D. Woodman, in Engerman and Genovese, pp. 427–54. In Rio, however, a 40% slave population did not seem to threaten order. Karasch, in ibid., pp. 369–93.

163. Christie, "Slavery," p. 43.

164. Ibid., p. 39. Elton, however, in traveling on the mainland, found that some slaves hired by Indians from Swahili slaveowners were worse off than slaves working for their own masters. Elton to Prideaux, 18 March 1874, FOCP 2499, p. 15.

165. Rodd to Rosebery, 31 December 1893, PP 1895, LXXI, 143, pp. 15–17; C. S. Smith, "Slavery," pp. 406–07.

166. For exposés of a scandal involving mistreatment on European caravans, see the *Anti-Slavery Reporter*, especially during 1894. See also Mathews, "Memorandum on Zanzibar Porters," 15 May 1894, FOCP 6557, p. 18, and Allen to Gresham, 2 April 1894, US Consul, 9. On hamali labor, see Kirk to Derby, 9 January 1878, FOCP 3928, pp. 306–07, and Fischer, *Mehr Licht*, pp. 65–66.

half their pay—part of which they received in advance. Above all, a caravan wasn't a clove shamba.[167]

If the confidence of masters in the loyalty of slaves is evident in the independence under which many of them worked, it is even more striking in the willingness of masters to allow their slaves to carry arms. The use of slaves in military and official capacities had long been common in Oman and elsewhere in the Islamic world, and the continued importance of such service in the face of new economic pressures indicates the persistence of older notions of what slaves could be expected to do. In 1811, the garrison in the fort at Zanzibar included between 400 and 500 slave-soldiers. The governor of the island was himself a slave, an Abyssinian eunuch named Yakut. After a long period of service, Yakut was succeeded by another Abyssinian slave, Ambar bin Sultan. Only after Ambar, did Seyyid Said begin appointing Arabs to this post, perhaps because the increasing Arab population of Zanzibar coveted this post. Not surprisingly, the Arab governors had significantly shorter reigns than the loyal Yakut.[168]

Slaves continued to serve as soldiers. In 1844, the Sultan's personal guard consisted of fifty African slaves. Seyyid Bargash had 300 slaves in his army, whom he rewarded by a provision in his will promising each freedom and a gift of $200 on his death.[169] In addition to having a permanent guard of slaves, the Sultan could distribute guns to his slaves whenever a threat arose. Seyyid Majid did precisely that when a split between the heirs of his father brought a threat of invasion from his brother, who was ruling the dominions in Muscat. Majid also called on other Arabs to arm their slaves when danger threatened.[170] The sailors of the Sultan's navy were largely slaves, although the officers were Arabs, some of whom owned the slaves who were manning their ships.[171] As late as the 1890s, the Sultan still had a palace guard of armed slaves, and some of the regular soldiers in his army were slaves of the Sultan, who took one-half of the pay the soldiers were receiving from the recently installed British administration.[172]

167. Zanzibaris who had a choice, wrote a German resident, preferred urban or caravan work to the fields. Fischer, *Mehr Licht,* pp. 65, 70.

168. Captain Smee, "Observations," 1811, reprinted in Burton, *Zanzibar,* 2:492; Letter from Captain Dallons, 1804, reprinted in Freeman-Grenville, *The East African Coast,* p. 198. See also Gray, *A History of Zanzibar,* pp. 97, 126–27.

169. Krapf, "Additional Remarks," CMS CA5/016/25; Will of Seyyid Bargash, reported by Euan-Smith, 7 April 1888, Gray Papers, Cambridge University Library, box 26; Euan-Smith to Salisbury, 31 May 1888, PP 1888. LXXIV, 255, p. 19.

170. Rigby to Bombay, 4 April 1859, Enclosures to Bombay Secret Letters, Ind. Off., L/P&S/5/140; Germain, "Zanzibar," p. 535.

171. Germain, "Zanzibar," p. 538; Speer to Seward, 26 November 1862, US Consul, 4.

172. Portal to Rosebery, 22 August 1892, FOCP 6341, pp. 286–87; Rodd to Rosebery, 3 April 1893, FOCP 6454, p. 84.

In addition to slaves, the Sultan relied on mercenaries from Baluchistan or the Hadramaut to serve in his army.[173] The least reliable group he could call upon consisted of his own Omani subjects, for the notion of a central state to whom all subjects owed loyalty was poorly developed. People supported their own kinship groups in times of trouble, and the Sultan was regarded as an Al-Busaidi as well as a Sultan. He had a degree of legitimacy as a ruler, but it was still necessary for him to rely on followers who were attached to him personally.

As one would expect, the other Omani subgroups behaved in analogous fashion. Internecine disputes were common, although much less so than in Oman, and subgroups mobilized not only their kinsmen but their dependents—clients and slaves—as well. The principal rivals of the Al-Busaidi, the Al-Harthi, relied heavily on slaves for political and military support. In 1854, during a crisis in the ruling dynasty, the Al-Harthi brought a large band of slaves from their plantations into Zanzibar town to demonstrate their power. A crisis was averted only with the help of the British consul and the Baluchi commander of the garrison, who ordered all plantation slaves out of town.[174] Five years later, the Al-Harthi joined forces with Seyyid Bargash in an unsuccessful rebellion against Bargash's brother, Seyyid Majid, who had recently succeeded to their father's office. Again, both fighting parties mobilized their slaves, and many of them were killed in this conflict among Omanis.[175] Dying to advance their masters' political interests, they showed that slaves—even plantation slaves—could still be loyal followers.

On the mainland, central authority was even weaker, being represented only by small mercenary garrisons in major towns, and slaveowning groups had an even greater need for supporters. The types of conflict that plagued coastal society in the nineteenth century were varied. They included attacks by hinterland peoples on coastal settlements, such as the Kwavi raids of the 1850s, and efforts by coastal people to extend their power inland—for example, the Mazrui raids on the Mijikenda. Local Swahili and Arab groups in Mombasa, Lamu, and elsewhere often resisted Omani authority, and some individuals, such as Suleiman bin Abdalla Al-Mauli, tried to set themselves up as local potentates independent of the Zanzibari sultanate. Ancient rivalries—for

---

173. The Sultan himself told the British consul that he relied on mercenaries because he could not trust Omanis. Hamerton to Willoughby, 20 August 1841, FO 54/4.

174. Gray, *Zanzibar*, p. 276. .

175. Rigby to Bombay, 4 April 1859, Enclosures to Bombay Secret Letters, Ind. Off., L/P&S/5/140; Ropes to State Department, 20 October 1859, US Consul, 4. Another incidence of slaves fighting on behalf of their masters is described in the case of the conflict between the Maviti and the Arabs and Indians of Kilwa. Churchill to Secretary of the Government of Bombay, 4 March 1868, FOCP 4202, p. 138.

example, that between Lamu and the nearby island of Pate—continued and were exacerbated as each side sought new allies. Even within communal groups, power struggles between factions took place—for example, between two factions among the Mazrui. In these cases, alliances—often shifting—among Arabs, Swahili, and inland Africans were formed, but each group invariably depended on its ability to mobilize its members and their followers. Political stability—as in Malindi—depended more on the balance of power among local groups than on governmental authority or common acceptance of the state.[176]

In Malindi, despite the planters' common economic interests, slaves remained important as loyal followers and soldiers. When Islam bin Ali Al-Kathiri, the Hadrami settler in Mambrui, fell into his dispute with the Omani governor, he went to Zanzibar to buy slaves who knew how to use guns. Suleiman bin Abdalla's challenge to Zanzibari authority depended on the armed strength of his slaves—who were also making him one of the leading grain-producers in the area.[177]

The political and military importance of slaves was greatest among the coast's most obstreperous group, the Mazrui, especially those led by Mbaruk bin Rashid of Gazi. Forced from Mombasa in 1837, they not only had to cope with strong Mijikenda subgroups in the hinterlands of their new homes, but remained anxious to reassert their former power. Mbaruk instigated major confrontations with Mombasa in the 1870s and 1880s and with the British in 1895–96. Mbaruk's Mazrui supporters recruited a wide variety of followers: converts to Islam from nearby Mijikenda, freed slaves, escaped slaves from rival coastal peoples, and others. They also purchased large numbers of slaves. The Mazrui's military requirements did not stand in the way of agriculture: slaves farmed under Mazrui headmen or on their own.[178] But whenever trouble flared up or the Mazrui went on one of their campaigns against their enemies, many of their slaves were given arms and fought side by side with their masters. Some slave-soldiers rose to positions of command. The evidence indicates that they fought loyally, especially in the rebellion of Mbaruk against the British. After his defeat, many slaves who could easily have deserted their hapless masters returned or

176. The best studies of conflict on the mainland coast are Spear; Ylvisaker; McKay, "Southern Kenya Coast," and Koffsky, forthcoming dissertation on Takaungu.

177. MAL 18, 26, 40. See also the biographies of these men in chapter 3. Suleiman was allied with Khamis bin Kombo, a Swahili of Mombasa, who himself had a large following of armed slaves. Price, Journal, 17 February 1889, reprinted in W. S. Price, p. 310; and n. 179, below.

178. Ludwig Krapf, Journal, entry for 24 June 1845, CMS CA5/016/168; Gissing to Kirk, 14 September 1884, FOCP 5165, pp. 240, 247; Report of Holmwood, incl. Zanzibar Annual Report, 1873–74, FOCP 2915, p. 86; Rashid bin Salim to Hinde, 29 October 1908, CP/1/62/46.

followed Mbaruk into exile in Tanganyika.[179] Mazrui slaves were evidently followers.[180]

One can find examples of slaves being used for military purposes in the Western Hemisphere too: the inclusion of slaves who were given promises of freedom in militias in the French Antilles; the use of slaves to fight Indians in the early days of South Carolina; or the reliance of some Brazilian slaveholders on their *bravi*, slaves, free blacks, mulattoes, and Indians, in the interfamily feuds that were endemic to the Brazilian aristocracy.[181] Yet, as colonial governments became more entrenched and the exploitation of slaves more intense, giving arms to slaves became a desperate last resort. On the contrary, the police forces of the state and paramilitary organizations of whites became increasingly directed against slave runaways and rebels.

Part of the difference was that slaves were not needed in the role of soldiers. Feeble as colonial and settler governments sometimes were, they were at least recognized as central authorities and could be expected to provide a measure of security.[182] On the coast of East Africa, communal and kinship groups relied on their collective strength for

179. On the role of slaves in the Mazrui rebellion, see the following letters of Hardinge: 1 May, 13 November 1895, and 17 February, 12 April 1896, in PP 1896, LIX, 41, pp. 1–2, 48, 62, 92. Some slave-soldiers rose to high rank in the Mazrui forces, notably Akida Songoro, a leading commander. Khamis bin Kombo Al-Mutafi, a leader of one of the twelve tribes of Mombasa and an ally of the Mazuri, similarly had 300 "armed slaves and retainers." Hardinge to Salisbury, 12 April 1896, ibid., p. 87; MacDougall to Piggott, 8 January 1896, CP/1/75/46. Koffsky's forthcoming study will also shed much light on political and social relationships among the Mazrui and their followers.

180. Farther south, the Swahili of the Mrima made use of slaves in fighting, while in the interior, Arab and Swahili trader-chiefs relied heavily on slaves, freed slaves, and other people detached from their own communal groups. Burton, *Lakes*, 1: 17, 2: 328–29; Melvin Page, "The Manyema Hordes of Tippu Tip," *International Journal of African Historical Studies* 7(1974): 69–84.

181. Wood, pp. 125–26; Freyre, *The Masters and the Slaves*, p. 312. Rather than arm slaves, American slaveowners generally preferred to use free blacks or blacks who were promised freedom. They needed to separate their supporters from their slaves, and at times sought to recruit mulattoes or free blacks as allies *against* their slaves. Leo Elisabeth, "The French Antilles," and Gwendolyn Midlo Hall, "Saint Domingue," in David Cohen and Jack Greene, eds., *Neither Slave Nor Free: The Freedmen of African Descent in the Slave Societies of the New World* (Baltimore, 1972), pp. 136, 173. In Venezuela, the need to recruit slaves and runaways into the armies fighting a civil war contributed to the collapse of the plantations. John V. Lombardi, "The Abolition of Slavery in Venezuela: A Non-Event," in Toplin, ed., *Slavery and Race Relations in Latin America*, pp. 232–33.

182. Where the state was extremely weak, as in medieval Europe, feudal lords relied on personal dependents—including, at times, slaves—for military support. Where Portuguese settlers were even more isolated than in Brazil, they recruited slave-armies. Bloch, *Feudal Society*, 1: 256; Allen Isaacman, *Mozambique: The Africanization of a European Institution: The Zambese Prazos, 1756–1902* (Madison, Wisc., 1972), pp. 54–55.

protection, while individuals venturing outside areas where their own social groups were stronger relied on personally loyal followers. But the use of slaves as soldiers in East Africa also shows an absence of fear of what they could do with their weapons that would strike the most paternalistic planter of the United States South as utter folly. This confidence—and the fact that it was not betrayed—is evidence that paternalism in East Africa was not a mere rationalization. Through their ties to their masters, slaves formed part of a social and political unit. Ties of dependence, the most salient dimension of Omani slavery, remained important, even as slaves became more valuable as laborers.[183]

From the slave's point of view, loyal service made good sense. If he could offer his master support, the master could offer him protection.[184] Not only did he belong to his master's own set of retainers, but through the master he belonged to the wider communal group: a slave of a Mazrui was himself a Mazrui and could benefit from the security offered by membership in a strong communal group. Deserting or rebelling against the masters would have required joining another similar group for protection. In fact, as noted below, many slaves who ran away did just that. Service was not only a realistic response to communal politics and conflict on the coast but was consistent with the political experiences of slaves in their homelands. Most coastal slaves came from peoples like the Yao, Nyamwezi, and Shambaa, who were undergoing conflict and political restructuring in the nineteenth century. Conflict was so intense that membership in a kinship group did not provide sufficient security, and free people needed the protection of a powerful chief. These patrimonial chiefs extended their own kinship networks to include other free followers and slaves as well.[185] This is not to say that the link between chief and free follower was the same as that between master and slave, but only that the slaves on the coast were all too aware of the consequences of failing to have a protector who was sufficiently powerful.

183. Prevalent as the slave-soldier is in Islamic countries, his role cannot be attributed to the content of Islam. Rather, the political organization of society is the most important variable, and slaves frequently served as soldiers in non-Muslim African societies where chiefs and kings had similar needs for personally loyal followers. Except for slave-soldiers belonging to the Sultan, coastal slaves used in fighting do not seem to have been military specialists, and no training programs for slave-soldiers existed, as with the Mamluks and Janissaries of the Middle East. Military action was one part of the functions of a follower, not a specialized task.

184. Living on outlying plantations, slaves were likely to be the first victims of an attack directed against their masters. Such was the case with Galla raids on Malindi. Kirk to Granville, 6 November 1873, PP 1874, LXII, 749, p. 103; Gissing to Kirk, 14 September 1884, FOCP 5165, p. 243.

185. Among the best studies of conflict and political recruitment in the East African interior are Feierman, *Shambaa Kingdom;* Alpers, "Trade, State and Society among the Yao," and Andrew Roberts, "The Nyamwezi," in Roberts, *Tanzania before 1900*, pp. 117–50.

Dependence on their owners for protection was not a happy situation for coastal slaves, but once torn away from their homelands, the alternatives were few. Masters, as well as slaves, knew this, and it was a major underpinning of the slaveowners' hegemony. The slaves' need for incorporation into a collectivity was the reason why their masters had the confidence to give them arms, and it was vital to maintaining discipline where the forces of physical repression were comparatively weak.[186]

Just as the military role of slaves reveals the continued political needs of the masters, so the role of slave women as concubines points to the social importance of dependents. Miscegenation was part of all slave societies, the sexual dimension of the subordination of slaves to their masters. Compared with both Catholic and Protestant societies of the Western Hemisphere, the important feature of miscegenation on the East African coast was that it was fully accepted within the norms of upright conduct, that it was regulated by law, and that the offspring of such unions were regarded as legitimate.

Islamic law, in contrast to its neglect of rules governing work, regulated sexual conduct with considerable precision. For the free woman, the only legal way of having sexual relations was marriage. The man, however, was allowed to marry four wives and keep concubines, who had to be his own slaves. Any female slave was legally at the sexual disposal of her master, although on the East African coast the consent of woman was apparently required.[187] By law, the child of a concubine by her master, provided he acknowledged his paternity, was free and equal before the law to the children of the master's free wives. A concubine who had borne her master's child was given a special status, *um wallid*, could not be sold, and would be freed upon her master's death.[188]

An indication of how much concubines were valued is the price the people of Zanzibar paid for them. In 1877, concubines sold for anything from $80 to $700, while laboring slaves fetched only $30 to $60.

186. Bloch links the need for protection with the origins of another form of dependency and oppression—serfdom (*Feudal Society*, 1: 255). The connection of the slave's marginal status to his utility as a soldier is also made in Meyers's study of Moroccan slave armies, "The ʿAbīd 'L-Buhārī."

187. Schacht, *Islamic Law*, p. 178; Hardinge to Salisbury, 23 April 1898, PP 1898, LX, 559, p. 77; MSA 21. The advantages of being a concubine—freedom for one's children and eventually for oneself—made refusal unlikely, while the atmosphere of slavery was not conducive to free choice in any case. Female slaves who were not concubines faced much the same drudgery as males—agricultural labor, menial jobs, and domestic service. See Newman, *Banani*, pp. 35–36; Charmetant, *D'Alger à Zanzibar*, p. 142; Cambrier, in Becker, 1: 404; Mackenzie, pp. 81, 88; Smith, pp. 406–07.

188. Brunschvig, p. 28; Hamilton, *Hedaya*, 1: 435; Weidner, pp. 4—5.

In the closing days of the slave trade, a shamba slave sold for £5 to £8, a *hamali*, £6 to £10, a slave for supervisory jobs, £8 to £12, a domestic servant, £12 to £25, and a concubine, £15 to £50.[189] In other words, slaves who were consumption items were worth more than slaves who were factors of production, and concubines were the most expensive of all.

Among the ordinary Arabs of Zanzibar, African concubines were numerous; the children of concubines may well have outnumbered the offspring of free wives.[190] According to a missionary, a concubine was usually chosen as a young girl and taken into the home. She was treated more or less as equal to the freeborn children until she reached puberty. She was then put into seclusion for a certain time and taken into the harem. If she had a child, she would be treated almost the same as a freeborn wife. If she did not, the master could marry her off to another slave or sell her.[191] Children of these mixed unions were not regarded as half-castes but as Arabs, and were the legal equals of their half-brothers and sisters by freeborn wives.[192]

On the mainland coast, African concubines were also common.[193] Evidence from court cases and interviews indicates that concubines— especially if they had borne a child—were generally treated in the same manner as free wives. If a concubine failed to bear children, however,

189. Kirk to Derby, 4 December 1877, FOCP 3928, p. 285; General Mathews, Memorandum, 23 April 1891, FO 84/2153. Other estimates—from 1811 onward—indicate that female slaves generally cost more than males, and attractive girls intended for concubinage were consistently the most expensive. Smee, "Description of the Island of Zanzibar," Ind. Off., L/MAR/c/586, p. 104; Lieut. A. B. Kemball, "Papers Relative to the Measures Adopted by the British Government between the years 1820 and 1844, for affecting the Suppression of the Slave Trade in the Persian Gulf," *Bombay Records*, N.S. 24 (1856): 649; Horace Putnam, Journal, August 1849, *NEMA*, pp. 427–28; Burton, *Lakes*, 2: 376; Elton, p. 55; Kersten, *Von der Deckens Reisen*, 1: 80.

190. Hardinge to Salisbury, 23 March 1898, PP 1898, LX, 559, p. 65; Devereux, p. 98; Mansfield to Hay, 28 April 1900, US Consul, 10; R. P. Waters, Journal, 24 May 1837, cited by Philip Northway, "Salem and the Zanzibar-East African Trade," *Essex Institute Historical Collections* 90 (1954): 382; Burton, *Zanzibar*, 1: 374; O'Sullivan, "Report," p. 41. Indians also cohabited with African women and left them to a friend or sold them when they left Zanzibar. Hamerton to Bombay Secretary, 15 February 1850, FO 84/830.

191. Emily Hutchinson, "Report to Monthly Meeting, 7 April 1909," Minutes, Vol. 2, Society of Friends Archives, London, PZ(F)/3. See also Kersten, 1: 81.

192. Hardinge to Salisbury, 28 March 1898, PP 1898, LX, 559, p. 65; Hardinge to Kimberley, 26 February 1895, LXII, 143, p. 29; O'Sullivan, "Report 1896," PP 1896, LIX, 395, p. 41; Burton, *Zanzibar*, 1:464.

193. Emery to Cooley, 5 February 1834, Emery Papers, RGS, London; Newman, *Banani*, p. 132; MSA 3, 11. Court records and registers of deeds contain references to concubines or children of concubines. Marriage, as opposed to concubinage, with freed slaves also took place. Such couples are mentioned in 17B 1895 and 136B 1897, Reg., Msa.

her status might—although not always—decline to that of a domestic, and she could be sold or married to someone else.[194] Concubines' children were legitimate and were regarded as Arabs or Swahili.[195]

The Koranic rules of descent did not always ensure that the children of concubines would be treated as social equals, however.[196] Strobel notes that in Mombasa their status was ambivalent, and that they therefore acquired familiarity with the social worlds of both the slaves and the free.[197] The gradations of status could be fine, depending on the person's ability to demonstrate that he or she belonged to the proper cultural milieu, as well as on the origins of the mother (local, Central African, or Ethiopian) and the way the father and his relatives chose to regard the child. The heritage of concubinage is evident and openly acknowledged in some leading Arab families. Such distinctions meant less in a town like Malindi—a frontier town settled by ambitious, and largely male, planters. There, full-fledged members of the wealthiest and most respected local families were borne of African slave women.[198]

The other extreme, according to an anthropological study by Abdul Hamid M. el-Zein, was found in Lamu. The sons of concubines were regarded as members of their father's kinship groups but not as the equals of their half-brothers by his free wives; daughters of concubines were slaves. Lamuans expressed their superiority over outsiders in terms of religious purity. They believed that a free mother was like a cooking vessel that would cook whatever her husband put inside her, while a slave mother was like a fire and would burn—render impure— the child of a Lamuan.[199]

It is not surprising that the inward-looking society of Lamu would have a more rigid view of purity than the agricultural outpost of Malindi or the cosmopolitan center of Mombasa. Nevertheless, it is unclear whether the evidence of el-Zein's informants applies to the period be-

194. *Halima binti Juma* vs. *Salim wa Ba Kassim Mazrui*, Civil Case 151 of 1903, Town Magistrate's Court, Mombasa; Chief Justice R. H. Hamilton to Combe, 5 September 1909, KNA, Judicial/1/201; *Fatuma binti Shahaleck Baluchi* vs. *Amina binti Vale and Nyanya binti Khamis*, Civil Case 341 of 1902, Town Magistrate's Court, Mombasa; MSA 11; Bi Kaje, interview by Margaret Strobel, 17 April 1973.

195. MSA 3, 11; MAL 18, 28, 43, 61.

196. Examples of discrimination against the children of concubines in other Islamic areas are cited by Goldziher, *Muslim Studies*, pp. 120–21, and Lewis, *Race and Color in Islam*, pp. 94–95.

197. Strobel, "Women's Wedding Celebrations," pp. 36–37.

198. MSA 3, 11; MAL 18, 28, 43, 61. McKay's findings on the southern Kenyan coast are similar to mine on the Malindi area. McKay, p. 119.

199. Abdul Hamid M. el-Zein, *The Sacred Meadows: A Structural Analysis of Religious Symbolism in an East African Town* (Evanston, Ill., 1974), pp. 31–33.

fore the abolition of slavery. Lamu has since fallen on harder times than other coastal towns, and its citizens see their decline in terms of a loss of purity. The theme of the purity-of-days-gone-by may be more of a sentimental view of the past than a nineteenth-century reality.[200]

However varied the actual social standing of concubines and their offspring, slaveowners were not oblivious to color. The slave market offers contradictory evidence. Brown Ethiopians and, above all, white Circassians and Georgians, were expensive indulgences for the elite of Zanzibar. Ethiopians sold for $40 to $150 in the 1840s, as much as $200 to $500 in the 1880s.[201] Brown and white concubines were important parts of the Sultan's entourage. Seyyid Said possessed sixty to seventy, and his sons and successors, Majid and Bargash, were borne of Circassian and Ethiopian mothers respectively.[202] Bargash supposedly had 44 women in his harem, and his will provided that at his death all concubines from foreign countries be offered free passage home, while those who wished to stay in Zanzibar be provided for.[203]

Concubines, then, were a source of sexual pleasure and a mark of status, but also a part of family life. In a society that was divided into kinship and communal groups, the strength of such groups was an essential part of politics. The size and composition of the household was a better indicator of prestige and influence than income and material goods. The price structure for slaves—in contrast to that of the Southern United States—emphasized the importance of women and their offspring.[204] Reproduction was a political and social act.

200. Ylvisaker's historical study of Lamu shows a society that was pragmatic in its relations with surrounding peoples and was closely connected culturally, politically, and economically with nearby Africans—non-Muslim as well as Muslim.

201. Captain Guillain, "Rapport Commercial," O.I., 2/10, vol. 1; Letter from a correspondent in Zanzibar, 11 June 1889, *Anti-Slavery Reporter*, 4th ser. 9 (1889): 124; Burton, *Zanzibar*, 1:467–68.

202. Farsy, *Seyyid Said bin Sultan*, pp. 10–13; Seward to Bombay, 4 August 1866, FO 54/23. For a fascinating glimpse of relations among these women of diverse origins and races, see the memoir by Seyyid Said's daughter. She claims that spite and jealousy characterized the interaction of these groups, but that the children made no distinction of color. Ruete, pp. 32, 34–35.

203. Msgr. R. de Courmont, "Le sultanat de Zanguebar," p. 383; Euan-Smith to Salisbury, 31 May 1888, PP 1888, LXXIV, 255, p. 19. The ruling family's desire for concubines from northern areas caused much embarrassment to British officials, who were trying to stamp out the trade in slaves in the opposite direction. Kirk to Derby, 21 February 1876, FO 84/1452; Miles to Granville, 27 September 1882, FOCP 4777, p. 252; Kirk to Bombay, 4 October 1869, FO 84/1307. Eunuchs were also used in the harems of the elite. Ruete, p. 12; Mackenzie, p. 91; Kirk to Granville, 7 April 1885, FO 84/1725.

204. Despite his exaggeration, Krapf's comment is revealing: "Every increase of property is immediately applied for the augmentation of wives and concubines." "Memoir on the East African Slave Trade," 1853, CMS CA5/016/179, pp. 49–50. On the other hand, male slaves in the United States were worth more than female, and slave prices in fact

The effects of concubinage on the social structure of the coast also differed from that of miscegenation in the Western Hemisphere. In the United States South, the children of illicit liaisons between masters and slaves were legally and socially defined as Negroes—the same as pure black slaves or ex-slaves. Elsewhere in the Americas, such children were called mulattoes or put in some other intermediary category, but they were still illegitimate and still slaves unless specifically freed by their master-father.[205] In neither case was the child of such a relationship considered a member of the father's family. However, under Islamic law, as actually practiced in East Africa, the children of concubines by their masters were legitimate and belonged to their father's communal group. Even if el-Zein's view of Lamu is valid, the son of a concubine still belonged to his father's kinship group. This fact influenced the nature of race relations in East Africa. Color prejudice clearly existed; it was expressed crudely in the market place and in the preference for light-skinned slaves for sensitive tasks as well as for concubines. But that is not the same as saying that race defined the boundaries of social groups. What counted most on the East African coast was who one's protector was and what communal group one belonged to, not what color one was. As long as the children of black women and brown men took the ethnic affiliation of their fathers, color was a poor guide to determining a person's social group.[206]

What, then, was a slave? He or she could be a field hand working in a gang under the master's eye, or an urban laborer working on his or her own. He could be a caravan leader, whom his master trusted to serve him in distant lands, or he could be a caravan porter on whom the master counted for money and little else. He or she could be a domestic servant, whose presence contributed to the prestige of the household, or he could be a retainer on whose loyalty the master relied whenever conflict arose. She could be the mother of her master's child. The common feature of all these roles is subordination.

Agriculture required a dependent work force, always present on the plantation even if the intensity of labor varied. Urban laborers had much freedom in their daily lives, but only because masters could count

---

followed quite closely the pattern of annual net earnings that could be expected from a slave of any given age and sex. Fogel and Engerman, 1: 76.

205. Winthrop D. Jordan, "American Chiaroscuro: The Status and Definition of Mulattoes in the British Colonies," in Foner and Genovese, pp. 189–201; and Degler, *Neither Black nor White*.

206. The dark color of Zanzibari Arabs was noted by Ruschenberger, p. 38; Rigby, "Report," pp. 328, 331; and Edward Vizetelly, *From Cyprus to Zanzibar by the Egyptian Delta* (London, 1901), p. 393.

on their loyalty. Both rural and urban sectors responded to the demands of the labor market, and the tightness of the master-slave bond adjusted to the situation. A concubine might be treated as the equal of a wife, but only because of her contribution to the household. The social and political dimensions of subordination were not always salient, but they were always there.

SLAVE RESISTANCE IN A PATERNALISTIC SOCIETY

To emphasize the ties that bound slaves to their masters is not to say that slaves passively accepted their owners' conception of paternalism, but only that they were unable to deny it altogether. Most worked to build a life of their own within the structure of paternalism—a process to be described in the following chapter—but substantial numbers took great risks to flee a situation they could not frontally attack. Escape, the most common form of resistance on both islands and mainland, was the slaves' principal means of restraining the masters' desire to increase productivity in an expanding plantation economy. The prevalence of resistance throughout the nineteenth century suggests that skirmishing along the boundaries of mutual expectations was continuous and that the customary duties and rights of slaves were in part the outcome of such struggles.

It is impossible to quantify the extent of acts of resistance on Zanzibar and Pemba, but it is clear that they were not isolated instances. Resistance occasionally took the form of committing crimes for which the masters were responsible by law. Burton said that slaves in Zanzibar town had been seen around fires, adding fuel and singing and dancing with delight. Some slaves even murdered their masters.[207]

More commonly they ran away. According to Loarer, most runaways were recent arrivals in Zanzibar.[208] Although an island, Zanzibar offered opportunities for escape. One of the few European visitors to the south of Zanzibar, a coral area where cloves did not grow, found es-

207. Burton, *Lakes*, 2: 331, 374–75. Similar actions by New World slaves are described by Patterson, pp. 261–66; Knight, p. 78; and Blassingame, pp. 107–08.

208. Loarer, O. I., 5/23, notebook 5. However, in a group of ten escapees from Pemba whom the British picked up thirty years later, half had been born on the island. Kirk to Salisbury, 8 May 1878, PP 1880, LXIX, 313, p. 227. In the New World, recent arrivals were also among the most likely to escape. The most acculturated slaves also ran away often, although frequently to cities where their knowledge of their masters' ways would enable them to disappear. Slaves in the middle were the least likely to escape or rebel. Mullin, *Flight*. The Zanzibari evidence agrees with the proposition that new slaves were most likely to flee, but there is no evidence that the most acculturated ones also did so. This may be the result of a high rate of manumission for slaves who had served for long periods.

caped slaves living there, subsisting on their crops of millet. They lived in detached huts, an indication that they did not feel in danger of attack. At the extreme north end of Pemba, some escaped slaves formed their own settlement, and the small government garrison at the other end of the island did not dare attack it. Other Pemba slaves took refuge on small islands off Pemba's coast.[209] Closer to the Arab estates themselves, the plantation of an English planter attempting to grow sugar was plagued by fugitive slaves from other plantations, who hid on his estate and stole goods. When the Universities' Mission to Central Africa bought a shamba, it received a number of fugitives.[210] At the end of the century, fugitives fled to government stations as well as to the missions. Others "simply disappeared," perhaps joining the large population of slaves, ex-slaves, and others living on their own in Zanzibar town.[211]

Many runaways tried to leave the island altogether. A desperate slave, at least up to 1873, could sell himself to an Arabian slave trader operating in Zanzibar—within half an hour according to one observer.[212] More positively, slaves had opportunities to steal a canoe or sailboat and make for the mainland coast, which was some forty to fifty miles away. British vessels, searching for slave dhows off Zanzibar and Pemba, picked up a number of canoes in which fugitive slaves were apparently trying to reach the mainland.[213] Others sought refuge with the naval vessels themselves. One officer wrote that on a survey of Pemba his boats were "besieged with slaves, who have requested to be taken on board, some from the land, some from canoes." Most of the fugitives complained of ill-treatment, and many showed signs of beatings, chains, or hunger. The descriptions of the naval officers strongly

209. Belleville, "Trip Around the Southern End of Zanzibar Island," pp. 71–72; Playfair, p. 257; Le Roy, "Au Zanguebar anglais," p. 620.

210. Sir Bartle Frere, "Memorandum Respecting Captain Fraser's Estate," 10 February 1873, PP 1873, LXI, 768, p. 35; Bishop Steere to Robins, 27 July 1878, UMCA Archives, Al (III), Box 2, fols. 480–82. The refugees included a woman who had been chained and beaten, a sick girl cast out by her master, and a man and woman who said they had lived free for six to seven years but were about to be taken as slaves to Pemba.

211. Zanzibar Government, Agriculture Department, *Annual Report*, 1898, p. 33; Cave to Lansdowne, 15 April 1901, FO 2/454. In Brazil, Salvador, a loosely structured city with a high black population also offered a potential refuge. Howard M. Prince, "Slave Rebellion in Bahia, 1807–1835" (Ph.D. diss., Columbia University, 1972).

212. Colomb, pp. 372–73.

213. Euan-Smith to Derby, 5 July 1875, FOCP 2915, p. 193; Comdr. Lang to Rear-Adm. Fremantle, 6 June 1889, FOCP 6052, p. 3; Capt. Brackenbury to Fremantle, 10 May 1889, PP 1889, LXXII, 279, p. 53; Comdr. Festing to Admiralty, 29 September, 3 October, 29 November, and 15 December 1894, *Documents relatifs à la répression de la traite des esclaves*, 1894, pp. 37–40; Capt. MacGill, "Further Report on the Detention of a Canoe and 5 Slaves by H.M.S. *Phoebe* on 14 April 1895," FO 107/46.

suggest that attempts to flee the islands were closely linked with specific instances of brutal treatment.[214]

Some made it all the way on their own. Burton found "a kind of East African Liberia" formed by runaways from Zanzibar behind the mainland coast. The community was sufficiently strong to threaten the caravan route between Mombasa and Usambara. In a mainland town across from Pemba, British officials found 103 runaways in 1897 and observed others arriving later in the year.[215] Possibly, escape became more common in the last years before abolition because the presence of British officials on the islands made the consequences of failure less severe. Some slaves did fail—descriptions of the punishment of slaves often cite escape as the most frequent offense.[216]

At least one, possibly two or three, violent rebellions occurred in Zanzibar. The known incident is similar to the formation of Maroon settlements in Jamaica, Brazil, and elsewhere in the Caribbean and South America by slaves who escaped en masse and defended themselves with force against recapture. It was not a direct attack on slaveowners, such as the rebellion of Nat Turner or the revolution in San Domingue.[217] A French naval officer writing in 1822 said that a few years previously slaves revolted, and the Arabs, assembled by the governor, chased them out of the woods, burning trees to get at them and shooting many.[218] This appears to be the same revolt described in 1860 by Richard Burton, who erroneously stated that it had occurred twenty years before. Burton said that the rebels were all recently imported Wazigua, a people living on the mainland of what is now Tanzania. They "rose against their Arab masters, retreated into the jungles, and, reinforced by male-

214. Capt. Sulivan to Rear-Adm. Macdonald, 3 February 1876, PP 1877, LXXVIII, 511, p. 333; Comdr. Wharton to Rear-Adm. Corbett, 17 October 1878, FOCP 3928, p. 546; Comdr. Lang to Capt. Woodward, 29 November 1886, FOCP 5161, p. 40; Miles to Granville, 16 July 1883, FOCP 4914, p. 165; Lieut. Nicholas to Comdr. Arbuthnot, 24 April 1889, PP 1889, LXXII, 279, p. 40; Comdr. Boyle to Rear-Adm. Macdonald, October 1876, FOCP 3686, p. 700, and many others.

215. Burton, Lakes, 2: 374; District Officer, Vanga, to Craufurd, 21 April 1897, and Tritton to Rogers, 30 October 1897, CP/1/97/183. See also Henry S. Newman, "Narrative of Visit of Theodore Burtt and Henry S. Newman to Zanzibar, Pemba, and the East Africa Protectorate, 1897," typescript in the library of the Society of Friends, London, MS 204, p. 51; Piggott to Smith, 11 February 1891, incl. Euan-Smith to Salisbury, 17 February 1891, FO 84/2146; Smith to Salisbury, 5 August 1891, FO 84/2149; O'Sullivan, "Report 1896," PP 1896, LIX, 395, p. 41.

216. Rigby, "Report," p. 331; Devereux, pp. 106–07; Mackenzie, p. 73; Newman, "Narrative," p. 43. Some slaves drowned while attempting to escape to the mainland. Comdr. Lang to Rear-Adm. Fremantle, 6 June 1889, FOCP 6052, p. 3.

217. Richard Price, ed., Maroon Societies (Garden City, N.Y., 1973); Patterson, pp. 266—83; Dunn, pp. 256–62; Marion D. deB. Kilson, "Towards Freedom: An Analysis of Slave Revolts in the United States," Phylon 25 (1964): 175–87.

218. Massieu to Ministre de la Marine et des Colonies, 9 October 1822, O.I., 17/89.

factors and malcontents, began a servile war, which raged with the greatest fury for six months." The revolt was put down by the governor of Zanzibar, Ahmed bin Seif, with soldiers from the Hadramaut.[219]

This revolt, then, took place in the early years of expanded slave populations and among a particular group that had as yet received little opportunity to become acculturated or submerged in Swahili society. One would expect such a group, sharing common experiences of freedom in their native land, to react in the most hostile and coherent way to enslavement.[220] The Arabs' reaction shows that collective resistance was a severe threat which had to be harshly repressed, but even in the heartlands of the sultanate, mercenaries had to be called in to do the job.

The known revolt occurred under the most favorable circumstances for collective action.[221] Later, slaves came from more diverse sources and could be integrated into a more established slave system. During the height of the clove economy no such revolts took place, and in the 1870s, Christie wrote, Arabs did not even fear them.[222]

219. Burton, *Lakes,* 1: 125. There are two reasons to suggest that this revolt actually occurred in the 1820s. Ahmed bin Seif was governor in the 1820s, not the 1840s. (Nicholls, *The Swahili Coast,* p. 272.) Moreover, there were many Europeans and Americans in Zanzibar around 1840, but their accounts fail to mention any slave revolt. If an event of sufficient importance to be related to Burton twenty years later occurred, it is unlikely that eyewitnesses or people who came shortly after the revolt would have missed it. Burton's description is similar to the less detailed statement by the Frenchman Massieu, but it is, of course, possible that a second revolt took place in the 1820s. Another description of a Wazigua revolt, apparently based on Wazigua informants on the mainland, came from a French missionary in 1886, who said the revolt occurred fifty years previously. This may also be the same revolt, or else another one by Wazigua. Père Picard, "Autour de Mandera," *Missions Catholiques* 18 (1886): 227.

220. In Père Picard's version of the revolt, the rebels had actually been captured in one raid and were about to be divided among their captors in Zanzibar when the revolt took place. This version, however, appears to have been inflated in the telling. Picard, pp. 226–27.

221. Similarly, revolts in Bahia were concentrated in the period 1807 to 1835. Economic expansion and high slave imports produced a high concentration of slaves in the city of Salvador and worsening urban living conditions. The region was also politically unstable. Slaves were mostly African-born, and many were of common origin or were Muslims. These factors do not constitute a complete explanation for the revolts, but they help to explain why they occurred at a specific time. Prince, pp. 60–82. See also Patterson, pp. 274–83.

222. Christie, "Slavery," p. 43. Baumann, who visited the islands in the early 1890s, mentions that a revolt took place in Pemba a long time before and that it, like the Zanzibar revolt, involved Wazigua. Given the time distance, it is possible that Baumann's informants were referring to the same Zanzibar revolt, which took place before their ancestors moved to Pemba (*Pemba,* p. 11). However, a famine among the Wazigua in the late 1830s, followed by a period of political turmoil, may have resulted in high concentrations of Wazigua in Pemba during the early days of clove planting there. Feierman, p. 137.

Flight—especially on an individual basis—was easier to accomplish in Zanzibar than in most of the Western Hemisphere, especially the Southern United States. As shown in the next chapter, slaves in Zanzibar lived in scattered clusters of huts and had considerable physical mobility. Their masters had few of the police forces, militias, and slave patrols that Western slave societies used. Nor could they count on nation-wide, impersonal mechanisms such as newspaper advertisements and law enforcement agencies in distant states to apprehend and return escaped slaves.

The actual act of escape, however, was all that was relatively easy. The islands were small and offered few places to hide. There is no evidence that the Wahadimu or Wapemba welcomed runaway slaves. Crossing to the mainland was risky, and once there, runaways, knowing little of the area, were likely to be reenslaved or killed by one of the coastal peoples. Slaves, like anyone else, were safe only if protected by their community, and the only available community was the plantation. To escape and begin life anew was a risky alternative to plantation life, but if a slave were desperate—faced with brutal punishment, excessive work, or loss of customary rights—he could walk away and take a chance on hiding out or trying to find a new home. Masters had to keep this in mind or risk losing substantial numbers of their slaves.[223]

The importance of joining or building a community was the principal reason why escape was a more effective sanction for slaves on the mainland. Political turmoil in parts of the coast meant that certain leaders and groups were glad to enlist slaves who could not abide their own masters, while the availability of sparsely populated land in some locations gave runaways a chance to build Maroon settlements.[224] Escape had a particularly great impact on the lives of Malindi's slaves, for the low population behind the coast, which had itself led to the intense exploitation of slave labor, also made escape a greater possibility. Given that the demands of extensive grain cultivation were more continuous and heavy than in Mombasa or Zanzibar, the regimentation of labor in Malindi might have degenerated into brutality were it not for slave resistance.

Resistance—mainly in the form of escape—was probably most severe

223. Several observers noted that masters and slaves were both aware that mistreatment was likely to lead to escape. Burton, *Zanzibar*, 1: 463; Christie, "Slavery," pp. 42–43; Holmwood to FO, 14 September 1887, FO 84/1854; Hardinge to Salisbury, 10 January 1896, PP 1896, LIX, 395, p. 24.

224. When some of Seyyid Majid's slaves found themselves with the better opportunities for escape which the mainland offered during their master's visit to Dar es Salaam, forty-one of them vanished into the nearby bush. Seward to Secretary to the Bombay Government, 10 November 1866, FO 84/1261.

in Malindi, but wherever plantation agriculture expanded, many slaves ran away. In the 1840s, Mombasa's period of agricultural growth, a village inhabited by runaway slaves from Mombasa and other Africans who had become detached from their own societies grew up to the south of the town. Other slaves fled Mombasa for Gazi, where the Mazrui, eager to obtain adherents, took them in.[225] Slaves continued to run away from Mombasa until the advent of colonial rule.[226]

Malindi's planters were plagued by runaways from at least the 1870s. Kirk noted in 1873 that Arabs had unsuccessfully attacked a runaway slave settlement and that in retaliation, the runaways, known as *watoro* (from *kutoroka*, "to run away"), were killing slaves on outlying plantations.[227] Local officials also tried to get the Galla to return runaways.[228] Most slaves fleeing Malindi went to the watoro villages in the vicinity of the Sabaki River. This land, located behind a range of small hills 10 to 15 miles inland, is fertile and now supports a substantial population; but it is not as good as the coastal plain and was therefore ignored by the planters. Before the large-scale northward migration of Mijikenda crossed the river around 1890, the population consisted mainly of scattered Galla and other nomads. Jilore, Makongeni, Chakama, Yameza, and Mlangobaya all came to be important Maroon villages in this area. Missionaries who passed through the region reported that there were three hundred watoro at Jilore in 1878 and a thousand at Makongeni in 1890; Fitzgerald found six hundred people in two of the villages in 1891.[229] These estimates seem high, and likely include offspring and persons from neighboring peoples. Nevertheless, these villages were substantial enough to fight off occasional attacks by the slaveowners of Malindi.[230] The hinterland north of the Sabaki River even acquired the name—still remembered today—of *Utoroni*, "the place of the runaway

225. The runaway settlement was known as Muasangombe, after its leader, who was not a runaway but a Digo (a Mijikenda subgroup). He had as many as 4,000 followers. Unstable conditions among the Mijikenda, which enabled a skilled man who could acquire a personal following to rise to power, made it possible for such heterogeneous communities to develop. Ludwig Krapf, "Journal," *Church Missionary Intelligencer* 1 (1849): 41; Map by Rebmann, 22 September 1848, CMS CA5/024/52; Spear, pp. 198–99. On slaves in Gazi, see Guillain, *Documents*, vol. 2/2, pp. 263–64.

226. Mackenzie to Euan-Smith, 6 December 1888, FOCP 6009, p. 26. See also Norman R. Bennett, "The Church Missionary Society of Mombasa, 1873–1894," in Jeffrey Butler, ed., *Boston University Papers in African History* (Boston, 1964), 1: 159–94.

227. Kirk to Granville, 6 November 1873, PP 1874, LXII, 749, p. 102.

228. Prideaux, Report on Zanzibar, 1873–74, FOCP 2915, p. 86.

229. Streeter to Wright, 10 August 1878, CMS CA5/027/11; Binns, "Report of a Visit Paid to Jilori," February 1877, CMS CA5/03/17; Binns to Lang, 19 February 1890, CMS G3/A5/0/1890/49; Alexandre Le Roy, *D'Aden à Zanzibar* (Tours, France, 1894), p. 304; Fitzgerald, *Travels*, pp. 119, 121, 124; MAL 17, 24, 30, 34, 35, 44, 45, 48.

230. MAL 24, 30, 35, 44, 45.

slaves." The name of a leader of the watoro, Ali Tete, is also remembered by many informants.[231]

Between Malindi and Mombasa was a watoro village called Koromio, but in 1852 the Mazrui of Takaungu stormed and burned it, killing and capturing some of the watoro and driving others into the bush.[232] Later, the largest Maroon settlement of all developed in that region. Fulladoyo was inhabited by slaves from Malindi, Takaungu, and Mombasa.[233] Although founded by a Mijikenda Christian in 1879, the number of watoro there grew to 17, then 44, then 350 out of a total population of 400.[234] Although scattered by a fierce attack by Arabs in 1883, the watoro hid in the area—none was recaptured. European authorities thought there were a thousand watoro in Fulladoyo in 1890, plus three thousand in the surrounding area, although these estimates included many Mijikenda.[235]

Another area of watoro settlements—the refuge of runaways from Lamu—was up the Tana and Juba rivers. Runaways built heavily stockaded villages and made their own spears and poisoned arrows while they farmed the surrounding land.[236]

Large numbers of runaways joined a powerful man or group that was seeking soldiers and followers. Mbaruk bin Rashid Al-Mazrui and Ahmed Fumoluti, Sultan of Witu, numbered many runaways among the personal followers upon whom they depended in their challenges to Zanzibari authority.[237] Watoro were pragmatic in their political alliances, joining Arab and Swahili leaders—even though they were slave-

231. Ali Tete was chief of the settlement at Chakama. A second watoro chief, Kamtande, leader of the village of Bura, is also well remembered. MAL 24, 28, 30, 34, 35, 45, 65.

232. Krapf, "Memoir," 1853, CMS CA5/016/179, p. 55.

233. Kirk to Granville, 9 November 1883, PP 1884, LXXV, 353, p. 128; G. Mackenzie to Euan-Smith, 12 February 1890, incl. Euan-Smith to Salisbury, 24 February 1890, FO 84/2059.

234. Menzies to Wright, 15 July 1880, CMS CA5/M6; Price to Miles, 7 March 1882, CMS G3/A5/0/1882/40.

235. However, 250 watoro joined Mbaruk after the demise of their own settlement. Kirk to Granville, 9 November 1883, PP 1884, LXXV, 353, p. 128; Mackenzie to Euan-Smith, 12 February 1890, incl. Euan-Smith to Salisbury, 24 February 1890, FO 84/2059.

236. Henry C. ArcAngelo, "A Sketch of the River Juba or Gochob, or Gowin, from a Trip Up the Stream in 1844," Cobburn's United Service Magazine, 1845, pp. 280–81; Map by J. R. W. Piggott, 3 July 1889, incl. McDermott to Mackinnon, 29 July 1889, Mackinnon Papers, Africa, IBEA no. 967, School of Oriental and African Studies, London.

237. Haggard to Kirk, 25 August 1884, FOCP 5165, p. 229; Miles to Granville, 17 November 1881, FOCP 4626, pp. 372–73; Price to Euan-Smith, 19 October 1888, reprinted in Price, Third Campaign, p. 188; Richard Brenner, "Richard Brenner's Reise in den Galla-Ländern, 1867–1868," Petermann's Mitteilungen, 1868, p. 175; "Richard Brenner's Forschungen in Ost-Afrika," in ibid., p. 458.

holders—who could offer them protection and a share of the spoils in exchange for their support.

However, slaves couldn't simply walk to the next plantation. The people of a town like Malindi may have shown little capability for collective political action, but they did recognize the strength and rightful residence of the town's constituent communal groups. They were not out to take one another's slaves, and watoro had to seek a rival potentate outside the area. What the coast lacked was not local communities, but a strong state.

Still another alternative for mistreated or dissatisfied mainland slaves developed with the establishment of several Christian mission stations in the hinterland of Mombasa after the 1840s. In 1888, British authorities found 907 runaways from the coast at the missions, including 548 from nearby Mombasa, 154 from Takaungu, and 163 from Malindi— some 80 miles distant.[238] They were taken in by the missionaries and African Christians, became Christians of varying degrees of piety, and above all became part of a community that could give them protection and a sense of belonging.[239]

Escape in East Africa seems simple only in comparison to the obstacles facing fugitive slaves in the United States. If a runaway failed he could be brutally punished, but he stood a reasonable chance of escaping from his master's reach.[240] The problem was to create the social conditions necessary for survival. Watoro communities faced severe challenges in coping with their environment: to survive until the first harvests, to live peacefully with their neighbors, and to repulse the intermittent attacks of their former masters.[241] Most important, the social fabric of African societies is woven in kinship ties, commonly accepted

238. Mackenzie to Euan-Smith, 6 December 1888, FOCP 6009, p. 26. Slaves continued to flee to the Mombasa missions from Malindi, Mambrui, and Takaungu well into the 1890s. MacDougall to Craufurd, 26 February, 25 March 1897, CP/1/75/46; Hardinge to Binns, 9 February 1899, PP 1899, LXIII, 303, p. 24.

239. MSA 2, 7, 8. For more on one of the mission settlements from the point of view of the son of a slave rescued from a slave dhow, see James Juma Mbotela, *The Freeing of the Slaves in East Africa* (London, 1956); and Bennett, pp. 159–94.

240. Runaways were often severely beaten if caught. Krapf, "Memoir," 1853, CMS CA5/016/179, p. 56.

241. If an individual runaway fell into the hands of Mijikenda, he was sometimes returned to his former master for ransom. Communities such as Muasangombe and Fulladoyo, although in populated areas, could take care of themselves and so had a basis for working out peaceful relations with their neighbors. The Sabaki villages were also strong and had only limited numbers of Galla to worry about. Similarly, all the major settlements had to fend off a few Arab attacks and did so only because of their strength as communities. The food problem could also be solved only by a group: new arrivals were fed out of common stores until their own crops came up. On these problems, see Krapf, "Memoir," CMS CA5/016/179, pp. 55–56.

institutions, rituals, and shared traditions.[242] So it took time for a refuge to become a community.

Escape, nonetheless, was frequent in all areas of the coast, although the largest watoro communities were in the area where exploitation was the most intensive. The extent of slave resistance belies facile generalizations that coastal slavery was "mild" or that slaves were content with their roles as dependents. Is a high rate of escape compatible with the concept of paternalism? Only if one confuses paternalism with benevolence by the masters and gratitude by the slaves is it inconsistent with resistance. If one stresses reciprocity—the expectations masters and slaves had of one another—there is no reason to expect a smooth or stable equilibrium. With two sides attempting to define their inherently conflicting versions of rights and duties, conflict was an essential part of paternalism.

The high rate of escape—especially on the mainland coast—in comparison to the Southern United States, can be attributed to three factors.[243] First, the timing of the appearance of Maroon communities—the 1840s near Mombasa and the 1870s near Malindi, as well as the Zigua revolt in Zanzibar in the 1820s—suggests that escape was indeed linked with the problem of defining obligations and rights. These were times of change in the agricultural sector, and escape may well have been a response of slaves to increasing demands being made upon them.[244]

Second, owing to the same expansion of agriculture, a high percentage of slaves at these times had only recently arrived from Central Africa. Escape was most likely to occur among those who were the least acculturated, the least indoctrinated with the idiom of paternalism, and had the fewest stakes (land, a spouse, children) in the plantation, the lowest rank in slave society, and the least knowledge of how to manipulate their masters.[245]

242. The difficulties of building such communities are discussed in Price, *Maroon Societies*.

243. These points are inferred from the timing and circumstances of the growth of watoro settlements. There is no direct evidence of the motives of runaways. My arguments are related to some of those presented in relation to New World slave revolts and escapes by Mullin; Patterson, pp. 274–83; Prince, pp. 60–82; R. Price, p. 24; and Genovese, *Roll*, pp. 588–95.

244. Wood notes that expanding agricultural production in South Carolina led to increased pressure on slaves during the period before a large-scale revolt in 1739. However, unlike the case of the coast, the machinery of social control grew stronger as well. Wood, p. 268.

245. The importance of these factors in the case of Virginia is developed at length by Mullin. See also Patterson, pp. 275–76, and Prince, pp. 61–65. However, a factor noted in

Third and most important, the balance of power was different from that in the United States. Geographic factors [246] plus the inability of slaveowners to act as a group made escape a more effective sanction for the slaves of East Africa than for their American counterparts. Only the relatively closely knit Mazrui had much success against mainland watoro settlements, while Zanzibaris had to use mercenaries to put down a revolt in the sultanate's heartland.[247] At all times, slaves could weigh their security and hardships on the plantations against their chances of a better life if they fled to a settlement of runaways, a new master, or a mission.[248] Escape was part of the unsteady equilibrium that was paternalism.

Whatever the motives of individual runaways, the net effect of such actions was to reinforce paternalism by militating against the worst excesses of slavery. Able observers such as Christie and Burton in Zanzibar and Fitzgerald and Hardinge on the mainland noted that slaveowners were well aware that they could not afford to put too much

---

some New World slave revolts—a high proportion of slaves coming from a common ethnic or religious background—appears only in the Wazigua revolt in Zanzibar. Later, when the mainland plantations were growing, the caravan routes brought slaves from a wide variety of areas. On ethnic and religious factors in the slave revolts of the Western Hemisphere see Prince, pp. 67–68, 72, and Monica Schuler, "Ethnic Slave Rebellions in the Caribbean and the Guianas," *Journal of Social History* 3 (1970): 374–85.

246. The ease of escape where labor was most intensive was undoubtedly a major reason why slave resistance generally took the form of escape rather than attempts to overthrow the slave system. The availability of hiding places was also one of the most important variables in the Americas. It explains why Jamaica had many revolts and Barbadoes few, while the immense size of the slave states of the United States, combined with their high white population by the nineteenth century, presented slaves with nearly insuperable barriers even before the mechanisms of social control are considered. Dunn, pp. 261–62; Genovese, *Roll*, p. 594; Blassingame, p. 119.

247. Oral and eyewitness accounts mention only a few efforts to recapture the watoro behind Malindi, all of which were beaten off by the runaways. Informants made it clear to me that there was very little that masters could do to prevent escape. Kirk to Granville, 6 November 1873, PP 1874, LXII, 749, p. 102; Rev. J. R. Deimler, "The Mission Field," *Church Missionary Intelligencer*, n.s. 29 (1904): 125–26; MAL 24, 30, 34, 35, 44, 45.

248. Slaves showed an acute awareness of changing opportunities to find alternatives. In Kenya during the late 1890s, as the power of the slaveowners to take reprisals against runaways waned and as British activities created new possibilities for employment, large numbers of slaves deserted their masters. Their pragmatism parallels the desertion of slaves in the Southern United States as the South fell to Union armies—actions which shocked slaveowners who had believed in the loyalty of their slaves. On the Kenyan situation, see Hardinge, "Report," PP 1898, LX, 199, p. 6; Hobley to Chief Secretary, Nairobi, 10 August 1917, CP/1/39/625; A. H. Le Q. Clayton, "Labour in the East Africa Protectorate, 1895–1918" (Ph.D. diss., St. Andrews University, 1971), p. 73. Other slaves, realizing that their masters were powerless to punish them, simply took it easy. Murray to Sub-Commissioner, Mombasa, 9 January 1902, CP/1/71/25. On the Old South, see Genovese, *Roll*, pp. 97–112.

pressure on their slaves.[249] Force was still used, and the threat of its use was always present, but slaves had a significant role in defining the limits to which they could be pushed and in forcing their masters to live up to their own Islamic norms.[250] This does not mean that slaveowners consciously gave in to their slaves. Rather, the necessity of taking slaves' rights seriously reinforced the master's self-image as a patriarch. Paternalism was strengthened both on the level of daily interaction—the testing of limits by masters and slaves—and on the level of ideology—the slaveowners' concept of slavery as an institution of dependence.

Even slaves who rejected paternalism still faced the same social pressures as their brethren who reached an accommodation with plantation society. Those who joined Arab or Swahili leaders participated in raids and battles, fighting other Arabs or Swahili, along with their slaves. The runaway slave communities staged raids on outlying plantations. Many slaves on these plantations were killed or kidnapped, and some were even sold.[251] That such communities were formed at all suggests that the common experience of oppression elicited some kind of collective response from a portion of the slaves. However, the Maroon village's ties were within itself, and an attack on the master's slaves was an attack on the master.[252] Whether they joined a new slaveowner or formed their own fledgling settlements, runaways knew that their security depended on their membership in a community, not on their ties with other oppressed people.[253]

249. Christie, "Slavery," pp. 42–43; Burton, *Zanzibar*, 1: 463; Fitzgerald, *Travels*, p. 32; Hardinge, "Report," PP 1898, LX, 199, p. 61. For similar views about the mainland, see also Kirk to Salisbury, 23 February 1880, FOCP 4498, p. 414; and about Zanzibar, Holmwood to FO, 14 September 1887, FO 84/1854, and Hardinge to Salisbury, 10 January 1896, PP 1896, LIX, 393, p. 24.

250. Even in the United States, slave resistance—especially slowdowns and resistance to overwork—had an important effect on limiting abuses and improving everyday living conditions. Genovese, *Roll*, p. 621.

251. New, *Life*, p. 49; Kirk to Granville, 6 November 1873, PP 1874, LXII, 749, p. 102; and Haggard to Kirk, 9 April and 25 August 1884; Gissing to Kirk, 14 September 1884, and Kirk to Granville, 23 September 1884—all in FOCP 5165, pp. 180, 227, 229, 243; MAL 5, 44, 45. The watoro of Makongeni, behind Malindi, cooperated with Mbaruk bin Rashid in a series of raids on harvests and slaves in Malindi in 1874, until the Sultan of Zanzibar sent soldiers to scatter the watoro and chase away Mbaruk. Greffulhe, p. 338. The harassment of plantations by runaway slaves in the Southern United States was noted by Blassingame, p. 119.

252. In some circumstances in the New World, runaways and plantation slaves did act together. But in other instances Maroons negotiated with the government, obtaining recognition of their independence in return for a promise to return future runaways. Price, p. 13; and Orlando Patterson, "Slavery and Slave Revolts: A Sociohistorical Analysis of the First Maroon War, 1665–1740," in Price, *Maroon Societies*, p. 272.

253. As Genovese notes, "Wherever paternalism exists, it undermines solidarity among the oppressed by linking them as individuals to their oppressors." *Roll*, p. 5.

Conclusions

The development of regulated, closely supervised labor in Zanzibar and of gang labor in Malindi reveals the extent to which the organization of Omani and Swahili society was responding to the dictates of the market. The customary workweek may not have been as long as in the Americas, but it was substantial, and the work, especially on large grain plantations, was as regimented as it was arduous. Punishment may have been used sparingly, but the threat was always present, and slaves had limited recourse against a master who abused the norms of his society. That masters did not drive their slaves harder still was in part the result of limitations in the Indian Ocean markets. Most important, the dynamics of plantation development themselves limited the extent to which slaves were reduced to mere factors of production by making the plantation into a close-knit social and economic unit.

Moreover, the varied needs slaveowners had long had of slaves persisted into the nineteenth century. Slavery was pushed and pulled in different directions. Slaveowners could organize their slaves into gangs or hire them out for profit, and the same individuals could enjoy the deference of their house servants and the political benefits of having armed retainers. The different forces varied from place to place. New forms of labor organization were most important in Malindi, where the most labor-intensive variant in agriculture coincided with the least developed social life. Change in the use of labor was the least in Mombasa, where the possibilities of agricultural expansion were limited and the rewards of urban life comparatively great. Change depended on the peculiarities of plantation crops: the seasonal labor demands of the clove tree and the delicacy of its branches reinforced plantation paternalism in Zanzibar and Pemba. Yet in Malindi the heavy labor requirements of grain cultivation were countered by a geographical and demographic situation that gave slaves some recourse against excessive demands.

Out of the varied needs slaveowners had of their slaves and the balance of forces between masters and slaves, customary notions of the slaves' rights and obligations emerged. Contemporary observers were able to learn with some precision what these community standards were, and the descendants of masters and slaves still remember these customs. Yet the equilibrium was unsteady, pulled in one direction by masters who wanted more work from their slaves and in another by slaves who resisted new demands and old obligations. Slaves were able to play an important part in defining the perimeters of paternalism because slaveholders relied on their skill as well as their brawn, because masters had high expectations of slaves' personal loyalty, and because slaveowners lacked the physical and political strength to control escape by force alone.

For the overwhelming majority of slaves who did not run away, accommodation was not a mere submission to force, but a recognition of their need for protection and membership in a social group. Despite the toil and degredation of plantation labor, paternalism offered them meaningful benefits in a difficult situation: a place to live with a modicum of security, plots on which to grow their own food, and a community of which one was a part. Masters would have been deceiving themselves if they believed their slaves were content, but in the social system of the East African coast, they had every reason to take their role as patriarchs seriously. The numerous injunctions of Islamic law to treat slaves kindly might have been ignored if they had run counter to economic and political practicalities, but they meant a great deal when religious ethics, the economic situation, and social relationships were mutually reinforcing.

The differences in the working lives of slaves in various parts of the coast suggest how responsive slaveowners were to economic incentives and conditions. Yet in all parts of the coast the diverse roles which slaves filled were similar, and in all areas the plantation had a strong social dimension. Slaveowners on the islands and mainland shared a common conception of the master-slave relationship that stressed the role of the Muslim patriarch.[254] The common social and ideological features of coastal slavery above all reflected the similarity of circumstances all along the coasts: patriarchy was everywhere a vital principle of social and political life.

Yet the religious context in which the master-slave relationship was viewed also showed the influence of the shared Islamic background and similar historical experiences with slavery, reinforced in the nineteenth century by the extent of communications among East African towns, the dispersal of Arab and Swahili communal groups, and the implications of common language and shared facets of coastal culture. Ideas of slavery were widely shared among coastal slaveowners, while the practice of slavery reflected the complexity of the slaveholders' needs and wants, the demographic and geographic constraints of particular localities, and the inescapable fact that the most important factors of production had wills of their own.

254. Because of the importance of property to buying or acquiring followers, even women slaveowners who exercised their property rights could fill "patriarchal" roles. See chapter 6.

6 Dependence and Freedom

Slaves on the East African coast were property, but they were not merely property. In some parts of the world the property rights of slaveowner over slaves were more fully developed than social ties, but no slave law was ever able to treat slaves solely as chattel and no slave society could avoid the necessity of creating some sort of social order.[1] Coastal slaveholders did indeed exercise their right to use and transfer slave property: deeds have been preserved by which slaves were sold, used as collateral for loans, bestowed as gifts, and passed on to the heirs of an estate.[2] However, some observers noted that the sale of slaves—once brought into Zanzibari society—was considered a social disgrace.[3] The fact of having dependents was as important as the right to dispose of property.

As owner and as superior, the master's control over his slaves was exercised as an individual. The slaves of one owner constituted a social group only through their common subordination to one person; their relationships with the wider society were mediated by their master.

The groups into which slaveowners brought their slaves were by no means uniform. The imagery—as we shall see—was patriarchal, but the structure was not that of a family or kinship group. A wealthy individ-

1. Davis, *The Problem of Slavery in Western Culture.*

2. Bi Salima binti Masudi of Malindi mortgaged sixty-four slaves, along with farms, land, and houses to Abdulla Hussein, the wealthy landlord from Shella, for $7,000 in 1886. Reg., Msa, 1A and 4A 1894. The coast's leading financier, Salim bin Khalfan, accepted four slaves, plus a house in Mombasa, as security on a mortgage of $450 in 1890. 234A 1893. An Mswahili borrowed $1,400 plus 280 pounds of ivory from another leading money-lender in 1886, and turned over four slaves for the creditor's use until the money was repaid. 165B 1897. Other mortgages with slaves as collateral are 217B 1897, 94B and 48B 1898, and 166A 1893. Gifts of a slave dating from 1849 and 1889 are recorded in 100A 1898 and 29B 1911. Inheritance of slaves comes up in 95A 1894 and a/c 227N of 1916, as well as the will of Mbarak bin Rashid from 1904 (copy lent by William McKay). Slaves could also be made over to a mosque for its benefit. Registers of Property, Wakf Commission, Mombasa, nos. 5 and 8.

3. Loarer, "Ile de Zanguebar," O.I., 5/23, notebook 5; Burton, *Zanzibar*, 1: 352; Christie, "Slavery in Zanzibar as It Is," p. 45. It is also a matter of debate how much slaveowners in the United States exercised their right to sell slaves, although there were established slave markets and professional slave traders. The scorn slaveowners heaped on slave traders pointed to their misgivings about carrying property rights to their logical conclusion. Stampp, *The Peculiar Institution*, pp. 256–71. For two views of the extent of slave trading, see Fogel and Engerman, *Time on the Cross* 1: 49–58, and Gutman, *Slavery and the Numbers Game*, pp. 102–40.

ual often included slaves—along with poorer kinsmen, clients, and others—in his personal entourage. Plantation agriculture rooted such groups in the owner's land and in a differentiated economic organization. In urban centers, the slaves of one master might not even constitute a work group. What counted was personal dependence; as individuals slaves neither constituted nor belonged to any corporate group.

Only through the master did slaves share in the political strength and social ties of communal groups.[4] The slaves of a highly independent man like Suleiman bin Abdalla were almost exclusively involved in a group of personal dependents, with weak ties to other Omani groups, strong opposition to the sultanate, and loose alliances with the followers of other political mavericks on the coast. But in Malindi, the slaves of various Washella settlers were part—although a subordinate part—of a communal group that maintained its political and social solidarity.

The personal bonds between master and slaves bound them, in some ways, more tightly than the owner's property rights, affecting their minds as well as their bodies. For slaves to be followers, they had to be incorporated into their master's society—be acculturated and socialized. If slaveowners sought deference as well as work, they had to make slaves adopt a patriarchal idiom—to address them in certain ways and to acknowledge their subordination on ritual occasions. Relatively paternalistic planters, like those of the Southern United States, could do more to undermine the cultural heritage and independent social life of their slaves than the more physically repressive planters of the Caribbean.

Yet even where the masters sought cultural domination and social subordination as well as labor, slaves did not simply accept the norms and conventions their masters sought to impose upon them. Slaves guarded the life they lived among themselves, and the hegemony of the slaveholders was never complete.

For slaves to develop some kind of life independent of their masters, it was necessary for people who had felt the impact of subordination to act as individuals and for people who came from diverse cultures and lived in distinct social units to find a basis of interaction. Their chances of success also depended on the needs, fears, and power of the slaveowners. On the coast of East Africa, the very strength of the multiple ties between masters and slaves made it possible for the slaveowners to give their slaves a relatively large degree of latitude in their daily lives,

4. In other African societies, kinship groups exercised more control over slaves, particularly as they were assimilated into society, than they did in coastal society. Still, because slaves could be bought on the market and had no inherent kinship ties, individuals were often in a position to exercise power over them and use that power to enhance their position vis-à-vis their own and rival kinship groups.

trusting that the slaves' vital need for membership—even as inferiors—in a wider group would ensure that they would stay within the bounds of a paternalistic social order.

ACCULTURATION AND DEPENDENCE

For the Muslim master, dependence was part of a religious and legal framework. Islamic law obliged the master to bring the slave into the Muslim community, teaching him Islam and ensuring that he followed its rules. The owner was the slave's guardian: only he could demand compensation if the slave suffered some wrong, and he was responsible by law for the slave's crimes or transactions. Slaves' legal responsibilities were consequently reduced, as were their religious obligations. The pilgrimage, for example, was not a duty of slaves as it was for free people. Certain violations of Islamic law were punishable by half the number of lashes free people were given for the same offense. Such rules underlined the slave's inferior status and dependence on his master but did not deny his ultimate spiritual equality. The master and the slave himself shared responsibility before God for the slave's conduct.

The first imperative was to convert the slave to Islam.[5] There is much evidence that this imperative was taken seriously by slaveowners in East Africa and that Islam became a central element in the lives of slaves and their descendants. Several visitors to Zanzibar observed that new slaves were circumcized, in line with Islamic practices, and taught the elements of the religion. On the islands and the coast, many slaves were sent to Koranic school. Others were taught by their own masters. Slaves also taught each other Islam.[6] Some observers felt that although slaves adhered to the external manifestations of Islam, such as prayer

5. Schacht, *Islamic Law*, p. 127; Mazrui, *Historia Ya Utumwa*, pp. 5–6; Niese, *Das Personen-und Familienrecht der Suaheli*, p. 44.

6. Loarer, O.I., 5/23, notebook 5; Michael W. Shepard, log of *Star*, 1844, *NEMA*, p. 262; Ludwig Krapf, "Additional Remarks on Zanzibar," CMS CA5/016/25; J. Courmont, "Rapport sur la Mission de Zanzibar," 8 June 1888, St. Esprit, 196/XI; Speke, *Journal of the Discovery of the Source of the Nile*, p. xxvi; Hardinge to Kimberley, 26 February 1895, PP 1895, LXXI, 143, p. 29; Rashid bin Hassani, "The Story of Rashid bin Hassani," p. 99; MAL 34, 35, 51. Slaves, like free Swahili and Hadramis but unlike the Omanis, were Sunni Muslims. The Ibadi version of Islam was a way of defining Omani identity—vis-à-vis free members of other communal groups as well as slaves. The predominance of the Sunni version among slaves may also reflect the fluid interaction of peoples—Swahili, Hadrami, slaves, and ex-slaves—in urban centers like Mombasa and Zanzibar town, as well as the open communications between cities and countryside. Hardinge to Kimberley, 26 February 1895, PP 1895, LXXI, 143, p. 29; August H. Nimtz, Jr., "The Role of the Muslim Sufi Order in Political Change: An Overview and Micro-Analysis from Tanzania" (Ph.D. diss., Indiana University, 1973), pp. 397–98; J. Spencer Trimingham, *Islam in East Africa* (Oxford; 1964), esp. p. 73.

and fasting, their knowledge of the doctrines was meager, and many pre-Islamic practices continued.[7]

Christie admitted that this might be true of new slaves, but he claimed that almost all second-generation slaves were strict Muslims.[8] It certainly would not be surprising for many slaves to be only partially Islamized. Even the free were far from uniformly learned in theological matters, and coastal Islam was everywhere influenced by pre-Islamic religious and magical practices.[9] The central point—on which all observers and informants agree—is that virtually all slaves *thought* of themselves as Muslims.[10] As at least one Christian missionary realized, the missions stood little chance of obtaining converts among the slaves, for all slaves considered themselves "vastly superior to all heathen and infidels." [11]

To get beyond the rudiments of Islam required leisure and money as well as piety, and such opportunities were open to few slaves. Nevertheless, a few slaves—mainly wazalia (locally born)—and manumitted slaves pursued studies in Koranic school; some made pilgrimages to Mecca; and a few became respected Islamic teachers.[12]

In this respect, there is no sharp distinction between the religious practices of Muslim slaveowners of East Africa and their Christian counterparts in the New World. The Catholic Church regarded slaves as potential converts, however indifferent Catholic slaveowners might have been, while in Protestant areas, planters' attitudes ranged from

7. Germain, "Note sur Zanzibar," pp. 353–54; LeRoy, *D'Aden à Zanzibar*, p. 181. See also el-Zein, *The Sacred Meadows*, pp. 37–38.

8. Christie, "Slavery," p. 42; Speke, p. xxviii. Because locally born slaves were Muslim, slaveowners would not accept ransom money from missionaries. Only newly arrived children were ransomed. Père Dupargue to Père Gère, 9 April 1872, St. Esprit, 195/III.

9. On syncretism in coastal Islam, see Lienhardt, "Introduction" to *The Medicine Man;* pp. 1–80.

10. El-Zein, although he asserts that Lamuan slaveowners thought their slaves incapable of learning anything but the rudiments of Islam, shows how they manipulated Islamic doctrines to counter their masters' notions of superiority.

11. Letter from Charles New in *United Methodist Free Church Magazine* 8 (1865): 345; J. T. Last, *Polyglotta Africana Orientalis* (London; 1885), p. 11; Fischer, *Mehr Licht*, p. 68; Oscar Baumann, *Usambara und Seine Nachbargebiete* (Berlin; 1891), p. 62. The freed slaves who inhabited the mission stations were mostly taken off dhows captured by the British navy before being exposed to the plantation environment, although runaways came to the missions as well.

12. Two of my informants, one an mzalia, the other an Arab, attended Koranic school together. I was also told of a Koranic teacher in the Malindi area who was an ex-slave from Lamu, while one of the most important religious leaders in Bagamoyo was a slave who had begun studying in Koranic school and then with leading scholars around 1886. MAL 18, 30, 50; Nimtz; Albrand, "Memoire sur Zanzibar," p. 73; Alexandre LeRoy, *Au Kilima-ndjaro (Afrique Orientale)* (Paris, 1893), p. 24; Kersten, *Von der Deckens Reisen,* 1: 81; Hardinge, Report on East Africa, PP 1898, LX, 199, p. 6.

hostility to a sincere wish to Christianize the heathen. Yet throughout the Western Hemisphere, but especially where new arrivals from Africa kept coming and planters ignored the social lives of slaves, distinct slave religions emerged with varying degrees of Christian and African influences, but above all reflecting the actual situation with which slaves had to cope.[13] No slave religion emerged in East Africa.

Masters and slaves both operated within the same normative and symbolic system, but not as equals. With greater religious obligations than slaves, with greater opportunities for learning and reflection, with more detachment from the rude experience of daily labor, and with generations of experience with Islam, masters—Arabs and Swahili alike—could claim superiority in the realm of religion, as they claimed superiority in status. Indeed, one of the most important terms for people of low status was *washenzi*—"heathens" or "barbarians." The same point was made by the names slaveowners gave their slaves. Islamic names, such as Mohammed or Ali or Aesha, were reserved for the free, while slaves were often named after a day of the week (Juma) or even after what they cost their master (Arobaini—forty [dollars]) or what they brought him (Faida—profit).[14] Status differences were expressed in terms of religion and civilization; but only by inculcating Islam could the point be made clear to the slaves. From the slaveowners' point of view, it was essential that slaves become Muslims—but not as good Muslims as the free.

Slaves, by accepting Islam, recognized that they had to find spiritual and social satisfaction within a cultural context they could not escape. By becoming Muslim they were adopting a portion of what, in coastal society, made their masters superior. They were thus differentiating themselves from the mass of heathens in the hinterland, from newly arrived slaves, and from their own pasts. Conversion was part of the process of learning to live within coastal society—but at a cost to the potential unity among slaves.[15] Still, slaves did not always accept Islam on their masters' terms and found within its myths and doctrines a way to assert their spiritual equality; nor did they assume that Islam negated the value of their "heathen" past. To these points I will return.

Similarly, no clear distinction emerged between the language of the

13. Genovese, *Roll, Jordan, Roll*, pp. 168–83. For a pioneering study of such a religion, see Melville H. Herskovits, *Life in a Haitian Valley* (New York, 1937), pp. 139–252.

14. Adolphe Burdo, *De Zanzibar au Lac Tanganyika* (Brussels, 1886), 1: 156. I have seen numerous slave names in the Land Office files, and heard more in interviews. Some slaves, particularly wazalia, had Islamic names, but this was unusual. Terms like *washenzi* are highly ambiguous: the point, in fact, is that status, culture, and religion are not distinct concepts but have overlapping meanings.

15. Genovese, *Roll*, pp. 170–71.

slaves and the language of the masters. Virtually all slaves learned Swahili. At times, groups of slaves from one place spoke their original languages, but slaves came from diverse parts of East Central Africa and relied on Swahili to communicate with their masters and each other. For all the variants of Swahili that exist, there is no slave version, comparable to the Creole languages of the descendants of slaves in the Caribbean.[16]

Religion and language were the two most important ways of defining who belonged to coastal society. New slaves also became accustomed to the climate, food, local customs, and above all to local institutions. The family was a key institution of socialization. After twelve-year-old Rashid bin Hassani was purchased in the Zanzibar slave market by Bibi Zem Zem, the Sultan's sister, he was brought to her plantation terrified by the ordeal of capture, separation from his kinsmen, and the voyage to Zanzibar from faraway Lake Nyasa. The nokoa called all Bibi Zem Zem's slaves together and asked those who were childless if they wanted a child. Rashid was adopted by a slave couple and remained with them as a son until he went off to work, marry, and move into his own home. Slaves who arrived as adults were given a wife or husband, a house, and a plot of land to grow their crops. They were carefully watched by trusted slaves until they had adjusted and ceased to try to run away.[17] As a child or as an adult, the new slave was given a material and emotional stake in plantation institutions, as well as a chance to learn how things were done.

In this way, slaves learned Swahili culture. They came to dress like other coastal people, to attend the festivals of the coast, to adopt Swahili marriage and funeral ceremonies, and to build Swahili-style houses for themselves.[18] Coastal culture was itself a mélange of diverse African and Asian elements, and the slaves made their own contribution, as we shall see later. This does not mean there was cultural uniformity—Hadramis, Omanis, Twelve Tribes Swahili, Bajunis, and other communal groups often preferred different foods, carried out ceremonies in different ways, and displayed other cultural variations. Nor did all people participate in the same ceremonies in the same manner. Slaves and

16. Hardinge, "Report," PP 1898, LX, 199, p. 6; Kirk to Derby, 4 April 1877, FOCP 3686, p. 563; MAL 35; MSA 37. On the varieties of Swahili, see Wilfred Whiteley, *Swahili: The Rise of a National Language* (London, 1969), pp. 3–4. For comparison, see Dell Hymes, ed., *Pidginization and Creolization of Languages* (Cambridge, 1971).

17. Rashid, p. 99. Slaves who tried to escape were punished. Loarer, O.I., 5/23, notebook 5; Germain, "Zanzibar," pp. 546–47; Mervyn Beech, MS on Swahili Life, Library of Fort Jesus, Mombasa.

18. Beech, "Slavery on the East Coast of Africa," p. 145; J. Blais, "Les anciens esclaves à Zanzibar," *Anthropos* 10–11 (1915–16): 105–07; Ruete, *Memoirs of an Arabian Princess*, p. 11; Quass, "Die Szuri's, die Kuli's und die Sclaven," pp. 450–52; Schmidt, *Sansibar*, p. 30.

freemen might attend the same wedding, but their roles within it only underscored the status distinction.[19] Nevertheless, Swahili culture was a wide net, and people of diverse origins, slaves included, were able to assimilate a life-style which they shared in many of its essentials with other coastal people.[20]

The importance of acculturation to Zanzibari society is clear in the terms that were used to describe slaves. A slave who was imported as an adult was called *mtumwa mjinga,* literally "stupid slave." A slave who had been purchased as a child and had grown up on the islands or coast was known as *mkulia,* "one who grew up here." Finally, a slave who was born on the islands or coast was an *mzalia,* "one who was born here." These terms implied increasing acceptance and trust—on the assumption that the person would act the part.[21] But even an *mzalia* was not a *mwungwana,* or descendant of free people. The line between those who were free of slave ancestry in the male line and those who were not was the fundamental status distinction on the coast (see my Conclusions).

It was mainly from the ranks of the wazalia that slaves were recruited to serve in the household or in positions of responsibility—as plantation supervisors, traders, or dhow captains. Among the 379 slaves the governor of Takaungu, Rashid bin Salim Al-Mazrui, claimed he owned, only 8 percent of the wazalia were listed as cultivators, compared to 65 percent domestic servants, and 23 percent artisans, sailors, or fishermen. Of the bought slaves, 87 percent were in the fields, 7 percent in domestic service, and 7 percent in trades or on the sea. These figures are not precise or typical—the Mazrui were more likely than any group to bring slaves they could trust into the household—but they do suggest that familiarity with coastal society was a key criterion for a nonplantation job.[22]

In turn, slaves who served in the household or in responsible roles were likely to be allowed a fuller part than ordinary workers in the ritual and social life of the freeborn: serious religious instruction, a more

19. Strobel, "Wedding Celebrations," pp. 38–39.

20. Much more research needs to be done on Swahili culture and the cultural interaction of Swahili and surrounding peoples. On Swahili-Mijikenda interaction, see Spear, "The Kaya Complex," pp. 126–33.

21. Kirk to Derby, 1 May 1876, FO 84/1453; Burton, *Lake Regions,* 2: 369–71: Baumann, *Sansibar,* p. 20; Christie, "Slavery," p. 33; Ludwig Krapf, *A Dictionary of the Swahili Language* (London, 1882), pp. 230, 271; Lyndon Harries, ed., *Swahili Prose Texts: A Selection from the Material Collected by Carl Velten from 1893 to 1896* (London, 1965), p. 37. See also Inter-Territorial Language Committee on the East African Dependencies, *A Standard Swahili-English Dictionary* (London, 1939), p. 536. A Swahili proverb reads, "Born here is the sensible slave," implying that an mzalia is more skillful than a new slave. Taylor, *African Aphorisms or Saws from Swahili-Land,* no. 350.

22. Claim for compensation by Rashid bin Salim Al-Mazrui, 1908, CP/1/62/46.

elaborate wedding ceremony, a more favored seat at ceremonial feasts.[23] Such slaves were placed in an ambivalent position: they were being accepted as coastal people and were being rewarded by more complete membership in coastal society; yet their entry into the social world of the freeborn could never be complete. They were receiving substantial incentives to accept the norms and behavior patterns of their owners. For others, manumission—which was wholly at the owner's discretion—promised an improved status, although frequently a new form of dependence, to slaves who pleased their masters. The pressures for cultural and social conformance affected most strongly those slaves who could provide continuity to slave traditions and a slave subculture. Acculturation and mobility were important parts of the slaveowners' control of society.

Not only did slaves have to be taught the culture of their masters, but they had to be placed in the society's institutions. Just as the slave family—as Rashid bin Hassani's account suggested—played a part in the socialization of new slaves, so it played a crucial role in making slaves part of a self-perpetuating social and economic institution, the plantation. If paternalism implies a concern with slaves as complete, if inferior, people and with society as an organic whole, one would expect masters to be concerned with continuity from generation to generation. The idea of importing a batch of slaves, making them work until they died, and then importing a new batch, is antithetical to paternalism. In a plantation context, the family is a sensible unit for reproduction and child rearing, for it gives the parents a stake in the status quo as well as providing a means of caring for children without taxing the master.[24]

At first glance, the evidence about Zanzibar and the mainland coast is negative. Most—but not all—travelers reported that family stability was not existant, promiscuity rampant, and the birth-rate low.[25] However,

23. Lodhi, "Institution of Slavery," pp. 10–11. Strobel notes that slaves who had shown their acceptance and understanding of Swahili culture participated more fully than others in the ritual life of a Swahili household. "Interaction of Slave and Freeborn," p. 17.

24. Paternalism, in this sense, is still not independent of the profit motive. The organic view of the plantation is encouraged whenever the cost of importing slaves exceeds the cost of rearing them. A paternalistic ideology is unlikely to emerge if the life-span—in part the result of a particular disease environment—is so short that the average slave dies before recouping the cost of his upbringing. Fogel and Engerman, *Time on the Cross*, 1: 20–29, 127–28; C. Vann Woodward, *American Counterpoint: Slavery and Racism in the North-South Dialogue* (Boston, 1971), pp. 78–106.

25. Rigby to Anderson, 21 March 1860, FO 84/1130; Rigby, "Report," 1860, in Russell, *General Rigby*, p. 334; Speer to Seward, 26 November 1862, US Consul, 4; Bishop Steere, Testimony to Select Committee on the Slave Trade, PP 1871, XII, 1, p. 76; Burton, *Zanzibar*, 1: 464; Newman, *Banani*, p. 31; O'Sullivan-Beare, "Report on Pemba," 1899, in PP

travelers made similar statements about the United States South—at least the first two—and recent research has shown them to be largely incorrect.[26] Perhaps travelers in the mid-Victorian era automatically assumed that a good institution like the family was necessarily incompatible with a bad one like slavery. A more accurate picture is hard to come by, since demographic data are wholly lacking.

The problem can be approached indirectly by noting that a relatively balanced ratio of male to female slaves is required for the plantation to become a self-perpetuating unit. In some parts of the Americas—where planters craved male labor and pregnancy was merely an impediment to work—the ratio of males to females among new imports and the slave population as a whole was high. In some of the English Caribbean sugar colonies during periods of expansion, 60 percent of the imports were male, only 13 percent children. Despite the fact that locally born slaves were evenly divided between sexes, the male-dominated imports distorted the sex ratios of the population. On Cuban sugar plantations during the sugar boom, males exceeded females by as much as two to one; on the coffee estates of Vassouras in Brazil the percentage of males hovered around 70 percent for African-born slaves and over 60 percent overall until the eve of abolition.[27] The opposite pole was the Southern United States in the nineteenth century: there sex ratios were nearly equal, and the slave population was self-reproducing.[28]

The slim evidence on sex ratios on the East African coast is closer to the pattern of the United States than to that of the Caribbean. An analysis of slaves taken off dhows illicitly engaged in the slave trade between 1874 and 1888 shows that 52 percent of the adult slaves were male, while children constituted over 30 percent of the cargoes.[29] Most

---

1901, XLVIII, 173, p. 21. Less negative views were expressed by Colomb, *Slave Catching*, p. 377; C. S. Smith to Kimberley, 26 May 1895, PP 1896, LIX, 395, pp. 8–9; and Schmidt, p. 48.

26. Fogel and Engerman, 1: 126–44; and Blassingame, *The Slave Community*, pp. 77–103.

27. K. G. Davies, *The Royal African Company* (London, 1957), p. 299; Knight, *Slave Society in Cuba*, p. 79; Stein, *Vassouras*, pp. 76, 155–56. For more on this intricate subject, see the studies in Engerman and Genovese, *Race and Slavery in the Western Hemisphere*, and Dunn, *Sugar and Slaves*, pp. 314–17.

28. Fogel and Engerman, 1: 26–27, 156. Natural increase was the main contributor to the growth of the slave population in the United States as early as the eighteenth century, and there is evidence that reproduction was a conscious goal of slaveowners. Ibid., pp. 25, 127–28.

29. These figures were calculated from the returns of naval officers engaged in antislave trade operations that are reprinted in PP, Slave Trade Series, 1874–89. They are not complete, but do give a sex breakdown of 3,498 slaves. Attempts were made to include only dhows destined for Zanzibar or the northern coast, but this was not always possible. For reasons that are not clear to me, the near-equality in sex ratios among adults

information on slave prices also suggests that adult laborers of either sex were equally valuable, although females intended as concubines commanded by far the highest prices.[30]

Data on slaves freed in Zanzibar and Pemba after the abolition of slavery in 1897 indicate that this near equality in sex ratios among adults imported from the mainland was maintained in the slave population as a whole. These figures—shown in Table 6:1—must be used cautiously, because of their late date and because the process of abolition, which required slaves to ask the British government for a certificate of freedom, involved much self-selection on the part of slaves.

TABLE 6:1

SEX RATIOS OF SLAVES FREED IN ZANZIBAR AND PEMBA

Category of Slaves	Males per 100 Females	Total Number
Zanzibar		
Total, 1897–1907	106	5,145
Born on mainland *	108	1,175
Born on island *	81	540
Shamba workers *	87	548
Other workers *	104	1,167
Living in city *	105	1,101
Living in country *	89	614
Pemba (total)	70	814

SOURCES: Last to Mathews, 10 January 1901, PP 1901, XLVIII, 173, pp. 29–30; Last to Raikes, 5 February 1902, PP 1903, XLV, 955, pp. 8–9; Last to Cave, 23 May 1908, FOCP 9401, p. 92; J. P. Farler, Slavery Reports on Pemba, 1900, 1901, PP 1901, XLVIII, 173, p. 31, and PP 1903, XLV, 955, p. 16.

* Based on slaves freed in 1900–01.

Besides the overall evenness of the sexual balance, the figures show a high proportion of females among shamba workers, as well as in the overwhelmingly rural population of Pemba. Unlike the sugar islands, the desire to employ the most efficient workers in agriculture did not distort the demographic structure of rural Zanzibar. The somewhat higher ratio of males among urban slaves probably reflects the large

---

did not apply to children, who were 61% male. A related set of figures—from slaves received by mission stations after having been taken from slave dhows—agrees closely with the statistics from naval sources. Kirk to Derby, 14 September 1877, FOCP 3686, pp. 658–59.

30. The evidence is not perfectly clear, since observers often failed to distinguish categories of slaves precisely. See Rigby, "Report," p. 333; Burton, Lakes, 2: 376; and Gen. Lloyd Mathews, Memorandum, 23 April 1891, FO 84/2153.

number of vibarua in Zanzibar town. The self-selection process of abolition may influence these figures: vibarua lacked close ties with their
masters but had to turn over a portion of their wages; females in the
town were often concubines, who were excluded from the abolition act
until 1909, or domestics, many whom of had close ties with their masters' households. The somewhat low proportion of males among slaves
born on the island—as well as in rural areas—may well reflect higher
mobility for males than for females, who remained on plantations or
became domestics or concubines.

Yet taken as a whole, the statistics suggest that family formation and
plantation continuity was, at the very least, demographically possible.
Not only did slaveowners maintain the female population of their estates, but they also bought a relatively high percentage of children,
despite the fact that these would not immediately be efficient workers.
Children, however, were easier to socialize than adults and would be
long-term members of the plantation community. Continuity in plantation life, not just short-term efficiency, influenced purchasing decisions
in the slave market.[31]

Marriage and family formation were not simply ways of breeding
slaves, but a way of placing personal relationships among slaves in the
context of the master-slave tie. Under Islamic law, the master was the
guardian of his slaves, and his permission was required for marriage,
just as the parents' consent was needed for free persons to marry.
Christie noted that masters themselves performed marriages for their
slaves, and that if a slave failed to find a mate on the plantation, the
master customarily purchased a slave from another plantation to whom
the slave had become attached.[32] Rashid bin Hassani's autobiography
includes a description of family life and then his own marriage in accordance with Islamic rituals.[33] On the mainland, a male slave cus-

31. A complete analysis of such decisions is impossible. For example, conditions on the
supply side may have affected the picture. It would not be surprising if societies of the
East African interior had a high demand for female slaves to add to the reproductive capacity of the lineages. This may help account for the high price of females in Zanzibar, as
well as for the slightly larger proportion of males in the import statistics.

32. Brunschvig, " 'Abd," pp. 26–27; Schacht, *Islamic Law*, p. 127. Christie, "Slavery," p.
33; Kersten, 1: 81, Colomb, pp. 376–77; Schmidt, p. 30; Fraser, "Zanzibar and the Slave
Trade," p. 20. Even after abolition, ex-slaves continued to obtain their ex-masters' consent before marrying. Zanzibar Government, "A Review of the System of Land Tenure,"
p. 20.

33. Rashid, p. 99. All sales of slaves that separated husband and wife or parents and
child were banned by the Sultan's proclamation in 1886—an indication that such sales
were contrary to Zanzibari norms but took place nonetheless. Sultan of Zanzibar to
Holmwood, 13 October 1886, PP 1888, XLIII, 283, p. 22. See also Christie, "Slavery," p.
46, and Speer to Seward, 26 November 1862, US Consul, 4.

tomarily paid his master a small fee (about $2) on the occasion of his marriage, as a recognition of the master's performance of his duties as guardian.[34] So strong was the acceptance of guardianship, that well after the abolition of slavery in Kenya, ex-masters often expected their ex-slaves to pay them this fee, and kadis still regarded the payment as part of the marriage ritual.[35]

Informants on the coast state emphatically that slaves married and raised children in a family setting.[36] Their own life-histories illustrate these points. Awade bin Maktub was the son of a father from near Lake Nyasa and a mother of Zulu origin born in Zanzibar.[37] The father was a slave of the Sultan in Zanzibar before the Sultan gave him to Bi Salima binti Masudi when she went, at the Sultan's behest, to Malindi. The mother was a *mtoto wa nyumbani* of the Sultan, that is, an mzalia who had been brought up in the household. She was nominally free but remained a dependent of the Sultan, who sent her to Bi Salima. In Malindi she married Awade's father. He worked in the fields while she remained in the household. Young Awade became a *mtoto wa nyumbani* himself, lived in Bi Salima's house, and was sent to Koranic school by her. Awade speaks with affection of both his own mother and Bi Salima, who was also like a mother to him. Under a slaveowner who took his or her social role seriously, a slave family could be a family within a family.[38]

The desire of masters to encourage families and reproduction did not necessarily imply that a slave population would in fact be self-

34. This fee was referred to as *kilemba,* meaning "turban." Beech, "Slavery," p. 148; and Fitzgerald, *Travels,* p. 28.

35. A former Arab official told me that this went on in the 1930s in Lamu. Slaves who had been freed by the government regarded the government as their new master and came to this official to obtain his consent for marriage. MSA 14. These practices had earlier produced a controversy within the administration. Assistant District Commissioner, Lamu, to Judge Hamilton, 30 April 1908, Judicial/1/402, KNA; Memorandum by Provincial Commissioner F. W. Isaac, 21 February 1912, CP/1/2/84.

36. MAL 34, 35, 38. Spouses are also mentioned in many documents. See, for example, 5A 1894, 993A 1911 (deed dated 1899), and 352A 1907, Reg., Msa. There is not enough data to study the structures of slave families or the ways in which slaves struggled to shape family life in their own ways. On the Southern United States, see Herbert G. Gutman, *The Slave Family in Slavery and Freedom, 1750–1925* (New York, 1976).

37. The mother may have been Ngoni, one of the peoples caught up in the dispersal of Southern African peoples after the rise of the Zulu leader Shaka in the 1820s.

38. MAL 30. In a variety of hierarchical societies, the institution of ritual coparenthood serves an analogous function in situating the family in the context of relationships between superior and inferior. As part of the baptism ceremony, a baby of lower-class birth is given a ceremonial sponsor from the upper class. The child acquires a special claim to the patronage of his coparent, while the patron sees the ties of dependence reaffirmed. Sidney W. Mintz and Eric R. Wolf, "An Analysis of Ritual Co-Parenthood (Compadrazgo)," *Southwestern Journal of Anthropology* 6 (1950): 341–68.

reproducing, for many of the determining factors lay outside of the master's control.[39] Most visitors to Zanzibar believed that the reproduction rate was low and the death rate high, but their opinions were not based on demographic data, for none exist.[40] A low reproduction rate, however, would not be surprising. Owing to the relatively short time between the large increase in plantation slavery and the advent of the British, a high proportion of slaves were mainland-born—two-thirds in the 1900–01 figures. Given the prevalence of tropical diseases in Zanzibar, a low fertility rate and a high rate of infant mortality could be expected.[41] Nor did all slave women share the attitudes toward the family expressed in the recollections of informants. Abortion and infanticide were occasionally practiced by slave women, for whom childbearing and rearing were additions to already heavy burdens.[42] These differences point to the contradictions of paternalism: the ability of slaves to build meaningful social relationships within plantation society and the rejection by some of the masters' self-interested notions of plantation continuity.

However close the ties between master and slaves, however similar their religious practices, language, and culture, their relationship was still that of the superior to his inferiors. This vertical distance was emphasized in speech. Deference was an essential aspect of a slave's behavior. Slaves greeted their masters with the expression *"Shikamuu,"* meaning literally "I embrace your feet," which has since become an expression of respect to elders. The master would reply, *"Marahaba,"*

39. On the difficulties of calculating birth and death rates, as well as making judgments about material welfare on the basis of such data, see Jack Ericson Eblen, "On the Natural Increase of Slave Populations: The Example of the Cuban Black Population, 1775–1900," and Stanley Engerman, "Comments on the Study of Race and Slavery"— both in Engerman and Genovese, pp. 211–48, 500–14.

40. See the sources cited in n. 25 above. Estimates of overall annual attrition are: 22–33% (1844), 30% (1857), 20% (1873), and 8–12% (1883). The decline may reflect a growing proportion of seasoned or locally born slaves in the population, but such rough estimates cannot reliably be compared. A French medical thesis on Zanzibar wisely avoids any such conclusions, citing the lack of data. The author did think that the population was growing, owing both to local births and immigration. Hamerton to Aberdeen, 2 January 1844, FO 54/6; Burton, *Zanzibar*, 1: 463; Kirk to Derby, 4 January 1878, FOCP 3928, p. 206; Miles to Granville, 1 March 1883, FOCP 4914, p. 124; Semmane, *Essai d'une Topographie Medicale*, p. 11.

41. Fogel and Engerman, 1: 26–27; Philip D. Curtin, "Epidemiology and the Slave Trade," *Political Science Quarterly* 83 (1968): 190–216. For contemporary views of disease in Zanzibar by physicians, see Semmane and Christie, *Cholera Epidemics*.

42. Burton, *Zanzibar*, 1: 464; Newman, *Banani*, p. 31; O'Sullivan-Beare, "Report," PP 1901, XLVIII, 173, p. 21. At best, women were allowed to stop working for only a month before delivery and for a month afterward. Christie, "Slavery," p. 47, and O'Sullivan-Beare, p. 21.

"Welcome." [43] Masters generally avoided the harsh words for slaves, *watumwa* in Swahili or *abd* in Arabic, and used *watoto*, "children," or *watu wangu*, "my people." Slaves referred to master and mistress as *bwana* and *bibi*, or else used the diminutives, *kibwana* and *kibibi*. [44] Such terminology does not mean that slaves were treated as family members, but it does imply that master-slave relationships were rationalized in terms of the patriarchal structure of the family.

Holidays were occasions for the masters to display generosity toward their slaves and for the slaves to express deference in their acceptance of hospitality. On the important holidays, the master staged a celebration for the benefit of his slaves. Animals were slaughtered, and meat and other food distributed at the master's house. [45] In Zanzibar town, however, slaves would "carouse and junket in their own quarter of town, each clan from the mainland keeping itself distinct." [46] These feasts were part of a general pattern of largess that was characteristic of Omanis, as well as Islamic beliefs that it was incumbent on the rich to give alms to the poor. Generosity was part of the sense of hierarchy.

The routine of greetings and festivals symbolized the many elements of dependence. The slaveowner was at the apex of a social group. How indelible an impression growing up within such a group could make emerges from the in-depth interviews Margaret Strobel has done with a Swahili woman of Mombasa, Bi Kaje. [47] The focus of social interaction was Bi Hindi, who—by exercising her property rights under Islamic law—had acquired slaves, farms, and houses and had attracted the allegiance of free kinsfolk. Bi Kaje's father was free, in terms of law and status, but essentially dependent on Bi Hindi, overseeing her farm, trading at her behest, and belonging to the group gathered around her. Bi Kaje's mother was a concubine, who knew the world of both the free and the slaves in Bi Hindi's household. Bi Kaje knew the thirty slaves and several waungwana well. The slaves participated together in weddings and other rituals; they were inculcated with Bi Hindi's notions of what "civilized" behavior was in a Swahili household—although some preferred their own rituals and forms of expression—and they received benefits—a wedding ceremony like that of the free, manumis-

43. Krapf, *Suahili Dictionary*, pp. 202, 331; Inter-territorial Committee, *Standard Dictionary*, pp. 420–21; Beech, "Swahili Life" (see n. 17, above).

44. Weidner, *Die Haussklaverei in Ostafrika*, p. 31. In the Southern United States, masters took such expressions of deference very seriously and their absence as a major breach. Genovese, *Roll*.

45. Last to Mathews, 22 February 1900, PP 1901, XLVIII, 173, p. 5; Schmidt, p. 30; MAL 24, 34, 45; MSA 12. Such feasts were also important to slaves in the United States South. Stampp, *The Peculiar Institution*, p. 365.

46. Burton, *Zanzibar*, 1: 366.

47. Strobel, "Interaction."

sion, assistance in old age—from Bi Hindi. Within the group, the free were clearly differentiated from the slaves, yet conformity to social norms—especially for concubines or those born into the household— narrowed the gap.

For all the social familiarity and reliance on Bi Hindi's patronage, economic life was starkly impersonal: half the slaves did not even work within the social group, but were hired out to others, remitting their wages to Bi Hindi. Social intimacy did not negate economic exploitation; both were part of a highly authoritarian structure couched in a familial ideology. The family, in many historical contexts, has provided the imagery to make subordination appear in a normative framework, to stress that the power of those on top is being exercised for the good of those on the bottom.[48]

The Muslim patriarch—extending protection and generosity to his dependents—was the crucial figure of the slaveholders' ideology. That a woman, like Bi Hindi in Mombasa or Bi Salima binti Masudi in Malindi, could be the leader of a social group underlines the great importance of property to social relations. Coastal society rigidly excluded women from political office, and it placed a high value on a man's control over the women—wives, concubines, daughters, and other kin—in his household. High status was often associated with the seclusion of women. Yet what counted above all was having dependent followers, and property was a means of acquiring them. Women generally held less of it than men, and the restraints on their actively controlling it were great; but those who succeeded in utilizing property effectively could even find freeborn men eager to accept a position of clientage.[49] From the point of view of the slaves, such a woman was not merely profiting from her property rights; she was the head of a group of dependent persons.[50]

For slaves, the personal and multifaced ties of dependence could rarely be avoided. Without belonging to a unified group under the

48. For an insightful discussion of the uses of the image of the family to justify violence toward subordinate people, see Michael Wallace, "Paternalism and Violence," in Philip. P. Wiener and John Fisher, eds., *Violence and Aggression in the History of Ideas* (New Brunswick, N.J., 1974), pp. 203–20.

49. In Malindi, men owned about seven times as many mashamba as did women (a/c, Malindi). On patriarchy, see Strobel, "Muslim Women," pp. 49–50.

50. The "paternalistic" position of women slaveowners held true in all but the political sense. Male informants in Malindi, including one brought up in Bi Salima's household, spoke of her strong control over her plantations, her leadership in the household, her role in raising—as Swahili families often do—the children of other parents, and her generosity. They used much the same terms as they did in describing men in similar roles. They hastened to add that her behavior was most unusual: only one other woman, in these accounts, exercised such active control over her property.

master or mistress, slaves would have stood alone in a society where people interacted as members of groups, not as individuals. For slaveowners, such ties were part of heshima, part of the ideological foundations of their power and status.

In the face of economic, social, and cultural subordination, some slaves rebelled. But more sought as much independence as they could find within a paternalistic system. The very strength of the bonds of dependence made its possible for such independence to exist without threatening the social or ideological basis of the slaveholders' position.

INDEPENDENCE UNDER SLAVERY

Slaves on the East African coast, even those whose working lives were rigidly controlled, had a certain amount of living space once their day's labor was done. For them, it provided more than a brief respite—namely, a chance to acquire a small degree of economic autonomy, to create a social life among themselves, and to resist, as individuals and as a group, the idea that they were inferior members of their owners' society.

Slaves, even those engaged in gang labor, were left alone to a considerable extent after they had completed their assigned ngwe or other task. The regimented home-life of many slave plantations in the Americas was unknown on the East African coast. Visitors to rural parts of Zanzibar saw slave huts scattered around the plantations, dispersed among the clove trees and the plots that were used by the slaves themselves. On the plantation of one of the largest landlords of Pemba—where the clove industry was the most intense—there was no one slave quarter, but only slave huts "dotted all over the place." [51] Similarly, slaves in Malindi lived scattered among the mashamba in clusters of two or three huts, or else in small villages containing only slaves. Each family had its own house, which they generally built themselves. By custom, masters had no right to enter a slave's hut unless in a "very extreme case, such as searching for a runaway." [52] In the Mombasa area, slaves often lived in villages containing slaves owned by various masters. They were governed by a slave headman elected by their own elders. He was expected to arrest any suspected criminals and send them to Mombasa for trial. [53]

---

51. Mackenzie, "Report on Slavery and the Slave-Trade," p. 75; Fitzgerald, *Travels*, p. 516; Baumann, *Sansibar*, p. 32; Grandidier, *Notice sur l'isle de Zanzibar*, p. 8.

52. Fitzgerald, *Travels*, pp. 20–21, 32, 34; MAL 24, 26, 28, 35, 38, 50.

53. Hardinge, "Report," PP 1898, LX, 199, p. 6; Hardinge to Salisbury, 12 April 1896, PP 1896, LIX, 41, p. 91. Slave Villages were also noted in the Vanga and Lamu areas. McKay, "Southern Kenya Coast" p. 155; Ylvisaker, "Lamu Archipelago," p. 98.

Urban slaves also had considerable autonomy. While house servants often lived with their masters, a visitor reported that they streamed into and out of the houses. Vibarua, mahamali, and artisans often lived in their own homes. As they became increasingly numerous in Zanzibar town, especially in the 1870s, a quarter of town where slaves were concentrated took shape. Some Hadramis, who worked in the port themselves or owned the port workers, also lived there, as did many slaves who had been freed by their masters and gravitated to the open environment of the town.[54] The combination of a high concentration of slaves and freed slaves in one section of town would likely have deeply frightened the citizens of a city in the Old South.[55]

Many slaves in Mombasa also lived on their own, often in houses they built on land rented or borrowed from Swahili or Arab landowners. The landlord was usually not the owner of the slave, and slaves of different masters often lived on the same plot, interspersed among Arabs, Swahili, and freed slaves. As in Zanzibar, a large portion of such slaves congregated in a particular quarter of the town.[56]

It is clear that the number of slaves who rented house plots was quite large, thanks to a list of rentals by Mombasa's leading landlord, Salim bin Khalfan Al-Busaidi, dating from 1899. As Table 6:2 indicates, a disproportionate number of female slaves rented such plots. Their numbers probably reflect women's importance as house servants—both

TABLE 6:2

LESSEES OF URBAN LAND OF SALIM BIN KHALFAN, MOMBASA, 1899

	Women	Men
Slaves	163	69
Freed slaves	139	53
Waungwana	91	154
Totals	393	276

SOURCE: Registers AS1 and AS2, Land Office, Mombasa.

54. Kersten, 1: 78; Christie, *Cholera*, pp. 239–40, 360, 366. On freed slaves, see below.

55. Wade, *Slavery in the Cities*. The combination of slaves and freed slaves was especially worrisome to Southern slaveowners. Eugene D. Genovese, "The Slave States of North America," in Cohen and Greene, eds., *Neither Slave Nor Free*, pp. 258–77.

56. This was Mji Mpya, New Town. These living patterns are evident in a large number of deeds filed in Reg., Msa. A typical deed of sale of a plot would mention that the house of "Maiki, slave of Kassim bin Rashid El-Mazrui" was on the property. Deeds that included descriptions of boundaries often mentioned that a slave was a neighbor. See, for example, 47A, 55A, 59A, 147A 1892, 71A 1894, 661A and 662A 1897. Of Bi Hindi's slaves, six lived in her house, nine in houses on her land or farms, and fifteen in houses they purchased, rented, or were given. Strobel, "Interaction," p. 10.

to their owners and for hire—but the figures show that many slave women had sufficient economic and social independence to rent land for their homes.[57] Some slave men were in a position to do so as well, but a higher proportion of men probably stayed on the mashamba, since Mombasa lacked the large corps of port laborers that Zanzibar possessed. Among waungwana, men frequently rented land, but women did so less often than slave women. The low status of the latter put them beneath the restrictive Islamic notions of seclusion, permitting them—along with men—to have a chance to build a home of their own.

Unlike the case of the coast, the increasing scale and intensity of plantation agriculture in the Americas tended to subject slaves to more restrictive living arrangements. Both slave villages and the independent houses in the towns were different from slaves' housing in parts of the New World. On some plantations in the Southern United States, slaves lived in single-family houses at some distance from their master's eyes, but the slave quarters were often placed within sight of the overseer's cottage. Where slaves were being exploited with the greatest intensity, as in Cuba during the sugar boom or southern Brazil in the coffee boom, slave quarters were closely supervised and even locked at night.[58] Some urban slaves lived on their own, but many others lived in barracks or in their master's enclosed compound.[59] In East Africa slaves could spend their leisure house in a place that was their own.

Similarly, the restrictions on freedom of movement that became characteristic of Western plantation societies did not apply in East Africa. In the British West Indies, market day was virtually the only time slaves were free to leave the plantation, and most areas had pass laws and other means of controlling the movements of slaves.[60] Visitors to Zanzibar were surprised by the extent of the physical mobility of slaves. Especially on Thursdays and Fridays—the two free days granted plantation slaves—they came to Zanzibar town in large numbers, bringing many items they had grown or made in their free time—fruit, vegeta-

57. Cities in the Southern United States also had a high proportion of female slaves. Wade, p. 23.

58. Quarters were sometimes locked in the United States as well, and they were patrolled in certain situations. Blassingame, p. 43. See also Stampp, p. 292; Fogel and Engerman, 1: 115–16; Stein, pp. 134, 168; Knight, p. 68; and Goveia, *Slave Society in the British Leeward Islands*, p. 184. The trend toward restricting slaves' lives is emphasized by Wood, *Black Majority*.

59. Wade, pp. 55–79; Starobin, *Industrial Slavery in the Old South*, pp. 57–62.

60. Goveia, p. 239; Patterson, *The Sociology of Slavery*, pp. 224–30; Stampp, p. 149. Despite all these restrictions, slaves still managed to visit friends and relatives on neighboring plantations.

bles, tobacco, mats, and the like. An "immense" number of slaves filled the streets. The market was a social center for the slaves as well as a place to sell goods.[61]

Burton was shocked at the extent to which slaves could roam around and behave as they wished: "The impudence and audacity of the wild slaves almost passed belief." He felt that they were a danger to public order, walking into open houses and carrying off goods or committing robberies at night. Another visitor to the town was surprised to see Negroes, presumably slaves, walking around with spears. In plantation areas, rival gangs of slaves sometimes fought each other with sticks, stones, and occasionally muskets. Pemba was also troubled by roaming bands of armed slaves.[62] Christie, however, found violent crime even more rare than in "civilized countries," and noted that petty theft was the only common crime. Even drunkenness was rare. But Kirk claimed drunkenness was common among slaves. If true, this would be a serious breach of Islamic norms and indicate the limited control masters had over their slaves. Perhaps Burton and Kirk simply assumed that the lower orders of society would necessarily behave badly if their betters did not keep a constant eye on them. Likewise, slaves in Malindi were able to walk around and go to town as they wished. In some cases, slaves living away from centers of population were given guns to protect themselves against wild animals.[63]

This freedom of movement and assembly, as well as the opportunity for slaves to obtain weapons, could get out of hand. In 1880, a larger number "of the better class of slaves" in Mombasa went off to some distant plantations for three days of "feasting and firing guns and consulting together." Their masters feared a rebellion but had no idea what to do about it. It came to nothing, but one can imagine that in the same circumstances slaveowners in the Americas would have had a clear idea of what to do.[64] In general, the slaves' independence caused little consternation. After all, if slaveowners could count on the loyalty of their slaves in fighting their political engagements for them, they should not

61. Journal of Lieutenant Christopher, 1843, incl. Bombay to Secret Committee, no. 54, 18 July 1843, Ind. Off., L/P&S/5/60; Rigby, "Report," p. 334; Christie, *Cholera*, pp. 318–19. In the West Indies, some areas allowed slaves to participate in analogous markets, notably in Jamaica, but some restricted such activities. Patterson, pp. 224–30; Goveia, p. 159.

62. Burton, *Zanzibar*, 1: 465–66: Ruschenberger, *A Voyage Round the World*, p. 38. Farler to Mathews, 26 January 1900, PP 1901, XLVIII, 173, p. 7.

63. Christie, "Slavery," pp. 42–43; Kirk to Granville, 13 December 1872, FOCP 4206, p. 109; Newman, *Banani*, p. 133; MAL 34.

64. Menzies to Wright, 18 June 1880; CMS CA5/M6. In the Americas, fear of assembly was particularly acute. Wade, p. 158; Stein, p. 204.

have feared dire consequences from letting their slaves move around as they wished during their free time.

Freedom of movement and residence was of course greatest for those slaves not tied to the system of plantation labor common in Zanzibar and Malindi. Farm workers who paid *ijara* or a proportion of the crops did not have to see their masters very often. Day laborers, as indicated earlier, often lived on their own and found work for themselves. In extreme cases, the bonds of slavery could become very weak. A caravan porter told his European employer that he had gone on the safari against his owner's wishes, and, thinking ahead to his master's claim to half his pay, he cockily asked, "Who can prevent me from eating it all up?" [65] So many urban slaves enlisted in caravans that in 1878 *hamali* labor became scarce. European merchants complained that slaves left without consulting their masters, while some slaveowners threatened to sell off their slaves unless measures were taken to prevent them from leaving on caravans. Nothing was done and the problem continued into the 1890s.[66] Rashid bin Hassani, a slave of Bibi Zem Zem, had his own house and kept the wages he earned doing odd jobs. In his own words, he was "merely under Bibi Zem Zem's protection." [67]

Even on clove plantations, the looseness of supervision sometimes presented slaves with opportunities to sell cloves to Indians behind their masters' backs at a price below that which their owners were asking. The Sultan tried to order all Indians to stay out of the plantation areas, but his power of enforcement was too weak and the role of the middlemen too essential for the ban to be effective.[68] On the mainland, a number of cases eventually came before colonial courts involving slaves who had lived as free men without having been legally manumitted. The courts had trouble deciding whether the person had in fact been freed.[69] These instances represent one end of a spectrum, but in

65. Paul Reichard, *Deutsch-Ostafrika: Das Land und Seine Bewohner* (Leipzig; 1892), p. 478. A slave who was working on a dhow that had to be repaired, hired himself out to another vessel, receiving the usual rate for a free sailor. He had already visited Arabia twice. Kirk considered this degree of freedom typical for slaves working as sailors. Kirk to Granville, 12 July 1873, FOCP 4207, p. 112.

66. Memorial by nine European merchants to the Sultan, incl. Kirk to Derby, 9 January 1878, FOCP 3928, p. 307; Norman R. Bennett, *Studies in East African History* (Boston, 1963), pp. 44–45.

67. Rashid, p. 79.

68. Seyyid Bargash to Churchill, 31 October 1871, incl. Churchill to Wedderburn, 17 November 1870, Ind. Off., L/P&S/9/49. Slaves in Jamaica also sold their masters' sugar, and this resulted in the passage of many ordinances restricting the market activities of slaves. Patterson, p. 224.

69. *Abdulla bin Mahomed* vs. *Juma bin Farajalla,* Civil Appeal 28 of 1911, *Kenya Law Reports,* 4: 68–71; *A. M. Jeevanjee and Co.,* vs. *The Crown,* Civil Appeal 30 of 1915, in ibid., 6: 86–89, 183–87.

general the masters' control over their slaves' nonworking activities was limited. No slaveowning class ever succeeded in making slavery into a total institution, but slaves on the East African coast had somewhat more living space than their counterparts in the Americas.[70]

From the slaves' point of view, flexibility of living arrangements was not simply accepted as a generous gift from the master. Nor did they view their dependence in the same terms as their owners did. For them, as for American slaves, paternalism marked the boundaries within which they could struggle to live their own lives and establish their own values.

The slaves made use of the limited opportunities they had to gain a modicum of economic independence outside of the master-slave relationship. Of course, the thrust of the plantation system was to develop economic dependence, not just by force but by the provision of plots on the master's land and by opportunities for advancement within the plantation hierarchy. Islamic law narrowly defined slaves' economic rights: any property acquired by a slave belonged to the master and could be taken by him at will.[71]

In actual practice, slaves in East Africa had more freedom to engage in economic activities and acquire modest amounts of money than they had by law. The theoretical right of the master to seize his slave's property at any time was exercised mainly at the time of the slave's death. In Zanzibar, Christie claimed, some slaves were wealthy. Even in the clove areas of Pemba, slaves could earn and keep a few pice by cutting firewood and selling it in the nearby village or by weaving mats for use in the drying of cloves.[72] Not only did they grow their own food in their spare time, but they could earn a little money by selling produce in the market. Most likely, urban slaves, who kept a portion of their earnings, had the best chance to accumulate money. Like other Zanzibaris who had acquired some wealth, slaves sometimes purchased other slaves for their own use. Slaves could also possess immovable property.[73]

As in Pemba, the slaves of Malindi could earn a little money from the surplus food they produced on their own small plots. Kirk said that a

70. See Elkins, *Slavery*.

71. Brunschvig, pp. 28–29; Niese, p. 43.

72. Christie, "Slavery," pp. 33, 47; Hardinge to Kimberly, 26 February 1895, PP 1895, LXXI, 143, pp. 28–29; Quass, p. 443; O'Sullivan, "Report on Pemba," 1896, PP 1896, LIX, 395, p. 42.

73. Christie, "Slavery," p. 47; Colomb, pp. 369–70; Speer to Seward, 26 November 1862, US Consul, 4; Rigby, "Report," p. 334; Rodd to Rosebery, 31 December 1893, PP 1895, LXXI, 143, p. 17; Quass, p. 443; Devereux, *A Cruise in the "Gorgon"*, p. 107; Deed of sale of a house by a slave to Bishop Tozer, 1865, in Gray Papers, Cambridge University Library, box 28.

slave could earn $10–12 per year from a plot, while a couple could get $30.[74]

The registers of transactions kept in Mombasa from 1891 onward contain a rich record of the economic activities of slaves. Slaves bought and sold houses, town land, and farmland. Most of these purchases and sales were modest, but some were substantial by contemporary standards.[75] Such property was often obtained by purchase from the slave's own savings, but occasionally, especially in the case of concubines, the plots were gifts of the master.[76] At least in theory, slaves could only sell land with the permission of their masters, but sometimes they even sold their masters' land, and courts later had problems determining which property legally belonged to the slave and which to the master.[77]

Slaves could also borrow money from Indian, Arab, or Swahili moneylenders, often mortgaging property as security. There are cases on record of a slave lending money to free men.[78] Most of these loans were small, but some deeds indicated that the slaves were conducting businesses of their own. Juma bin Nasib borrowed $504 from the Imperial British East Africa Company in 1892, repayable in one year, and mortgaged his shamba, three cows, and his dhow.[79] Another slave of the same master borrowed $30 plus 140 pounds of ivory, and later $92 from two separate Indians. A dhow captain of slave status obtained credit for 140 pounds of ivory and 70 pounds of giraffe horn from the town's leading Omani moneylender, mortgaging a house in Mombasa and a shamba outside of the city.[80] A slave of a Zanzibari was appointed to be his master's agent and supervisor of his master's slaves at Mam-

74. Kirk to Granville, 6 November 1873, PP 1874, LXII, 749, pp. 101–02.

75. Bokeit bin Khais sold land worth $330 in Mombasa in 1898. 365A 1898, Reg., Msa. In Malindi, one Yusuf bin Kombo claimed that he inherited a 150-acre plot from his father, who was the slave of a Bajuni. The government allowed the claim, but Malindi scuttlebut says that Yusuf had claimed his master's land after abolition. a/c 126D of 1914. A loan of $1078 to Faraji, slave of Komboro bin Mwenye Uvi, a Swahili of Mombasa, was the eighth largest transaction in a series of 566 deeds. 4B 1893, Reg., Msa.

76. a/c 88, 89M 1913, 107D 1915 (Malindi); a/c 22 of 1922 (Mambrui); and 101A 1898, 54A 1906, Reg., Msa.

77. Opinion of the Kadi of Kenya, Sheikh Suliman bin Ali, filed with a/c 20N of 1915 (Mombasa); a/c 17, 19, 20, 24, 25, 41, 48 N of 1915 (Mombasa); *Mohamed bin Mansur* vs. *Administrator General of East Africa*, Civil Cause 154 of 1917, Resident Magistrate's Court, Mombasa; *Talib bin Mwenye Jaha, wasi of Sud bin Muslim* vs. *Mishi wa Abdulla*, Civil Cause 662 of 1911, Town Magistrate's Court, Mombasa.

78. Hassan bin Ismail, from Kilwa, borrowed about $10 from Abd Salam bin Athman, slave of Zaharan bin Sheikh, due in three months, and mortgaged his house in Mombasa. 97A 1904, Reg., Msa. See also 19B 1893 and 5B 1896.

79. The deed is dated 1889, 151A 1892. Juma, slave of binti Ali binti Khamis Al-Mandhry, also owned a dhow. 122B 1899.

80. 58A 1893; 56A 1893; 398A 1892. Johari, "servant" of an Arab, borrowed over 800 pounds of ivory. 200B 1897.

brui. Meanwhile, he traded on his own account and accumulated much property.[81] Another slave appointed a free Swahili as his agent to collect fifteen peices of ivory that were due him.[82] The records also mention a partnership among a free person, a slave, and a freed slave. I have seen records of thirteen transactions by this trio, together or individually. They borrowed money four times, in amounts varying from $51 to $375, mortgaging various mashamba, houses, daggers, and personal effects as collateral, and gained financing for ivory deals on nine occasions, for quantities of ivory between one-half and ten frasilas. They obtained these loans from an assortment of Indians, Arabs, and Swahili.[83]

The activities of these slave-entrepreneurs indicate the possibilities open to slaves, not a large-scale participation in business. Table 6:3 compares the transactions executed by slaves with those of free Arabs and Swahili, as recorded in the Mombasa deed registers. Overall, slaves were involved in under 5 percent of the transactions recorded. The properties they bought and sold were very modest, and the higher average values for loans they raised represent the work of a small

TABLE 6:3

TRANSACTIONS BY SLAVES, MOMBASA

| | By Slaves | | By Arabs and Swahili | |
| | | Mean Value | | Mean Value |
Type of Transaction	Number	(Rs)	Number	(Rs)
Bought urban property *	30	52	146	263
Bought shamba *	8	66	119	232
Sold urban property *	30	64	276	420
Sold shamba *	4	52	186	430
Borrowed against property *	9	200	159	509
Borrowed—no collateral	12	433	202	453
Borrowed ivory	17 †	—	111	—

* Based on 20% sample of the A-series, 1891–1905. Others based on B-series, 100% sample, 1892–1899, after which B-series was no longer kept.

† Includes all the ivory transactions of the trio mentioned in the text.

81. The master's son seized much of the property and was sued by Juma. The case was pending at the time the letter describing it was written, and the outcome is unknown. Weaver to Craufurd, 13 January 1899, CP/1/74/43.

82. 54B 1894. See also 152B 1899.

83. The three were named Rubea bin Juma, slave of the Kilifi tribe of the Mombasa Swahili, Fundi Khamis, freed slave of Ali bin Salim Al-Timami, and Masai bin Mtwana, a man from the coast of Tanzania, whose name suggests he might have been of slave origin himself. 2, 17, 141, 180, 207, 233, 234 B 1894; 5, 6, 9 B 1898; 11B 1899; 8, 238A 1894. On the activities of a rich slave in Vanga, see McKay, pp. 118–19.

number of traders. The registers, however, probably underestimate the participation of slaves, for they were the furthest removed from the ways of the colonial bureaucracy and had the least valuable properties. Moreover, many transactions probably occurred between slaves and their masters or between two slaves, and would be handled informally.[84] Nevertheless, the evidence of entrepreneurial ·initiative by some slaves does not negate the fact that the overwhelming majority were poor.

Even those slaves who did accumulate some property could not be sure of passing it on to their children, since the property of a deceased slave passed to his master. A number of documents indicate that property was in fact inherited this way—which may well have reduced the incentives for slaves to amass wealth.[85] So deeply ingrained were these rules of inheritance that over twenty years after the abolition of slave status, ex-masters were still successfully claiming to be their former slaves' heirs.[86]

That slaves bought and sold their homes and farms, borrowed money, and traded, despite the labors they had to perform for their masters, indicates how much they wanted to minimize their economic dependence. To buy a house and a shamba was to reduce one's reliance on the master's fulfilling his obligations. Economic activities were symbolic, as well as practical, acts. For the objects of economic transactions to instigate them was a demonstration of personal initiative and ability outside of the slaves' demeaning role in the social order.

Culturally and ideologically, slaves did not fully internalize their position as subordinate members of their master's society. They did not totally accept the notion that their owners' culture was the only standard of civilization, and at the same time they denied that slaves, by definition, failed to meet those standards.

One of the most important expressions of cultural continuity was dance. Every Friday night, after a day of rest, the slaves of the Malindi arca came into town from the plantations. They congregated with

84. Lodhi claims that in Zanzibar, high-ranking slaves lent money to their juniors, without contracts or interest. Lodhi, p. 15.

85. *Me'Twana bi Muombwa* vs. *Me'Mtwana bi Muombwa*, Civil Case 430 of 1902, Town Magistrate's Court, Mombasa; *Talib bin Mwenye Jaha wasi of Sud bin Muslim El-Kilindini* vs. *Mishi wa Abdulla*, Civil Case 662 of 1911, Town Magistrate's Court, Mombasa; a/c 24 of 1923, 82D of 1914, 132M, 140M of 1913 (Malindi); a/c 42N of 1916 (Mombasa); and Reg., 42B 1896, 61B 1898, 83B 1899, 228A 1894.

86. MSA 14. The Mazrui let some of their slaves work on their own and then claimed the estate when the slave died, although they had other slaves working under closer supervision. Rashid bin Salim to Hinde, 29 October 1908, CP/1/62/46; and notes on an interview with Rashid bin Salim, 1908, ibid.

other slaves who came from the same parts of the interior of East Africa and danced the traditional dances of their home areas. Eventually, some of these dances became incorporated into Swahili culture, being danced by slaves and waungwana alike.[87] Dances were also part of Zanzibari slave society, and slaves in Zanzibar had work-songs as well, which they sang in unison as they worked in town.[88]

The continuing importance of female initiation ceremonies among slaves points to the ambiguity of their cultural position. For waungwana, sexual maturity was a private matter. While a slave woman (called a *somo*) was often employed to instruct a freeborn girl in sexual matters, the onset of puberty occasioned no ceremonies. The sexual instruction of slave girls was handled by *makungwi* (singular *kungwi*), slave women who belonged to an initiation society and were trained by older members. While a member of this association might also serve as a somo to a free girl, that relationship was individual. With slaves, puberty was marked collectively under the direction of makungwi.

Strobel argues that the female puberty rites were amalgams of the related practices of the peoples who provided the coast with most of its slaves. The waungwana scorned these rites and did not let their daughters participate in them. The slaves who were involved affirmed their belief in the rituals of their homelands, in the face of the disdain of their owners. For makungwi, membership in an initiation society provided a way to express solidarity with other slave women and to aspire to leadership roles outside of the structures of cultural and social dependence. Only well after abolition—and to a lesser extent than with slave dances—did initiation ceremonies attract waungwana women.[89]

Slave dances and initiation rites provided alternative cultural values and forms of association to slaves. Yet coastal slaves did not develop a clearly defined subculture. The boundaries remained unclear: even

87. MAL 24, 34, 35. One informant had played as a muscian at dances of former slaves, playing both coastal and Nyasa music (MSA 37). The dances of slaves in Malindi are described at some length by a former district officer there, R. Skene, in "Arab and Swahili Dances and Ceremonies," *Journal of the Royal Anthropological Institute* 47 (1917): 418–20, and were also mentioned by New, *Life, Wanderings and Labours in Eastern Africa*, p. 66. Strobel argues that certain wedding dances popular in Mombassa were brought there by slaves. Slave women had their own dances, which they performed among themselves, but certain styles later became more widely diffused. "Wedding Celebrations," pp. 28–41. Dances and songs were features of every Western slave society as well, although slaves' freedom to congregate was sometimes more restricted. Goveia, p. 184; Stein, p. 204; Genovese, *Roll*, pp. 569–73.

88. Godfrey Dale, *The Peoples of Zanzibar* (London, 1920), p. 16; Charmetant, *D'Alger à Zanzibar*, pp. 142–43; Schmidt, pp. 75–76. On the mainland opposite Zanzibar, slaves also performed the dances of their homelands. Baumann, *Usambara*, p. 62.

89. Strobel, "Muslim Women," pp. 282–87, and "Interaction," pp. 14–17.

slaves who fully participated in dances and rituals of the hinterland were also involved in Islam and other basic elements of coastal society. Other slaves responded more to the pressures toward acculturation. To celebrate puberty privately could be part of a process of raising one's status. Slaveowners gave enough recognition to slaves—especially to those living in or born into the household—who became familiar with the ways of the coast to make such efforts meaningful.

The dangers that a strong subculture might have posed to the slaveowners' cultural hegemony helps explain why coastal slaveholders did in fact show such interest in acculturating their slaves, and why—unlike planters in the Southern United States—they rewarded slaves who had learned their standards. For ties of dependence to retain their primacy, the ties among the slaves could not be allowed to grow too tight.

We still need to know much more about the origins of rites, myths, forms of expression, and symbols in Swahili culture and more about how different groups within Swahili society understood and manipulated these elements of culture. The available evidence suggests that slaves realized that improving their precarious position in society depended on mastering the ways of the society they had been brought into, but that it was equally necessary, in order to protect themselves against their owners' claims to superiority, that they develop a life among themselves and reaffirm the value of their own cultural heritage. The evidence also shows that cultural interaction was not a one-way process: slaves gave as well as received. The cosmopolitan culture of the coast was enriched, not just by immigrants from Asia, but by slaves brought against their will from the deep interior of Africa.

At the same time, the most central element of the Swahili and Arab slaveowners' culture and ideology—Islam—could itself be turned from an underpinning of patriarchy into a defense of spiritual equality. Religious ideology, as Genovese points out, "invariably is politically ambiguous." [90] If conversion brought slaves into the masters' ideological orbit and widened the gap between old and new slaves, it also created the basis for a challenge to the slaveowners' notions of their own religious superiority.

Slaves in the Southern United States used Christian themes—often combined with African elements—to celebrate the small joys within great suffering, to understand their masters' violation of Christian principles, to cope with natural as well as human misfortune, and to

90. This ambiguity undoubtedly caused the confusion among American slaveowners about the value and danger of converting slaves to Christianity. Some thought religion would teach slaves their place, others that it would make them forget it. In a sense, both were right. Genovese, *Roll,* p. 181.

provide a basis for collective strength. One only wishes that so much could be said about the East African coast, but no documents, so far as I know, give a slave's version of Islam in the nineteenth century. The best insights come from studies of coastal religion in the twentieth century and show how people of slave descent confronted the strong legacy of inferiority which slavery left. How fully these analyses apply to an earlier era is unclear, but they do suggest how people who were defined as "inferior" within a particular cultural tradition dealt ideologically with the concept of subordination.

El-Zein has shown how the descendants of masters and slaves in Lamu have used the Creation myth to bolster their conflicting notions of status. The waungwana claim that God created three colors of dust. Slaves are structurally associated with black dust and Europeans with red—both are connected with earthly impulses, with being close to nature. The free are associated with white dust, heavenly light, and purity.

The children of slaves, on the other hand, play down the distinctions among the kinds of dust, and stress the purity of belief. If Adam, God's own creation, could turn against Him, then anyone can do so. Conversely, the more love people have for the Prophet, the greater their purity.[91] In short, the two sides stress different elements of the same basic myth to make opposite points: that religious purity is a matter of descent and a matter of an individual's love for the Prophet.

These conflicting views were manifested during religious ceremonies, during which the waungwana, who controlled the mosques and ceremonies, relegated ex-slaves to positions commensurate with their supposedly inherent impurity. However, around 1891, when a learned and well-born religious leader began to allow slaves equal participation in ceremonies and even to study the Koran with him, ex-slaves flocked to him. In the changing socioeconomic situation of Lamu in the early twentieth century, slaves were able to change their religious position by actively participating in a movement that stressed their piety rather then their descent.[92]

A similar development occurred in Bagamoyo, although this time the local leader was himself an ex-slave. He rose to prominence not through the hierarchy of local scholars, which was closely associated with the town's waungwana elite, but through an expanding sufi brotherhood, the Qadiriyya. The brotherhood was by no means a movement of the lower classes, but in Bagamoyo it represented an al-

91. El-Zein, pp. 198–218.
92. Although the leader, Sharif Saleh ibn 'Alwi Jamalilil, welcomed slaves as equals in religious education and ritual, he still opposed intermarriage with them. Ibid., chap. 3.

ternative to a closely knit local elite. Sheikh Ramiya had been a slave who was freed in the 1880s and was able to obtain a thorough religious education. The rise of the Qadiriyya gave him a chance to prove his abilities, and he eventually became the most respected scholar in town. His following included many ex-slaves, but it was the extent of social change that enabled him to rise to general prominence and gain the respect—if reluctant—of waungwana.[93]

It was thus possible for slaves to become assimilated into coastal society without internalizing their roles as subordinate members of it. Nor did they discard all that was theirs. The descendants of slaves with whom I talked on the Kenyan coast were conscious of being coastal people and proud of being Muslims, but they also had a strong sense of their origins and collective identity.

I had expected that wazalia would be sensitive to the social inferiority which slave descent implied and would therefore be reluctant to admit their slave ancestry, hiding behind the broad cover of being "Waswahili." Instead, my informants of slave origin spoke freely and with pride of their origins. They referred to themselves as "Wanyasa" (singular Mnyasa), from the home area of most of the slaves. Even slaves from other areas accepted this designation. They learned from their parents about the traditions of their homeland, danced traditional dances, and sometimes spoke their home language in addition to Swahili. My old informants were only second-generation coastal people, a fact which contributed to the strength of Wanyasa consciousness.[94]

One informant told me that he had wanted to visit his parents' home in what is now Malawi but had been deterred by the cost. A few ex-slaves made the attempt. Amina binti Muhandu had been carried away during childhood and became a slave in Mombasa. In 1911, four years after abolition, she and her husband managed to get to Nyasaland. She looked for her relatives but failed to find any. After two years, she tried to return to Mombasa, where her children had remained, but she was trapped by floods in which her husband died. Neither she nor her children could afford to pay for her passage back, and while the bureaucracies of two British colonies discussed her case, Amina died.[95]

The slave trade had opened up an enormous and tragic gulf between people like Amina and their roots. The changes that both the coast and

93. Nimtz.
94. MAL 30, 34, 35, 38, 51, 61; MSA 37.
95. MSA 37; Resident, Port Herald to Superintendant of Native Affairs, Zomba, 6 October 1914; District Commissioner, Mombasa, to Provincial Commissioner, Coast, 5 December 1914; Superintendant of Native Affairs, Zomba, to Chief Secretary, Zomba, 29 October 1914, CP/1/12/270. Another attempt to return home, with no information about what happened, is mentioned in Hardinge to Piggott, 13 August 1894, CP/1/Addms 2.

the interior had undergone, the passage of time, the dislocation of people, and the large distances involved, as well as the stakes that slaves had developed in coastal culture and coastal life, made return impossible. Still, many slaves retained a sense of where they came from and, through the concept of being Wanyasa, expressed the common denominator of their shared identity.[96]

Slaves on the East African coast simultaneously experienced a high degree of dependence and independence. The two elements appear to be contradictory, and in many slave systems they were. Jamaican slaves were able to live on their own and farm their own plots when their long hours of toil were over; but this largely reflected the planters' indifference to any dimensions of the slaves' lives except the amount of work they did. In the Southern United States, many of the aspects of dependence described on the East African coast—concern for material welfare, family formation, and patterns of deference—were present. Perhaps intentionally, this emphasis on dependence undermined slaves' chances to take care of themselves, even if the slaves still managed to forge a sense of community among themselves.[97] However, on the coast of East Africa dependence did not imply total control over slaves' lives, and independence did not imply indifference.

Plantation slavery on the East African coast was an extension and redefinition of older forms of dependence which shaped relations among the free as well as with the slaves. Dependence meant periodic demonstrations of respect and deference, integration of slaves' families into the plantation, an expectation that slaves would take their master's part in political feuds, and above all the presence, preferably on the master's property, of people whom he could consider watu wangu. In some situations, as in Malindi, dependence conflicted with the need for labor; in Mombasa, having dependents settled on the land was more consistent with the demands of the local economy. But everywhere, the slaves' need for membership in a group that could provide protection, land, and integration into society went far toward maintaining the attachment of slave to master. The slaveowner's control lay in his actually fulfilling his role: herein lay the reciprocity of a paternalistic order. Force was still important, particularly in maintaining the authority of

96. To informants of waungwana origin, the term *wanyasa* was derogatory, emphasizing that slaves were not full members of coastal society. Wazalia turned this viewpoint on its head, finding pride in their hinterland origins as well as in their coastal culture. Above all, it gave them a sense of identity.

97. Genovese, "The Treatment of Slaves in Different Countries," in Foner and Genovese, *Slavery in the New World*, p. 204. See also Patterson, p. 93, Dunn, p. 249, and Genovese, *Roll*, passim.

the slaveowner within his plantation, but a tight apparatus of social control to keep an entire class under guard was neither possible nor necessary.

The slaveowners of the Old South came from the most bourgeois society then existing. That they came to enjoy the aristocratic pleasures of commanding a dependent following points to the powerful dynamic generated by the plantation life; but they could not ignore the society around them: the growth of a central government that could provide security for individuals, increasing political participation, and ever-expanding geographic mobility. The lives of the slaves had to be carefully restricted because the lives of the free were not.[98]

Even if the master-slave relationship on the East African coast did not strain its historical and societal context as much as slavery in the United States, the newly developed plantation society of East Africa was still beset by contradictions and tensions. Owners wanted work as well as deference, meted out punishment as well as protection, and emphasized slaves' cultural and religious distinctiveness as well as their similarity. Slaves, faced with the necessity of living in coastal society, found they had a niche within it, not as equals but at least as members. They also found that they did not have to accept their economic role and social position passively, but could—within limits—use their hands and minds to obtain a measure of self-reliance in their daily lives.

MANUMISSION

Slavery, under Islamic doctrines, was morally and legally sanctioned. Yet Islam, like Christianity, was not entirely at ease with slavery.[99] The Koran restricted the circumstances under which slaves could be taken, and it promised a heavenly reward to the master who freed his slaves. The freeing of slaves was particularly encouraged as expiation from such offenses as homicide, perjury, and some types of sexual misconduct. Manumission was also a gesture of gratitude for recovery from an illness or for other reasons.[100] Manumission, however, was an especially pious act precisely because it was not required. Since slavery was basically accepted, the man who freed a slave showed himself to be a man of exceptional piety.[101]

98. On the increasing restrictions on the rights of slaves in eighteenth-century South Carolina—a process that paralleled increasing exploitation and repression, see Wood, *Black Majority.* The connection between growing freedom for whites and oppression for slaves in colonial Virginia is stressed by Morgan, *American Slavery.*

99. Franz Rosenthal, *The Muslim Concept of Freedom* (Leiden, 1960), p. 29.

100. Hamilton, *The Hedaya,* 1: 420; Mazrui, p. 7; W. Arafat, "The Attitude of Islam to Slavery," *The Islamic Quarterly* 10 (1966): 14.

101. As a result of this attitude toward manumission, coastal people had difficulty understanding the liberation of slaves by the colonial government. Since their masters had

The freed slave enjoyed the legal rights of the free born, although the former master remained his patron or guardian. The ex-master was legally responsible for overseeing the ex-slave's marriage arrangements.[102] Ex-slaves could keep and bequeath all the property they acquired after they were freed, but the master was the legal heir in the absence of children or certain other categories of heirs.[103]

In actual practice, a slaveowner had to consider several factors before freeing some of his slaves. The conflicting wishes are illustrated by the case of Zanzibar's largest slaveowner, the Sultan himself. Seyyid Said's will specified that at his death, all his slaves, male and female, should be freed, *"excepting* those who are at his plantations, for the sake of almighty God and in hope of His mercy"*: God's mercy was very much desired, but so too was a large clove harvest. Each freed slave was allowed to keep whatever property he or she possessed, and in addition all concubines were given $100 each, while other Ethiopian slaves of either sex received $50 apiece. Certain Georgian and Ethiopian slaves were bequeathed the produce of one of the Sultan's plantations.[104] Seyyid Bargash freed a few slaves each year, and he too provided that at his death all his slaves—except those used in agriculture—be freed. They were allowed to keep their homes and personal possessions. In addition, each of his town slaves, estimated to number 3,000, was bequeathed $10, and the 300 slaves in the army plus the 50 or 60 concubines got $200 each. Six houses and seven mashamba were set aside to provide for the maintenance of the concubines.[105] These wills con-

not freed them in accordance with Islamic law, the status of such slaves had changed only in terms of the foreign law. As the government paid masters compensation, most people understood what had happened as a purchase and referred to slaves who had been freed in this manner as "slaves of the government" or "slaves of the Consul." See Hardinge to Kimberley, 20 February 1895, PP 1895, LXXI, 143, p. 30, and many deeds in the Mombasa registers referring to individuals in this way.

102. Guardianship, like the ownership of slaves, passed to the ex-master's heirs after his death. It was an even stronger relationship than clientage under Islamic law, for it could not be broken even if the ex-master so desired, whereas a patron could terminate a relationship with a client. Paul G. Forand, "The Relation of the Slave and the Client to the Master or Patron in Medieval Islam," *International Journal of Middle East Studies* 2 (1971): 64–66.

103. As a result, there were sometimes disputes over whether certain property had been acquired before or after the slave had been freed. Brunschvig, p. 30; Schacht, p. 133; Mazrui, p. 8. An example of such a dispute is *Mohamed bin Mansur* vs. *Administrator General of East Africa*, Civil Case 154 of 1917, Resident Magistrate's Court, Mombasa.

104. Translation of the will of Seyyid Said in Coghlan, "Proceedings," Ind. Off., L/P&S/5/145, pp. 35–36. Emphasis added.

105. These figures are far from exact. Reichard, p. 475; Kirk to Derby, 27 April 1875, FOCP 2915, p. 152; Will of Seyyid Bargash, reported by Euan-Smith, 7 April 1888, Gray Papers, Cambridge University Library, box 26; Euan-Smith to Salisbury, 31 May 1888, PP 1888, LXXIV, 255, p. 19. On the implementation of the will, see Portal to Salisbury, 17 June 1889, FOCP 6010, p. 27.

tained many other provisions for aiding the poor and providing for prayers and pilgrimages in the name of the deceased; manumission of slaves was part of a larger pattern of charity, but it stopped short of freeing the slaves who picked the cloves.

Among the Sultan's subjects, manumission was apparently a common occurrence, although quantitative evidence is sparse. A French visitor reported that first-generation slaves were usually freed, and that it was rare for locally born slaves to die in servitude. Consul Pelly believed that 50 percent of the slaves landed in Zanzibar were eventually freed. The English physician Christie and the German explorer Baumann found a large population of freed slaves in Zanzibar.[106] Even as slave supplies dwindled in the 1890s, seven hundred voluntary manumissions were registered with the government during one five-month period. After slavery was abolished and masters became eligible for compensation for slaves freed under government auspices, many masters chose instead to free their slaves in the old manner, preferring a heavenly compensation to money.[107] The only strong negative evidence comes from the time of the great expansion of the clove economy in the 1840s. At that time, wrote Hamerton, manumission was "of uncommon occurrence." [108]

On the mainland as well, manumission was not merely an ideal but a regular occurrence. The rich records of the Mombasa Land Office include a large number of deeds of freedom, wills freeing slaves, and records of transactions made by freed slaves. Deeds of freedom—made by Arabs, Swahili, and even freed slaves—often invoked the idea of a divine reward for an act of generosity:

> Rashid bin Ali bin Rashid ElManthirji declares that he has made free his slave named Athman of the *Mnyassa* tribe . . . in consideration to seek from the Most High God an Excellent reward in conformity with the saying of the Prophet . . . "whosoever frees a slave who is a believer, God has freed such a one from every cala-

106. Christie, "Slavery," pp. 50–51; Baumann, *Sansibar*, p. 21; Germain, "Zanzibar," p. 547; Pelly to Forbes, 12 February 1862, Pelly Papers, FO 800/234. That over 30% of slaves freed in Zanzibar after abolition were wazalia, clearly shows that manumission was far from universal in the first generation.

107. Rodd to Rosebery, 31 December 1893, PP 1895, LXXI, 143, p. 17. On Zanzibar island, 5,141 slaves were freed by the government between 1897 and 1907, while the government registered 5,468 slaves who had been freed by their masters. However, in Pemba, 5,930 slaves were freed by the government and only 754 by their masters. The discrepancy may be accounted for by irregularities in registration, but it still suggests that the masters of Pemba, with their greater reliance on clove growing and plantation life, hung on more tenaciously to their slaves than their more cosmopolitan counterparts in Zanzibar. PP 1909, LVI, 581, p. 50.

108. Hamerton to Aberdeen, 2 January 1844, FO 54/6.

mity—the calamity of hellfire—to happiness and comfort." . . . [No-one shall have power over Athman] except as guardian. [1903]

Hidaya binti Hoonzi Elchangamwe declares that she has freed her slaves Kijate and her daughter Mjakazi, irrevocably freed slaves at the date and time this document was drawn; the Liberator accepts from God that she will be placed in Paradise and no-one should interfere with them, and she has given them her *shamba* at Changamwe in the district of Mombasa. [1898] [109]

One of the many wills freeing slaves upon the master's death revealed clearly the dual nature of the slave as a person worthy of the owner's generosity and as a transferable object: Mbaruk bin Rashid, the Mazrui leader, ordered that three concubines be freed—each was to receive a slave as a gift. [110]

On both Zanzibar and the mainland, slaves were often freed as atonement for wrongdoing, in gratitude for recovery from an illness, as a reward for loyal service, or as a provision of a will. Concubines who had borne their master a child were legally entitled to freedom on their master's death. [111] Freed slaves received a certificate from the kadi, which they often wore in a small silver case around the neck. [112] Freedom was something to be cherished.

It was also possible, if the master agreed, for slaves to make a binding arrangement by which they would be freed once a certain sum of money had been paid to the master. [113] I have seen four deeds from Mombasa and one from Malindi by which slaves purchased their freedom for between $21 and $70. In two other deeds, slaves purchased

109. 57B 1903; 163A 1907, Reg., Msa. One Arab woman in Mombasa freed fifteen slaves by one deed and four more in separate deeds. Some deeds mention that the freed slave was a concubine. 18–21B 1911; 25B and 17B 1911; 62B, 6B, 37B 1903; 5B 14B, 20B, 49B, 86B 1904; 1B, 35B, 36B, 47B 1905; 15B 30B, 37B, 49B 1907. (The deeds were filed on the above dates, but were generally written many years before.) The earliest deed that I have seen dates from 1871 and is filed with the case of *Juma bin Farjalla* vs. *Abdalla bin Mohamed*, Civil Cause 348 of 1911, Town Court, Mombasa. Slaves were freed by deed even after the legal abolition of the status of slavery in Kenya in 1907. See, for example, 15B, 16B, 856 A 1911, and 611 A 1908.

˙ 110. A copy of the will was shown to me by William McKay. For other wills, see 29A 1893; 29B 1893; 56B 1899; 8B 1901.

111. Christie, "Slavery," p. 46; Rigby, "Report," p. 334; Colomb, p. 373; Missionaires d'Alger, *A l'assaut des pays nègres* (Paris, 1884), p. 55: Hardinge to Kimberly, 26 February 1895, PP 1895, LXXI, 143, p. 30.

112. Rigby, "Report," pp. 330, 334; Devereux, pp. 107–08; Niese, p. 45.

113. These provisions were regulated by Islamic law. Schacht, pp. 42–43; Colomb, p. 370; Hardinge to Kimberley, 26 February 1895, PP 1895, LXXI, 143, p. 30. Seyyid Said apparently issued a decree saying that all able-bodied slaves could free themselves by paying their owner $100, but this decree was ignored. Euan-Smith to Salisbury, 20 June 1890, FO 84/2062.

their freedom and their personal property—which would otherwise be retained by the master—for $75 and $89.[114]

Oral evidence confirms that slaves could be freed on special occasions like a pilgrimage or a marriage and as a reward for long service. Self-purchase was also mentioned, although some informants said it was infrequent.[115] However, several of the ex-slaves in Malindi stated emphatically that manumission was rare.[116] It is tempting to argue that Malindi, with its intensive agriculture, had a lower rate of manumission than Mombasa, where masters were less reliant on slave labor and more conscious of their social standing. Most freedom deeds do come from Mombasa, but as local records are much better there than in Malindi, this is far from conclusive.[117]

Freedom did not necessarily mean the end of economic dependence. The ex-master remained the ex-slave's guardian, and beyond that many ex-slaves retained close ties with the former master. Trusted slaves who had been freed often remained in the service of the ex-master, and their relationship became similar to clientage. Christie described this relationship as similar to that of an Arab of inferior family to one of high standing.[118] By custom, Zanzibari landowners were expected to give their freed slaves the plot they had used as slaves or another piece of land to cultivate for their own benefit. Hardinge said that this was usually freehold, but other sources indicate that a portion of each estate was made into a *wakf* (an irrevocable, inalienable gift) for freed slaves to use. Such slaves were expected to perform an annual service for the ex-master, more as a token of dependence than as a source of labor.[119]

On the mainland, the custom of giving a freed slave some property or a present was referred to by one informant as *uhuru na kitu*, "freedom with something."[120] Such gifts were specified in the freedom deed or will; Kashi binti Mwijaa Al-Changamwe, for example, gave her freed

114. Reg., Msa., 61B 1903, 58B 1906, 582A 1906, 14B and 38B 1907; Reg., Mal, 7B 1903; *Mohamed bin Ali* vs. *Mboni binti Maftaha*, High Court, Mombasa, 1914. Self-purchase was important in Latin America but not North America. Tannebaum, *Slave and Citizen*, pp. 51–56, 68.

115. MAL 5, 12, 18, 30, 40, 44; MSA 3, 14, 26, 28. See also Beech, "Slavery," p. 148.

116. MAL 24, 34, 35. Another said that some masters freed their slaves and some did not. MAL 38.

117. The Malindi land records from 1912–15 indicate that many freed slaves owned land, but it is not clear how many of them were freed by their masters rather than by the government.

118. Colomb, p. 373; Christie, "Slavery," p. 35.

119. Hardinge to Salisbury, 24 March 1899, PP 1899, LXIII, 303, p. 28; "Report by Mr. Last respecting the working of the Decree in 1903," 23 May 1904, PP 1905, LVI, 551, p. 3; Fitzgerald, *Travels*, p. 525; Weidner, p. 27.

120. MAL 18.

slave a shamba with seventy-five coconut trees on it worth $69; Mo-
hammed bin Isa Al-Imami gave his slave Ramathan his freedom, a
boat, and three head of cattle.[121] Sometimes, the deed specified that the
freed slave would be given use of the property during his or her lifetime, but that it would revert to the master's family after the slave's
death.[122] Some masters devoted wakf land to their slaves. One of Salim
bin Khalfan's largest plantations in Malindi was reserved for that purpose, and his will also specified that all his domestic slaves be freed and
given $ 10 "by way of reward at their freedom." [123] Not all masters
were so generous: other deeds indicate that some freed slaves were
made to return property they had been using as slaves.[124]

The custom of uhuru na kitu may have given freed slaves a chance to
take care of themselves, but the context emphasized that they were the
recipients of patriarchal generosity. In a social sense, many ex-slaves
remained attached to their masters' families. They were known as the
mahuru (singular *huru*), *mahadimu* (singular *hadimu*), or *maskini* of their
former master.[125] Documents did not simply refer to ex-slaves by their
own names but, for example, to "Rajab, freed slave of Bashir bin Salim
El-Harthi," or "Uledi *wa* Ali bin Mbarak" (*wa* means "of").[126] Such terminology emphasized that manumitted slaves remained part of their
master's "people." The relationships involved continued deference on
the part of the freed slave. He was expected to pay homage to the master or his next of kin at ceremonial occasions such as marriages and fu-
nerals.

The ex-master also retained the obligations of a guardian. He was

121. 1004A 1907; 15B 1911; 56B 1899; Reg., Msa, and a/c 195M of 1913 (Malindi).

122. 20B 1904, Reg., Msa, a/c 5N of 1916 and 181N of 1915 (Mombasa); MSA 14.

123. Will dated 1891 filed with Probate and Administration Case 114 of 1920, now
kept in High Court, Nairobi. On the shamba, see MAL 5, 12, 32, 34. Juma Kengewa,
MAL 34, whose parents were slaves of Salim bin Khalfan, was interviewed at his house on
the shamba, which is occupied by a few descendants of slaves and many Giriama squatters. Said bin Hemed, governor of Mambrui and Malindi, also provided a shamba for his
ex-slaves. Translation of Arabic copy of the wakf deed dated 1904 in DC/MAL/4/1 in
KNA. Gifts of houses and farms to freed slaves have also been recorded. 80A 1906 and
437A 1908, Reg., Msa.

124. 771A, 801A, 1076A, and 1211A 1911. The late date of these deeds may indicate
a breakdown of dependency relations in the face of the government's abolition of slavery.
Masters may have started to take their property rights more literally.

125. The first two terms simply mean "freed slave"; the third literally means "poor
people," but in fact refers to those who were pitied and received benefits from God. A
master might also refer to his ex-slaves as his *watoto*, "children." Weidner, p. 26; Last,
"Report," p. 3; Krapf, *Swahili Dictionary*, p. 92, 104; Inter-territorial Committee, *Standard
Dictionary*, pp. 122, 138; Beech, "Slavery," p. 149; New, *Life*, p. 56; MAL 18.

126. These terms are used in Reg., Msa. See also a deed from Zanzibar, dated 1861,
translation in Gray Papers, Cambridge University Library, box 28.

supposed to arrange or approve a marriage for his ex-slave, help him if he became sick or indigent, obtain compensation in case of legal action, arrange for a funeral, and be his heir should none other be available. At times, ex-slaves continued to live in the household.[127] Documents illustrate the continuity in relationships: ex-slaves sometimes obtained loans from their ex-masters; one freed slave gave his former master power of attorney to act on his behalf, while another was given power of attorney by his mistress to act for her; a large shamba owned by an ex-slave was inherited by his "liberator." [128]

Through the ex-master, the ex-slave retained his association with a wider communal group. The Mazrui *jamaa* included many Mazrui ex-slaves, as well as slaves and other followers. Members of the jamaa were given land for their own use and for the use of their heirs, subject only to the proviso that it could not be sold to someone outside the jamaa. They paid no rent, but would be expected to be loyal to the Mazrui.[129]

Such ex-slaves would enjoy the continued protection of their ex-master. Especially in unsettled areas, such as the region north of Mombasa, where the Mazrui and their followers periodically became embroiled in conflicts with the people of Mombasa and the Mijikenda, the lack of a protector could have dire consequences. An African missionary of the Church Missionary Society near Mombasa reported that freed slaves who moved about in the area were sometimes reenslaved by "strong ones." [130] In short, manumission freed the slave from his former work obligations, but he often remained a dependent and the ex-master his protector.[131]

Not all ex-slaves lived under conditions of dependence, just as not all slaves had close personal relations with their masters. Urban areas gave freed slaves the greatest latitude, as they did slaves: towns were comparatively safe; hired labor was in demand; and urban society was relatively heterogeneous and flexible. In Zanzibar town, many ex-slaves, ei-

127. Weidner, p. 26; Germain, "Zanzibar," p. 547; Newman, *Banani*, pp. 32–33; Rodd to Rosebery, 31 December 1893, PP 1895, LXXI, 143, p. 17; "Slavery Report for 1902 by Mr. Farler," FOCP 8177, pp. 106–07; MAL 18; MSA 12.

128. Ramathan, freed slave of Rashid bin Sood Shikeli, borrowed $118 from Rashid and mortgaged a shamba. Amina, freed slave of Rashid bin Ali bin Mona Al-Darani, borrowed $22 from her ex-master and mortgaged a house. Reg., Msa, 107A 1906, 353A 1899. See also a/c 96, 97, 103M 1913, Malindi. The slave who was given a power of attorney—ironically—was to obtain compensation for his ex-mistress for her slaves who had been freed by the government. 756A 1909, 180B 1898. The inheritance case is Probate and Administration Case no. 69 of 1917, High Court, Mombasa.

129. See the testimony inclosed in District Commissioner, Kwale, to Provincial Commissioner, Coast, 27 June 1935, Land Office, Nairobi, file 30646.

130. George David to Wright, 10 October 1878, CMS CA5/M5.

131. Quass, p. 445.

ther former residents of the town or new migrants from the plantations, joined the pool of labor that worked in the port, provided caravan porterage, and performed odd jobs. They apparently lived in much the same manner as the vibarua slaves, but did not have to turn over a large portion of their earnings to their masters. Some participated in the dangerous but potentially profitable illicit slave trade. Of 174 people convicted of slave dealing in 1889–90 and 1895–97, 24 percent were apparently manumitted slaves and another 8 percent were slaves freed by the British. This mixture suggests that freed slaves participated in a common substratum of Zanzibari society whose money was not always earned within the rules of the colonial state. The more successful ones could accumulate enough capital to buy slaves themselves or go into trade.[132]

The Mombasa records indicate that ex-slaves were able to purchase or rent town plots on which to live. Nearly two hundred freed slaves rented plots from Salim bin Khalfan in 1899.[133] A number bought mashamba in the surrounding countryside with which to support themselves. The plots they bought—like those provided by former masters— were generally small, but some freed slaves managed to acquire substantial land. Nolea Mema, freed slave of Mbaruk bin Mohamed Al-Shikeli, left an estate worth over $5,000, including a shamba, a share in a house with land, and cash. His personal wealth, however, did not end his relationship with his former master's kinsmen. He left money to the Shikeli mosque and to his executor—a member of the Shikeli group— as well as to charities and other individuals.[134] Another freed slave bought a shamba with 87 coconut trees for $240, and a third sold a plantation for $72. An enterprising former slave bought a shamba for $46 from his former master and sold it to an Indian a few months later for over $240.[135]

Other ex-slaves in the Mombasa area obtained permission to cultivate land controlled by the Nine Tribes of the Mombasa Swahili.[136] Still others went to work for traders. Kombo bin Karai, freed slave of Khamis bin Saad Al-Mandhry, was entrusted with $464 worth of trade goods by a leading trader and money-lender. Jumaa, freed slave of a

132. Speke, p. xxvii; Christie, *Cholera*, p. 308; Kirk to Salisbury, 8 January 1886, FOCP 5459, p. 293; Missionaires d'Alger, p. 55; Baumann, *Sansibar*, p. 21. The slave-trading figures were calculated from a tabulation of judgments in *Documents relatifs à la répression de la traite des esclaves*, 1897, pp. 220–50.

133. See Table 6:2. In the 20% sample of land transactions from Mombasa (1891–1905), twenty-eight involved freed slaves who owned urban houses or plots.

134. Probate and Administration Case no. 17 of 1924, High Court, Mombasa.

135. 607A 1908; 329 A 1899; 1122A, 1123A, and 1187A 1907; 397 A 1908, Reg., Msa.

136. Instances of this are described in a/c 28, 29, 30N of 1915 (Mombasa).

Swahili, seems to have traded on his own, for he mortgaged his house against a loan of forty-five pounds of ivory worth $115.[137] Freed slaves also owned slaves of their own.[138] However, independence did not mean an easy life. In Mombasa, the urban properties and the farms they bought and sold were modest, although more valuable than those of slaves: overall, the average property bought or sold by a freed slave was worth Rs 102, compared with Rs 59 for slaves and Rs 360 for Arab and Swahili waungwana.[139]

The abundant land of Malindi offered opportunities to ambitious freed slaves as well as to others. *Mzee* (Elder) Juma Mja, freed slave of a Bajun of Lamu, came as a poor man to Mambrui and became a large-scale slaveowner and one of the wealthiest men in town. He had mosques in Mambrui and Malindi constructed in his name, a sign of wealth and respectability in an Islamic society. People still tell stories, with several variations, about his conflict with Said bin Hemed Al-Busaidi, governor of Mambrui. Jealous of a man of lowly birth acquiring such riches, Said forbade Mzee Juma to allow his slaves to hold the customary dances and celebrations after the clearing of new bush each year. Mzee Juma sent several dhows loaded with the produce of his fields to the Sultan of Zanzibar, along with a request for justice. The Sultan responded by giving him a letter insisting that the governor give him equal treatment.[140]

Similarly, Feruzi, an Ethiopian slave of the Sultan of Zanzibar, came to Malindi after being freed and became a wealthy slaveowner. He, too, built a mosque and is well remembered today.[141] From questioning people today about individuals like Mzee Juma and Feruzi, it is clear that they are among the more notable figures of Malindi's past. Yet while they are respected, especially for having built mosques, their servile origin has not been forgotten. An ex-slave, even a wealthy one, was not the same as a mwungwana.[142]

137. 93B 1894; 302A 1899. See also Krapf, "Memoir," CMS CA5/016/179, p. 50.

138. Freed slaves freed their slaves in deeds 37B 1903, 49B 1904, and 216A 1905. Another freed slave mortgaged two of his slaves plus a shamba for $85 in 1890. 466A 1897.

139. A-series, 20% sample, 1891–1905. These figures exclude slaves freed by the British. The number of sales involving ex-slaves was 44, compared to 72 for slaves. The records also contain 11 mortgages on landed property averaging Rs 144 and 8 loans with no collateral, with a mean value of Rs 158.

140. MAL 12, 24, 36, 37, 38, 40, 44, 45, 46. Three plots, totaling 128 acres, were registered in the name of his daughter, a/c, Mambrui. To take the story one step further, one of Mzee Juma's ex-slaves later sold a shamba for Rs 300. a/c 69D 1912.

141. MAL 35 (son of a slave of Feruzi) and MAL 18, 30, 34. The mosque of Feruzi is mentioned in District Officer, Malindi, to Secretary of the Wakf Commission, 8 January 1934, MAL/2/1ADM7/1, KNA. His property figures in a/c 3 of 1957, Malindi.

142. MAL 44, 45, 50.

The East African coast would fall somewhere in the middle along a broad continuum between societies that assimilated slaves or their descendants as equals and societies where slaves—and even freed slaves—were a distinct group, set apart by racial differences, specific subcultures, and separate structures of relationships. The coast, and certain other Islamic areas of Africa, differ from most other African societies in making a sharp legal distinction between a slave and a freed slave. More typically, captives passed through stages—which often took more than one generation—of acceptance into society. Sometimes they were fully incorporated; sometimes invidious distinctions remained attached to their descendants. Rarely was there a single moment that corresponded to manumission. Nevertheless, the legal differences are probably less important than the social similarities. Coastal slaves went through a number of stages of social acceptance even without manumission, and dependence frequently continued even after the slave acquired the legal persona of the free.[143]

The Southern United States was situated toward one end of the continuum. Although manumission, especially during the Colonial and Revolutionary periods, was far from unusual, most Southern states in the nineteenth century passed measures to restrain masters from freeing slaves and to restrict the legal, social, and economic rights of blacks who supposedly had been freed. Such measures reflected increased fear of conspiracies between slaves and freedmen, class conflict among whites, and the inability of Southerners—particularly in the context of the racial and positive-good defenses of slavery—to cope with the anomalous position of blacks who were outside their logical place in the social order. In some Southern cities, clientage relationships developed between white elites and the better-off freedmen, but in general freed blacks were treated as a distinct group. In New Orleans, where race relations were closer to Latin American patterns, the large and relatively well-off community of freed slaves was on occasion dealt with as a group that might make a useful ally. The importance of intermediate groups—defined by color or ex-slave status—was even more evident in the Caribbean and in South America.[144]

143. Slaves were sometimes treated as free without having been legally manumitted. See above, and Strobel, "Interaction," p. 9. For comparison with other African societies, see the studies in Meillassoux, *L'esclavage*, and Miers and Koptytoff, *Slavery in Africa*, as well as my criticisms of the way absorption of slaves has been studied in "Studying Slavery in Africa."

144. See the fine study of Ira Berlin, *Slaves without Masters: The Free Negro in the Antebellum South* (New York, 1974); Cohen and Greene; Tannenbaum; Toplin, *Slavery and Race Relations;* and Raymond T. Smith, "Social Stratification in the Caribbean," in Leonard Plotnicov and Arthur Tuden, eds., *Essays on Comparative Social Stratification* (Pittsburgh, Pa., 1970), pp. 43–76. The efforts of certain New World planter classes to use

The costs of manumission to the slaveowners of the East African coast were high. It lessened the chance that coastal plantations could have a self-reproducing labor supply, but there is no evidence that the practice declined when the supply of new slaves was threatened. That manumission was a common and socially rewarded act reflects not just Islamic ideals, but the social and political necessity of living up to them. Manumission—as well as the modest degree of mobility allowed within slave status—helped prevent the formation of a homogeneous slave class. Without a change in status slaves would have developed, over generations, even stronger traditions, even stronger unity among themselves, than they did. The spirit of resistance among slaves might have been more threatening if the condition and status of slaves had remained unchanged throughout the lifetime of each slave and across generations. New slaves were expensive, but at least they had directly experienced the violence of enslavement, came from diverse linguistic and cultural groups, and did not know the ways of the coast.

Slaveowners lacked the power to maintain a system that provided no mobility for slaves, but they could decide which slaves were to be freed or allowed to better their position. For freed slaves, membership in a communal group or in the entourage of a powerful man was still important, although they could insist on better terms than slaves could. Some ex-slaves exercised more de facto independence than others, but manumission, in general, did not end the reciprocal obligations of superior and inferior.[145] In coastal society, it was less important that a freed slave belonged to a particular social category (mahadimu or mahuru) than that he was the freedman of a specific person. Freed slaves were part of a hierarchy, not a single—and potentially dangerous— group.

By freeing a slave, the master lost his labor, but not the psychological, social, and political benefits of having followers. At the same time, his voluntarily giving up title to a valuable commodity demonstrated his wealth, generosity, and piety. It reinforced his heshima, affirming the slaveowners' rationale for their superiority. Manumission was an integral part of slavery on the East African coast.

---

freed blacks as a group to help control slaves as a group contrasts with the continuity of dependency across such divisions on the East African coast.

145. The situation of freed slaves bears comparison with that of mulattoes in Brazil. Because of the white elite's control of patronage, mulattoes became valued clients instead of a threatening social class. See Emilia Viotti da Costa, "The Myth of Racial Democracy in Brazil: A Problem of Social Mythology," Paper Presented at the Annual Meeting of the Southern Historical Association, Washington, D.C., 14 November 1975.

Conclusions:
Slavery, Class, and Race on the
East African Coast

A slave was both a person and a thing, a factor of production and a member of society. Slaves were extensions of their owner's will, but they also had wills of their own. In all slave societies, slavery was pulled in various directions by old norms and new needs and by the opposing strengths of masters and slaves. The balance between the divergent roles of slaves in a given society at a given time can be situated on a continuum between the slave as a person absorbed into his buyer or captor's social group and the slave as a worker.

Ila of Central Africa	Oman ca. 1800	Zanzibar ca. 1870	U.S. South 19th century	Jamaica 18th century
Slaves as kinsmen	Slaves as dependents	Productivity and dependence both valued		Slaves as workers

The left side of the continuum is characterized by the use of slaves to expand kinship groups. Here, slaves worked alongside their masters and, in the absence of distinct social and economic roles, were readily absorbed. In more differentiated societies, slaveowners incorporated slaves into their followings but slaves were more clearly distinguished from the free. Slaves were part of a hierarchical social order but they were not specifically a laboring class. As one moves to the right along the continuum, the productive activities of slaves become relatively more important. Their distinct economic role separated them from their masters and exacerbated the tendency—always present in their foreign origin and special legal status—to regard slaves as a distinct social category. Still, masters and slaves formed a social unit: personal ties crossed status lines. At the extreme end of the continuum, the slaveowner was a businessman for whom slaves were a labor force and nothing else. The plantation was not a vertically integrated community.

The process described in this book was a movement toward the right along this line. Within the coastal region, the process went further in Malindi than in Mombasa, while Zanzibar fell in between. As this continuum makes clear, the evolution of coastal slavery, with its variations, was part of a much wider range of possibilities.

Like the Southern United States, the East African coast reflected the complex interplay of the social and economic dimensions of slavery. The patterns of human interaction and the ethos of Southern society, as Eugene Genovese stresses, were very different either from the areas of the Western world where wage-labor prevailed or from slave societies that were more completely dominated by the market. The plantation was a community; the master was a "lord" providing protection and sustenance to his dependent following; and the master-slave relationship embraced all facets of life, not just labor.[1] Genovese's comparative perspective should be extended in the opposite direction: to situate antebellum slavery in respect to societies where relations of dependence were even more important. Such a comparison suggests, not simply that the East African coast was more paternalistic than the Southern United States when both plantation economics were at their peaks, but that the character of paternalism and the process out of which it developed in these two societies differed fundamentally.

In both areas, slaveowners sought social as well as economic rewards. Relationships between superior and inferior were personal, and customs and laws defined the obligations they had toward one another. As an ideology, paternalism defined slaves as socially inferior human beings, but at least it defined them as human beings.

The plantation economy created its own imperatives—hard work and efficient organization. In much of the Old South and in the parts of East Africa where the incentives were strongest, notably Malindi, the result was rigidly organized, closely supervised labor—something vastly different from anything the coast had previously known and from ways of exploiting serf and free labor in Europe. Personal bonds had to confront the depersonalizing tendency of a differentiated labor force.

The demands of plantation agriculture varied: slaves on the East African coast—even in the grain fields of Malindi—did not face as hard or as continuous a work schedule as slaves in the cotton fields of the South, let alone on sugar plantations in the Caribbean. On clove plantations, the heavy labor requirements of the harvest left a large labor force tied to the plantation all year, and planters made less effort than their American counterparts to take advantage of the slack season. Regardless of the crop, the slaveholders of the Swahili coast—responsive as they were to commercial incentives—did not have as dynamic a system to respond to as did the planters of the Americas; their sense of personal worth and status was not so closely linked with the continuous accumulation of wealth; and they lacked the power to repress the resistance of slaves to ever more onerous demands.

1. Genovese, *Political Economy of Slavery* and *The World the Slaveholders Made.*

By the mid-nineteenth century, plantation labor was the dominant function of coastal slaves, as it had been in the Americas since the early days of slavery. The development of the plantation did not altogether eclipse the varied roles in which slaves had served in Oman and East Africa. Slaveowners employed some slaves in positions of trust or intimacy, while others merely handed over their earnings. The variety of tasks which slaves performed was not unique, but the confidence that coastal slaveowners had in their slaves—outside of the context of plantation discipline—would have struck Southern planters as foolhardy.

In all slave societies, the possession of slaves was a source of prestige as well as income. In East Africa, slaves made an especially important contribution to the social and political strength of individuals, households, and communal groups. Most strikingly, Arab and Swahili slaveowners were willing to arm their slaves. Individuals and communal groups relied on the support of slaves for political and military strength. Only the Sultan had slaves who were specialized soldiers, and even he did not try to organize them into a trained and indoctrinated corps like the Mamluks or Janissaries. Plantation slaves were sometimes armed when the need arose: the functions of worker and soldier were both part of the general concept of the slave as a dependent follower. Slaveowners needed the might of their slaves; they did not fear it.

In most slave societies, women were subordinated to the desires of their masters. But the implications of miscegenation were quite different. While Southern slaveowners fornicated with their slaves, such liaisons were taboo and the children who issued from them were still slaves. On the East African coast, concubinage was legal and socially acceptable. The offspring of a master and his concubine were considered free and legitimate, although their standing in the community varied with the social situation. These differences cannot be attributed to greater sexual permissiveness or social tolerance in Islam as compared with Christianity, but to the concepts of kinship that were written into Islamic law and remained vital parts of the society of nineteenth-century East Africa. Children added to the strength of the family and the communal group. This was not a calculation that a son would serve his father, for that would have required a long delay. Rather, this conception of descent stemmed from a belief that the family *as a group* would be strengthened by expanding the range of members included within the system of partilineal descent. Such a view held little relevance to the narrower concepts of kinship in Western societies.

Whatever slaves did, they had to be controlled. Everywhere, slaveowners relied on a combination of force, economic dependence, and social constraints. The slaveowners of the Southern states could call on substantial reinforcements to back up the disciplinary power of the master. On the coast of East Africa, punishment was crucial to maintaining the owner's authority within the plantation, but behind the master was a weak state and a divided free population. However, if masters were weak, slaves were vulnerable: with no roots of their own, they needed membership in the only social group available. The instruments of repression facing coastal slaves were relatively weak, but the bonds of dependence were strong.

Slaveowners could think of themselves as protectors. They were also providers. The laws and customs of the Southern United States and the East African coast required slaveowners to look after the material welfare of their slaves. That they could violate these norms with legal impunity did not mean that they were insensitive to community standards or to the necessity of fostering dependence. Again, a shade of difference appears in the way the two sets of planters met their obligations: Southern slaveowners provided food and housing directly to their slaves, who in turn supplied the necessary labor under plantation discipline. Coastal masters provided slaves or slave families with the land and the security they needed to look after their own welfare. They created a strong economic link to the plantation, but one that allowed a measure of self-reliance.

Slaveowners in the two regions were concerned with the social life of slaves and the propriety of their conduct. They taught them their own language and—with varying degrees of genuine concern—elements of their own religion. They sought to incorporate the basic institutions of slave life—notably the family—into the vertical bonds of the plantation, and they showed an interest in the long-term viability of plantation society, not just the short-term productivity of the work force.

Slaveowners also valued the symbolic element of the master-slave relationship. The obligations of the master toward his slaves were emphasized in feasts and other ceremonies he provided. Slaves were obliged to show deference in their acceptance of such "generosity" and in the way they addressed their owners. The masters, especially on the Swahili coast, reciprocated by referring to their slaves as "my people" or "my children."

These relationships were encouraged both by the intimate, semi-isolated nature of plantation life and by community norms. Not all masters responded. They were affected by diverse influences, from feelings of affection or anger to the desire to increase profits.

But the way slaveowners acted—and even the way they thought of themselves—were invariably shaped by those whom they sought to control. Slaves could play upon, and reinforce, the slaveowners' paternalistic self-image: the offer of personal deference could bring a personal response. They could also reject the slaveowners' notions of superiority and benevolence, withholding deference from the master and reminding each other of the injustice and oppression they were undergoing. Slaves had to accept many of the obligations imposed on them; they resisted others. Slaveowners sought to make slaves internalize cultural and ethical standards that underscored the planters' hegemony; they had no choice but to accept much of the way slaves chose to live among themselves.

The customary limitations on the work load reflected this reciprocity. So too did the social and cultural life of slaves. In both spheres, the balance of power between slaves and masters on the East African coast was not as decisively tilted in the masters' direction as in the Southern United States. On the one hand, coastal slaves had much more independence once their daily work was done: to make their homes away from their masters' eyes, to move about freely, to congregate together, to perform ceremonies that were important to them, to sell the produce of their plots, and occasionally to do business on their own. On the other hand, coastal slaves—especially those brought up in their owners' households—were better rewarded for their acceptance and understanding of their owners' culture. Such slaves could be allowed fuller participation in the social and ritual life of the freeborn and a better chance to obtain a position of responsibility. Slaves were placed in distinct social categories, depending on their degree of contact with Swahili society.

The results, for coastal slaves, were ambiguous. They or their descendants could—under the master's control—enter further into the social life of the society they had been forced to join than could American slaves. They still could not attain the status of the freeborn. The modest degree of social mobility undermined—to an extent—the slaves' own cultural heritage and the development of a semi-autonomous slave subculture. The incentives to adopt Swahili customs affected most strongly those slaves who could have given slave subculture continuity over generations.

Still, coastal slaves—like their American counterparts—engaged in an ideological and cultural struggle on two levels. They used their mastery of their owners' cultures, particularly of their religious ideas, to judge the slaveowners greed and cruelty by the standards of Islam or Christianity and to assert their own moral equality. At the same time, slaves were able to preserve, create, or reinterpret forms of expression that were distinctly their own. Cultural resistance helped slaves turn their position as outsiders into a positive sense of community.

To build a life within the confines of relations of dependence or to try to break these bonds constituted, as Genovese observes, "two forms of a single process by which the slaves accepted what could not be avoided and simultaneously fought individually and as a people for moral as well as physical survival." [2] Slavery was in many ways a confrontation between two opposed wills, two opposed aspirations. Escape and rebellion were part of this confrontation. On the East African coast, as in the Southern United States, some slaves ran away from masters who beat them brutally or tried to expand the customary work requirements. Even in parts of the coast where slavery was the least regimented, notably Mombasa, substantial numbers of slaves still refused to live under their masters' control.

Escape was never easy, but in the Old South, geography, the population distribution, and the nation-wide institutions on which their owners could call posed formidable obstacles to runaways and rebels. On the coast, especially the mainland, the primary problem was to find a community that could provide a substitute for the protection, economic security, and membership in a social group, that slaves had—on demeaning terms—on the plantation. Some slaves built their own communities; others changed the terms of their subordination by joining the entourage of a powerful man outside of their owner's community or by fleeing to a mission. Escape—the most extreme of the many ways slaves asserted control over their own lives—was a more viable option for slaves on the East African coast than in the antebellum South. Resistance played a crucial role—especially when conditions favored the growth of their owners' plantations—in limiting the regimentation and intensity of labor.

The fundamental differences between the nature of plantation slavery within the Atlantic and Indian Ocean economic systems did not lie narrowly in the operations of the market principle or even in the organization of plantation labor. Both systems generated strong incentives, and planters responded by developing new, more efficient forms of labor organization. But the two regions differed substantially in degree. Once tobacco, rice, or cotton cultivation proved its profitability, the slaveowners of the Southern United States needed to control their slaves more tightly because they were extracting more labor from them to feed the needs and wants of developing Europe. The expansionist trends in the clove economy of Zanzibar fluctuated with clove prices, tying slaves more closely to the plantation as an economic and social unit than to high-incentive export production. Where the opportunities for exploiting regimented labor were greatest, in Malindi, further development was constrained by the limitations on demand and transport in the preindustrial economies of the Indian Ocean network, as well as by rising slave prices and the resistance of the slaves.

2. Genovese, *Roll, Jordan, Roll*, p. 658.

One must look beyond the point of production to forms of class rule. Even if one acknowledges precapitalist elements in the social relations of the Southern plantation, one cannot ignore the plantation's global context: a centralized political system, a complex and highly interdependent market economy, geographic mobility for individuals, contractual relationships among individuals, and an ideology stressing individual autonomy. On the one hand, protection, access to land or jobs, and entry into social relationships were not, for American society as a whole, under the control of powerful "lords" or of kinship and communal groups. On the other hand, the planter class—for all its internal differences, problems with poor whites, and conflicts with Northern elites—had developed, at least by the nineteenth century, relatively effective control of the apparatus of state government—legislatures, bureaucracies, police forces, and judiciaries. Impersonal mechanisms could maintain order, guarantee the functioning of the market, and preserve individual autonomy.

As a result, planters had little need for personal retainers and little interest in the contribution of slave women to their kinship groups' reproductive capacity. And planters *as a class* were equipped to take forceful measures to control slaves *as a class,* and they could count on the help of whites *as a race* to maintain order among blacks *as a race.* Yet the very structures which made slaveholders strong made it necessary for them to use their strength. The tight watch slaveholders kept on their slaves, their anxiety about freed blacks, and the vigilant control they maintained over the repressive apparatus of the state all point to the relative weakness of ties of dependence.[3]

On the East African coast, the state's power did not grow with the plantation system, and government was identified with a particular dynasty. The Sultan's officials provided some security and stability within coastal towns, and Islamic judges could discipline individual slaves, but it was more difficult for them to coerce and intimidate slaves as a group.

At the same time, an independent-minded man could build a personal power base through his retainers, while communal groups relied on their solidarity and followers to protect themselves against such individuals, each other, the Sultan, and outsiders. Slaveowners needed slave retainers and valued the contribution of slave women to their group's numerical strength.

And slaves, their own kinship and communal affiliations severed, needed their owners for physical and social survival. Because dependence was so deeply rooted in the social structure, slaveowners did not

---

3. The importance of institutional mechanisms to social control helps explain why political issues like the Fugitive Slave Law were argued with such virulence.

face the same pressure as Southern planters to curtail their slaves' autonomy in daily life. Their own need for followers—and the slaves' ability to resist—made it necessary for planters to pay close attention to these bonds, whatever the imperatives of plantation agriculture.

The differing historical contexts in which plantation agriculture developed had a profound impact on the ideology of slaveholders. Southerners were not unaware of the precedents for relations of dependence within English history. Some proslavery writers sought to develop an aristocratic ideology, stressing the superiority of their patriarchal system to the crass materialism and competitive individualism of the North.[4] But they were struggling against the currents of developing capitalism and political democracy. As George Fredrickson writes, "The South's fundamental conception of itself as a slaveholding society was unstable." [5] To argue that society was organized on hierarchical principles in which each social category had its rightful place made considerable sense in view of the social relations within the plantation, and some sense in terms of the patronage that leading planters extended to their poor white neighbors. But it was less consistent with the increasingly commercialized and competitive economy the slaveholders were building and with the political system they were trying to control. By the eighteenth century, planters were overcoming their need to exploit white labor directly, and finding that they needed the political support of the lower orders of whites.[6] Poor whites—eager and able to assert their autonomy—were not likely to be attracted to a political philosophy that told them they were inferior members of a hierarchy. With expanding political participation in the nineteenth century, a cotton boom that made slave labor all the more essential, and a challenge from abolitionists to the moral and political position of the slaveowners, equality among whites became increasingly linked with subhuman status for blacks.[7] The growing ideological importance of racism reflected, in large part, the failure of hierarchical political philosophy to serve as an adequate conceptual framework for American society.[8]

4. George Fitzhugh, *Cannibals All! or, Slaves Without Masters,* ed. C. Vann Woodward (Cambridge, Mass., 1960).

5. Fredrickson, *The Black Image in the White Mind,* p. 58.

6. Morgan, *American Slavery-American Freedom,* pp. 344, 367, 380–81.

7. Fredrickson, chapter 2. David Donald argues that the hierarchical defense of slavery in the 1840s and 1850s was not a defense of slavery as it was, but as it might have been, were it not for the increasing commercialization of the South. "The Proslavery Argument Reconsidered," *Journal of Southern History* 37 (1971): 16–17.

8. This is not to deny the complexity of the formation of American racial attitudes, but only to emphasize the contradictions in ruling-class ideology. Genovese's stress on the anticapitalist nature of Southern ideology probably leans too heavily on Fitzhugh and neglects other strands in Southern thought that were simultaneously more bourgeois and

In contrast, bourgeois conceptions of man as an individual with no fixed place in the social order were foreign to Omani and Swahili political ideas. Political ideas focused on communal solidarity and personal dependence.

Islam provided an ideological framework for defining the role of slaves in society. The Koran and other texts maintained that slaves had a definite place in the social order, with rights as well as obligations. These provisions provided a measure of continuity, even if they were no guarantee against the eroding force of the pursuit of profits. Islam provided fixed standards against which the self-serving reinterpretations of slaveowners had to be measured. Since no distinction was made between religion and law, slave codes were derived from the Koran— not from a sovereign legislature controlled by a planter class.[9]

That the provisions of Islamic law—especially those pertaining to the social position of slaves—were taken seriously, as they often were, did not result simply from piety or good will. The slaves did more than the Koran to ensure that slaveowners would meet their obligations. The strength of Islam lay in the mutual reinforcement of ideology and social structure. A religious framework enabled the slaveholder to see his own behavior, not in terms of reciprocity, but as conduct that was expected of a Muslim in a position of authority over his dependents.

To understand the relative suppleness in the concept of slavery in coastal society and the multiplicity of roles that slaves filled, it is also necessary to look at the way plantation slavery evolved. In the Old South, slavery arose out of a quest for agricultural labor, and this process created a strong association between the category of slave and menial labor performed under close supervision.[10] On the East African coast, plantation slavery developed out of a broader concept of dependence. Slaves had long served as skilled artisans, retainers, and concubines, as well as laborers. Slaves who were in positions of trust, who engaged in business transactions on their own behalf, or who managed their own social lives, did not contradict preconceptions about the slaves' place in society or their natural abilities. Perhaps continued economic transformation could have eroded old social structures and norms, but the plantation economy became enmeshed in its own structural weaknesses and vulnerability to outside forces even before the coast's rulers succumbed to European imperialism.

---

more racist. See in particular his essay, "The Logical Outcome of the Slaveholders' Philosophy," in *World*, pp. 118–244, and also Woodward's introduction to Fitzhugh.

9. On the importance of planter classes to shaping New World slave codes, see Goveia, "The West Indian Slave Laws," In Foner and Genovese, *Slavery*, pp. 113–37.

10. The roles that slaves actually performed were more varied than the preconceptions of Southerners.

The congruence of ideology and long-standing social practices in East Africa meant that the notion of slaves as socially inferior dependents was deeply ingrained.[11] This ideology equipped masters to understand why their slaves would acquiesce to a system that defined them as inferior, without having to postulate that slaves were different sorts of individuals from their masters. The world was hierarchical, and the fact that particular individuals were on the bottom and others on the top was God's will. This was not just a matter of Islamic fatalism but an accurate understanding of social and political reality. The self-image of the master as protector was not just a rationale for exploitation; it was, from the slave's point of view, all too true. Masters did not need to believe that slaves really felt like a member of the family, only that—in the absence of their own kinship groups—slaves needed a place in the social order.

For slaveowners in the Southern United States, it was more difficult to understand why their slaves did not rebel. That was why "Sambo" was such an important figure in white mythology. The idea of the slave as naturally docile, content, lazy, and irresponsible protected Southerners from their fear that the slave might be a person like them—someone who would not tolerate slavery. It may be true, as David Brion Davis suggests, that all slave societies had their versions of Sambo, but some needed him more that others, and not all identified Sambo with a particular race. The Southerners' need for Sambo reflected not only the high level of repression in society—producing fear, more repression, and more fear—but also their lack of confidence that the slaves accepted, even grudgingly, their place in the social order.[12]

That forms of slavery in the Southern United States and on the coast of East Africa bore as much similarity to each other as they did reveals something of the power of the master-slave relationship in the plantation context. Genovese suggests that Southern paternalism developed on the plantation itself, out of the most bourgeois society then existing

11. The moral sanction that the Koran gave slavery, combined with its deep roots in social structure, helped to obviate challenges comparable to those of abolitionists in Europe and America. Some modern Muslim apologists have argued that the growth of Islam was a step toward abolition, since it restricted the conditions under which slaves could be taken, provided ways in which they could be freed, and protected their welfare. They might have reversed their argument: the ideological security of slavery under Islam meant that the imposing of community standards on slaveowners was not a threat. For an apology written in Swahili by a member of a leading slaveowning family on the coast of Kenya, see Mazrui, *Historia ya Utumwa*.

12. Davis, *Problem of Slavery*, pp. 59–60. On stereotypes of slaves in the United States, see Blassingame, *Slave Community*, pp. 139–41, and Ronald Takaki, "The Black Child-Savage in Ante-Bellum America," in Gary B. Nash and Richard Weiss, eds., *The Great Fear: Race in the Mind of America* (New York, 1970), pp. 27–44.

and in the face of contradictory social, political, and economic pressures. On the coast of East Africa, relations of dependence had pervaded society even before the advent of the plantation. Agricultural expansion, in some ways, undercut these relations, making slaves into a regimented labor force, but in other ways, the development of the plantation transformed, but did not destroy, the multiple dimensions of the master-slave relationship.

Paternalism, in both regions, was an important characteristic of the way superiors thought of themselves and acted toward their inferiors. But the concept of paternalism reveals little about the way the Southern ruling class employed state power, class solidarity, and the support of other whites to control slaves. It gives only a partial insight into the South's ideology and racial attitudes. In East Africa, paternalistic relations existed within different kinds of social groups. There, the ties among slaveholders were weak, but the ties of inferior to superior and the bonds of communal affiliation were relatively strong. If plantation paternalism pushed Southern society away from the directions in which American society as a whole was moving, it could not overcome those tendencies. And if plantation development on the East African coast made the organization of slave labor bend with the pressures of the grain, coconut, and clove markets, it could not negate the pervasiveness of the ties of dependence.

In the Old South, the plantation never became a close-knit, hierarchical community that functioned as a basic unit of society. On the Swahili coast, neither the owners nor the owned came to form a class capable of thinking of itself as a collectivity and acting accordingly.

Class, E. P. Thompson reminds us, is not a thing whose presence or absence can be readily observed, but a relationship that develops historically.[13] Plantation agriculture—by its very nature—tended to polarize society into distinct and antagonistic classes. That slaves were foreigners—often marked by distinctive appearance—reinforced these divisions. The relationship of class developed more fully in the Southern United States and the other offshoots of Europe in the Western Hemisphere, then it did on the East Coast of Africa.

As in many precapitalist societies, the closest bonds among the coastal slaveowners were cultural: the ties of insiders against outsiders, long-time Muslims against newly converted heathens. The shared sense of being a true member of coastal society was essential to the cultural hegemony of the free. It provided a justification for their economic

13. E. P. Thompson, *The Making of the English Working Class* (New York, 1963), pp. 10–11.

control and their status and set forth the terms under which new-comers would be assimilated.[14]

The free developed a strong sense of social distinctions. Society was divided into the freeborn (waungwana), and slaves and their descendants, whether watumwa, wakulia, wazalia, or mahuru.[15] The social distinction was even more durable than legal status, for it did not end with manumission, and it was made all the more important by the need of the free—including those who owned no slaves—to differentiate themselves from the vast number of outsiders being brought to the coast to labor in the fields.

Although the master-slave relationship was part of a wider range of relationships of superior to subordinate, the slave was set apart most clearly and with the narrowest limitations on mobility. Neither he nor his descendants could become a mwungwana.[16] As in many Islamic societies, the testing ground of social distinctions was marriage. Men could marry beneath their status but women could not. A mwungwana woman could only marry a mwungwana man. A mwungwana man could marry a mwungwana woman of equal or lower status, or else marry a freed slave or take slave concubines. The first was preferred, but the others were legal and common.[17] So strong was this rule that anthropologists studying coastal villages some forty years after the abolition of slavery in Kenya found few marriages that violated it.[18]

14. The importance of cultural hegemony in maintaining status divisions and hierarchy in different kinds of societies with ineffective central governments is clear in Bloch, *Feudal Society,* and Thompson, "Patrician Society, Plebian Culture."

15. A mwungwana is someone free of slave descent in the male line. The importance of this distinction is emphasized by New, in *Life, Wanderings and Labour,* p. 56; Schmidt, *Sansibar,* pp. 56–57; and Becker, *La Vie en Afrique,* 1: 23. On the use of these terms in Swahili literature, see Knappert, "Social and Moral Concepts," pp. 128–29. Allen ("Swahili Culture Reconsidered," p. 134) tries to argue that the term waungwana referred, not to those free of slave descent, but to those who practiced the urban Swahili culture. The main point, however, is that descent and culture were inextricably intertwined.

16. For waungwana, many factors determined status, including age, family, length of time one had been a "coastal person," and so on, many of which could be altered with time. Even clients of relatively low origin could be absorbed into a family over one or more generations.

17. As a result, the descendant of a slave woman could be of higher status than his mother—if her master had fathered him—while the children of slave men could not be upwardly mobile. These principles are known as *kafā'a*—equality or suitability of marriage. For general discussions of this concept in Islam, see: Levy, *The Social Structure of Islam,* pp. 62–64, 67–68; and Farhat J. Ziadeh, "Equality (Kafā'ah) in the Muslim Law of Marriage," *American Journal of Comparative Law* 6 (1957): 503–17. On East African interpretations, I was much enlightened by the chief Kadi of Kenya, Sheikh Abdulla Saleh Al-Farsy, MSA 21.

18. Wijeyewardene, "Some Aspects of Village Solidarity," pp. 192–94; Bujra, "An Anthropological Study of Political Action," p. 111.

These status divisions were defined in terms of the master-slave distinction, not in terms of a particular mode of production. As I argued in chapter 2, plantation ownership, important as it was to the wealthy elite, provided in itself neither the material nor the social basis of their position. Plantations—especially in Zanzibar or Mombasa—were not the only sources of wealth, while land, slaves, and the income derived from them were a part—albeit a major one—of a broader concept of heshima in terms of which status was measured. Power originated, not in the solidarity of planters or from their collective control of institutions, but from control over personal followers, combined with kinship and communal ties. Political relations were fluid, linking people spread along a gradation of statuses to a man of power.

The closest bonds, both personal and political, were not between equals, but between superior and inferior. The dependents of a given slaveowner were involved together in ritual and social interaction. The growth of plantations increased the intimacy of contacts that crossed status divisions, while the movement of slaveowners into rural areas decreased contacts within status groups. When political conflict erupted, it was generally along communal lines, or else it involved the personal followers of rival individuals. Masters and slaves were most often on the same side. In the slaveowners' idiom, *watu wangu*, "my people," did not refer to members of one's own status group, but to one's dependents.[19]

The failure of planters to coalesce as a class weakened their ability to confront the masses of slaves they were importing. They proved ineffectual in combating the most serious threat to their control, escape. A revolt in the heartlands of the Zanzibari Sultanate could only be put down with the aid of mercenaries. On the mainland, watoro settlements developed on the edge of the plantations, and the slaveowners' attempts to stamp them out were intermittent and insufficient. And in their daily interaction with slaves, masters could not forget their own reliance on slave support, even if it meant that slaves had to be allowed to rise through gradations of status and new slaves had to be brought in to maintain the labor force.

Slaves, during the course of the nineteenth century, developed a sense of collective identity, responding to the vast influx of their number into coastal plantations, their shared experience of regimented and arduous labor, and their common religious and cultural subordination. Their strongest solidarity—like that of their masters—was cultural. The term they used to describe their collective identity—over and above the diversity of their backgrounds—was revealing: *wanyasa*. They

19. The term *jamaa* (loosely meaning "extended family") also included slaves and freed slaves with genuine kinsmen.

did not describe themselves by their status or role in coastal society (*wa-tumwa*—slaves) or by race (*watu weusi*—black people), but by origin. Their foreign origin—which epitomized their subordinate position in coastal society—was for them a source of common identity and pride.

The dances, initiation ceremonies, and other forms of ritual and social life that the slaves shared among themselves were antithetical to paternalism, but they did not form the basis of a developing subculture. The reality of dependent social relations was too powerful and could not help but produce some kind of identification with coastal society and the slaveowners' communal groups.[20] But the partially formed subculture did not die out—some slaves could move in two worlds—and eventually it exerted its influence on Swahili culture as a whole.

That substantial numbers of slaves ran away to communities of their own suggests that some kind of collective spirit existed, and that it was not devoid of political content. But for other slaves, fleeing a master meant seeking a new protector. Even the Maroon settlements found that their survival depended on their strength as communities, not on their ties with other slaves.

Conflict was frequent between watoro communities and plantation communities, and within the latter, conflict between individual masters and slaves was continuous. But conflict between slaves as a group and masters as a group did not develop. Slaves were unable to coalesce as a class or to confront their owners collectively, but they were able to influence their reciprocal relations with their owners and to protect themselves against the idea that social dependency implied their own inferiority as people.

The structures of dependency within coastal society absorbed the polarizing influence of plantation development, blunting—although not eliminating—the tendency for society to divide into new groups based on class. Similarly, the vast influx of blacks brought to labor in the fields did not cause racial divisions to crystallize, as they did in the Americas.

Racial distinctiveness is a particular form of the more universal condition of the slave—his being an outsider. But biological differences had particular implications, within a differentiated economy, to the structural divisions of society. The Southern United States went the farthest of Western slave societies toward making the black-white di-

20. The legacy of this identification was as clear in interviews with descendants of slaves as was their consciousness of being wanyasa. They even internalized the historical traditions of their owners' communal groups: wazalia informants in Malindi, when questioned about the town's origins, invariably gave the versions of the parents' masters.

chotomy the most fundamental group boundary in society. In other American societies, the rich were also white and the poor black, but intermediate groups were recognized and some mobility allowed, through the expedient of redefining as white those whom the elite wished to recruit.[21]

Blackness, slave status, and menial work tended to coincide in coastal society as well. As agriculture expanded, a larger proportion of slaves became field workers, and virtually all of them were black. Nor were the people of the coast free from color prejudice. They expressed it in the prices they paid for slaves of differing colors and features. A few Swahili proverbs hint that slaves were looked upon as inherently inferior, even though this violated the spirit of the Koran. The legacy of such prejudices can still be heard in the form of disparaging remarks made by waungwana about "Waafrika," although such disdain was based on origins, culture, and religion, as well as color.[22]

However, racial lines in coastal society were blurred. The masters were ethnically mixed, and waungwana were not necessarily light-skinned, although all thought of themselves as ethnically distinct from the Africans of the interior. Swahili—whether Bajuni, Washella, members of the Twelve Tribes, Wapemba, or Wahadimu—ranged in color from brown to black. Even Arabs could have dark skins and negroid features, since children of Arab men by black concubines were considered Arabs. Finally, the entourage of a powerful man, as well as a communal group, included, among the people from whom support was expected and who were involved in a network of social relations, light-skinned Arabs or Swahili, black slaves, black freed slaves, perhaps a few light-skinned slaves, and black clients recruited from nearby societies. Racial distinctions were recognized, but they were a rough guide to a person's status or group affiliation.

Prejudice was not formalized into a doctrine justifying domination on the basis of the inherent inferiority of the subordinate group. The elite's concept of dependence—self-serving as it was—remained relevant to social and political reality. Only after the creation of the colonial state, when the structure of political action changed drastically, did divisions of race and class become crucial determinants of the bounda-

21. When a society was overwhelmed by plantation agriculture, as in Cuba during the nineteenth century, discrimination against blacks—even freed ones—and racist doctrines could become more virulent. Franklin W. Knight, "Slavery, Race, and Social Structure in Cuba During the Nineteenth Century," in Toplin, Slavery and Race Relations, p. 213. See also Degler, Neither White Nor Black, and da Costa, "Myth of Racial Democracy."

22. For proverbs, see Taylor, African Alphorisms, no. 313, 349, 449. See also Bujra, pp. 101, 112.

ries of political and social groups and basic components of conflicting ideologies.[23]

The impact of plantation slavery on the East African coast differed substantially from its effect on the Southern United States. It is well to remember that in the blend of personal and impersonal dimensions of slavery in both regions, subordination was the fundamental premise. Whether a master called his slave "my child" or "boy" or "nigger," the slave was not a child. He or his ancestor had been wrenched away from his family, from people whom he considered his own, and offered the consolation of life as an inferior and a dependent. However much the master might value his slaves as people and as followers, he was also a plantation owner whose profits derived from the labor of his slaves. Behind the security, personal ties, and social rewards of plantation life lay the sanction of force. On the coast of East Africa, as in other slave societies, slaves lacked the physical and social strength to overturn the structure of society, but they still struggled to obtain some control over the way they worked and lived.

23. To argue that the master-slave division in nineteenth-century Zanzibar directly led to the conflicts that brought about the revolution of 1964 skips a lot of history. The legacy of plantation development was indeed an Arab landowning elite which became the target of a movement that included the descendants of slaves, plus larger numbers of immigrants from the mainland and Swahili who had been outside the plantation system. Still, the processes that turned division into conflict belong to the colonial situation. See Lofchie, *Zanzibar: Background to Revolution.*

Appendix 1
Sultans and Consuls

Sultans of Muscat and Zanzibar

Said bin Sultan, ruled 1806–56

In 1856, the Sultanate was divided between Muscat and Zanzibar. Said bin Sultan was followed by four of his sons in Zanzibar:

Majid, 1856–70
Bargash, 1870–88
Khalifa, 1888–90
Ali, 1890–93

Political Agents and Consuls-General of the British Government in Zanzibar

Lieutenant-Colonel Atkins Hamerton, 1841–57
Lieutenant-Colonel C. P. Rigby, 1858–61
Sir Lewis Pelly, 1862 (acting)
Colonel R. L. Playfair, 1863–65
Mr. H. A. Churchill, 1866–70
Sir John Kirk, 1870–86
Sir Claude McDonald, 1887–88
Sir Charles Euan-Smith, 1889–91
Sir Gerald Portal, 1891–92
Sir Rennell Rodd, 1893
Sir Arthur Hardinge, 1894–1900

Information for both lists is taken from Sir Reginald Coupland, *The Exploitation of East Africa 1856–1890: The Slave Trade and the Scramble* (London: Faber and Faber, 1939); and F. B. Pearce, *Zanzibar: The Island Metropolis of Eastern Africa* (London: Unwin, 1920), p. 276.

Appendix 2
Anti-Slave Trade Measures, 1822–1890

1822   Treaty between British and Sultan of Muscat banning all export of slaves by the Sultan's subjects to Christian nations (including India and Mascerene Islands).

1839   Extension of above treaty restricting area of Indian Ocean in which the slave trade was allowed and giving the British Navy the right to search Omani dhows.

1841   First British consul sent to Zanzibar.

1847   Treaty, signed in 1845, between the British and the Sultan of Muscat goes into effect, banning shipment of slaves outside the African dominions of the Sultan.

1860–61   Consul Rigby confiscates slaves belonging to Indians in Zanzibar. This policy was not continued by his successors after 1861. British naval vessels begin to confiscate slaves and burn dhows that were in violation of 1845 treaty. Attempts made to force Northern Arabs out of Zanzibar harbor.

1862–64   Regulations by Sultan of Zanzibar designed to hinder Northern Arabs. Only East African subjects of Sultan allowed to obtain licenses to carry slaves within his African dominions. No slave shipments allowed January-April, the period of favorable winds to the North.

1868   Decree of Sultan ordering that anyone involved in export trade (Northern Arabs or Zanzibaris who sell slaves to them) be punished. Provisions for enforcement established.

1873   Sir Bartle Frere pressures Seyyid Bargash to sign treaty abolishing all shipments of slaves by sea and giving the British Navy the right to search vessels and bring them to Zanzibar for trial if they contained slaves. Public slave markets closed.

1874   Consul Kirk renews policy of confiscating slaves of Indians.

1876   Treaty between the British and the Sultan of Zanzibar bans all slave caravans on land. Penalties to be imposed on slavers. Sultan's officials enforce it on mainland, while the navy continues to capture slave dhows.

1888   Imperial British East Africa Company given concession to coast of what is now Kenya by the Sultan. Posts set up in Mombasa, Malindi, and elsewhere. Blockade of Tanganyika coast as a consequence of the German takeover and resistance by the local people.

1889   Proclamation by the Sultan declaring that all children born to slaves after 1890 would be free. Never publicly announced or enforced.

1890   Zanzibar becomes a British Protectorate. Proclamation of Sultan declares all slaves acquired after 1890 are free. All sales of slaves banned and inheritance of slaves limited to the master's children only. Slaves of Mijikenda (or other local) origin declared free on Kenya coast.

Note on Sources

A glance at the bibliography of a monograph on slavery in the Americas is enough to turn the Africanist green with envy, even if he is aware of all the disputes and complaints which historians of the Americas have about their sources. Africanists lack the plantation records that allow a picture to be drawn of economic activities on particular plantations; the diaries, memoirs, and narratives that give inside views of plantation life from differing perspectives; and the censuses, probate records, and other quantifiable sources that allow assessments to be made of demographic patterns and the economic characteristics of plantation regions.

But for the memories of a few exceptional informants and scattered records, I would have had no idea of the activities on specific plantations or the life-histories of specific planters, leaving only more general accounts of visitors or the recollections of informants about what plantation society was like. Because Africanists depend on outsiders for contemporary accounts, they can rarely see a process of change through all its phases but must infer what must have happened between periods that are adequately documented. A convincing analysis must be built up from a combination of sources, each of which has severe liabilities.

The problem of interpreting the accounts of travelers, missionaries, and officials are not particularly unusual: their knowledge of language and customs was often imperfect, their preconceptions about African society and the institution of slavery in general were often strong, their acquaintance with rural areas was usually brief, their figures on trade and population were often offhand estimates, and their closest contacts among local people tended to be with the slaveholding elite. Nevertheless, used with discrimination, their evidence is extremely valuable. Some visitors were acute and relatively detached observers, and conflicting prejudices among the more biased made it possible to obtain a fairly balanced picture—at least for Zanzibar, where the accounts were most numerous.

Few local records have been preserved. The historical interests of the local people focused on genealogical and community histories, not on preserving trade records and accounts of individuals' lives. By far the best source of contemporary documents is the Mombasa Land Office, which contains several deed files dating to the 1890s, including a few deeds from earlier periods. One set of deeds, the A-series, includes sales, mortgages, and rentals of agricultural land, urban plots, and houses. A second set, the B-series, contains loans not involving land as collateral, trading agreements, manumission papers for slaves, and a variety of other documents. Such records cover Mombasa from 1891 onward and Malindi from 1903. These deeds provide crucial examples of practices involving slaves. The freedom papers show that slaves actually were freed in accordance with Islamic theories, while the transaction records indicate that slaves and freed slaves could participate in the economy.

The data can also be used quantitatively, and I am in the process of using them to make a systematic study of land and credit in Mombasa to 1919, working in collaboration with John Zarwan. Karim Janmohamed has also collected this data. In the present study, I have used all 566 deeds of the B-series that involved a transaction of some sort (1892–99, after which it was phased out), plus a 20 percent sample of the A-series (1891–1905), amounting to 1,097 cases. The deed collections are biased toward transactions involving people who were most willing to acknowledge the colonial bureaucracy, although registration was compulsory. The processed data shed considerable light on the participation of various ethnic groups in the economy of Mombasa toward the end of the slavery era.

I have also been able to obtain an idea of patterns of land ownership from the Land Office's complete transcripts of hearings held between 1912 and 1924 for the purpose of assigning titles to individual plots of land in the agricultural zones of Mombasa and Malindi. Since few landowners had deeds of purchase, claimants usually had to point out their boundaries to investigators and bring witnesses to the hearings if their claims were disputed. The procedure was somewhat biased in favor of local elites, but some standards of proof existed and many smallholders received titles. The data provide, for example, a general idea of the distribution of land among Swahili and Arab subgroups and an idea of the size of plantations, although all groups had lost land since the abolition of slavery in 1907.

The study of slavery on the mainland coast was enriched by approximately one hundred interviews I conducted in Mombasa and Malindi in 1972–73. In Swahili society, there are no formal oral traditions, but a number of men—some very old, some middle-aged—have a lively interest in the past and recall much information related by their parents or other elders. Most informants were only one generation removed from the period of slavery; several had been born slaves. Many interviews were structured around genealogies and descriptions of the lives of the informants' ancestors or the more important members of their communal groups. Such data are a guide to the economic activities of members of different ethnic groups.

Informants of different origins—sons of slaves as well as slaveowners—also gave their views of customs pertaining to slave labor, farming techniques, living arrangements of slaves, land usage, and other matters. Informants of free and slave descent gave very different interpretations of slavery, while members of different communal groups often had conflicting interpretations of local history. When such informants agreed on a particular point, this was a good indication that, for example, a certain custom was widely accepted. When they disagreed, they pointed to sensitive areas.

The biggest problem with oral evidence is change. All documents may contain inaccurate observations, but oral testimonies can also be distorted in the process of transmission. It is often hard to tell whether a particular custom applied to the nineteenth century or the more recent past, or whether expressions of group hostility reflect conflicts that have become salient since the abolition of slavery. For this reason, written and oral sources must be used together. An informant's evidence can render meaningful a cursory observation by a traveler, but the traveler's evidence makes it possible to establish the relevance of the oral data to the more distant past. More important, many aspects of culture and social relationships as they existed in the nineteenth century will remain beyond the grasp of historians, while others will be understood in vague and uncertain terms.

The techniques of interviewing could only be informal. I tried to follow the informants' own interests as much as possible. Most interviews were done in Swahili, and I only rarely used an interpreter or tape recorder—both of which could interfere with the atmosphere of trust and mutual interest in the past. Interviews were written up immediately afterward, and the notes are in my possession.

Following is a list of informants and brief notes to identify the value of their information. In the text they are cited by numbers and the place of interview: MAL (Malindi and vicinity, including Mambrui) and MSA (Mombasa and vicinity). I regret the impersonal nature of the citations, for these people are very alive to me, but for most readers, the information below is more important than the names.

Malindi Informants (MAL)

1. Mohamed Maawia. An Mshella. Works for the Land Office and knows the intricacies of land tenure and usage well, in addition to the history of the Washella people. (Interviewed in Mombasa).

(MAL)   2. Gulamhussein Tayabji. Very old Indian of the Bohora community. Son of the first Indian to settle in Mambrui.

3. Said Khalid Abdalla. Of mixed Shella-Omani origin.

4. Nassor Said Nassor Al-Busaidi. From a minor branch of the politically dominant Omani communal group.

5. Swaleh Mohamed Gagi. A Baluchi descended from one of the original soldiers sent to Malindi by the Sultan. Knowledgeable in Baluchi history in Malindi, the founding of Malindi, and Malindi social history generally. Provided a perspective somewhat outside of the four principal communal groups in Malindi.

6. Mohamed Hemed. Baluchi. Former dhow captain.

7. Erastus Tsuma. Giriama. Chief of Malindi. A young man, but well acquainted with Giriama elders.

8. Tayabali Rajabali Mulla Bhaiji. Borhora. Son of a trader in Malindi in the 1880s. Well informed about his community, trade, and agriculture.

9. Ali Salim Salim. Mshella farmer.

10. Jivanji Gulamhussein Jivanji. Bohora. Grandson of the most important Indian import-export merchant and financier, Jivanji Mamuji.

11. Abdulla Athman Al-Amudy. Hadrami trader well versed in his community's role in Malindi society.

12. Mohamed Lali. Bajuni. Gave an elaborate history of the founding of Malindi that shows signs of a fine imagination. A good guide to stories about important figures of the nineteenth century as well as local customs.

13. Salim Alyan Nahwy. Son of MAL 18.

14. Rev. Kalume. Provided important leads to Giriama informants.

15. Abdalla Omar Nabahani. A young man, but able to provide information about a group from the Lamu area that came to Malindi.

16. Bakari Rarua. A Giriama Muslim and an elder. Very knowledgeable about Giriama relations with Arabs and ex-slaves.

17. Abdalla Seif. One of the oldest Washella, in his eighties. He was able to identify important people in Malindi's history and was an expert on local customs, agriculture, and the town's social organization.

18. Alyan Hemed Al-Nahwy. The oldest Omani, in his eighties. Also extremely knowledgeable about people, customs, and society, particularly concerning Omanis.

19. Omar Dahman Al-Amudy. A leader of the Hadrami community.

20. Omar Ali. Very old Mshella.

21. bin Omari. Expert on history of Malindi's mosques but too ill for extensive interview.

22. Mohamed Said Nassor Al-Busaidi. Older brother of MAL 4 and well informed on Omanis in Malindi. (MAL)

23. Abbas Abdulhussein Adamji Saigar. Bohora trader.

24. Omar wa Fundi. An mzalia, son of a door-maker owned by a leading Mshella. Superb source on the life of slaves.

25. Said Abdalla Mohamed Saiban. Hadrami trader.

26. Khalifa wa Lali Hadaa. Descendant of early Bajuni settlers. About eighty and one of the best informants about slavery and nineteenth-century society.

27. Mohamed Abubakar Abbas. An old Mshella well versed in his community's history and society in the old days.

28. Yahya Said Hemed Al-Busaidi. Son and grandson of the first two governors of Mambrui. Knows the story of his important family and other Omanis. Age seventy-five.

29. Omar Ahmed Barium. Hadrami. Provided valuable information on Omani-Hadrami relations.

30. Awade Maktub. Mtoto wa nyumbani of bi Salima, a leading slave-owner. In his eighties. Provided a vivid account of slave life, relations between masters and slaves, watoro, and other questions.

31. Suede Nasibu. Mzalia, son of the slave of a Bajuni.

32. Mselem Khalfan Jaafari. Omani. His grandfather was an overseer for Salim bin Khalfan.

33. Salim Sabiki. Bajuni sailor and fisherman.

34. Juma Kengewa. Son of slaves on plantation of Salim bin Khalfan. Very good on life of slaves.

35. Jabu Masoya. Son of a slave who was an overseer on a shamba owned by an ex-slave. Gave a moving, bitter account of life under slavery.

36. Sheriff Mohamed Said Al-Beith. Islamic teacher in Mambrui. Young man who knows the history of the village well.

37. Omar Salim Batheiff. Hadrami. Descendant of old settlers in Mambrui.

38. Juma Mbaraka. His parents were slaves of an Omani.

39. Ahmed Salim Bawazir. Hadrami trader and landowner.

40. Salim Mohamed Islam Al-Kathiri. Grandson of Islam bin Ali, an important figure in Mambrui's history and a fine informant on his family, slavery, and Mambrui society.

41. Ali Athman. Bajuni of Mambrui.

42. Mussbhai Tayabji Walliji. Son of first Bohora in Mambrui (brother of MAL 2). Very knowledgeable on trading organization in Mambrui.

43. Mahfudh Mohamed Ali Basharahil. Grandson of leading Hadrami farmer and trader in Mambrui.

(MAL)   44. Dewel Said Badwill. Very old Hadrami, nearly one hundred, living in Mambrui. A fine informant on most topics, who has seen as well as heard.

45. Joint interview: Athman Mohamed Nabhani, Maalim Abud Abdalla (Bajuni) and Mohamed Abubakar Yusuf (from Lamu). These three informants added to each other's comments and confirmed several points regarding the early history of Mambrui, social life in the town, various important people, problems with watoro, etc.

46. Kassim Umar. Bajuni. Told about role of Bajunis in Mambrui and about the outlying areas of the town, where he lives.

47. Ahmed Mbarak Handwan. From the richest Hadrami family in Malindi in the late nineteenth century.

48. Rev. Timothy Ngoma. Pastor of the church at Jilore, the first mission station near Malindi. Knows the mission's history, including the interaction of mission people with watoro.

49. Alfred Yongo. Giriama elder.

50. Dola Bakari. Bajuni of Mambrui.

51. Mzee Jabu. Son of slaves in Mambrui.

52. Omar Bwana Mkuu. Bajuni who knew much about the origins of Mambrui, Bajuni history, and the life of a small-scale cultivator.

53. Maalim Mohamed. Bajuni. Useful on dhow trade.

54. Gari Kai. Giriama elder.

55. Mzeze Kwicha. Giriama elder.

56. Suleiman Amur Al-Daremki. From a leading Omani family.

57. Rev. Ishmael Toya. Very old Mgiriama who went to school at the Jilore mission and knew area well.

58. Hassan Said Al-Homar. Hadrami living in Mambrui hinterland.

59. Isa Said Al-Hasibi. Omani living near Mambrui. Relative of bi Salima binti Masudi and important source on her life.

60. Suleiman Ali Mselem Al-Khalasi. Grandson of bi Salima's husband and son of a kadi of Malindi.

61. Mohamed Khamis Muhando. An mzalia of Mzigua origin. Well informed about early Malindi history and slavery.

62. Kazungu wa Kiganda. Giriama elder.

63. Mohamed Omari Toya. Giriama Muslim.

64. Mohamed wa Mweni. Giriama Muslim.

65. Bisiria Toya. Giriama elder who was very knowledgeable about Giriama-Arab relations and the slave trade in the Malindi hinterland.

66. Mohamed Omar Al-Amudy. Interviewed in Shella, Lamu, about migration of Washella to Malindi.

67. Abdulla Kadara. Interviewed in Lamu about founding of Malindi.

Mombasa Informants (MSA)

1. Lance Jones Bengo. Grandson of William Jones, who was taken from a slave dhow by the British and later became a missionary. Interesting on life at mission stations.
2. James Juma Mbotela. Son of a slave taken off a captured dhow and brought up at Freretown. Age eighty-four and a fine informant about the northern mainland of Mombasa, as well as mission life.
3. Mohamed Rashid Al-Mazrui. About sixty and the leading Mazrui historian in Mombasa. Also knows much about agriculture and slavery.
4. Ahmed Abdalla Al-Mazrui. A young, well-educated relative of MSA 3, who has learned much from his elders and has great insight into coastal society.
5. William George Kombo. Son of slaves of Giriama, brought up at mission station.
6. Gibson Koboko. Mrabai. Married to daughter of slaves.
7. Newland Gibson Ngome. Good informant on life at Rabai mission.
8. Mzee Benjamin Chimwenga, son of Ndoro. Mribe. Excellent on interaction of Arabs, Mijikenda, and watoro in the coastal hinterland.
9. Shiabuddin Shiraghdin. Part Punjabi, part Mombasa Swahili. An expert on Swahili customs and traditions. One interview was conducted jointly with Hyder Mohamed Kindy, a Swahili spokesman.
10. Samuel Levi. Mission resident who also knew much about relations of mission people to local Arabs.
11. Mohamed Ali Mirza. Baluchi. Grandson of Abdulrehman Mirza, a leading trader and money-lender in late nineteenth-century Mombasa. Well informed about Baluchi history, trade, and slavery.
12. Salim Mohamed Muhashamy. Former chief Arab official of the coast of Kenya under British rule and member of a leading Omani family.
13. Shariff Abdalla Salim. Leading member of the Hadrami community.
14. Al-Amin Said Al-Mandhry. Fifty-six years old, an excellent informant with whom I spoke many times. A former Arab official, familiar with Islamic law and coastal practices, and well informed about agriculture, slavery, Omani-Swahili relations, trade, and the history of the Mandhry communal group.
15. Said Mohamed Al-Mandhry. Expert in Mandhry history. Provided a detailed Mandhry genealogy.
16. Shariff Mohamed Abdalla Shatry. Member of a very active Hadrami trading family.

(MSA) 17. Shariff Abdulrehman Abdalla Shatry. Brother of the above.

18. Mohamedali Bhaijee. Bohora trader who dealt in copra.

19. Ali Jemedar Amir. Of mixed Baluchi-Swahili descent. Well versed in Mombasa history despite his age.

20. Famy Mbarak Hinawi. Son of Mbarak bin Ali Hinawy, former Arab official. Young, but had interesting comments on an Arab family that included ex-slaves in household.

21. Abdalla Saleh Al-Farsy. The leading Islamic scholar of the coast. From Zanzibar, but now chief kadi of Kenya. An expert on Islamic law, local practices, and Zanzibari history.

22. Yahya Ali Omar. Swahili scholar. Knowledgeable on Swahili agriculture and customs.

23. Mohamed Hemed Timami. From a Suri family with long ties to Mombasa.

24. Said Karama. Swahili poet.

25. Mohamed Khammal Khan. Baluchi. A teacher with a sound knowledge of Swahili customs and local history.

26. Mohamed Kassim Al-Mazrui. Former chief kadi of Kenya and a leading Islamic scholar who has written a book on Islamic slavery.

27. Mohamed Ahmed Ali Al-Mandhry. Grandson of a leading Omani landowner and trader, Ali bin Salim bin Ali Al-Mandhry.

28. Muhiddin Mohamed Al-Changamwe. Expert on history of this Swahili subgroup, as well as agriculture and slavery. Provided information on some of the wealthy Swahili of the nineteenth century.

29. Wazee of Majengo. Joint interview with four elders from this district of Mombasa, arranged by the chief of Majengo. General agreement on customary requirements of slaves emerged from the discussion.

30. Mohamed Said Al-Busaidi. Administrator of remaining portion of the estate of Salim bin Khalfan, who provided information about his holdings and the social composition of the neighborhoods where he held land.

31. Ibrahim Shaib. Old Bajuni living near Mombasa. told of relations of Arabs, Swahili, Mijikenda, and slaves on mainland north of Mombasa.

32. Mchangamwe Umar. Of Digo origin, but born in Kisauni, and knowledgeable about agriculture and intergroup relations in the area.

33. Wazee of Kisauni. Joint interview with eight elders of various communal groups arranged by the chief of Kisauni. They agreed that Kisauni had originally been a Mijikenda area and that Arabs encroached on the land.

34. Said Salim Ruwehi. From a leading Omani family of Zanzibar   (MSA)
    which combined plantation agriculture with scholarship.
35. Said Mohamed Baghozi. Hadrami who told me about the Hadrami
    place in Mombasa society and their interaction with Omanis and
    slaves.
36. Ahmed Said Riami. From an important Zanzibari family.
37. Juma Rubai. An mzalia living in Mombasa, whose father was a
    slave in Malindi. Age seventy-three. Made interesting comparisons
    between slavery in Mombasa and Malindi.
38. Maalim Mzagu and Mzee Juma. Two long-time dock workers.

In addition to the above, Margaret Strobel generously showed me transcripts of her interviews with Shamsa binti Mohamed Muhashamy, Bi
Momo, and Bi Kaje.

Bibliography

Government Archives

Public Record Office, London

ADM 1/70, Letters of Lieut. J. B. Emery, 1824–26
ADM 1/62, Report on Pemba by Captain W. Fisher, 1809
ADM 52/3940, Journal of Lieut. J. B. Emery, 1824–26
CO 167, Mauritius
CO 533, Kenya
FO 2, Africa
FO 54, Muscat
FO 84, Slave Trade
FO 107, Zanzibar
FO 403, Confidential Prints, Africa (cited by number of the print)
FO 541, Confidential Prints, Slave Trade (cited by number of the print)
FO 800/234, Papers of Sir Lewis Pelly

India Office Records, London

Political and Secret: L/P&S/5, L/P&S/ 9
Marine: L/MAR/c/586, log of Capt. T. Smee, 1811
Residency Records: Bushire, 5/15/1/0
                      Muscat, 5/15/3/A
Bengal Commerical Records: P/174/16, 18
Bombay Proceedings: P/381/33, P/385/12, 26
Bombay Commerce, Reports: P/419/41–91

Foreign and Commonwealth Office, London

Edward Batson, "The Social Survey of Zanzibar," MS, 1961

Archives de l'Ancien Ministère d'Outre-Mer, Paris

Réunion
Océan Indien

Archives du Ministère des Affaires Etrangères, Paris

Correspondance Commerciale, Muscate
Correspondance Commerciale, Zanzibar

283

Archives Nationales, Paris

    Colonies: C4, F2c/12
    Affaires Etrangères: B3/438

United States National Archives, Washington

    Dispatches of United States Consuls to Zanzibar (microfilm)

Kenya National Archives, Nairobi

    Coast Province, Deposits 1 and 2
    Provincial and District Annual and Quarterly Reports, Seyidie Province (later Coast Province)
    Political Record Books, Seyidie Province
    Judicial Department Records

High Court of Kenya, Nairobi

    Probate and Administration Files
    Records of the High Court, Mombasa, plus scattered files from Town Magistrate's and Resident Magistrate's Court, Mombasa

Land Office, Nairobi

    LO 30646, file on Mazrui land, Gazi

Land Office, Mombasa

    Adjudication causes pursuant to Coast Land Settlement Act of 1908: Malindi, 1912–15; Mombasa, 1916–18; Mambrui, 1922–24
    Registers of Deeds, Mombasa:
    A-series (land), 1891–1912
    B-series (miscellaneous), 1892–1912
    AS and AS 2 (rentals), 1899
    Register of Deeds, Malindi: A-series, 1903–12

Wakf Commission, Mombasa

    Register of Wakf Properties, Mombasa

Fort Jesus, Mombasa

    Mervyn Beech, "Swahili Life," MS, n.d. [ca. 1915]

Other Archives

Church Missionary Society, London

    CA5/01, Miscellaneous letters
    CA5/02–27, Letters from individual missionaries to 1880
    CA5/M1–6, Minute books
    G3/A5/0/1881–, Correspondence, 1881–

Universities' Mission to Central Africa, London

    Correspondence, Zanzibar

Friends' Library, London

    MS Narrative of visit of Theodore Burtt and Henry S. Newman to Zanzibar, Pemba, and the East Africa Protectorate, 1897, MS vol. 204
    Correspondence, Pemba

Rhodes House, Oxford University

    British and Foreign Anti-Slavery Society Papers, G2–5
    Richard Thornton, Journals, MSS.Afr.s49
    Gerald Portal, Papers, MSS.Afr.s103–14
    Mombasa Social Survey, 1956–58

School of Oriental and African Studies, University of London

    Papers of Sir William Mackinnon

Cambridge University Library

    Papers of Sir John Gray (including typescripts of documents from Zanzibar archives)

Royal Commonwealth Society, London

    Papers of Sir John Gray (including typescripts of rare documents and unpublished papers by Sir John Gray)

Royal Geographical Society, London

    Letters from Lieut. J. B. Emery to W. D. Cooley, 1833–35

Archives de la Congregation du Saint-Esprit, Paris

    Correspondence and dossiers, Zanzibar, boxes 61, 194–97, 649

Department of History, University of Nairobi

Sheikh Al-Amin bin Ali, "History of the Mazru'i Dynasty of Mombasa," trans. J. M. Ritchie, n.d. [ca. 1940]

University of Dar es Salaam Library

Selected records from the Indian National Archives, Foreign Department, 1834–69, prepared by Dr. Abdul Sheriff, 2 reels of microfilm
Swahili Collection: "Maisha Yangu," by Persis Chimwai, no. 178, and "Historical Notes," by Khalid Kifara, no. 180

Private

Mohamed Hussien Tharia Topan, "Biography of Sir Tharia Topan, Knight," MS, 1960–63, in possession of the author's son, Dr. Farouk Topan, Nairobi

Official Documents

Parliamentary Papers, Great Britain

Series on the Slave Trade in East Africa, 1828, 1837–38, 1843–44, 1865–94
Series on Slavery and Abolition in Zanzibar and Pemba, 1895–1905
1871, XII, 1. Report of the Special Committee on the East African Slave Trade
1873, LXI, 767. Correspondence respecting Sir Bartle Frere's Mission to the East Coast of Africa, 1872–73
1888, LXXIV, 255. Further Correspondence respecting Germany and Zanzibar
1893–94, LXII, 575. Reports on the Zanzibar Protectorate
1896, LIX, 41. Correspondence respecting the Recent Rebellion in British East Africa
1898, LX, 199. Report by Sir A. Hardinge on the Condition and Progress of the East Africa Protectorate from Its Establishment to the 20th July, 1897
1898, LX, 361. Report by Vice-Consul O'Sullivan on the Island of Pemba, 1896–97
1903, XLV, 745. Report on Slavery and Free Labour by W. J. Monson, Assistant Secretary of the East Africa Protectorate
1903, XLV, 759. Report by Mr. A. Whyte on His Recent Travels along the Sea-Coast Belt of the British East Africa Protectorate

Publications of the Governments of India and Bombay (available in the India Office Library, London, except as noted)

Selections from the Records of the Bombay Government, n.s. 24, 1856.
Selections from the Records of the Government of India: Reports on the

Administration of the Persian Gulf Residence and the Muscat Political Agency, 1875–84

William M. Coghlan, "Proceedings connected with the commission appointed by the Government to investigate and report on the disputes between the rulers of Muscat and Zanzibar." Bombay: Education Society Press, 1861

Captain P. D. Henderson, "Précis of Correspondence relating to Zanzibar Affairs from 1856 to 1872," 1872

John Robb, "A Medico-Topographical Report on Zanzibar." Calcutta, 1874 (copy in British Museum)

J. A. Saldanha, ed., "Précis on the Slave Trade in the Gulf of Oman and the Persian Gulf, 1873–1905." Simla, 1906

Foreign Office, Diplomatic and Consular Reports, Annual Series

Zanzibar, 1891, no. 982, and Supplementary Report, no. 991
Zanzibar, 1892, no. 1194
Pemba, 1900, no. 2653

Publications of the Zanzibar Government (Published by the Government Printer except as noted)

Agriculture Department, Annual Report, 1898——

Zanzibar Law Reports containing cases determined in the British Consular Court and in H.B.M.'s Court and in the Supreme Court of his Highness the Sultan and in Courts Subordinate thereto, 1868 to 1918, compiled by Sir William Murison and S. S. Abrahams. London: Waterlow, 1919

Report on the Non-Native Census, 1921

Memorandum on Certain Aspects of the Zanzibar Clove Industry, by G. D. Kirsopp. London: Waterlow, 1926

Statistics of the Zanzibar Protectorate, by R. H. Crofton, 1921, 1931

The Land and Its Mortgage Debt, by C. F. Strickland. London: Waterlow, 1932

Report on the Indebtedness of the Agricultural Classes, by C. A. Bartlett and J. S. Last, 1933

A Note on Agricultural Indebtedness in the Zanzibar Protectorate, by Sir Ernest M. Dowson, 1936

A Review of the System of Land Tenure in the Islands of Zanzibar and Pemba, by W. R. McGeach and William Addis, 1945 (written in 1934)

Report on the Inquiry to claims to certain land at or near Ngezi, Vitongoji, in the Mudiria of Chake Chake in the District of Pemba, by J. M. Gray, 1956

Publications of the British East Africa Protectorate (published by the Government Printer except as noted)

Report on the Native Cultivation, Products and Capabilities of the Coast Lands of the Malindi District, by W. W. A. Fitzgerald, 1891

Official List of Lands Adjudicated under the Land Titles Ordinance of
    1908, Supplement to Official Gazette of the East Africa Protectorate,
    Supplement 5 to Gazette of 31 May 1916
Census Returns, 1911
Report on the Census of Non-Natives, 1921
Kenya Law Reports, containing cases determined by the High Court of
    East Africa, and by the Court of Appeals for Eastern Africa, and by the
    Judicial Committee of the Privy Council on Appeals from the Court,
    compiled by R. W. Hamilton, 1897–1921. Reprinted, Dobbs Ferry, N.Y.:
    Oceana, 1967

Miscellaneous

Documents relatifs à la repression de la traite des esclaves publiées en ex-
    écution des articles LXXXI et suivants de l'acte général de Bruxelles.
    Brussels, 1892——
United States House of Representatives, Report upon the Commerical
    Relations of the United States with Foreign Countries, 1865–1900

Published Works, Dissertations, and Conference Papers

Abdurrahim Mohamed Jiddawi. "Extracts from an Arab Account Book,
    1840–1854." *Tanganyika Notes and Records* 33 (1953): 25–31.
Akinola, G. A. "Slavery and Slave Revolts in the Sultanate of Zanzibar in the
    Nineteenth Century." *Journal of the Historical Society of Nigeria* 6 (1972):
    215–28
Albrand, Fortené. "Extraits d'une Memoire sur Zanzibar et Quiloa," *Bulletin de
    la Société de Géographie* (Paris), 2d ser. 10 (1838): 65–83.
Allen, Miss. "Glimpses of Harem Life." *Central Africa* 1 (1883): 147–48.
Alpers, E. A. *Ivory and Slaves in East Central Africa.* Berkeley: University of Cali-
    fornia Press, 1975.
———. "Trade, State and Society among the Yao in the Nineteenth Century."
    Journal of African History 10 (1969): 405–20.
Anderson, J. N. D. *Islamic Law in Africa.* New Impression. London: Frank Cass,
    1970. First published, 1959.
'Arafat, W. "The Attitude of Islam to Slavery." *The Islamic Quarterly* 10, nos. 1
    and 2 (1966): 12–18.
ArcAngelo, Henry C. "A Sketch of the River Juba or Gochob, or Gowin, from a
    Trip Up the Stream in 1844." *Cobburn's United Service Magazine* (1845), part
    1, pp. 278–83.
Bathurst, R. D. "The Ya'rubi Dynasty of Oman." D. Phil. dissertation, Oxford
    University, 1967.
Baumann, Oscar. *Die Insel Pemba.* Leipzig: Duncker and Humblot, 1899.
———. *Die Insel Sansibar.* Leipzig: Duncker and Humblot, 1897.
———. *Usambara und seine Nachbargebiete.* Berlin: Reimers, 1891.
Baur et LeRoy, les R. P. *A travers le Zanguebar: Voyage dans l'Oudoé, l'Ouzigoua,
    l'Oukwèrè, l'Oukami et l'Ousagara.* Tours: Alfred Mame et Fils, 1887.

Becker, Jerome. *La vie en Afrique, ou trois ans dans l'Afrique Centrale*. 2 vols. Paris-Brussels: J. Lebèque, 1887.

Beckford, George L. *Persistent Poverty: Underdevelopment in Plantation Economies of the Third World*. New York: Oxford University Press, 1972.

Beech, Mervyn W. "Slavery on the East Coast of Africa." *Journal of the African Society* 15 (1916): 145–49.

Beehler, W. H. *The Cruise of the "Brooklyn"*. Philadelphia: Lippincott, 1885.

Belleville, A. "Trip Around the South End of Zanzibar Island," *Proceedings of the Royal Geographical Society* 20 (1875–76): 69–74.

Bennett, Norman R. "The Church Missionary Society in Mombasa, 1873–1894." *Boston University Papers in African History*, vol. 1. Edited by Jeffery Butler. Boston: Boston University Press, 1964.

———, and Brooks, George E., eds. *New England Merchants in Africa: A History through Documents, 1802–1865*. Boston: Boston University Press, 1965.

Bent, J. Theodore. "Expedition to the Hadramaut," *The Geographical Journal* 4 (1894): 315–33.

Berg, Fred James. "Mombasa under the Busaidi Sultanate: The City and Its Hinterland in the Nineteenth Century." Ph.D. dissertation, University of Wisconsin, 1971.

———. "The Swahili Community of Mombasa, 1500–1900." *Journal of African History* 9 (1968): 35–56.

———, and Walter, B. J. "Mosques, Population and Urban Development in Mombasa." *Hadith 1*. Edited by B. A. Ogot. Nairobi: East African Publishing House for the Historical Association of Kenya, 1968.

Berlin, Ira. *Slaves without Masters: The Free Negro in the Antebellum South*. New York: Pantheon, 1974.

Berlioux, Etienne Felix. *The Slave Trade in Africa in 1872*. London: Edward Marsh, 1872.

Binns, Rev. Harry K. "Slavery in British East Africa," *Church Missionary Intelligencer*, n.s. 23 (June 1897): 462.

Birken, Andreas. "Das Sultanat Zanzibar im 19 Jahrhundert." Ph.D. dissertation, Eberhard-Karls-Universität zu Tübingen, 1971.

Blais, J. "Les anciens esclaves à Zanzibar," *Anthropos* 10–11 (1915–16): 504–11.

Blassingame, John W. *The Slave Community*. New York: Oxford University Press, 1972.

Bloch, Marc. *Feudal Society. Volume 1: The Growth of Ties of Dependence*. Translated by L. A. Manyon. Chicago: University of Chicago Press, 1961.

Boteler, Thomas. *Narrative of a Voyage of Discovery to Africa and Arabia Performed by His Majesty's Ships "Levin" and "Barracouta" from 1821 to 1826*. 2 vols. London: Bentley, 1835.

Boxer, Charles R. *Race Relations in the Portuguese Colonial Empire, 1415–1825*. Oxford: Clarendon Press, 1963.

———, and de Azevedo, Carlos. *Fort Jesus and the Portuguese in Mombasa, 1593–1729*. London: Hollis and Carter, 1960.

Breen, T. H. "A Changing Labor Force and Race Relations in Virginia, 1660–1710." *Journal of Social History* 7 (1973): 3–25.

Brenner, Richard. "Richard Brenner's Reise in den Galla-Landern,

1867–1868," and "Forschungen in Ost-Afrika." *Petermann's Mittheilungen* (1868), pp. 175–79, 456–65.

Bridenbaugh, Carl, and Bridenbaugh, Roberta. *No Peace Beyond the Line: The English in the Caribbean, 1624–1690.* New York: Oxford University Press, 1972.

Brode, Heinrick. *Tippou Tib: The Story of His Career in Central Africa.* Translated by H. Havelock. London: Edward Arnold, 1907.

Brown, Walter T. "The Politics of Business: Relations between Zanzibar and Bagamoyo in the Late Nineteenth Century." *African Historical Studies* 4 (1971): 631–44.

Browne, J. Ross. *Etchings of a Whaling Cruise with Notes of a Sojourn on the Island of Zanzibar.* Cambridge, Mass.: Harvard University Press, 1968. First published in 1846.

Brunschvig, R. " 'Abd," *Encyclopedia of Islam,* 1: 24–40. Leiden: Brill, 1960.

Buckingham, J. S. *Travels in Assyria, Media and Persia.* London: Henry Coburn and Richard Bentley, 1830.

———. "Voyage from Bushire to Muscat." *Oriental Herald* 22 (1829): 79–103.

———. "Voyage from Muscat to Bushire." *Oriental Herald* 19 (1828): 39–57.

Bujra, Janet. "An Anthropological Study of Political Action in a Bajuni Village, Kenya." Ph.D. dissertation, University of London, 1968.

Burdo, Adolphe. *De Zanzibar au Lac Tanganyika.* Vol. 1 of *Les Belges dans l'Afrique Centrale.* Brussels: Maes, 1886.

Burton, Richard. *The Lake Regions of Central Africa.* 2 vols. London: Longman and Green, 1860.

———. *Zanzibar: City, Island, Coast.* 2 vols. London: Tinsley Brothers, 1872.

Caplan, Ann Patricia. *Choice and Constraint in a Swahili Community: Property, Hierarchy, and Cognatic Descent on the East African Coast.* London: Oxford University Press for the International African Institute, 1975.

Chanler, William Astor. *Through Jungle and Desert.* London: Macmillan, 1896.

Charmetant, Le P. *D'Alger à Zanzibar.* Paris: Librarie de la Société Bibliographique, 1882.

Christie, James. *Cholera Epidemics in East Africa.* London: Macmillan, 1876.

———. "Slavery in Zanzibar as It Is." In *The East African Slave Trade,* edited by E. Steere. London: Harrison, 1871.

Christopher, W. "Commanding His Majesty's Ship *Tigris* on the East Coast of Africa." *Journal of the Royal Geographical Society* 14 (1840): 76–103.

———. "Extracts from a Journal Kept during a Partial Inquiry into the Present Resources and State of Northeastern Africa." *Transactions of the Bombay Geographical Society* 6 (1843): 383–409.

Clayton, A. H. leQ. "Labour in the East African Protectorate, 1895–1919." Ph.D. dissertation, St. Andrews University, 1971.

Cohen, David W., and Greene, Jack P., eds. *Neither Slave nor Free: The Freedman of African Descent in the Slave Societies of the New World.* Baltimore: Johns Hopkins University Press, 1972.

Colomb, Captain John C. R. *Slave Catching in the Indian Ocean.* London: Longmans, 1873.

Cooper, Frederick. "Plantation Slavery on the East Coast of Africa in the Nineteenth Century." Ph.D. dissertation, Yale University, 1974.

————. "Studying Slavery in Africa: Some Criticisms and Comparisons." Paper presented to the Program of African Studies, Northwestern University, 9 February 1976.

Coupland, Sir Reginald. *East Africa and Its Invaders*. Oxford: Clarendon Press, 1938.

————. *The Exploitation of East Africa, 1856–1890: The Slave Trade and the Scramble*. London: Faber and Faber, 1939.

Courmont, Msgr. R. de. "Second Tournée dans le vicariat apostolique du Zanguebar." *Missions Catholiques* 18 (1886): 594–97, 604–05, 615–20.

————. "La situation politique et religieuse au Zanguebar." *Missions Catholiques* 21 (1889): 109–12.

————. "Le Sultanat de Zanguebar," *Missions Catholiques* 18 (1886): 382–84, 393–95, 404–06, 412–14.

————. "Une tournée dans le vicariat apostolique du Zanguebar." *Missions Catholiques* 17 (1885): 462–66, 485–89, 497–502, 521–25, 536–38, 545–48.

Courret, Charles. *A l'est et a l'ouest dans l'Océan Indien*. Paris: Chevalier-Marescq, 1884.

Courtenay, P. P. *Plantation Agriculture*. London: Bell, 1965.

Craster, J. E. *Pemba: The Spice Island of Zanzibar*. London: Fisher Unwin, 1913.

Curtin, Philip D. *The Atlantic Slave Trade: A Census*. Madison: University of Wisconsin Press, 1969.

da Costa, Emelia Viotti. "The Myth of Racial Democracy in Brazil: A Problem of Social Mythology." Paper presented to the Annual Meeting of the Southern Historical Association, Washington, D.C., 14 November 1975.

Dale, Godfrey, *The Peoples of Zanzibar*. London: Universities Mission to Central Africa, 1920.

David, Paul A., Gutman, Herbert G., Sutch, Richard, Temin, Peter, and Wright, Gavin. *Reckoning with Slavery: A Critical Study in the Quantitative History of American Negro Slavery*. New York: Oxford University Press, 1976.

Davis, David Brion. *The Problem of Slavery in Western Culture*. Ithaca, N.Y.: Cornell University Press, 1966.

Degler, Carl N. *Neither Black nor White: Slave and Race Relations in Brazil and the United States*. New York: Macmillan, 1971.

————. "Slavery and the Genesis of American Race Prejudice." *Comparative Studies in Society and History* 2 (1959): 49–67.

de Langle, Fleuriot. "La traite des esclaves à la côte orientale d'Afrique." *Revue Maritime et Coloniale* 38 (1873):785–828.

Devereux, W. C. *A Cruise in the "Gorgon"*. London: Dawsons of Pall Mall, 1968. First published, 1869.

de Vienne, Charles. "De Zanzibar à l'Oukami: route des lacs de l'Afrique equatoriale." *Bulletin de la Société de Géographie* (Paris), 6th ser. 4 (1872): 356–69.

Dougherty, John A. *The East Indies Station; or The Cruise of H. M. S. "Garnet" 1887–90*. Malta: Muscat Printing Co., 1892.

Dundas, F. G. "Explorations of the Rivers Tana and Juba." *Scottish Geographical Magazine* 9 (1893): 113–26.

Dunn, Richard S. *Sugar and Slaves: The Rise of the Planter Class in the English West Indies, 1624–1713*. Chapel Hill: University of North Carolina Press, 1972.

Eastman, Carol M. "Who are the Waswahili?" *Africa* 41 (1971): 228–35.

Elkins, Stanley M. *Slavery: A Problem in American Institutional and Intellectual Life.* Chicago: University of Chicago Press, 1959.

Elton, Frederic. *Travels and Researches among the Lakes and Mountains of Eastern and Central Africa.* Edited by H. B. Cotterill. London: Murray, 1879.

———. "On the Coastal Country of East Africa, South of Zanzibar." *Journal of the Royal Geographical Society* 44 (1874): 227–52.

El-Zein, Abdul Hamid M. *The Sacred Meadows: A Structural Analysis of Religious Symbolism in an East African Town.* Evanston, Ill.: Northwestern University Press, 1974.

Emery, J. B. "A Short Account of Mombas and the Neighboring Coast of Africa." *Journal of the Royal Geographical Society* 3 (1883): 280–82.

Engerman, Stanley L., and Genovese, Eugene D., eds. *Race and Slavery in the Western Hemisphere: Quantitative Studies.* Princeton, N.J.: Princeton University Press, 1975.

Erhardt, J. "Reports Respecting Central Africa." *Proceedings of the Royal Geographical Society* 1 (1855): 8–10.

Farler, J. V. "Native Routes in East Africa from Pangani to the Masai Country and the Victoria Nyanza." *Proceedings of the Royal Geographical Society,* n.s. 4 (1882): 730–42.

Farsy, Abdulla Saleh. *Seyyid Said bin Sultan.* Zanzibar: Mwongozi Printing Press, 1942.

———. *Terehe ya Imam Shafi na Wanovyuoni Wakubwa wa Mashariki ya Afrika.* Zanzibar: Federal Department, 1944.

Fawcus, W. P. Jones. "Experience in Zanzibar and East Africa." *Manchester Geographical Society Journal* 24 (1908): 5–11.

Feierman, Steven. *The Shambaa Kingdom: A History.* Madison: University of Wisconsin Press, 1974.

Filliot, J.-M. *La traite des esclaves vers les Mascareignes au XVIIIe siècle.* Paris: ORSTOM, 1974.

Finley, M. I. "Slavery." In *International Encyclopedia of the Social Sciences,* 14: 307–13. New York: Macmillan, 1968.

Fischer, G. A. *Mehr Licht im Dunklen Weltteil.* Hamburg: Friedericksen, 1885.

Fisher, Allan G. B., and Fisher, Humphrey J. *Slavery and Muslim Society in Africa.* Garden City, N.Y.: Doubleday, 1971.

Fitzgerald, W. W. A. *Travels in the Coastlands of British East Africa and the Islands of Zanzibar and Pemba.* London: Chapman and Hall, 1898.

Fogel, Robert W., and Engerman, Stanley L. *Time on the Cross: The Economics of American Negro Slavery.* 2 vols. Boston: Little, Brown, 1974.

Foner, Laura, and Genovese, Eugene D., eds., *Slavery in the New World: A Reader in Comparative History.* Englewood Cliffs, N.J.: Prentice-Hall, 1969.

Forand, Paul G. "The Relations of the Slave and the Client to the Master or Patron in Medieval Islam." *International Journal of Middle Eastern Studies* 2 (1971): 59–66.

Fosbrooke, H. A. "Richard Thornton in East Africa." *Tanganyika Notes and Records* 58–59 (1962): 43–65.

Fraser, Captain H. A. "Zanzibar and the Slave Trade." In *The East African Slave Trade,* edited by E. Steere. London: Harrison, 1871.

Fraser, James B. *Narrative of a Journey into Khorosan in the Years 1821 and 1822*. London: Longmans, 1825.

Fredrickson, George M. *The Black Image in the White Mind: The Debate on Afro-American Character and Destiny, 1817–1914*. New York: Harper & Row, 1971.

———. "Why Blacks Were Left Out." *New York Review of Books*, February 7, 1974, pp. 23–24.

Freeman-Grenville, G. S. P. *The East African Coast: Select Documents*. London: Oxford University Press, 1962.

———. *The French at Kilwa Island*. Oxford: Clarendon Press, 1965.

Freyre, Gilberto. *The Masters and the Slaves: A Study in the Development of Brazilian Civilization*. Translated by Samuel Putnam. Abridged from the 2d ed. New York: Knopf, 1964.

Gaume, Msgr. *Voyage à la côte orientale d'Afrique pendant l'année 1866 par le R. P. Horner*. Paris: Gaume Frères et J. Duprey, 1872.

Gavin, R. J. "The Bartle Frere Mission to Zanzibar." *Historical Journal* 5 (1962): 122–48.

Genovese, Eugene D. *The Political Economy of Slavery*. New York: Pantheon, 1965.

———. *Roll, Jordan, Roll: The World the Slaves Made*. New York: Pantheon, 1974.

———. *The World the Slaveholders Made*. New York: Pantheon, 1969.

———, ed. *The Slave Economies*. 2 vols. New York: Wiley, 1973.

Germain, A. "Note sur Zanzibar et la côte orientale d'Afrique." *Bulletin de la Société de Géographie* (Paris), 5th ser. 16 (1868): 530–59.

———. "Quelques mots sur l'Oman et le Sultan de Maskate." *Bulletin de la Société de Géographie* (Paris), 16 (1868): 339–64.

Gissing, C. E. "A Journey from Mombasa to Mount Ndau and Kusigao." *Proceedings of the Royal Geographical Society*, n.s. 6 (1884): 551–66.

Gobineau, A. de. *Trois ans en Asie, de 1855 à 1858*. 3 vols. Paris: Grasset, 1823.

Goveia, Elsa V. *Slave Society in the British Leeward Islands at the End of the Eighteenth Century*. New Haven: Yale University Press, 1965.

Grandidier, Alfred. *Notice sur l'isle de Zanzibar*. Saint-Denis: Roussin, 1868.

Gray, Sir John. *The British in Mombasa, 1824–1826*. London: Macmillan for the Kenya Historical Society, 1957.

———. *A History of Zanzibar from the Middle Ages to 1856*. London: Oxford University Press, 1962.

Gray, Richard, and Birmingham, David, eds. *Pre-Colonial African Trade*. London: Oxford University Press, 1970.

Greffulhe, H. "Voyage de Lamoo à Zanzibar." *Bulletin de la Société de Géographie et d'Etudes Coloniales de Marseille* 2 (1878): 209–17, 327–60.

Guillain, Charles. "Côte de Zanguebar et Mascate, 1841." *Revue Coloniale* 1 (1843): 520–71.

———. *Documents sur l'histoire, la géographie et le commerce de l'Afrique Orientale*. 3 vols. Paris: Bertrand, 1856–58.

Gutman, Herbert G. *Slavery and the Numbers Game: A Critique of Time on the Cross*. Urbana: University of Illinois Press, 1975.

Haines, Captain S. B. "Description of the Arabian Coast." *Transactions of the Bombay Geographical Society* 2 (1852): 60–211.

————. "Memoir to Accompany a Chart of the South Coast of Arabia." *Journal of the Royal Geographical Society* 9 (1839): 124–56.

Hambly, Gavin R. G. "Islamic Slavery: An Overview." Paper presented to a faculty seminar, Yale University, 1972.

Hamilton, Alexander. *A New Account of the East Indies, 1688–1723.* Edinburgh: Mosman, 1727.

Hamilton, Charles, trans. *The Hedaya, or Guide.* London: Bensley, 1791.

Handlin, Oscar, and Handlin, Mary. "Origins of the Southern Labor System." *William and Mary Quarterly,* 3d ser. 7 (1950): 199–222.

Hardinge, Arthur. *Diplomatist in the East.* London: Cape, 1928.

Harkema, R. C. "De Stad Zanzibar in de Tweede Helft van de Negentiende Eeuw en enkele Oudere Oostafrikanse Kuststeden." Doctor of Letters dissertation, Rijksuniversiteit te Groningon, 1967.

Harries, Lyndon, ed. *Swahili Prose Texts: A Selection from the Material Collected by Carl Velten from 1893 to 1896.* London: Oxford University Press, 1965.

Harris, Marvin. *Patterns of Race in the Americas.* New York: Walker, 1964.

Hoetink, H. *Caribbean Race Relations: A Study of Two Variants.* Translated by Eva M. Hooykaas. London: Oxford University Press, 1967.

Hollingsworth, L. W. *Zanzibar under the Foreign Office, 1890–1913.* London: Macmillan, 1953.

Holman, James. *Voyage Round the World.* London: Smith, Elder and Co., 1835.

Holt, P. M., Lambton, A. K. S., and Lewis, Bernard, eds. *The Cambridge History of Islam.* 2 vols. Cambridge: Cambridge University Press, 1970.

Hopkins, A. G. *An Economic History of West Africa.* London: Longmans, 1973.

Hore, E. L. *Tanganyika: Eleven Years in Central Africa.* London: Stanford, 1892.

Hourani, Albert. "Race and Related Ideas in the Near East." In *Comparative Perspectives on Race Relations,* edited by Melvin M. Tumin. Boston: Little, Brown, 1969.

Human Relations Area Files. *Subcontractor's Monograph No. 51. Eastern Arabia.* New Haven: HRAF, 1956.

————. *Subcontractor's Monograph No. 52. Southern Arabia.* New Haven: HRAF, 1956.

Hume, R. O. "Extracts from the Journal of Mr. Hume." *Missionary Herald* 36 (1840): 60–62.

Hutchinson, E. *The Slave Trade of East Africa.* London: Low, Marston, Low, and Searle, 1874.

Hyder Kindy, *Life and Politics in Mombasa.* Nairobi: East African Publishing House, 1972.

Hymes, Dell, ed. *Pidginization and Creolization of Languages.* Cambridge: Cambridge University Press, 1971.

Ibn Battuta. *Travels in Asia and Africa, 1325–1354.* Translated and selected by H. A. R. Gibb. London: Routledge, 1929.

Ingrams, William H. *Arabia and the Isles.* 3d ed. London: Murray, 1966.

————. *Zanzibar: Its History and Peoples.* London: Witherby, 1931.

Inter-Territorial Language Committee on the East African Dependencies. *A Standard Swahili-English Dictionary.* London: Oxford University Press, 1939.

Isaacs, Nathaniel. *Travels and Adventures in Eastern Africa*. London: Churton, 1836.

Jablonski, M. "Note sur la géographie de l'Isle de Zanzibar," *Bulletin de la Société de Géographie* (Paris), 5th ser. 12 (1866): 353–70.

Jackson, Frederick. *Early Days in East Africa*. London: Arnold, 1930.

Jones-Bateman, P. L., ed. and trans. *The Autobiography of an African Slave-Boy*. London: Universities' Mission to Central Africa, 1891.

Jordan, Winthrop D. *The White Man's Burden: Historical Origins of Racism in the United States*. New York: Oxford University Press, 1974.

———. *White Over Black: American Attitudes toward the Negro, 1550–1812*. Chapel Hill: University of North Carolina Press, 1968.

Jourdain, John. *The Journal of John Jourdain*. Edited by William Foster. Cambridge, Eng.: Haklyut Society, 1905.

Kayamba, H. M. T. "Notes on the Wadigo." *Tanganyika Notes and Records* 23 (1947): 80–96.

Kelly, J. B. *Britain and the Persian Gulf, 1795–1880*. Oxford: Clarendon Press, 1968.

———. *Sultanate and Imamate in Oman*. Chatham House Memorandum. London: Oxford University Press, 1959.

Keppel, Sir Henry. *A Sailor's Life under Four Sovereigns*. London: Macmillan, 1899.

Kerdudal, L. de. "Quiloa ou Keloua." *Revue Coloniale*, February 1844, pp. 244–56.

Kersten, Otto, ed. *Baron Carl von der Deckens Reisen in Ost Afrika*. 3 vols. Leipzig and Heidelberg: Winter, 1871.

"The Clove Industry of Zanzibar." *Kew Bulletin* (1893), pp. 17–20.

Kirk, John. "Agricultural Resources of Zanzibar." *Kew Bulletin* (1892), pp. 87–91.

Klein, Herbert. *Slavery in the Americas: A Comparative Study of Virginia and Cuba*. Chicago: University Chicago Press, 1967.

Knappert, Jan. "Social and Moral Concepts in Swahili Islamic Literature." *Africa* 11 (1970): 125–36.

———. *Traditional Swahili Poetry*. Leiden: Brill, 1967.

Knight, Franklin W. *Slave Society in Cuba During the Nineteenth Century*. Madison: University of Wisconsin Press, 1970.

Krapf, Ludwig. *A Dictionary of the Swahili Language*. London: Trübner, 1882.

———. *Travels, Researches, and Missionary Labours During an Eighteen Years' Residence in Eastern Africa*. Boston: Tricknor and Fields, 1860.

Landen, Robert G. *Oman Since 1856: Disruptive Modernization in a Traditional Arab Society*. Princeton, N.J.: Princeton University Press, 1967.

Last, J. T. *Polyglotta Africana Orientalis*. London: Society for Promoting Christian Knowledge, 1885.

LeRoy, Alexandre. *D'Aden à Zanzibar*. Tours: Mame, 1894.

———. *Au Kilima-ndjaro (Afrique Orientale)*. Paris: Senard and Derangeon, 1893.

———. "Le Long des côtes: de Zanzibar à Lamo." *Missions Catholiques* 21 (1889): 8–12, 18–20, 30–33, 40–44, 52–56, 65–70, 77–81, 89–92, 101–04, 114–17, 129–32.

————. Au Zanguebar anglais." *Missions Catholiques* 22 (1890): 435–37, 448–634.

————, and Courmont, Msgr. R. "Mombase (Afrique Orientale)." *Missions Catholiques* 19 (1887): 534–36, 547–49, 560–61.

Levy, Reuben. *The Social Structure of Islam.* 2d ed. Cambridge: Cambridge University Press, 1957.

Lewicki, Tedeusz. "Al-Ibadiyya." In *Encyclopedia of Islam,* 3: 648–60. Leiden: Brill, 1971.

————. "The Ibadites of Arabia and Africa." *Cahiers d'Histoire Mondiale* 13 (1971): 51–130.

Lewis, Bernard. *The Arabs in History.* New York: Harper & Row, 1958.

————. *Race and Color in Islam.* New York: Harper & Row, 1971.

Lienhardt, Peter A. "Family Waqf in Zanzibar." East African Institute for Social Research, *Conference,* 1958.

————, ed. *The Medicine Man: Swifa ya Nguvumali.* Oxford: Clarendon Press, 1968.

Livingstone, David. *The Last Journals of David Livingstone, in Central Africa from 1865 to His Death.* London: Murray, 1874.

Lloyd, Christopher. *The Navy and the Slave Trade.* London: Longmans, 1949.

Loarer, Captain. "L'Ile de Zanzibar." *Revue de l'Orient* 9 (1851): 240–99.

Lodhi, Abdul Aziz. "The Institution of Slavery in Zanzibar and Pemba." *Research Report No. 16,* The Scandanavian Institute of African Studies, Uppsala, 1973.

Lofchie, Michael F. *Zanzibar: Background to Revolution.* Princeton, N.J.: Princeton University Press, 1965.

Lombardi, John V. "Comparative Slave Systems in the Americas: A Critical Review." In *New Approaches to Latin American History,* edited by Richard Graham and Peter H. Smith. Austin: University of Texas Press, 1974.

Lugard, Lord Frederick. *The Rise of Our East African Empire.* Edinburgh: Blackwood, 1893.

Lyne, Robert. *An Apostle of Empire, Being the Life of Sir Lloyd William Mathews.* London: George Allen and Unwin, 1936.

————. "Causes Contributing to the Success of the Zanzibar Clove Industry." *Bulletin of the Imperial Institute* 8 (1910): 143–44.

————. *Zanzibar in Contemporary Times.* London: Hurst and Blackett, 1905.

Ly-Tio-Fane, Madeleine, ed. *Mauritius and the Spice Trade: The Odyssey of Pierre Poivre.* Port Louis, Mauritius: Esclapon, 1958.

McClellan, F. C. "Agricutural Resources of the Zanzibar Protectorate." *Bulletin of the Imperial Institute* 12 (1914): 407–29.

McDermott, P. L. *British East Africa or IBEA. A History of the Formation and Work of the Imperial British East Africa Company.* New ed. London: Chapman and Hall, 1895.

MacDonald, J. R. L. *Soldiering and Surveying in British East Africa, 1891–1894.* London: Arnold, 1897.

McKay, William Francis. "A Precolonial History of the Southern Kenya Coast." Ph.D. dissertation, Boston University, 1975.

Mackenzie, Donald. "A Report on Slavery and the Slave Trade in Zanzibar,

Pemba and the Mainland of the British Protectorates of East Africa." *Anti-Slavery Reporter* 4th ser. 15 (1895): 69–96.

McLeod, Lyons. *Travels in Eastern Africa.* London: Hunt and Hackett, 1860.

Madan, A. C., ed. *Kiungani, or Story and History from Central Africa.* London: Bell, 1887.

Mangat, J. S. *A History of the Asians in East Africa, 1886 to 1945.* Oxford: Clarendon Press, 1969.

Marras, Etienne. "L'Isle de Zanzibar." *Bulletin de la Société de Géographie de Marseille* 5 (1881): 192–200.

Martin, B. G. "Notes on Some Members of the Learned Classes of Zanzibar and East Africa in the Nineteenth Century." *African Historical Studies* 4 (1971): 525–46.

Martin, Esmund Bradley. *The History of Malindi: A Geographical Analysis of an East African Coastal Town from the Portuguese Period to the Present.* Nairobi: East African Literature Bureau, 1973.

Maurizi, Vincenzo [pseud. Sheikh Mansur]. *History of Seyd Said, Sultan of Muscat; Together with an Account of the Countries and People on the Shores of the Persian Gulf, Particularly of the Wahabees.* London: Booth, 1819.

Mazrui, Muhammad Kasim. *Historia ya Utumwa Katika Uislamu na Dini Nyengine.* Nairobi: Islamic Foundation, 1970.

Mbarak Ali Hinawy. *Al-Akida and Fort Jesus Mombasa.* London: Macmillan, 1950.

Mbotela, James J. *The Freeing of the Slaves in East Africa.* London: Evans Brothers, 1956.

Meillassoux, Claude, ed. *L'esclavage en Afrique précoloniale.* Paris: Maspero, 1975.

Meyers, Allen. "The ʿAbīd 'L-Buhārī: Slave Soldiers and State-Craft in Morocco, 1672–1790," Ph.D. dissertation, Cornell University, 1974.

Middleton, John. *Land Tenure in Zanzibar.* London: Her Majesty's Stationary Office, 1961.

———, and Campbell, Jane. *Zanzibar: Its Society and Its Politics.* London: Oxford University Press for the Institute of Race Relations, 1965.

Miers, Suzanne. *Britain and the Ending of the Slave Trade.* London: Longman, 1975.

———, and Kopytoff, Igor, eds. *Slavery in Africa: Historical and Anthropological Perspectives.* Madison: University of Wisconsin Press, 1977.

Mignan, R. *A Winter Journey through Russia, the Caucasian Alps and Georgia, Thence into Koordistan.* London: Bentley, 1839.

Milburn, William. *Oriental Commerce.* London: Black, Perry and Co., 1813.

Miles, S. B. *The Countries and Tribes of the Persian Gulf.* London: Cass, 1966. First published 1919.

Mintz, Sidney W., and Wolf, Eric R. "An Analysis of Ritual Co-Parenthood (Compadrazgo)." *Southwestern Journal of Anthropology* 6 (1950): 341–68.

Missionaires d'Alger. *A l'assaut des pays nègres, journal des Missionaires d'Alger dans l'Afrique Equitoriale.* Paris: Ecoles d'Orient, 1884.

Mollat, Michel. "Les relations de l'Afrique de l'est avec l'Asie: essai de position de quelques problèmes historiques." *Cahiers d'Histoire Mondiale* 13 (1971): 291–316.

Mondevit, Saulnier de. "Observations sur la Côte du Zanguebar." *Nouvelles Annales de Voyages*. Paris: Gide fils, 1820.

Morgan, Edmund S. *American Slavery-American Freedom: The Ordeal of Colonial Virginia*. New York: Norton, 1975.

Müller, Fritz Ferdinand. *Deutschland-Zanzibar-Ostafrika: Geschichte einer deutschen Kolonialeroberung, 1884–1890*. Berlin: Rütten and Loening, 1959.

Mullin, Gerald W. *Flight and Rebellion: Slave Resistance in Eighteenth–Century Virginia*. New York: Oxford University Press, 1972.

New, Charles, "Journey from the Pangani, via Usambara, to Mombasa." *Journal of the Royal Geographical Society* 45 (1875): 414–20.

———. *Life, Wanderings and Labours in Eastern Africa*. London: Hodder and Stoughton, 1873.

———. "Missionary Notes." *United Methodist Free Church Magazine* 10 (1867): 285–87, 425–32, 497–504, 569–71.

Newman, Henry Stanley. *Banani: The Transition from Slavery to Freedom in Zanzibar and Pemba*. London: Headley Brothers, 1898.

Nicholls, C. S. *The Swahili Coast: Politics, Diplomacy and Trade on the East African Littoral, 1798–1856*. London: Allen and Unwin, 1971.

Nieboer, H. J. *Slavery as an Industrial System*. Rev. ed. The Hague: Nijhoff, 1910.

Niebuhr, Carsten. *Travels through Arabia*. Translated by Robert Heron. 2 vols. Edinburgh: Morison and Son, 1792.

Niese, Richard. *Das Personen- und Familienrecht der Suaheli*. Berlin: Pintus, 1902.

Nimtz, August H., Jr. "The Role of the Muslim Sūfī Order in Political Change: An Overview and Micro-analysis from Tanzania." Ph.D. dissertation, Indiana University, 1973.

Nolloth, M. S. "Extracts from the Journal of Captain M. S. Nolloth, H. M. S. *Frolic*." *Nautical Magazine* (1857), pp. 1–12, 73–78, 136–43, 191–98, 247–56.

Northway, Phillip. "Salem and the Zanzibar-East Africa Trade." *Essex Institute Historical Collection* 90 (1954): 361–88.

Ogot, B. A., ed. *Zamani: A Survey of East African History*. New ed. Nairobi: East African Publishing House/Longmans, 1974.

Oroge, E. A. "The Institution of Slavery in Yorubaland with Particular Reference to the Nineteenth Century." Ph.D. dissertation, University of Birmingham, 1971.

Osgood, J. B. F. *Notes of Travel or Recollections of Majunga, Zanzibar, Muscat, Aden, Mocha, and Other Eastern Ports*. Salem, Mass.: Creamer, 1854.

Owen, William F. W. *Narrative of Voyages to Explore the Shores of Africa, Arabia, and Madagascar*. 2 vols. London: Bentley, 1833.

Palgrave, William G. *A Narrative of a Year's Journey through Central and Eastern Arabia (1862–1863)*. 2 vols. London: Macmillan, 1865.

———. "Observations Made in Central, Eastern and Southern Arabia during a Journey through that Country in 1862 and 1863." *Journal of the Royal Geographical Society* 34 (1864): 111–54.

Pares, Richard. *Merchants and Planters*. Cambridge: Cambridge University Press, 1960.

Patterson, Orlando. *The Sociology of Slavery: An Analysis of the Origins, Develop-

ment and Structure of Negro Slave Society in Jamaica. Rutherford, N.J.: Fairleigh Dickinson University Press, 1967.

Pearce, F. B. *Zanzibar: The Island Metropolis of Eastern Africa.* London: Fisher Unwin, 1920.

Pelly, Lewis. "The Persian Gulf as an Area of Trade." *Proceedings of the Royal Geographical Society* 8 (1863–64): 18–21.

————. "Remarks on the Tribes, Trade and Resources around the Shore Line of the Persian Gulf." *Transactions of the Bombay Geographical Society* 17 (1863): 32–112.

Phillips, Ulrich B. *Life and Labor in the Old South.* Boston: Little, Brown, 1929.

Phillips, Wendell. *Oman: A History.* London: Longmans, 1967.

Picard, Père. "Autour de Mandera." *Missions Catholiques* 18 (1886): 225–28.

Pickering, Charles. *The Races of Man and Their Geographical Distribution.* London: Chapman, 1849.

Playfair, R. L. "Extracts from the Administrative Report of the Political Agent for the two past years ending with the 31st of May, 1864." *Transactions of the Bombay Geographical Society* 17 (1864): 277–87.

————. "Report on the Result of the Observations and Inquiries Made during a Tour in the Various Countries around Zanzibar, especially those more or less connected with the Slave Trade." *Transactions of the Bombay Geographical Society* 17 (1864): 256–68.

————. "Visit to the Wanika Country in the Vicinity of Mombasa and the Progress Made by the Christian Missionaries at the Place." *Transactions of the Bombay Geographical Society* 17 (1864): 269–76.

Postans, Lieutenant T. "Some Account of the Present State of the Trade between the Port of Mandavie in Cutch and the Eastern Coast of Africa." *Transactions of the Bombay Geographical Society* 3 (1839–40): 169–75.

Price, R. *Report of the Rev. R. Price of His Visit to Zanzibar and the Coast of East Africa.* London: London Missionary Society, 1876.

Price, Richard, ed. *Maroon Societies.* Garden City, N.Y.: Doubleday, 1973.

Price, W. Salter. *My Third Campaign in East Africa.* London: Hunt, 1891.

Prince, Howard M. "Slave Rebellions in Bahia, 1807–1835." Ph.D. dissertation, Columbia University, 1972.

Prins, A. H. J. *Sailing from Lamu: A Study of Maritime Culture in Islamic East Africa.* Assen: Van Gorcom, 1965.

————. *The Swahili-Speaking Peoples of Zanzibar and the East African Coast.* London: International African Institute, 1961.

Prior, James. *Voyage Along the Eastern Coast of Africa.* Vol. 2 of *New Voyages and Travels.* London: Phillips. 1819.

Pruen, S. Tristram. *The Arab and the African: Experiences in Eastern Equatorial Africa During a Residence of Three Years.* London: Seeley and Co., 1891.

Quass, E. "Die Szuri's, die Kuli's, und die Sclaven in Zanzibar." *Zeitschrift für Allgemeine Erdkunde,* n.s. 9 (1860): 421–60.

Rabaud, A. "Zanzibar." *Bulletin de la Société de Géographie de Marseille* 3 (1879): 158–77.

Raffray, Achille. "Voyage chez les Ouanika sur la côte de Zanguebar." *Tour du Monde* 35 (1878): 284–304.

————. "Voyage en Abyssinie, à Zanguebar et aux pays des Ouanika." *Bulletin de la Société de Géographie* (Paris), 6th ser. 10 (1879): 291–313.

Rashid bin Hassani. "The Story of Rashid bin Hassani of the Bisa Tribe, Northern Rhodesia," recorded by W. F. Baldock. In *Ten Africans*, edited by Margery Perham. London: Faber and Faber, 1963.

Rawson, Geoffrey. *Life of Admiral Sir Harry Rawson*. London: Arnold, 1914.

Reichard, P. *Deutsch Ostafrika*. Leipzig: Spamer, 1892.

Renault, François. *Lavigerie, l'esclavage africain et l'Europe*. 2 vols. Paris: Boccard, 1971.

Rice, C. Duncan. *The Rise and Fall of Black Slavery*. New York: Harper & Row, 1975.

Ridley, H. N. *Spices*. London: Macmillan, 1912.

Rigby, Christopher P. "Remarks on the Northeast Coast of Africa and the Tribes by Which It Is Inhabited." *Transactions of the Bombay Geographical Society* 6 (1844): 67–92.

————. "Report on the Zanzibar Dominions, 1 July 1860." Reprinted in *General Rigby, Zanzibar and the Slave Trade*, edited by Mrs. Charles E. Russell. London: Allen and Unwin, 1935.

Roberts, Andrew, ed. *Tanzania before 1900*. Nairobi: East African Publishing House, 1968.

Roberts, Edmund. *Embassay to Eastern Courts of Cochin-China, Siam, and Muscat, 1832–1834*. New York: Harper and Brothers, 1837.

Rodd, Sir James Rennell. *Social and Diplomatic Memoirs, 1884–1893*. London: Arnold, 1922.

Rodinson, Maxime. *Islam and Capitalism*. Translated by Brian Pearce. New York: Pantheon, 1973.

Ropes, Edward D., Jr. *The Zanzibar Letters of Edward D. Ropes, 1882–1892*. Edited by N. R. Bennett. Boston: Boston University Press, 1973.

Ruete, Emily. *Memoirs of an Arabian Princess: An Autobiography*. New York: Appleton and Co., 1888.

Ruschenberger, W. S. W. *A Voyage around the World, Including an Embassy to Muscat and Siam in 1835, 1836, and 1837*. Philadelphia: Carey, Lea and Blanchard, 1838.

Russell, Mrs. Charles E., ed. *General Rigby, Zanzibar and the Slave Trade*. London: Allen and Unwin, 1935.

Said-Ruete, R. *Said bin Sultan (1791–1856), Ruler of Oman and Zanzibar: His Place in the History of Arabia and East Africa*. London: Ousley, 1929.

Saint-Martin, Vivien de. "La côte orientale d'Afrique entre la Cap Delgado et la Cap Guardafui." *Annales des Voyages* 107 (1845): 269–88.

Salem, Elie Adib. *Political Theory and Institutions of the Khawārij*. Johns Hopkins University Studies in Historical and Political Science, vol. 74, no. 2. Baltimore: Johns Hopkins University Press, 1956.

Salil-ibn-Razik. *History of the Imams and Seyyids of 'Oman from A.D. 661–1856*. Edited and translated by George Percy Badger. London: Hakluyt Society, 1871.

Salim, A. I. *The Swahili-Speaking Peoples of Kenya's Coast, 1895–1965*. Nairobi: East African Publishing House, 1973.

Salt, Henry. *A Voyage to Abyssinia and Travels into the Interior of That Country.* London: Cass, 1967. First published 1814.

Schacht, Joseph. "Bibliothèques et manuscrits abadites." *Revue Africaine* 50 (1956): 375–98.

———. *An Introduction to Islamic Law.* London: Oxford University Press, 1964.

———. "Notes on Islam in East Africa." *Studia Islamica* 23 (1965): 91–136.

———. *Origins of Muhammadan Jurisprudence.* Oxford: Clarendon Press, 1967.

Schmidt, Karl Wilhelm. *Sansibar: Ein Ostafrikanisches Culturbild.* Liepzig: Brockhaus, 1888.

Semanne, Constantin-Abel. *Essai d'une topographie medicale sur l'Ile de Zanzibar (côte orientale d'Afrique).* Thesis for a doctorate in Medicine. Paris: Imprimeur de la Faculté de Médecine, 1864.

Serjeant, R. B. "Société et gourvernement en Arabie du Sud." *Arabica* 14 (1967): 284–97.

Shepherd, William A. *From Bombay to Bushire and Bussura.* London: Bentley, 1857.

Sheridan, Richard B. *Sugar and Slavery: An Economic History of the British West Indies, 1623–1775.* Baltimore: Johns Hopkins University Press, 1974.

Sheriff, Abdul Mohamed Hussein. "The Rise of a Commercial Empire: An Aspect of the Economic History of Zanzibar, 1770–1873." Ph.D. dissertation, University of London, 1971.

Siegel, Bernard J. "Some Methodological Considerations for a Comparative Study of Slavery." *American Anthropologist* 47 (1947): 357–92.

Skene, R. "Arab and Swahili Dances and Ceremonies." *Journal of the Royal Anthropological Institute* 47 (1917): 413–34.

Smee, Captain Thomas, and Hardy, Lieutenant. "Report on the Eastern Seaboard of Africa." *Transactions of the Bombay Geographical Society* 6 (1844): 23–61.

Smith, Charles Stewart. "Explorations in Zanzibar Dominions." *Royal Geographical Society Supplementary Papers* 2 (1889): 99–125.

———. "Slavery." In *The History of the Universities' Mission to Central Africa, 1859–1909,* edited by A. E. M. Anderson-Morshead. London: Universities' Mission to Central Africa, 1909.

Smith, M. G. "Slavery and Emancipation in Two Societies." *Social and Economic Studies* (Jamaica) 3 (1954): 239–90.

Smith, W. Robertson. *Kinship and Marriage in Early Arabia.* Cambridge: Cambridge University Press, 1885.

Spear, Thomas. "The Kaya Complex: A History of the Mijikenda Peoples of the Kenya Coast to 1900." Ph.D. dissertation, University of Wisconsin, 1974.

Speke, John H. *Journal of the Discovery of the Source of the Nile.* London: Blackwood, 1863.

Stampp, Kenneth. *The Peculiar Institution.* New York: Vintage, 1956.

Stanley, H. M. *How I Found Livingstone.* London: Sampson, Low and Searle, 1879.

Starobin, Robert S. *Industrial Slavery in the Old South.* New York: Oxford University Press, 1970.

Steere, Edward. *Some Account of the Town of Zanzibar*. London: Bell and Daldy, 1869.

———. *Swahili Tales as Told by the Natives of Zanzibar*. London: Society for the Propagation of Christian Knowledge, 1869.

Stein, Stanley J. *Vassouras: A Brazilian Coffee County, 1850–1900*. Cambridge, Mass.: Harvard University Press, 1957.

Storms, Capitaine. "L'esclavage entre le Tanganyika et la côte est." *Le Mouvement Anti-esclavagiste* 1 (1888–89): 148.

Strandes, Justus. *The Portuguese Period in East Africa*. Translated by Jean F. Wallwork. Nairobi: East African Publishing House, 1961. First published 1899.

Strobel, Margaret Ann. "The Interaction of Slave and Freeborn Members of a Swahili Domestic Unit." Paper presented to the Annual Meeting of the American Historical Association, Atlanta, Georgia, 28 December 1975.

———. "Muslim Women in Mombasa, Kenya, 1890–1973." Ph.D. dissertation, University of California at Los Angeles, 1975.

———. "Women's Wedding Celebrations in Mombasa, Kenya." *The African Studies Review* 18 (1975): 35–45.

Sulivan, G. L. *Dhow Chasing in Zanzibar Waters*. London: Sampson, Low, Marston, Low and Searle, 1873.

Sykes, Colonel. "Notes on the Possessions of the Imam of Muskat, on the Climate and Productions of Zanzibar, and on the Prospects of African Discovery from Mombasa." *Journal of the Royal Geographical Society* 23 (1853): 101–19.

Tannenbaum, Frank. *Slave and Citizen: The Negro in the Americas*. New York: Knopf, 1946.

Taylor, W. E. *African Aphorisms or Saws from Swahili-Land*. London: Sleldon, 1891.

Thompson, E. P. "Patrician Society, Plebian Culture." *Journal of Social History* 7 (1974): 382–405.

———. "Time, Work Discipline and Industrial Capitalism." *Past and Present* 38 (1967): 56–97.

Thomson, Joseph. *To the Central African Lakes and Back*. London: Cass, 1968. First published 1881.

Tidbury, G. E. *The Clove Tree*. London: Lockwood and Son, 1949.

Tippu Tip. *Maisha ya Hamed bin Muhammed el Murjebi yaani Tippu Tip*. Translated by W. H. Whiteley. *Supplement to the East Africa Swahili Committee Journal*, vols. 28–29 (1958–59).

Toeppen, Kurt. "Deutsch Witu-Land." *Deutsche Kolonialzeitung* 2 (1889): 325–28.

Toplin, Robert Brent, ed. *Slavery and Race Relations in Latin America*. Westport, Conn.: Greenwood, 1974.

Toussaint, Auguste. *Histoire des îles mascareignes*. Paris: Berger-Levrault, 1972:

———. *History of the Indian Ocean*. Translated by June Guicharnaud. London: Routledge and Kegan Paul, 1966.

Trimingham, J. Spencer. *Islam in East Africa*. Oxford: Clarendon Press, 1964.

Tuden, Arthur, and Plotnicov, Leonard, eds. *Social Stratification in Africa*. New York: Free Press, 1970.

Villiers, Alan. "Some Aspects of the Arab Dhow Trade." *The Middle East Journal* 2 (1948): 399–416.

Vizetelly, Edward. *From Cyprus to Zanzibar by the Egyptian Delta.* London: Pearson, 1901.

Von der Decken, Karl. "Untergang der v. der Decken'schen Expedition, September 1865." *Petermann's Geographische Mittheilungen* (1866), pp. 66–77.

Wade, Richard C. *Slavery in the Cities: The South, 1820–1860.* New York: Oxford University Press, 1964.

Wakefield, Thomas. "East Africa." *The Missionary Echo* 1 (1894): 38–41, 156–57, 181–84.

———. "Recent Journey from Lamu to Golbantis in the Galla Country." *Journal of the Manchester Geographical Society* 4 (1888): 1–13.

———. "Rev. Thomas Wakefield's Fourth Journey to the Southern Galla Country." *Proceedings of the Royal Geographical Society* 4 (1882): 368–72.

———. Routes of Native Caravans from the Coast to the Interior of East Africa." *Journal of the Royal Geographical Society* 40 (1870): 303–39.

Wakefield, Mrs. Thomas. *Memoirs of Mrs. Rebecca Wakefield, Wife of the Rev. T. Wakefield by her Brother Robert Brown.* London: Hamilton and Adams, 1877.

Warburg, O. "Vegetationsbilder aus Deutsch-Ostafrika. Gewüznelkonplantage in Sansibar." *Deutsche Kolonial-Zeitung* 8 (1895): 241–42.

Ward, Gertrude, ed. *The Letters of Bishop Tozer.* London: Universities' Mission to Central Africa, 1902.

Weidner, Fritz. *Die Haussklaverei in Ostafrika.* Jena, Germany: Fischer, 1915.

Wellsted, J. R. *Travels in Arabia.* 2 vols. London: Murray, 1838.

Werner, Alice. "The Wahadimu of Zanzibar." *Journal of the African Society* 15 (1916): 356–60.

———, and Hitchens, eds. and trans. *The Advice of Mwana Kupona upon the Wifely Duty.* Medstead, Hampshire, Eng.: Azania Press, 1934.

Whiteley, Wilfred. *Swahili: The Rise of a National Language.* London: Methuen, 1969.

Wijeyewardene, G. E. T. "Some Aspects of Village Solidarity in Ki-Swahili Speaking Communities of Kenya and Tanganyika." Ph.D. dissertation, Cambridge University, 1961.

Williams, Eric. *Capitalism and Slavery.* New York: Capricorn, 1944.

Willoughby, Sir J. *East Africa and Its Big Game.* London: Longmans, 1889.

Wolf, E. R. "The Social Organization of Mecca and the Origins of Islam." *Southwestern Journal of Anthropology* 7 (1951): 329–56.

Wolf, Lieut. "Narrative of a voyage to explore the shores of Africa, Arabia, and Madagascar, performed by His Majesty's Ships *Leven* and *Barracuda*, under the direction of Capt. W. F. W. Owen, RN." *Journal of the Royal Geographical Society* 3 (1833): 197–223.

Wolff, Richard D. *The Economics of Colonialism: Britain and Kenya, 1870–1930.* New Haven: Yale University Press, 1974.

Wood, Peter. *Black Majority: Negroes in Colonial South Carolina from 1670 through the Stono Rebellion.* New York: Knopf, 1974.

Woodman, Harold D. *King Cotton and His Retainers: Financing and Marketing the Cotton Crop of the South, 1800–1925.* Lexington: University of Kentucky Press, 1968.

Woodward, C. Vann. *American Counterpoint: Slavery and Racism in the North-South Dialogue.* Boston: Little, Brown, 1971.

Yates, William. *Dadu: or, Stories of Native Life in East Africa.* London: Crombie, 1886.

Ylvisaker, Marguerite. "The Political and Economic Relationship of the Lamu Archipelago to the Adjacent Kenya Coast in the Nineteenth Century." Ph.D. dissertation, Boston University, 1975.

Ziadeh, Farhat J. "Equality (Kafā'ah) in the Muslim Law of Marriage." *American Journal of Comparative Law* 6 (1957): 503–17.

Periodicals

Anti-Slavery Reporter, 1870–1910

Bulletin de la Congregation du Saint-Esprit, 1866–90

Church Missionary Gleaner, 1875–81

Church Missionary Intelligencer, 1849–1906

Church Missionary Record, 1844–49

United Methodist Free Church Magazine, 1869–90

Index